INSIDE THE
COLD WAR

ALSO BY JOHN SHARNIK:

Playing for Life (with William F. Talbert)
Remembrance of Games Past

INSIDE THE
COLD WAR

AN ORAL HISTORY

JOHN SHARNIK

Introductions by
PETER JENNINGS
and TED KOPPEL

ARBOR HOUSE ❦ NEW YORK

10 9 8 7 6 5 4 3 2 1

Library of Congress Cataloging in Publication Data

Sharnik, John.
Inside the cold war.

1. World politics—1945–   . I. Title.
D1053.S448 1987 909.82 87-922
ISBN: 0-87795-866-1

EDITORIAL AND PHOTO RESEARCH BY LYRYSA SMITH

With love and thanks:
Barbara
and
In memoriam:
Dick Cohen
and Oliver Howard
Quem lucem persequibamur?

CONTENTS

AUTHOR'S NOTE

This book originated with a television program, the ABC News special "45/85," a three-hour review of world events. Like the broadcast, the book is based substantially on the accounts of expert witnesses interviewed by ABC journalists. Except when quoted only incidentally, these witnesses are identified both by their current status and their role at the time of a particular event or historic episode.

The normal jumble of speech is almost always clarified by seeing a person's face on the television screen and hearing his or her voice. You can tell, by emphasis or expression, what the speaker meant even when the words don't come out exactly right. In print, an individual's spoken words are apt to require the help of editing.

The interviews incorporated into this account were excerpted or compressed by me from lengthy verbatim transcripts. Deliberate repetitions for emphasis have been preserved, but meaningless repetitions, stammers, and misstatements promptly corrected by the speaker have been eliminated.

With two routine exceptions, wording has not been changed. One exception is to correct obvious slips of the tongue or the kinds of minor grammatical lapses that occur in informal conversation, in which the subject of a sentence may be separated from the verb by a long digression. So, for example, I have felt free to correct a "he" to "they" when that is obviously what the speaker meant, or to change a singular verb to a plural when required, not for nicety but in order to make sense.

The second exception is a matter of doing justice to interviewees (or, in some instances, to interpreters) speaking English as a foreign language and having normal difficulties making the transition. Even an erudite French diplomat, for example, is apt to slip up on a verb tense or to insert extra articles, referring, let's say, to *"the* democracy" or *"the* world peace." Russians tend to leave out articles altogether, as in "conflict between Soviet Union and United States." Locutions like these were fixed as a matter of courtesy and clarity.

The only reason any changes in transcript were made was to reflect the speaker as accurately as possible while enabling the reader to understand what was said.

INTRODUCTION
by
Peter Jennings

The book you're about to read will trace for you what's happened in the forty years from the end of World War II in 1945 to the milestone year of 1985 and beyond. It is essentially a chronicle of what we call, not always accurately, the cold war, that tug for power, ideology, and commerce between the Communist and non-Communist worlds.

But although this struggle permeates the history of the time, it is not the only hallmark of the period. There were great strides forward in communications, medicine, and social status. There were also significant deviations in decent human behavior. The rise of modern terrorism not only gave the world a new kind of warfare but in the process deliberately selected totally innocent pawns as its immediate victims.

I've spent much of my career covering for television the events of this period. I've witnessed the dramas, trod the locales, and talked to the people who've made this history—the captains of state who moved the pawns, and the pawns themselves as they basked in glory or shuddered in misery. And reflecting upon all of this in the reportage and research for the ABC television broadcast "45/85" from which this book stems, I find myself thinking of the good and the bad that the period has produced.

First, the good.

There is the end of colonialism. To be sure, powerful countries, particularly the United States and the Soviet Union, still seek to dominate smaller countries in their respective spheres—but there is not the bald exploitation of people and land that there was when the big countries literally owned their colonies. Today India is a free country, the Philippines are free, Algeria—indeed all of Africa—is free.

Yet another good is the probable end of world war. Not the end of *all* war, to be sure, for several rage at this moment. But even though many people genuinely quake at the specter of nuclear holocaust, all three living former Presidents plus the sitting President agreed in interviews for "45/85" that there will be no nuclear world war, and even as dedicated a cold warrior as former Senator Barry Goldwater says he no longer feels the Soviet Union is out to blow up the world.

The truth is that we may have finally reached that point where, even though we are able to wage so horrible a war, man, for all his inhumanity, may not dare do so. It is not only the nuclear capability that makes all civilized nations too frightened to make war, but other technological achievements also alleviate the danger. Today there could be no Pearl Harbor. In December 1941 the Japanese fleet was able to assemble in the Kurile Islands and then steam undetected for a week toward Hawaii. Today that armada would be detected immediately by satellite surveillance. There can be no such sneak attack today.

Which brings us to yet another general good, the tremendous advancements in technology for peace as well as for war, not only the miracle of a man walking on the moon, but perhaps the equal miracle that allowed us on earth to see and hear him as he did it.

Technological advances have not only made it possible for us to soar through space and transplant hearts and communicate instantly over any distance, but they have also led to some seemingly mundane developments that have had profound results. Take air conditioning and the jet plane. They converted Arizona from a sleepy backwater to the nation's most prosperous and growing area. Air conditioning made possible a full and productive workday in a scorching climate, while the jet plane made the state easily accessible to the country's marketplaces. There are whole nations, new but equally ambitious, which hope some day to emulate our Sun Belt.

The world has seen much social change, though not enough. In this country, few remember that in 1945, when World War II ended, a black person could not stay in a midtown hotel, eat in a restaurant, try on a suit in a clothier's, live in a white neighborhood, or get even the lowest clerical job—not only in Selma and Atlanta, but also in New York and Chicago. The revolution that eradicated those outrages took barely half the forty years this book explores, and was, despite the agony we perceived at the time, relatively painless when compared to similar revolutions in other times and in other lands. The struggle to liberate women is not similarly complete, but the progress has been dramatic.

Yet, lest we bask too much in the world's successes of the period, we cannot ignore the failures.

، Perhaps foremost is our absolute failure to eliminate poverty. Poverty is relative. A poor black on welfare in Harlem is not as poor as a poor black in a rural southern shanty, who is not as poor as a cemetery dweller in Cairo, who is not as poor as a street person in Calcutta.

But misery is misery, and a hungry child is a hungry child no matter what your measuring stick—and here we don't seem to have made any discernible progress.

We have also failed to develop any rational means of solving international disputes. The big hope at the start of this period was the formation of the United Nations. It is far from the same hope at the end of the period, though the UN often does good works which go unnoticed.

There remains the devastating problem of polarization between peoples, not only between Communist and non-Communist, but between black and white in South Africa, between Arab and Israeli in the Middle East as well as between Moslems and between tribes.

Not only is there no effective power to mediate, there is also all too little understanding—of Islam, for example—by those who should have the capacity to moderate.

In 1945, there were two great powers—the United States and the Soviet Union—and they could dictate to their lessers. But now it is the small nations that often dominate the world stage. Their weapon is not the frontal assault of the Russian advance into Germany or the American bomb at Hiroshima: it is a new, open-to-everyone type of warfare called terrorism. It started not recently, as we too often think, but at the end of World War II. The Israelis used it to wrest the mandate from Britain. Castro used it to overcome the much more powerful Batista in Cuba. The rebellious use it in Central America and India. It is not a phenomenon unique to the Middle East by any means.

So, while the period from 1945 to 1985 has been momentous in many ways, most of the basic conflicts remain. For the most part, the struggle between capitalism and communism continues in the same places. There is still an encircled Israel on one hand, and desperate, stateless Palestinians on the other. There is still a Latin America rich in resources and poor in social and economic justice. But if we have dramatically reduced the prospect of another world war, eased the cruel burden of racism, and eliminated many diseases along the way, surely the collective desire of the next forty years is for social progress to match the technological magnificence of the previous forty.

INTRODUCTION
by
Ted Koppel

When the Second World War ended and the cold war was gathering, I was five and living in London with my parents (both of whom were refugees from Hitler's Germany). Although the war, and the events leading up to it, had shattered their lives, it had barely ruffled the surface of mine. I slept under my father's steel desk, in a small office he had in our house; the discomfort of running out into the garden and huddling for hours in the concrete bomb shelter there had proved more compelling to my middle-aged parents than the threat from incoming V1 and V2 rocket-bombs. Actually, the dampness of the bomb shelter and the inconvenience of frequent false alarms must have been considerable. The bombs were landing in our neighborhood. Every house but one on Haslemere Gardens bore the shattered evidence of explosions. I remember expressing some personal resentment over the absence of broken windows in our house. To a five-year-old, their failure to inflict *any* damage on our home seemed like a personal reproach.

Here are some other memories of the most destructive war in the history of man:

I recall my father going off on his rounds as an air raid warden, with a steel helmet and a broom. The broom was intended to sweep incendiary bombs from rooftops (preferably before they burned through) down to the street, where a second air raid warden, armed with helmet and garbage can lid (or dust-bin cover, as it was known in that place and those times) could smother the otherwise harmless device. I do not recall if my father and his colleague ever engaged a fire-bomb, or, for that matter, if the procedure was ever successfully completed by anyone. But I remember that was the plan.

I recall that only a couple of streets from where we lived seemingly endless convoys of U.S. military trucks rolled up-country along what was then known as the North Circular Road. I was among the thousands of English children who learned, early on, the rewards of standing by the roadside yelling, "Any gum, chum?" To this day, I have an unsated yearning for Chiclets, Hershey bars, Spam, and condensed (not evaporated) milk. Nor are there enough negative images in the world to ever wipe out or overcome the early adoration and worship I paid the American GI.

I remember subjecting my mother to painful embarrassment by openly expressing my yearning to live in America, as we stood one morning on a bus queue. I think it was bananas I lusted after on that particular occasion. But no matter—bananas, chocolate, Spam, comics, Daisy rifles—everything wonderful lay beyond vision and almost beyond imagining in America.

Not that England was, in any respect, bad. On the contrary, England was *Great;* the centerpiece of Great Britain, which itself was the centerpiece of the British Empire. America was a favorite uncle, indulgent and rich. Britain was, plain and simply, the greatest country in the world. I didn't know then that the sun never set on the British Empire, but it would have seemed a perfectly reasonable assumption.

Then, one day the war was over and the lights came on again. Grownups had been singing about it for years, but I'd never known what they'd meant: "When the Lights Go On Again All Over the World." Now the war *was* over and the lights *were* on again. There was no longer any need for the "blackout." My father took me out on the streets one evening and the world glittered. Street lamps and house lights no longer masked behind midnight blue shades; automobile headlamps without masking tape. It was the lights that drew a five-year-old's attention; but the England revealed by those lights was exhausted, dingy, and bankrupt.

During the next few years, British-controlled Palestine would give way to the new Jewish state of Israel. The Indian Raj collapsed, was subdivided into India and Pakistan, with each becoming independent of Britain. From Singapore to Kenya, from the Persian Gulf to the Suez Canal, British influence diminished and then disappeared.

By the early 1950s I was in a British boarding school, yearning to breathe free. On the longer holidays I would visit Germany, where my father was engaged in a legal battle to reclaim what the Nazis had stolen. It hardly occurred to me then that the Germans might be rebuilding their shattered country more quickly, more efficiently, and above all, more permanently than the British. Nor was it easy for a twelve-year-old conqueror swaggering through the streets of occupied Frankfurt to understand the political transition that was taking place. Germany had already been transformed into an ally, and in similar Orwellian fashion, old allies were now regarded as having never been anything but enemies.

One summer evening in 1952 while I was vacationing with my parents in Frankfurt, we heard a string of explosions that lit up the sky. One of our German neighbors ran screaming into the street: *"Die Russen! Die Russen kommen!"* ("The Russians! The Russians are coming!") They weren't. Actually, it was the Americans, celebrating the Fourth of July with a fireworks display at a nearby botanical garden. We were all on one side now: the British, the Americans, and the Germans. Benevolent old "Uncle Joe" Stalin was now as much of a threat to us as he was to the freshly de-Nazified *Bundesrepublik.* In the wink of an eye, our former allies in Russia and China became our cold-war adversaries. Meanwhile, our former enemies in Japan and Germany and Italy were now our allies. Indeed, although I didn't think of it in such terms as a twelve-year-old, postwar reconstruction in Germany was already far ahead of what was happening across the English Channel at home.

I do remember this, however. Food was rich and plentiful in Germany by 1952. There was no rationing. At about the same time, I remember sugar rationing being lifted for the first time since before the war in England. People took pillow cases to the sweet shops. It is not by coincidence that the English have among the worst teeth of any people in the world. Candy is a national passion; and as suddenly as it became available, it was gone. In less than a week, rationing was reinstated. Only seven years after the end of the war, the vanquished had already established a "chocolate gap" over their British victors. To this day, they have only widened the gulf on almost every economic level.

Then, suddenly, it was 1953 and my parents and I were aboard the *Queen Mary,* headed for the United States. I do not recall having played any major role in the deliberations that preceded the decision to emigrate; but as the father of four myself now, I doubt that my parents would have solicited the opinion of a thirteen-year-old.

It was not, I regret to say, the Statue of Liberty that drew my earliest interest. After all, it was not some bloodthirsty dictatorship from which I was escaping; merely a British boarding school. What captivated my attention (as indeed it was designed to do) was the most enormous coffee cup I had ever seen. Erected on the New Jersey shoreline, it stands there to this day, a single drop of coffee hanging from its rim: "Maxwell House Coffee. Good to the Last Drop."

Ironically, it was another commercial, the next day, that made me believe we had made a terrible mistake in coming to the United States. The radio jingle burbled the virtues of an antacid: "Eat too much, drink too much? Try Brioschi's, try Brioschi's." It was an intensely depressing concept. What kind of country had we come to, where people worried about having eaten or drunk too much? It was not a problem that afflicted the world from which we had come.

It is, however, astonishingly easy to become acclimatized to excess. It took a little time to learn the differences between the English and American languages. (Many exist on the scatological level—in England you "have" a piss, in America you "take" one.) But becoming an American is largely a matter of learning to lose the inhibitions you acquired in the land of your birth. It is all right, I found, to be openly proud of yourself here. "If you can do it," as Texans are fond of saying, "it ain't braggin'." Even now, though, almost thirty-five years later, having long ago become an American by choice rather than accident of birth, the innocence of this "can do" spirit still troubles me. It seems to carry with it a corollary astonishing in a land of immigrants: namely, that others are less competent than we.

The victory that the United States helped achieve over the Axis powers in 1945 confirmed America's self-image as a nation uniquely endowed and blessed by the Almighty. We have sometimes since then acted as though we had Him under an exclusive, long-term contract. We were to learn otherwise and to our enormous sorrow in Korea and Vietnam, in Iran and Lebanon, in Cuba and Afghanistan. U.S. sponsorship, we were about to learn, could sometimes be as much of a liability as a help. The huge self-confidence that Americans project causes a great deal of resentment around the world. To this day we continue to be astonished by the fact that we are neither universally loved nor appreciated; but we are beginning to learn.

Those four decades of the cold war have taught us something about the scope and the limits of our power, unequaled by any similar span in our history. In 1945 we were rich, innocent, and relatively unscarred by the war, which never came to our own shores. We were sole possessors of The Bomb and filled with a missionary zeal to recast Europe and Japan, and as much of the rest of the world as would allow, in our own image. In Europe and Japan we exceeded our own wildest expectations. We are having some difficulty coming to grips with the notion that our former dependent students may outstrip us economically, but we will learn.

The rest of the world, however, has split into pieces we may never learn to manage. Communism is not the monolithic bloc we once believed, but in its diversity it has proved to be an even more puzzling challenge. The Third World either plays the game of pro- and anti-Communist, or fails to arouse our interest.

For all that, what you are about to read is the story of America coming into its own as the single most important economic, political, and military force in the world. Those four decades are when it happened. Had I been a little older, perhaps, or a little more perceptive, I might have observed the phenomenon rolling across the Atlantic in the wake of the *Queen Mary,* as we left England and came to the United States, for the world's center of gravity was making precisely the same journey.

·PART I·

DRAWING
THE LINE
Truman and Stalin

1945-52

·1·

HERITAGE OF VICTORY

In the humid evening of August 14, 1945, a half million people crowded into New York's Times Square to wait for news they could have heard at home over their living-room radios. It was as if they needed the presence of witnesses to assure themselves that what they expected to happen—what they'd spent years hoping for and days anticipating—had really, finally occurred.

A moment after 7 P.M., the headline flashed in moving lights on Times Tower: OFFICIAL—TRUMAN ANNOUNCES JAPANESE SURREN-DER. The five-word message touched off a demonstration that outdid New Year's Eve for noise and high spirits. "A victory roar . . . beat upon the eardrums for the next 20 minutes," according to the next day's account in the *Times*. Hats, flags, packages were tossed in the air. A blizzard of paper began to fall from the windows of hotels and office buildings, where workers had stayed late in hopes they would have something to celebrate. "Men and women embraced—there were no strangers in New York yesterday," said the journalistic voice of a city not noted for friendliness.

And the ranks of celebrants kept growing. Several hours later, according to police estimates, there were two million friends milling noisily through the streets of midtown New York.

One emblematic face emerged from that crowd in a *Life* magazine photograph. It was the face of an anonymous sailor who moved through Times Square exuberantly kissing every pretty girl in his path. An unremarked face in the same crowd was that of a thirty-two-year-old navy officer named Richard M. Nixon, ashore between tours of duty in the Pacific. That evening he showed the star-crossed combi-

3

nation of qualities he would later reveal to the world: a talent for being in the right place at the historic moment and somehow having things go wrong.

Lieutenant Commander Nixon joined the throng in Times Square that evening . . . and had his pocket picked.

The official proclamation of V-J Day—Victory over Japan—would not come until a formal surrender ceremony almost three weeks later, on September 2, 1945. But after six years of the most devastating war in history, the world was impatient to start celebrating.

In Washington that evening, after making his terse, dramatic announcement, President Harry Truman went out on the White House lawn and exchanged congratulations through the fence with the jubilant crowd of thousands that was gathering along Pennsylvania Avenue. The crowd stayed put, the President had to make two curtain calls, and he wound up delivering a speech from the portico. In between, he called his mother in Independence, Missouri. When she left the phone, she told a waiting reporter, "That was Harry. I'm glad Harry decided to end the war."

In London it was midnight when the news broke. On the twelfth stroke of Big Ben, Prime Minister Attlee began his announcement, and within minutes the rooftops and terraces were filled with pajama-clad Britons. In the morning they filled the cobbled pavements outside Buckingham Palace, cheering King George VI and Queen Mary. Then, joined by American GIs based on their island, British civilians and soldiers in the hundreds of thousands marched along Piccadilly and into Trafalgar Square, where the singing and dancing went on all night.

In Moscow, there was no immediate official celebration to bring crowds into Red Square. But the news was repeated continuously on radio through the middle of the night. And *Pravda* next day hailed the victory as the result of cooperation among the great powers and declared that "the foundations for postwar security" were now in place.

Russian and American officers in occupied Germany (which had surrendered three months earlier) raised toasts together in the garish cabarets of occupied Berlin. Paris lit up the war-darkened Eiffel Tower, and the bells finally rang again in Ottawa's war-silenced Peace Tower.

In Chungking, firecrackers popped and Americans in uniform were mobbed by their Chinese allies, who pressed precious black-market cigarettes on them as tokens of friendship and gratitude. Recently liberated people of the Philippines paraded through the streets of Manila beating time to a victory chant on the fenders of automobiles. Australians began a round of public partying that wouldn't stop—not for days; in Sydney, the high spirits got out of hand as a mob destroyed fire trucks despatched to dampen them down. And on the Pacific island of Okinawa, where the battle had barely ended, GIs lit up the skies with tracer bullets in an exuberant farewell to arms and were answered by nervous gunners on U.S. ships offshore, still on the alert against *kamikaze* attacks. To Okinawa's wartime casualty toll of 38,000 Americans, peace added six more dead, thirty wounded.

The casualties of victory scarcely marred the worldwide jubilation. There cannot have been many moments in history when so much of the human race was united in spirit as they were at that moment marking the end of World War II. The air was heady with relief, with the joy of survival, a sense of great expectations.

Even among those with an awareness of history's capriciousness, few would have imagined that the next period in the chronicle of human affairs would be characterized not by harmony but by conflict, by continuous tension overhung with a threat not merely of terrible destruction but of total annihilation. Four decades later, it would be hard for a new generation of school children to imagine—even hard for their elders to remember—that Russians and Americans had once been allies, and Germany and Japan their common enemies.

Among the great conflicts in world history, the cold war is an anomaly. It has no precise starting date. There was no Pearl Harbor attack . . . no shot heard 'round the world like the famous volley fired by the American colonists at Lexington . . . no incendiary incident like the assassination of the Austrian archduke at Sarajevo, which lit the fuse of the First World War.

Unlike traditional warfare, this was a clash of *ideas and policies,* a form of conflict in which the antagonists were careful never to engage each other in battle—not directly, though sometimes through proxies.

But the cold war hardly differed from conventional warfare in its impact on American government. On the American agenda, national security often took precedence over "civilian" values like human rights and the quality of life. Foreign policy, instead of pursuing its own objectives, was tied to the behavior of a foreign country, the Soviet Union, whose motives were assumed to be invariably hostile.

The "cold" of this war was more than the absence of fire. It was the

spirit-numbing chill of disappointed hopes about the way the world
would operate after the exhilarating achievement of victory. It was
the icy blast of international *insecurity,* which did more than alarm
governments and influence their decisions—it sent chills of anxiety
through the lives of individual citizens all over the planet.

In 1985, ABC News launched a massive review of the events of the
previous four decades—the first forty years of the cold war. In interviews with some 130 expert witnesses on both sides of the conflict,
East and West—government leaders and lesser officials; participants
and bystanders in the period's lesser wars, in revolutions, diplomatic
conferences, cabinet meetings, private conversations at high levels
. . . in these interviews, facts previously unknown or little understood
emerged into the light of history, in some cases from under the cover
of official secrecy. The review was broadcast in the form of an extraordinary television special entitled "45/85."

These same interviews, including many that had to be left on the
cutting-room floor and many others that could be broadcast only in
brief excerpts, form the basis of this account.

The testimony of the men and women—East and West—who waged
the cold war tells us that they based their decisions on assumptions
about the other side's capabilities and intentions that sometimes
proved to be mistaken. They often failed to appreciate each other's
motives, sometimes misinterpreting genuine conviction for mere
cynicism or opportunism. And, like soldiers in any war, the strongest
impression finally left on them by their experience, in many cases, was
how much they had in common with the enemy.

Inadvertently, the testimony also reflects the *difference* in their
experience, which is the difference in the two conflicting systems.
Witnesses on the Western side were often critical of their government's policies and freely discussed the "errors" of the past forty years.
On the Communist side, the testimony, while often revealing about
details, never took issue with the official line.

Premonitions

People didn't begin talking about "the cold war" until 1947, when
the phrase emerged in a speech by the American financier-statesman,
Bernard Baruch. But they instantly recognized it as the state the world
had been living in for the last couple of years. In hindsight, the elements of potential conflict seemed to have been gathering beneath the
surface of events even before that exhilarating day of victory. While

the temperature of the headlines had been sunny, the barometer had apparently been dropping all through the last six months of the war.

When the Allied leaders met at Yalta in February 1945, they may have realized the war was entering its final chapter, but neither the political chieftains nor their military experts had any way of knowing how brief that chapter would be.

It was only weeks since the American army had escaped from the Bulge, where the German *Wehrmacht* staged what would turn out to be its final offensive. The Western Allies had not yet crossed the Rhine.

On the eastern front, the Russians had made a grinding advance through Poland and were just beginning to probe the defenses of the German homeland.

In the Pacific, the Philippines were being liberated; the costly battle for Okinawa had not even begun. Japan, 500 miles beyond, was a mountain still to be conquered.

News photographs of the summit meeting in the mild winter of the Russian Crimean resort were wonderfully reassuring: FDR looking even more patrician than ever in a dark woolen cloak that draped his shoulders, his handsome face ennobled by hollows that turned out to be the sign of serious illness . . . Churchill, indomitable-looking in his naval get-up . . . Stalin, gruff but deceptively benign behind his large moustache.

Their purpose was to plot the strategy of the next—and, they hoped, decisive—phase of the war and, in broad outline, the future of the conquered countries. Roosevelt had an even more pressing objective in mind. His Combined Chiefs of Staff and his Pacific army commanders in the field, General Douglas MacArthur and General Albert Wedemeyer, all were urging him to secure a Soviet declaration of war on Japan at the earliest opportune moment, at any bearable cost. The military planners were envisioning an invasion of Japan that might cost the United States a million casualties. General MacArthur, the brilliant architect of America's military advance across the Pacific, warned that the invasion would be followed by a lengthy guerilla campaign in which the Japanese people would defend their homeland from hills and caves the way the Japanese army had defended their outlying islands. America's ultimate weapon, the atomic bomb, did not enter into the discussions. It was still treated as a secret, and it was still a dubious quantity. "The bomb will never go off," FDR had been told by his chief of staff, Admiral William D. Leahy, "and I speak as an expert on explosives." At best, the explosive power of the A-bomb was calculated at a modest one or two kilotons—the equivalent of 1,000 to 2,000 tons of TNT.

The price Roosevelt agreed to pay in exchange for Soviet entry into the Japanese War did not seem exorbitant in the circumstances. Added together, the main items would give Moscow a much-strengthened hand in northeastern Asia, where the Russians had historically contended for influence with the Japanese. The Russians would gain some Japanese island territories, railroad rights in Manchuria, and a zone of occupation in Korea, the small country bordering on China that—like much of China itself—had been occupied by the Japanese. The risks in this arrangement, so far as the West's Chinese allies were concerned, seemed taken care of by Stalin's agreement to recognize the Nationalist government of Generalissimo Chiang Kai-shek and to urge Chiang's Communist rival, Mao Zedong, to cooperate with the government.

For what was then referred to as the European theater of operations, the Yalta agreement laid down the broad outlines of a postwar Allied occupation of Germany until some permanent arrangement should be made for the future of that country. Some German territory was to be awarded to Poland as a compensation for Polish territory to be incorporated into the USSR.

A provisional government was set up for the newly liberated Polish people. It was an uneasy coalition of leftists from a committee the Russians had set up in the city of Lublin and more conservative elements from the Polish government-in-exile in London. In Poland and in the other countries of Eastern Europe—Germany's former captives and satellites—the postwar future was to be decided by free elections.

From the American point of view, it may be hard to understand why it should have taken any such negotiation to bring the Soviet ally into the war against Japan—to persuade Moscow to open a second front on Russia's Asian flank. It had been no easier for the Russians to understand the Allies' caution about opening a second front in Europe during the earlier years of the war when Russia had its back to the wall.

The Yalta agreement was later characterized by Churchill as "extremely favorable to Soviet Russia" but necessary in pursuit of a war that was expected to last in Europe through the summer and fall of 1945 and in the Pacific for another eighteen months after that. Roosevelt expressed regrets about the deal for Poland but said it was "the best I can do . . . at this time."

Two months after he came home from Yalta, Roosevelt was dead of a massive cerebral hemorrhage, suffered while he was sitting for a portrait at the southern White House in Warm Springs, Georgia. His

last words were simple and unhistoric: "I have a terrific headache."
One of his last presidential thoughts, imparted to an aide, was about
Stalin's disturbing behavior in the weeks since their meeting in Yalta.
Almost up to the moment of his death, FDR was worried about the
political role the Soviets were playing in the liberated areas of Eastern
Europe and in the United Nations Organization, as it was then being
called during the process of formation.

Admired and beloved, Roosevelt was publicly mourned in every
Allied capital, including Moscow. Even his bitter enemies, the Japanese, paid tribute to "the great man" in radio messages.

Harry Truman, who was sworn in as Roosevelt's successor that evening in a one-minute ceremony at the White House, was a Kansas City
merchant-turned-politician with a businessman's style as brisk and
no-nonsense as his own brief inaugural service.

Truman arrived in the presidential office with no great inclination
to sentimentalize "our Russian allies." As a senator from Missouri he
once said, before the United States had become involved in the war,
"If we see that Germany is winning [the war], we ought to help Russia.
And if Russia is winning, we ought to help Germany. And in that way,
let them kill as many [of each other] as possible."

Picked rather cavalierly by the 1944 presidential candidate as his
running mate, Truman, astonishingly, had met with Roosevelt only
twice as Vice-President when he succeeded to the Oval Office. Apparently the new President knew nothing of the atomic bomb then being
perfected in the workshops of Los Alamos (although the testimony of
a personal friend suggests that he may have had some inkling of a
powerful secret weapon). Two weeks into his presidency, Truman got
a briefing on the bomb. His reaction, later reported by an aide, was
tough-minded almost to the point of cynicism: "If it explodes as I think
it will, I'll certainly have a hammer on those boys"—that is, the Russians.

In those early weeks of his presidency, he had his first encounter
with a high Soviet official—the foreign minister, Vyacheslav M. Molotov. The issue was one that had troubled FDR up to his dying day. It
was Poland, where—in the process of liberation—the Red Army was
busy nullifying the prospect of free elections called for under the Yalta
agreement. An open breach was developing between the two Polish
factions, and the Soviets were hurrying to install Communists in key
positions, shouldering aside the moderates.

During the meeting in the Oval Office, Molotov objected to
the blunt language of Truman's protest. "Carry out your agree-

ments," Truman snapped, "and you won't get talked to like that!"

By mid-April, the Red Army had swept beyond Poland and was deep inside Germany, within fifty miles of Berlin. The Western Allies, having stormed across the Rhine in recent weeks, were also surging toward Hitler's capital from the other side. The satellite capitals of Vienna and Prague were within the grasp of both Allied forces, East and West.

But the road to Berlin, like other matters of Allied strategy, was a subject of conflict between the Supreme Commander of the Western Allied Armies, General Dwight D. Eisenhower, and the British prime minister, Winston Churchill.

SIR JOHN COLVILLE
London banker, author
1945: Assistant private secretary to the prime minister

Eisenhower refused to go for Berlin, although Churchill pressed him to, in telegram after telegram and conversation after conversation. It had been agreed that the Western Allies would make for Berlin. It was absolutely agreed by everybody. And then quite suddenly Eisenhower personally telegraphed to Stalin that he'd decided to move the direction of the Western armies southward to Leipzig and Dresden because he didn't think Berlin was any longer of strategic importance. Stalin, of course, was delighted and said that, yes, he thought that was absolutely right and he himself would move his best troops away from Berlin, southwards. He did exactly the opposite. He strengthened his Berlin forces and put his best troops there, because to the Russians it was very important to get to Berlin before we did.

And then, of course, the same thing happened over Prague, so that the feeling was—Churchill's feeling was—that we had unnecessarily given away a great deal of Europe to Communist domination, and I'm afraid he blamed this largely on Eisenhower.

The subsequent history of Eastern Europe—the reduction of Poland, Hungary, Czechoslovakia to satellites and the precarious status of Berlin—would often be traced to two events: the Yalta agreement and that military decision on the road to Berlin. But when Eisenhower sent out a direct order reining in the Ninth Army from the outskirts of the German capital and restraining ebullient General George S. Patton's Third Army from the approaches to Prague, Ike was acting from the same considerations that had ruled Churchill at Yalta: He was planning for a much longer war.

Hitler's armies were in retreat but not yet neutralized. It was in the south of Germany, in the mountainous "redoubt" of the Bavarian Alps, that the Führer had ordered the *Wehrmacht* to make a stand. Allied intelligence and planning for some time had been pointing toward some such climactic battle. But the Nazi leadership had fallen apart, the morale of the German armies was shattered, and whole divisions began surrendering to the Allies.

On the day Hitler committed suicide in his bunker, May 1, 1945, the reports of American foreign correspondents in the field still dwelt on the Nazi "redoubt" and the anticipated "last stand."

The end came abruptly. Just seven days later the German forces surrendered unconditionally—to the Western Allies in Reims, France, and to the Russians in Berlin.

As the European war ended, the organizational conference of the United Nations was being held in San Francisco in an argumentative atmosphere. One of the main issues was which of the two Polish factions should be recognized as the country's representatives.

Still, a certain amount of abrasion is taken for granted as part of any alliance. The overriding fact about the East-West relationship at that point was not its conflicts but its mutual interest in consolidating the victory over Germany and making it stick.

Eisenhower visited Moscow as Stalin's honored guest to receive the tribute of the Soviet government. It was expressed in the form of a medal, the Order of Suvorov. At a meeting in Frankfurt with his Soviet counterpart, Marshal Zhukov, Ike was further honored with a remarkably valuable decoration, the jeweled Order of Victory, which had been given to no more than seven persons—and no non-Russians—before. Ike came away impressed with Russia's friendship with the United States.

Truman sailed to meet the Russian and British leaders at Potsdam, a suburb of Berlin, soon after the victory in Europe, and came away with a certain grudging fondness for Stalin.

At Potsdam, where the new American leader made his first appearance among the Big Three, a new British spokesman also joined the ranks in mid-conference. Clement Attlee replaced Winston Churchill when the Labour party upset Churchill's Conservatives in the general elections.

The meeting brought the Yalta agreement up to date and filled in some sketchy outlines. Ground rules were set up for the occupation of Germany—the country was to be divided into four zones, to be administered by the U.S., Britain, France, and Russia. Berlin was divided likewise into occupied sectors, with access to the city guaranteed to the Western Allies through Russian-occupied territory. For issues affecting the whole country, an Allied Control Council was set up.

It was at Potsdam that a new and awesome force was introduced— at first almost casually—into the arena of international politics. En route to Europe, Truman had got word that the atomic bomb had been tested at Alamogordo, New Mexico. Its success could be measured by the destruction of all desert life, both plant and animal, within a mile of ground zero, the point of the blast.

When Truman dropped word in conversation with Stalin that the United States had developed "a new weapon of unusual destructive force," he did not explain the mysterious source of its power. Stalin may have known about the development of an atomic weapon before Truman did, through Soviet espionage channels that had penetrated the nuclear establishment. But he was just as cool in his response. He wished the Americans good luck with their new weapon against the Japanese.

Whether to use the bomb or not was a decision that was still being debated within the administration. General George C. Marshall, as chairman of the Combined Chiefs of Staff the nation's highest ranking military officer, had expressed qualms to his civilian superior.

JOHN J. MCCLOY
Retired banker and government official
1945: Assistant secretary of war

General Marshall used to say to me, "Don't let them ask me, Mr. McCloy, whether or not we should drop the bomb on Japan. I don't know, and I don't think the scientists know, either, because they come forward with these big words like "primordial." What does "primordial" mean? Something before anything was organized, primordial is. It's primitive. It's something strange. It's a cosmic result. What does it mean—that they'll blow up the world? Nobody knows.

And to this day, the top scientists don't know any more than they did then —[only] that a nuclear exchange would produce a disaster of such consequences that nobody can really accurately identify or describe it.

But in the fiery light of that time, Hiroshima was a foregone conclusion. America was in its fourth year of grinding warfare against the

Japanese; Britain was in its sixth. The prospect of those million casualties in an invasion of Japan—the only visible alternative—was just too much to face. Tokyo had just defied a joint U.S.–British declaration offering Japan reentry into the community of nations via unconditional surrender. An accompanying warning of immediate destruction had been ignored. The American scientific and military experts had concluded there was no feasible way to conduct a nonlethal demonstration of the A-bomb—that is, a drop on uninhabited territory—that might impress the Japanese enough to make them give in. Perhaps more importantly, it would have meant wasting half of America's meager stockpile, which at that time amounted to precisely two bombs.

Only four days after the end of the Potsdam meeting, on the morning of August 6, the bomb fell on Japan. A ten-foot-long black device weighing four and a half tons destroyed four square miles of the city of Hiroshima (population: 344,000) by fire and blast. The force of the bomb had been wildly underestimated by Secretary of War Henry Stimson in his briefing of the President a few months before. It was the equivalent not of one or two thousand tons of TNT, but of 20,000 tons. The death toll was 80,000. Hiroshima, the first victim of the atomic age, was not a totally innocent one. The city was the headquarters of the Japanese Second Army, which was practically wiped out by the single bomb.

While the image of the lethal mushroom-shaped cloud burned itself into the world's consciousness, the United States paused, looking for some sign of a white flag through the nuclear pall. But the government of Japan was gripped by an internal struggle between a growing peace faction and the recalcitrant military leadership, which was prepared to take the country down with it in a suicidal blaze of samurai honor.

The Americans did not wait long. The next act in the world's first nuclear drama was one that history might find harder to forgive than Hiroshima. It was a kind of strategic bluff.

The second atomic bomb, dropped on the city of Nagasaki, just three days after the first, killed 35,000 people, and it jolted the Japanese government out of its paralysis. Even the military hard-liners shrank from the image of their crowded cities blowing up, one by one, in a nuclear holocaust. The next bomb, they assumed, would land on Tokyo. They did not realize they had survived the worst. With the bombing of Nagasaki, the Americans had expended their atomic arsenal. It would have taken months to manufacture the next bomb.

There were several more days of suspense—another invisible struggle behind the scenes in Tokyo—and Washington finally received the
message of surrender. It touched off the joyful worldwide victory
celebration from Times Square to Chungking. Japan's capitulation had
been hastened by an event that occurred the day of Nagasaki: In
keeping with the Yalta and Potsdam agreements, the Soviet Union had
declared war on Japan, sending troops across the border of Japanese-
occupied Manchuria.

Two weeks later, as the United States battleship *Missouri* was
steaming into Tokyo Bay carrying General MacArthur to accept the
formal surrender, the Japanese government had to put down a cabal
of militant holdouts. They had organized a formation of planes for a
kamikaze run against the surrender ship.

The ceremony proceeded, the surrender was signed. The most destructive war in history had finally staggered to an end, dragging with
it the beginnings of history's next great tragedy, the cold war, and
providing it with a symbol, the mushroom cloud. A later generation
might find it hard to understand why the painful lessons of war had
not assured a transition to a stable peace. The answer is as simple as
the cold war is complex: It was not a time for moralizing or pondering
the instructive benefits of experience, only a time for celebration.

BRIAN URQUHART
Assistant secretary general of the UN
1945: British army enlisted man

I remember thinking when I learned of the use of nuclear weapons at
Hiroshima: *Thank God! That will end the war!*

In those days, it wasn't unfashionable to think it was a good idea. It is now.
But, you know—you know, then we'd been fighting for six years, and I must
say everybody—everybody who'd been in the army, at any rate, or the
forces—was to some extent brutalized. We were all perfectly used to seeing
people killed and towns blown up. I mean, that was our daily experience.
And to find something that actually would put an end to it, no matter how
frightful it was . . . it seemed to be the natural thing to do.

It seemed natural to look forward not to applying the lessons of war
but to enjoying the luxury of peace.

·2·

ABOUT-FACE

People are united by their totems and their shibboleths—peace chants, ban-the-bomb signs, law-and-order bumper stickers, anti-Communist slogans. All through the Second World War, it was "V for Victory." Winston Churchill had popularized the two-fingered gesture. On BBC radio broadcasts it was expressed in the opening phrase of Beethoven's Fifth (V) Symphony: Dit-dit-dit-*dah* (the letter V in Morse code). For six years, no other goal had been necessary. For everything that troubled the world, victory was the solution. With the end of the war, it became part of the problem.

The defeat of the Axis powers brought their societies to a standstill. Governments, economies, local administrations, even school systems lay paralyzed, waiting for orders from the Allies. In liberated countries the very machinery of victory brought hostile political factions into contact with each other—elements that had been kept in suspense like dangerous chemicals during the war years. In China, the end of the war had left 1.2 million Japanese troops in place; at the stroke of peace, the U.S. army and navy began transporting whole divisions of Chiang Kai-shek's Nationalist army northward into Manchuria to haul in the beaten enemy and confiscate their weapons. Manchuria was the stronghold of Chiang's longtime internal enemy, the Communists, led by Mao Zedong, with an army of their own. The factions were bound to collide.

In the liberated countries of Europe, the political left had emerged from the war with new claims and expectations. Leftists had carried a heavy share of the anti-Nazi resistance—partly out of conviction, partly because they were Hitler's selected targets. They thought their sacrifice entitled them to a greater share of power, if not the power itself. And the hard conditions of daily life in postwar Europe seemed to favor them as advocates of radical change.

The Continent was "a washout," in the phrase of an American observer. From the Rhine on east into Russia, cities looked as if they had been trampled by giants. In the streets of Germany, housewives in ersatz wool sweaters worked alongside elderly men in threadbare suits and remnants of *Wehrmacht* uniforms—worked in "rubble brigades," moving the collapsed bricks and stones off the streetcar tracks, arranging them in neatly squared-off mounds or walls. GIs who were stationed in postwar Germany would never be able to shake the peculiar sensation that lodged in the nostrils. It was a compound of coal smoke and cooking odors and old clothing—the smell of want.

Italy, damaged by its long flirtation with fascism and its alliance with Hitler, was no better off.

Europe's victors were suffering along with their beaten enemies. Russia was exhausted, its landscape in ruins, its populace depleted by war casualties. France, Belgium, the Netherlands—all had taken a pounding; all were economically listless, politically nervous. Britain, the only country among the European Allies to have been spared German invasion, had not escaped ruin from the air. The nation of doughty spirits seemed too weary to dig itself out—or too hungry. Rationing—of meat, butter, sugar, clothes, petrol, *everything*—remained as much a fact of life as it had been all through the war.

Washington officials visited Europe to survey the postwar scene and help shape an American role in the postwar world.

JOHN J. MCCLOY

We visited all the areas, not only where our troops had been but a good many areas where the troops of the Soviet Union were already. And I came away with a very vivid impression of how tremendous and really awe-inspiring the prestige of the United States was at that stage. It seemed that everybody who had a trouble thought the United States was going to be in a position to solve it, and I was alarmed at the height of the expectancies and really of the almost massive prestige that we had at that time. And I was fearful of the fact that we wouldn't by any means be able to deliver all of the expectancies.

The United States alone was entering the postwar period unscathed. The American continent was not only unsoiled by enemy troops but undamaged by enemy bombs. For all the 400,000 American lives that had been sacrificed, for all the American resources that had been poured into the Allied war effort, the United States had emerged an unshaken tower of strength. Perhaps it was even *strengthened.* Stimulated by wartime demand, the gross national product had more than doubled over the prewar, Depression-struck level. An incredible 60 percent of the world's economic output was being produced by the United States. Two-thirds of the automobiles in the world were American.

America's initial response to the world's "expectancies" was to shrink from them. The postwar spirit was expressed in a two-syllable headline word that emerged in the GI newspaper the *Stars and Stripes,* and led its front page almost daily. The word was "demob," short for demobilization, as in: PENTAGON PROMISES DEMOB SPEED-UP AND GIS PROTEST LAG IN DEMOB PROGRAM.

A vast transoceanic armada was carrying American servicemen home from Europe and Asia at an even faster rate than it had transported them to the theaters of war at the height of the war effort. As soon as the ink was dry on the Japanese surrender document, a reduction of 5 million men—more than half the strength of the armed forces—went into effect. The American forces in Europe were being thinned out from the day of victory over Germany. They would be reduced from 2.8 million to 400,000 as quickly as they could be transported. Another 1.5 million would be left on occupation duty, mainly in Japan.

"Peace," said *Time* magazine, "had hit the services like another Pearl Harbor."

Along with its "war-surplus" men and women, America's services unloaded vast amounts of matériel. Some U.S. army bases in Europe looked like vast used-car lots, filled with almost everything that moved on wheels or treads—trucks of all sizes, ambulances, cranes, earth-moving equipment, everything for sale at cut-rate prices. The navy sold surplus construction equipment, tankers, landing craft. This super-garage sale was the basis for some postwar private fortunes built up by enterprising Europeans. Surplus jeeps were reserved for occupation GIs. One ex-soldier studying at the Sorbonne under the GI Bill of Rights bought a three-quarter-ton truck for $500, repaired it, and resold it in Paris to help finance his *Wanderjahre* in France.

Whole navy flotillas were stored under wraps—"in mothballs"—at their home bases. Transport planes were sold to the commercial airlines. Formations of bombers and fighters were blown up on the ground.

The job of liquidating the huge military inventory was supervised by a St. Louis businessman, a Democratic party stalwart.

STUART SYMINGTON
Retired banker and government official
1946: War surplus administrator

The main idea was how to get rid of, without scandal, about a hundred billion dollars of matériel that we didn't want all over the world and also cancel out the orders in this country of things we had planned to buy and things we had stored.

Nothing is worth more than you can get for it or need for it, and planes were getting very rapidly obsolete, because we were moving fairly rapidly into the jet age, you see.

We knew, as the result of the dropping of the Hiroshima bomb at first and then Nagasaki, we knew that, whatever war had been, it would never be the same again. One of the sad things that developed was the idea that because of the nuclear weapons we could eliminate a great deal of conventional war. That was not true.

Of course, when the war was over, there was no remote knowledge that we'd ever be in another conflict in a relatively short time. As usual, we were fighting a war to end all wars.

Speedy as it was, the demobilization process wasn't fast enough for the overseas GIs. In places where large numbers of American troops were concentrated, like Frankfurt and Paris, "demob" protests built into actual riots. Symington says they were provoked by "some newspaper people who made a career out of demanding that the troops be brought back, which was really disgraceful," and who coaxed the soldiers "to demand your rights! Write your senator! Write your congressman! There's no need for you to be over there now!"

Another high-level civilian with the War Department at that time, Paul Nitze, goes even further: "They had some Communists in the staff of the publication of the armed services, the *Stars and Stripes*. I believe it to be true. In fact, I know that the then-secretary of war [Robert P. Patterson] was absolutely convinced of it."

That view from the Pentagon foreshadows suspicions that were soon to pervade almost every foreign policy decision and many domestic ones as well. Perhaps even more, it reflects the historic schism between governments that make wars and the soldiers who fight them.

The *Stars and Stripes* was a worldwide "chain" of daily newspapers published in autonomous editions under the army's auspices and the authority of various theater commanders. The several European editions, under Eisenhower's benevolence, operated in a free-wheeling style with an avowedly antiestablishment bias. That is, they represented the interests of their "consumers," the GIs. Their staffs, made up of enlisted men and officers with civilian newspaper experience, may have sheltered one or two ink-stained wretches who had joined the Young Communist League at college in the style of their Depression generation. There may even have been an old copy reader or rewrite man who continued to believe in the faded dreams of marxism. If so, they could not have pushed demobilization any harder than it was already being pushed by the great mass of Americans, in uniform or at home.

RICHARD M. NIXON
1946: Navy veteran, California attorney

The people of the United States are basically isolationists at heart. This is not to be critical of that point of view; it's just a statement of fact. After World War I, we wanted to come home. After World War II, we all wanted to come home. I remember very well *I* wanted to come home.

Some politicians rode the wave of public sentiment. "Bring the boys home!" was a popular position that few elected officials dared to oppose openly. At Potsdam, President Truman was asked by a GI reporter from the *Stars and Stripes* if dependents would be brought over to Europe. "No, young man," Truman said firmly, "I'm going to bring *you home,* where you belong!"

Stuart Symington recalls discussing the situation with his father-in-law, Senator James Wadsworth of New York, who observed that one of the most damaging words in the American vocabulary was "mom" because "every mother wanted her boy home." Senator Claude D. Pepper of Florida sailed to Europe on the first postwar commercial voyage of the *Queen Elizabeth,* just reconverted from a troop transport. After surveying the situation in the Russian-occupied countries, he "incurred the wrath of some of the GIs by saying that I didn't think we ought to release the men as rapidly as we were doing. I thought we'd have to pay for it later on."

Getting Back to Business

"Reconversion" was the civilian counterpart to demobilization, and if there was any ideology behind that, it was the exuberant spirit of free enterprise unleashed. One of the first postwar acts of the Truman administration was to revoke the manpower controls which made it impossible for nonessential industries to hire people away from war plants. Restrictions on materials were soon loosened up. With unrestrained enthusiasm, the American economy shifted gears and product lines. Factories that had been turning out tanks, armored personnel carriers, and all sorts of military equipment now began to roll out goods and gadgets to satisfy the vast consumer appetite that had built up all through the years of wartime austerity: automobiles, refrigerators, washing machines, toasters . . . and one long-promised electronic device which had been withheld from the market because of Pearl Harbor: television.

A whole new generation of consumers was waiting to buy them—a generation of Americans in uniform impatient to get out and resume interrupted careers, start families, find homes. They were eager to contribute their bit to the postwar business boom, the baby boom, the housing boom. In Levittown, the prototype housing development rising in assembly-line modules from a Long Island potato field, a veteran would soon be able to buy a basic four-room house for $6,995—in installments of $60 a month. No down payment.

Wasn't that what the war was all about? "The preservation of the American way of life"—mom, apple pie, two cars in every driveway and a dishwasher in every all-electric kitchen. The rest was so obvious it hardly needed saying: political systems based on free elections. In 1946, these seemed like reasonable expectations—not just for America but for the rest of the world.

Almost as they had after the First World War, Americans were now doing an about-face. But this time it was not so much in revulsion from the world as in absorption with themselves. Some nagging twitch of conscience told the nation it would not really escape the role it had taken on willy-nilly with Pearl Harbor. The world was recognizably full of potential dangers: a possible revival of German militarism, unredeemable traditionalism in Japan . . . and the Soviet Union's increasing willfulness, its self-seeking behavior.

With a glance back over their shoulders at the world that was taking shape, Americans placed their faith not in the Bomb, which was temporarily out of stock anyway, but in the newly organized United Nations.

It was more than a national about-face from war. It was an abdication of military power. The Combined Chiefs of Staff, alarmed at the speed with which their military machine was being dismantled, repeatedly sent reports to the President alerting him to the dangers. But, according to a Truman aide, "the sentiment on the Hill was such that it would have been absolutely impossible to reverse the rate of decrease—it just was politically not feasible."

By the summer of 1946, there was not a single combat-ready division left in the army nor a combat-ready group in the air force. As for the navy: Paul Nitze remembers coming home from a government mission to Japan, paying a call on Secretary of Defense James Forrestal, and finding him in a state of head-shaking dismay. "He'd been trying to put together a task force to go on an exercise up to Alaska, and this was to consist of one carrier and three destroyers. And they couldn't put together enough boiler crews to get the goddamn things to sea. You knew we were in deep trouble."

Around the same time, Colonel Dean Rusk, a college administrator in civilian life, was released from the army and joined the State Department's Division of International Affairs. It was not a propitious moment for international security: "Joseph Stalin sat over there and looked across at the West and saw the divisions melting away. In retrospect, it's clear to me that we subjected Stalin to intolerable temptations through our own weakness. And it has taken us many years to pick up the pieces from that great mistake involved in our demobilization after V-J Day."

·3·

REENGAGEMENT

It was inevitable that the United States and the Soviet Union would come into conflict, but not at first because of ideology. Both superpowers held a passionate belief in their own systems, but the American mood was unambitious, and the Russians were more immediately concerned with their own security than with spreading the faith. The idea of world revolution bringing a triumph of the proletariat lies forever close to the surface of the Communist sensibility. But Communist expansion in the late forties may have been less of a strategic objective than a consequence of the search for security—helped by the vacuum left by the withdrawal of American power.

What put the two superpowers on a collision course was their conflicting policies for dealing with conquered and liberated nations. Their objective was the same—both wanted first and foremost to protect themselves against the kind of danger that Axis aggression had brought into the world. But they differed sharply on methods, on how to avert another Pearl Harbor, another Nazi invasion.

The Russians would feel secure with nothing less than a giant buffer zone—what French generals call a *glacis,* a slope that defenders can command through their gunsights. What Moscow envisioned in Central Europe was a kind of Maginot line of pro-Soviet territory separating the Germans from the Soviet Union.

The Americans held a different view of security. They were moved almost instinctively by a kind of nineteenth-century liberal belief in the rehabilitation of criminals, including criminal societies. Aggression could be tamed by reforming the aggressors.

The American approach was clearly demonstrated in the occupation of Japan, where Truman had resisted Stalin's effort to stake out a role and where U.S. policy consequently had a free hand. It was exercised by General MacArthur in the name of democracy but in a haughty, autocratic style.

TOSHIO NISHI
Historian and author
1945: Junior high school student in Japan

The Americans came and everybody was very scared—that I had learned from my sisters. They were very scared. They were sure they'd get raped. And my brother told me that the school teacher told him, "You'll be castrated, boy"—all boys would be castrated—"so when an American comes, you hide in the mountains." And girls should wear boys' clothes and so forth.

And my father, uncles—uncles who went to war—were very scared. I mean, scared in the sense: *Well, this is it, we lost the war, probably we were to be executed for good reason—for losing the war, as the Japanese did. Losers do not count.*

What happened instead, under the occupation, left Nishi with an impression of America's "immense power and wealth, even though in my childhood wealth was always in terms of food—chewing gum, bags of wheat flour, chocolates, biscuits, skim milk, and, I remember, roasted almonds, raisins, strawberry jam. You know, I think I can still recall the taste of them."

The occupation also left its legacy of ideas.

TOSHIO NISHI

Even though we were starving, everybody came to school. Of course, that's not from the occupation—that's from a long history of Japanese emphasis on learning, education. And, of course, parents support it, society supports it. The most frequently mentioned word in educational practice or ideals was "democracy." And, of course, in our kids' mind, democracy did not make any sense as an abstract notion, so the teacher says, "Well, for instance, when you start fighting, you don't hit each other. You discuss. Negotiate. Talk about it. What went wrong here?"

Most teachers who taught us were enthusiastic for democracy as if they felt that liberation themselves. Felt that they could be free as well and teach as they liked. But I remember, when I broke a window-pane while I was fighting, I was taken to the principal's office, and he

said, "Boy, you sit on the floor!" And so I sat on the floor. On my knees.
    And he said, "Breaking the window is not democracy." I said, "It was an accident, sir." He says, "No." So we argued about it. And he got very irritated and said, "If this was before the war, I could severely punish you. I could hit you. In fact, I could bust your face, boy."
    And I remember that incident, because I heard so many stories from my [older] brother how tough his high school was. Total discipline. Total obedience. No talking back. You know, when the teacher said study, they studied like maniacs. The best legacy U.S. occupation left for Japan is the Japanese baptism in democracy.

The benevolence of the American occupation sometimes bordered on naiveté. The Communists were active in the ravaged country, where crowds of hungry, homeless people wandered the streets of burned-out cities. And at one point, through simple lack of awareness, General MacArthur's military government nearly delivered control of one of the most influential government functions, broadcasting, into the hands of Communists.

In the countries of Eastern Europe, the contrasting Russian policy was being implemented. "Liberation" was extended into military occupation. The purge of Nazi collaborators was often bloody, and it broadened into a repression of any political elements, left or right, that might be expected to resist pro-Soviet policy.

The dividing line between contrasting policies was becoming a political boundary line.

The Iron Curtain

The realization began to dawn that Europe was being unredeemably divided, East from West. The first general alarm was sounded on March 5, 1946. It happened, implausibly, at a parochial midwestern site, the campus of Westminster College in Fulton, Missouri. The event proved to be a landmark of the cold war.

CLARK CLIFFORD
Washington attorney
1946: Special counsel to President Truman

The president of this rather obscure college thought it would be a great idea if for the commencement address he had the world's leading citizen, Winston Churchill. So he sat down and wrote a letter to the President of the

United States and said, "I would like to have Winston Churchill come make the commencement address." I would estimate that his odds of success were about one in a million. But it so happened that President Truman wanted to have a closer association with Winston Churchill. He had only known him for two or three days at the Potsdam conference [before Churchill was replaced as Prime Minister by Clement Attlee].

This invitation came in. It seemed exactly appropriate. It went back to Missouri, where President Truman had come from. He then passed the invitation on to Winston Churchill and urged that he accept it.

So he came on over. I might say that the trip out—President Truman and Mr. Churchill and six of us staff members—was one of the greatest experiences that a human being can have. It took three and a half days to go out and three and a half days to come back. We did it by train. And Mr. Churchill, at the very beginning of the trip, raised the question whether or not President Truman still played poker. President Truman said, yes, he played a lot of poker. Winston Churchill said, "Well, I've played poker. I started playing poker in the Boer War." He said, "I wonder if we might play some poker on this trip out to southern Missouri." And the President said, "I'm sure we can arrange it."

So that afternoon, when Mr. Churchill was taking his siesta, he got all six of us together—President Truman's aides—and he said, "Men, this fellow is probably a very good poker player. And," he said, "I want you to do your best. I expect every man to do his duty."

I felt like I was being talked to by the commander of the U.S.S. *Constitution* before we went into battle with the British fleet.

We played poker every evening and got to know Mr. Churchill well. He turned out to be a really quite poor poker player. But the idea after a while was to carry it along and make it a pleasant occasion.

But they got to know each other very, very well; and it was very valuable. I think maybe Mr. Churchill may have discussed the speech that he made with the President before we reached Fulton, Missouri; but the rest of us did not know it. It was completely new to me.

It was on that campus platform in Fulton, Missouri, that Winston Churchill described the failure of Allied hopes: "From Stettin in the Baltic to Trieste in the Adriatic, an Iron Curtain has descended across the Continent. . . . Police governments are prevailing; and so far, except in Czechoslovakia, there is no true democracy. . . . This is certainly not the liberated Europe we fought to build up."

Furthermore, Churchill warned, "throughout the world, Communist fifth columns are established and work in complete unity and absolute obedience to directives they receive from the Communist center."

JOHN SHARNIK

The "Iron Curtain" rang as dramatically as those other Churchillian wartime phrases promising Britons "nothing but blood, toil, tears, and sweat" and paying tribute to them in "their finest hour." The rolling Churchillian prose called on Americans to face the fact that the Yalta agreements, the very foundation of the Allies' scheme for the postwar world, were being nullified. The future of the liberated nations of Eastern Europe was being decided not by free elections but by the presence of the Red Army. And Soviet influence now extended as far as its troops had advanced.

The warning was accompanied by a call for an Anglo-American military alliance to present an armed front against Communist expansion. "From what I have seen of our Russian friends and allies . . . I am convinced there is nothing they admire so much as strength, and nothing for which they have less respect than weakness."

The message met with something less than unanimous assent in the West. The British Foreign Office, one of its postwar members recalls, considered the speech "absolutely disastrous," "a stone thrown in the pond" of Allied efforts to deal with the Russians.

In Washington and around the country the speech was widely criticized as "warmongering," an "invitation to war against the Soviet Union." Indeed, Stalin called the speech "a declaration of war."

Some Americans found it instructive.

RICHARD M. NIXON

I was at that time running for Congress of the United States in the 12th District of California. I had just come out of the service. I had never run for office before. I was taking on Jerry Voorhees, a very popular incumbent who had held the office for ten years.

My reaction to the speech was rather curious at the time. The Communist issue had not yet become a big one. I appreciated the fact that the Russians had been our allies in World War II, as most people did. And I thought Churchill was too belligerent when I read the speech in the *Los Angeles Times*. I wondered if he wasn't seeing dangers there, or exaggerating a situation and seeing dangers that really weren't there. However, he proved to be right.

That speech, the Iron Curtain speech, alerted me to the Communist problem in the world, the fact that the Soviet Union, who had been our allies, were now our adversaries. The need for me was to think not just about the problems of the 12th District and what do we do about the citrus and the irrigation, the dams, et cetera of that particular district but what do we do about the world? It was then that I think I began to think for the first time in terms of foreign policy being my major interest.

Senator Claude Pepper, an independent-minded New Dealer, by no means one of Truman's personal favorites, was asked by the President several days after Fulton what he thought of it. Pepper said he thought it was "unwise and unfortunate." What he felt, though he didn't say it, was that the speech had merely reinforced Truman's own anti-Soviet mind-set.

The maverick Democrat from Florida had been disturbed by some of the things he saw and heard on his postwar fact-finding trip through Eastern Europe ("paid my own expenses, practically all of it"). President Eduard Beneš of Czechoslovakia had told him "that Stalin had personally promised him that if he would allow them [the Soviets] to manage their foreign policy, he would not interfere with their domestic policy."

Senator Pepper had not found that necessarily reassuring. Apparently, the Russians "were determined that for the first time they would get their clutches on Eastern Europe."

At the same time, Pepper was also disturbed by what he considered to be the hard line evolving in the administration's foreign policy. At the end of the war, U.S. lend-lease aid to the Soviets had been abruptly cut off rather than phased out. The impact on the Russian economy was painful.

CLAUDE D. PEPPER
Democratic congressman from Florida
1946: Democratic senator from Florida

Stalin had told me in detail how much pig iron they were producing and how much oil they were producing and how many cars they had and how many locomotives. He had it all at his fingertips. And then he told of the terrible devastation and the small amount of those things that they had after the Germans left. So the Russians suffered worse than any of the Allies. And not only that, Stalin said, "We lost fifteen million killed. Fifteen million of our people were dead at the end of this war, on account of this war of Hitler."

To my surprise, he said, "You know, your country didn't even reply in the last six months to a request I made for a six-billion-dollar"—either "loan" or "grant" (I don't remember which he said). But he said, "I submitted the request for a loan (or a grant) of six billion dollars, and it's been now six months, and I never even had a reply from your country."

Well, that was shocking to me, that my country would be that inconsiderate of a major nation like the Soviet Union, one which had been our valued ally a little while before. So I made inquiry about it when I got back home, and, indeed, I mentioned it on the floor of the Senate. And the State Department said, "Yes, there was something about a message from him on that subject, but it got lost." Well, I—I'm rather too skeptical of a matter [of that nature] getting lost.

In his meeting with Stalin, Pepper asked why the two wartime Allies couldn't seem to work together in peace. Stalin pointed out that they had been held together during the war by the bond of "a common enemy," adding that now "there were many things to divide us; but as Christ said, 'Seek and ye shall find.' "

Pepper was so startled that he asked his interpreter, George Kennan, the U.S. embassy counsellor, if that really was what the Communist leader had said. "He sure did," Kennan told him.

It was one of the few times a Soviet leader was known to cite any authority higher than Marx or Lenin.

Senator Pepper's forebodings about the possible effect of Churchill's speech were not unfounded. According to Clark Clifford, "the impact upon the President was substantial." It seemed as if, once the alarm had been sounded, United States officials began looking for signs of Kremlin activity everywhere. They had no trouble finding it.

In the countries of Eastern Europe, an ominous pattern had been established. In the provisional governments, Communists were invariably installed in charge of the interior ministry, giving them control of the police and with it the power to suppress political opposition. The Yalta promise of free elections was going by the boards.

In the Middle East, the Russians demanded a share in the control of the Dardanelles, the Turkish straits leading into the Black Sea. They proposed to abrogate a post–World War I treaty that kept the straits open to international traffic. They balked at withdrawing their troops from a border province of Iran.

In the UN, the Russians rejected a remarkable United States proposal to surrender its own monopoly of nuclear power and submit it to international control. The Russians weren't willing to give up their own nuclear development until they too had achieved an atomic bomb and proved themselves a first-class power.

In occupied Germany, the Soviets were pursuing economic policies at odds with the Western Allies. There were also discomfiting personal incidents. There was an occasion when Marshal Zhukov, the Russian supreme commander in Germany, affronted by a bit of GI horseplay he considered to be an insult to Stalin, demanded that General Eisenhower have the offender immediately executed. Ike of course declined; Zhukov stormed angrily out of the room saying he would have no more to do with the Americans.

It was shortly after Churchill's Fulton speech that President Truman commissioned his special counsel, Clark Clifford, to draw up a report enumerating all of the points of East–West conflict, the Soviet violations of treaties and agreements, in spirit or in substance. By the time it was finished, the report was broadened into an overall appraisal of the East–West relationship, including the views of officials in the Departments of State, War, Navy, and the various intelligence agencies. It arrived on the President's desk under a heavy lid of secrecy.

There was nothing in the report that the President didn't already know. But the force of those consolidated incidents shook him up a good deal, as Truman himself might have said. He sat up most of the night reading the report and found its conclusions so hot that he decided he couldn't afford the risk of a leak. He ordered all copies turned over to him at once.

GEORGE ELSEY
Retired president of the American Red Cross
1946: White House aide under Clark Clifford

The point [of the report] was, we had to recognize the Soviets were on an expansionist binge, if you will. They were going to extend their sphere of influence as far as they possibly could. And at any point where they sensed weakness on the part of the United States and Western Europe, they would press forward. And it would not only be in Western Europe, it would be in the Middle East and, to the extent they could, it would be in Southeast Asia, India, as well.

The Truman Doctrine

It was only a few months after the shock of the tightly classified Elsey report that a British envoy walked into the President's office and delivered another jolt. This time the President went public with the message. The subject: chaos and communism in the eastern Mediterranean.

Once again the basic facts were already known. The immediate concern was Greece, where the Nazis had replaced their failing Italian ally as an occupation force during the latter stages of the war. They had been dislodged by a combination of local resistance and British military pressure. And the British, the traditional power in the eastern Mediterranean, had been supervising the restoration of constitutional government in Greece under King George II and his successor, King Paul.

But a Communist army of guerrillas, striking from bases in the mountainous northern area of Greece, was disrupting life in that country, pressuring the government and threatening to seize power. Further, a similar emergency was starting to develop in nearby Turkey.

Now came the shocker: Britain, its economy staggering in the postwar gloom, could no longer afford the cost of supporting the Greek government in its efforts to hold back the Red surge. The United States would have to pick up the tab or see another country disappear behind the Iron Curtain. *Two* countries, in fact, when Turkey inevitably followed.

Truman's response to the alarm was decisive and historic. It characterized the feisty quality that came to be associated with this erect, compact man with the thin-lipped smile, the steel-rimmed glasses, the snappy, haberdasher's style of dressing—a neatly folded handkerchief always visible in the pocket of his double-breasted suits, a World War I veteran's button in his lapel. He was a man with an extraordinary sense of history—better grounded in the American past, according to his associate Clark Clifford, than any modern President except possibly the professorial Woodrow Wilson.

When Truman was young, poor eyesight had kept him from playing with the other kids, and he had spent the time reading. "I am one of the few people," he once boasted to Clifford, "who ever actually read the *Encyclopaedia Britannica.*" Like a later American President who was also kept from combat on the playing fields as a boy—Lyndon Johnson—he grew up with a painful sense of his own limitations. He sometimes seemed overawed by the office he'd inherited. "As Harry Truman," he once confided to an aide, "I'm nothing. But as President Truman I have no peer." He had developed the pugnacity of a man who grew up feeling a need to prove himself.

Truman's reading of history made him well aware of the traditional restraints of American foreign policy. The entire succession of America's chief executives had observed George Washington's injunction against getting involved in Europe's troubles—observed it even in the breach as Wilson and Roosevelt had when they felt America's interests and America's ultimate security were endangered by European events. To this point, in keeping with the historic hands-off policy, the Truman administration had shied away from requests for postwar help from the European allies. The free-handed wartime Lend-Lease program was converted into businesslike loans.

But Harry Truman saw the crisis in Greece as a sign of approaching danger and also as a challenge. The eastern Mediterranean was the corridor to the vital oil resources of the Arab countries. It was the eastern anchor of Europe's defense line.

In March 1947, addressing a joint session of Congress in a speech nationally broadcast by radio, the President declared that America's vital interests required it to "support free peoples who are resisting subjugation by armed minorities or outside forces." That pronouncement became known as the Truman Doctrine. It was Truman's response to advice from his allies in Congress that the only way he could hope to secure passage of a foreign aid bill was "to scare hell out of the American public." Within months, a program of substantial aid to Greece and Turkey, eventually amounting to some $400 million, was steered through the Congress.

As would often prove the case throughout the course of the cold war, the situation in Greece was not quite as clear as American policy makers saw it. "Our information," Clark Clifford remembers, "was that it was being fomented by the Soviets." In fact it was a genuine civil war, one of those situations in which native leftists were trying to seize by force what they could not hope to gain by legitimate means.

The guerilla general was a Marxist tobacco worker named Markos Vafiadis, who had learned hit-and-run tactics as an anti-Nazi partisan. His forces were reckoned by the government at 27,000; he claims 47,000. Unquestionably, General Markos's guerilllas got outside help, but the source was a lot closer than Moscow. The Soviet Union at first turned a deaf ear to the guerillas' appeals for assistance, apparently feeling that the timing for revolution was bad. Stalin furthermore was not eager to provoke the United States into getting involved in the eastern Mediterranean.

Where the Greek guerillas did find a ready source of supply, training, and—when they needed it—sanctuary was in Greece's close Communist neighbors: Bulgaria, Albania, and especially Yugoslavia. American officials were apparently unaware of the widening rift between the Yugoslavs and their Soviet brothers. When an American military aircraft was driven back from the boundaries of Yugoslavian air space and another was shot down with the loss of four American lives, Washington attributed the incidents to the Kremlin. Milovan Djilas, then a vice-president of Yugoslavia under Marshal Tito, now insists this was simply not so. The Yugoslavs, he says, were defending their own sovereignty against what they considered to be an arrogant violation from the air by American pilots.

People in Greece would have had little interest at that time in any such fine points of demonology. For them, the issue was life and death. Each side charged the other with massacres. The guerrillas practiced a particularly heinous form of atrocity, kidnapping children and, in effect, holding them hostage to persuade their families to join the Communist cause, to undermine public morale, and also to put pressure on the government to make concessions.

EVANGELOS AVEROFF-TOSSIZZA
Author, former deputy prime minister of Greece
1947: Member of Greek parliament

You don't know what life was for three years here in Greece. It was something unbelievable. You couldn't travel in the countryside—you had to travel in convoy. You couldn't make more than ten, fifteen kilometers an hour traveling by car in the convoys. The economy was destroyed. Something was produced but very little, because the country was controlled by the [guerrilla] bands. Communications were very bad.

So we relied very much on the foreign exchange [provided by] the Truman Doctrine to import foodstuffs and whatever materials we needed for production. Of course, there were very big limitations. There were food cards—how do you call them?—ration books.

I was a young member of parliament then; and as I put it to some American congressmen who came here, "We'll put in the blood; you put in the arms." If that had not happened, Greece would have fallen.

American ships were waiting in Greek ports to deliver aid as soon as Congress gave its official okay. Arms, food, other economic aid— the flood of American supplies had an instantaneous effect, reaching down to the level of the Greek villager and foot soldier. Jack Matathias, who later emigrated to New York, was then a twenty-six-year-old draftee in the Greek army. In his unit, "in a matter of a couple of days, everything changed." Old, broken-down vehicles were replaced by big GMC trucks loaded with supplies. Socks, shirts, everything the soldiers had been forced to scrounge for themselves was now issued to them, along with better and more plentiful weapons.

Greek morale was lifted. The tide began to run out on the rebels. In February 1948 on a visit to Moscow, Marshal Tito and his vice-president, Djilas, were told by Stalin: "Fold up the revolutionary movement in Greece! Fold it up!" But it was more in spite of Stalin than because of him that Yugoslavia withdrew its support and doomed the rebellion. For the form of independent communism that would become known as Titoism was gathering force; within a few months, the Yugoslavs made an open break from the Kremlin and undertook economic relations with the West. They also closed their borders to the Greek guerrillas, depriving them of sanctuary.

The Greek Communist movement, meanwhile, was split by conflicts between General Markos's military leadership and his political counterparts. Late in 1949 the underground Communist radio announced that, in order to avoid "destroying the homeland," armed hostilities against the government would stop.

The Greek episode stands as a landmark in the great sweep of the cold war. Historians would later disagree in trying to trace the East-West conflict back to its origins. To the Soviet's strongarm actions in Eastern European countries? The Anglo-American team-up against Moscow? The withholding of postwar aid from America's wartime ally? The Russians' abrasive occupation policies in Germany?

But there is no question that by the end of 1947 the cold war was on in earnest. The Greek civil war was the first serious engagement. The Truman Doctrine set a course for American resistance to Communist expansion by helping threatened countries, and that would become the cornerstone of American foreign policy over the next four decades.

The first test of that policy, in Greece, was a successful one, but the lessons of that experience were not always easy to apply.

EVANGELOS AVEROFF-TOSSIZZA

The Truman Doctrine convinced the Greek people that the fight was possible and that it should take place . . . [but] the decisive factor was that the majority of the Greek people was determined to fight up to the last man. In other words, if you have not the will to fight, you don't win, whatever arms you have. If you have a Cadillac, a very powerful Cadillac, but you are a cowardly driver, and I have a very small, old car, I will arrive first and not you.

·4·

EXTENDING THE COMMITMENT

In an age that is comfortably sheltered from the weather by air conditioning and oil furnaces, it is hard to imagine that world affairs could have been at the mercy of the elements in recent times. Yet that was exactly the case in Western Europe in two successive winters of wet, numbing cold, of frequent storms erupting out of endlessly leaden skies. In the seasons of 1946–47 and 1947–48, winter was a historic force. People huddled in their food-short kitchens in coal-short houses and in rubble shelters. Transport stumbled, production faltered, economies shriveled. The mood of Europe was mean and politically downbeat. France, where the extreme left had a strong foothold in the Assembly and in the leadership of the national union, the General Confederation of Labor, was beleaguered by strikes and parliamentary conflict. It looked as if the Communists might be in a position to take over sometime in '48. Italy was the same.

What rescued Europe from that two-year-long peril was a massive American program. It was launched in the wake of the Truman Doctrine in the late spring of 1947 in the merciful hiatus between those two terrible winters. The immediate aim was humanitarian, but there was no denying its ideological edge. To keep Europe from freezing, starving, and falling apart economically meant keeping the political left from taking over.

CLARK CLIFFORD

The original concept was a brainchild of the fertile mind of Dean Acheson [then an undersecretary of state]. He discussed it at some length with President Truman. I sat in on some of those meetings. And President Truman thought well of the idea.

And I remember one time saying, as we were getting near the end of it, saying to President Truman that this obviously was going to be one of the very important accomplishments of his administration and I hoped it might bear his name. It might be "the Truman concept" or "the Truman approach" or something of that sort. . . . And he said, "No." He said, "We have a Republican majority in the Senate and one in the House, and anything that bore Truman's name would be given the deep six." He said, "It never would get off the ground, so we've got to find a different way to do it."

It was he who decided to give the whole matter, practically in its final form, to George Marshall for George Marshall to take up and deliver at the Harvard Commencement.

George C. Marshall retained the nearly universal respect he had won in wartime as chief of staff of the U.S. army. The one notable failure in his distinguished career was a lengthy, arduous, and ultimately futile effort to bring the Chinese Nationalists and their Communist opponents into some kind of working arrangement. Relieved of that sisyphean job, he was made Truman's secretary of state.

Marshall had the face of a Norman Rockwell portrait and the character to go with it. An associate describes him as so staunch that "Georgie Patton said he'd rather face a Nazi Panzer division barehanded than have an interview with George Catlett Marshall," so resolute in judgment that "his decisions were never made on what was popular at the moment but where did it take you five years from now."

Marshall's speech at illustrious Harvard proved to be as momentous as the one delivered by Churchill at obscure little Westminster College the year before, though the immediate reaction to his message was unpromising. The assembled graduates, alumni, the university officials, and visiting dignitaries mostly sat on their hands, applauding only the passages of anti-Communist rhetoric that by now were standard in addresses by American public officials.

PAUL NITZE
Arms-control adviser, Reagan administration
1947: State Department economic adviser

It was more complicated than that. After all, the speech, as you remember, did contain an offer to not only the USSR but to the European satellites of the USSR. It offered aid to them. And it contained a sentence saying that the Marshall Plan is not addressed against any country or any ideology. It is against hunger and need and danger.

So that speech did, in its terms, emphasize the positive aspects of the program, not the anti-Communist aspects of the program.

Now a lot of us were involved in the initial drafts of that speech. But Secretary Marshall did the final editing of it. It was his speech. And the operative part of it was only about three paragraphs long. It's an extraordinary speech. There wasn't any "plan" at the time. Nobody had any idea as to how you actually do the darn thing. But it was a brilliant concept. It was exactly what was needed at that time. The press didn't pick it up. It got really little publicity. It was not until Ernie Bevin in England picked it up and then asked the other European countries to join him in creating a group to look into how *they* could pick this up and work and do their part of developing ideas which then the United States might be able to support and give aid to translate a concept into a program.

Marshall's message to Europe was a promise of massive economic aid if European nations would get together, take inventory of their resources, and plot their own recovery. Ernest Bevin, foreign secretary in the Attlee Labour government, immediately organized a conference in Paris of European officials, East and West, to pick up Marshall's cue.

LORD FRANKS
Former British ambassador to the U.S.
1947: Member of House of Lords,
Chairman of European Recovery Program

Bevin said, "Anything you want you can have. There'll be an airplane ready for you between London and Paris. Any minister, any civil servant, any industrialist—name them. They'll be flown over."

He was assured of the continuing United States interest in Europe—which is what General Marshall's speech meant—if a satisfactory reply could be constructed. That's why he was excited.

Our business at the conference was to work out how much the European countries at the conference, the sixteen nations, could do for themselves and what the deficit was which we would ask the United States to supply.

First of all, the productive economy was broken down. There were thousands of bridges down in France. There weren't any machine tools; they'd been taken away. There wasn't steel coming out at the steel plants because the coal wasn't coming out of the ground. And then there'd been a disastrous winter; the grain wasn't growing in the fields. So the problems were really two: how do people get enough food to live and how do they get the wherewithal of productive industry to go to work? The things that were needed were, first of all, food—wheat—and, secondly, steel, and thirdly, machine tools. With these things, people could live and work.

We thought the deficit was of the order of $28 billion, of which some could be supplied by the International Bank and the International Fund—but it was well over $20 billion for the United States.

The sixteen participating nations included Scandinavian countries, Iceland, Greece, Turkey, and—remarkably—the Allied zones of recently defeated Germany—but none of the Iron Curtain countries. The Communists had gone as far as sending Soviet Foreign Minister Molotov to a brief preliminary planning meeting, but when it ended, so did Russia's participation in the Marshall Plan. Molotov's expressed reason was curiously oblique. The American offer, he insisted, was not serious because it had come only from the administration, not from the Congress, which held the purse strings.

The Western Allies tried to persuade him—in the words of Hervé Alphand of the French delegation—"that we must first give some reasons for the government of the United States to go before Congress. But, apparently, he thought he had better views of the American democracy than we had."

Anyway, when Molotov said *"Nyet,"* he was speaking for the whole Communist bloc. Alphand says: "We had received from Poland, from Czechoslovakia, from Hungary, from all the so-called people's democracies enthusiastic approval of the Marshall Plan; and a few days after, under the pressure of Stalin, we received from the same countries letters saying that it was United States imperialism, that they couldn't accept it, et cetera, et cetera." Alphand was left with the feeling that his British colleagues had already reached—that "this division of Europe was now an undeniable fact."

Russian sources would later concede that the Marshall Plan, as a Soviet journalist puts it, "did help in a certain way" to rebuild the European economy, but they insist—not unrealistically—that its ultimate purposes were political and military. Its implicit intention, in the interpretation of a Russian foreign service official, was to shut the Communists out of Western governments, and its effect, as in Greece and Turkey, would have been to tie recipients militarily to the U.S. It was also quite possible, within the terms of the Plan, that the Soviets, with their sources of food, would have wound up a contributor rather than a recipient.

The East stayed away, and the sixteen remaining nations quickly put their facts and figures together.

LORD FRANKS

We worked from nine o'clock in the morning till two or three at night for eight weeks solid, Sunday included. And what spurred us on was the knowledge that in November Italy would be out of bread grains and that France would be out in the early spring of '48 so that people would literally starve unless we could get our report out and unless there was a favorable response in America.

About the twenty-first of September, all the Ministers came back and signed the report. Then they sent it back to General Marshall [as] the reply to his speech. Then in the autumn I was sent out to explain and justify what we had said in the report, and I saw General Marshall in the State Department, and I was cross-questioned by the Senate Foreign Relations Committee and the Foreign Affairs Committee of the House of Representatives.

I went to Defense, to Treasury, to Commerce, and then I was sent out all over the United States explaining what we'd done—all the way from Massachusetts to California and from Arizona to Vermont.

It was quite extraordinary, because people were interested and concerned and didn't always understand. For example, I had to explain to a farmer, a wheat grower in Kansas, that if an Italian offered him lira notes for his wheat, what he would do with them in the local drugstore. He'd want dollars, and the Italians hadn't any dollars. This is what the aid program was all about.

Congress did not blithely finance the participating nations' whole $20-billion shopping list. Opponents of the Marshall Plan derided it as "Operation Rathole." But a sequence of events was driving public opinion into the camp of the cold warriors. It was almost as if the Communists were conspiring against themselves.

In Hungary, which—to the dismay of Moscow—had elected a non-Communist government after the war, the Soviet manipulated Communist politicians into power. "An outrage," Truman called it. Soviet control would soon be solidified by a purge of the Party leadership, getting rid of nationalist-minded officials in favor of those advocating close ties to Moscow.

A massive propaganda network, the Communist Information Bureau or Cominform—successor to the notorious old revolutionary apparatus, the Comintern—was put into operation in the satellite capitals. Party members and sympathizers in France and Italy were propagandized to sabotage the Marshall Plan.

The French cabinet was toppled by a wave of strikes. Its successor was soon in trouble. The threat of a general strike in the mean winter of 1947–48 forced the premier, Robert Schuman, to request special police powers to head off threatened violence from the left.

The situation in Italy grew so sensitive that the United States postponed the withdrawal of a large segment of its occupation force.

In February of '48, the facade of independence and neutrality was stripped from Czechoslovakia in a brutal Communist coup—Czechoslovakia, the last outpost of democracy behind the Iron Curtain, by Churchill's accounting in his Fulton speech. The foreign minister, Jan Masaryk—a man whose name was familiar in the West as son of the Czech republic's founder—was found dead, either murdered or forced to commit suicide. Eastern Europe's political tragedy took on a personal face.

Within six weeks, Congress passed the Marshall Plan, ultimately appropriating some $12.5 billion for the European Recovery Program.

LORD FRANKS

What the Marshall Plan did as it came into effect was to give hope and confidence. The wheat flowed across the ocean, the steel flowed across the oceans, machine tools came, and people were fed; people could work, and activity and confidence revived. And by 1950, industrial production was a third up on 1937, the best year before the war. As compared with 1947, steel production was up by two-thirds; and agriculture was up by thirty-three-and-a-third percent. The effect was astonishing.

A State Called Israel

Ironically, as the Marshall Plan was drawing the West together and tugging the U.S. and the Soviet Union further apart, the Americans and Russians found themselves lining up side by side on a dramatic issue, while confronting Britain on the other side of the line.

The Labour party was then reluctantly facing a job that Winston Churchill had said he would never do: presiding over the dissolution of the British Empire. India was gone. Palestine was next.

In that underdeveloped piece of Middle Eastern real estate, Britain wasn't technically the proprietor but only the administrator in the name of the old League of Nations under a mandate acquired at the end of the First World War. There Britain straddled a pair of powder kegs. Both the Arab majority (perhaps 700,000) and the Jewish minority (400,000) were animated by long-repressed claims to nationhood. To the Palestinian Arabs, the land was their liberated province of the pre–World War I Ottoman Turkish Empire, their home for many generations, the site of Muslim holy places. To the Jews, it was the biblical homeland from which they had been scattered ages ago; since the turn of the century they had been drawn back there and away from an inhospitable Europe by the Zionist movement. Both sides held IOUs from the British dating back to 1917, the Arabs in the form of a promise to set up independent Arab states, the Jews in the form of a promise of a national homeland by the foreign secretary, Lord Balfour. The Zionist claim had taken on added moral force with the end of World War II. Even *more* than a homeland, Palestine was the only visible refuge for the survivors of the Nazi holocaust.

Two years after the war there were still perhaps a half million Jews barracked in camps in Germany, Austria, and Italy—not concentration camps but DP (Displaced Persons) quarters operated under Allied auspices. Among another 3 million Jews behind the Iron Curtain, a growing number were uneasy about their prospects and felt the hopeful attraction of Zionism. Finally, thousands of Jews were in transit through a risky pipeline, an underground route from Central Europe to Mediterranean ports in France and Italy. There they would be smuggled to Palestine in Zionist-chartered ships—smuggled, necessarily, because the British had clamped down on Jewish immigration under pressure from the increasingly belligerent Arab majority.

It was the most desperate of gambles. Only five shiploads out of sixty-three actually got ashore. Thousands of Jewish refugees, intercepted en route to Palestine, were flung back once more into the frustration of life in the camps—usually on the British-held Mediterranean island of Cyprus. From there, a mere trickle of 750 a month was allowed into Palestine.

Their cause was dramatized by the tragedy of one ship named the *Exodus 1947,* out of Marseilles, which was forcibly turned back at

Haifa on the very shore of the Promised Land—its 4,500 refugees subdued by hoses, rifle butts, and tear gas. They were shipped back to France, which refused to accept them and returned them to a camp in Germany.

As it happened, the crucial episode of this tragedy—the interception at Haifa—was witnessed by members of a special UN commission. As a result, a pro-Zionist sentiment was now established in the UN.

Close as its ties were to Britain, the United States was a traditional enemy of empire. Its own independence, after all, had been won in an anticolonial war. The American flag ever since had been a banner to subject peoples around the world. America's anticolonial policy was so firmly rooted it hardly needed to be enunciated—it was handed over from administration to administration like the keys to the White House door.

The United States could hardly remain aloof from the Palestine issue. As British power sank in the eastern Mediterranean, signaled by the disengagement from Greece, a vacuum was being created, and American power was being drawn in. The substantial Jewish-American minority, the largest Jewish national community in the world, pressed Washington in the same direction. Zionist sentiment in this country ran strong, and the plight of Europe's refugees evoked sympathy from Americans of all faiths.

Harry Truman was among them. His consciousness had been raised (as a later generation would have put it) when his old Kansas City business partner, Eddie Jacobson, persuaded him to see the Zionist leader Chaim Weizmann.

But if United States official policy on Palestine sometimes seemed ambivalent, it was because an internal conflict was going on within the administration while the fate of Europe's Jews and the future of Palestine hung in the balance—with passions rising and exploding.

CLARK CLIFFORD

[President Truman] felt very deeply about Israel; he wanted to do whatever he could do to assist in the development of a homeland for the Jews. In that engagement, he was constantly thwarted by the State Department and the Defense Department; they thought it was inimical to our country's interests. And they opposed him at every turn.

Now, this might be difficult for the American people to assume—that a department could oppose the President. But there are any number of devious manners in which they could see that his plans at this particular stage might be halted—or it might be slowed up, it might be retarded.

They thought it was an unwise course of action to have an independent state of Israel in the Middle East. The Defense Department particularly said that we should side with the Arabs. They were looking at it from a military standpoint—that's where the oil was. And that area of the world has been an area that's been fraught with difficulty from time immemorial, and they wanted us to be on the other side.

The State Department thought that we should side with the British, who also did not want an independent state in the Middle East. I think that one could speculate as to whether or not, if he had chosen to take a different route, whether that would have brought peace to the Middle East. I don't believe so. I think that it was appropriate that there be an independent nation there.

An Anglo-American commission investigated, deliberated, and came up with a "compromise" that distressed everybody. The Jews grew desperate. Zionist guerrilla warfare against British military forces on the scene escalated. An extremist group known as the Irgun emerged under the leadership of a Polish Jew named Menachem Begin, laying claim not just to a Jewish homeland but to the whole biblical kingdom at its largest (which would include Jordan). In an act of deliberate terrorism, Begin's underground organization blew up the British administrative headquarters at the King David Hotel in Jerusalem, causing the deaths of ninety-one civil servants—British, Arab, Jewish.

The British government in London, exhausted from clutching the live grenade called Palestine, gingerly handed it over to the UN. There the United States dismayed its ally by lining up with the Soviet bloc in voting to partition the area between Arabs and Jews. Not only that, but according to word received at the Foreign Office in Whitehall, Harry Truman personally called the president of at least one small country and pressured him to vote the right way. The Russians were moved not by any great zeal for the Jewish cause but by the opportunity to strike a public blow against imperialism, to disrupt the British sway in the Middle East, and possibly to establish a bridgehead for themselves.

The British government, feeling abandoned, isolated, and disgusted, tired of playing the heavy, gave up the mandate. Instead of staying on to police a transition, the British pulled their troops out of Palestine in six months. Before they left, they drained the territorial treasury and shut down the post office, telephone system, and rail-roads. Behind the British withdrawal, Arab armies were massing. Jews were digging in.

On May 14, 1948, within hours of the moment the British governor general hauled down the Union Jack and climbed aboard a departing cruiser, a meeting of Zionist organization leaders was convened at the Tel Aviv Museum. David Ben-Gurion, a short, barrel-chested man with a wild crown of white hair, pounded a gavel and, as head of a provisional government, proclaimed an independent state to be called Israel after its Biblical ancestor.

The act touched off an outburst of emotion pent up through two thousand years of Jewish exile. It also touched off a blaze of warfare. But Israel entered the war reinforced by a decision that had just been hammered out 7,500 miles away inside the Truman White House.

CLARK CLIFFORD

I remember the whole matter came down to a meeting in the President's office. Secretary of State Marshall was there, Assistant Secretary Lovett was there—and their top advisers. [The President] had asked that I come in and give his position on the recognition of Israel, and the meeting may have lasted two hours and was as bitter and harsh a meeting as I ever attended during the time that I was there.

I had read President Truman's comments in different speeches, press conferences. I assembled the arguments that I knew were in his mind. And I presented them at that time. I remember one of the main arguments was, as he said, "The time has come to end persecution of these people." He said that this country's always been opposed to persecution and "Let's do it. Let's step up now and end persecution."

His theory was that in the Old Testament the Jews had been promised a homeland of their own; and he said, "This is the time for us to comply with" what he believed to be a declaration in the Old Testament. He was a great Bible student and believed in it a good deal. He also felt that the British had not played it fair because back in 1917 there'd been the Balfour Declaration, which was a very clear recognition of their right some day to have a home-land; and he said, "That's another reason." So he said ultimately, "I'm going to do all in my power, and I intend to be successful in seeing that they have a homeland."

Well, we had a very bitter three days or so at that particular time in May of 1948. Ultimately, General Marshall came around and said, "I will not support our recognition of Israel, but I will not oppose it." The President said, "Thank you, General. That's all that I want you to do."

That was not the end of the internal conflict, however. Marshall's underlings were not ready to give up the fight for a compromise that, they felt, could keep Washington from British and Arab interests.

DEAN RUSK
University professor
1948: Assistant secretary of state
for UN affairs

The British mandate was to expire at six o'clock on a certain day in May 1947–'48 [May 14]. Well, Clark [Clifford] called me from the White House in my office in the State Department at quarter to six and said, "The President wants me to tell you that a state of Israel will be proclaimed at six o'clock, and the United States will give it immediate recognition. And he wants you to inform our delegation at the United Nations."

And I said, "But, Clark, this will cut right across what our delegation has been trying to achieve for the past several weeks up there at the UN on the instruction of President Truman and for which we've already got more than forty votes in the General Assembly." Clifford said, "Nevertheless, that is the instruction of the President."

About five minutes past six, a delegate came screaming down the aisle waving an Associated Press ticker, went to the podium, and read this ticker announcing the formation of the state of Israel and United States recognition and called on the United States delegation for an explanation.

Well, bedlam just broke out in the General Assembly. I remember one of the American political staff physically sat on the lap of a delegate of Cuba to keep him from going to the podium immediately and withdrawing Cuba from the United Nations.

Senator Warren Austin [head of the U.S. delegation] left the Assembly because he thought that it was important for the UN to know that this was a presidential decision and that our delegation had not been trying to hoodwink everybody for the past several weeks.

About quarter past six Secretary George Marshall got me on the intercommunications box. He said, "Rusk, get up there to New York at once and prevent our delegation from resigning en masse." So I got the next plane out. But by the time I'd gotten there, they'd sort of cooled off again, and we weren't faced with the resignation of our delegation.

The war that broke out in Palestine that same day took on a kind of prophetic cold war shape—but skewed, as if projected through a distorting lens. Jewish pilots took to the air in Nazi Messerschmitt 109s "very kindly given to us," recalls one of those pilots, Ezer Weizman, the nephew of the Zionist patriarch, "with the blessing of the Soviet Union through Communist Czechoslovakia." They were flying against Egyptian pilots firing at them from British Spitfires.

"We literally fought for our lives," Weizman observes, "and where did we get assistance from if not from the Communist world?"

Another veteran of that war recalls that for months he and his colleagues were so deeply absorbed in their new country's life-and-death struggle they had no idea that at the same time a crisis of global dimensions had broken out in Germany.

This time the superpowers confronted each other.

Airlift to Berlin

Germany, late June 1948.

This is still very much a beaten country living on ration stamps. What rebuilding is going on—a few shops and houses here and there among the overgrown rubble—is being done with black-market materials bartered for precious bacon, butter, coffee, and cigarettes. Americans are still startled to see dignified men carrying briefcases stoop to retrieve a discarded cigarette out of the gutter.

And yet the economy of the Western Zone is beginning to stir back to life. The Marshall Plan is about to take hold. The Allies have stepped up coal production in the Ruhr to help the rest of Europe ward off the blows of another bad winter. Occupation air traffic is turning Frankfurt into a major hub for the world's airlines. The country has held its first trade fair, offering cameras, tires, pharmaceuticals, even Opel automobiles for export, among a range of products from false teeth to complete hydroelectric plants. A couple of wartime industrialists, the airplane designers and manufacturers Willy Messerschmitt and Ernst Heinkel, are talking about going into the household-appliance business.

The slowly brightening picture reflects the Western Allies' evolving policy toward Germany: not mere punishment or isolation but rehabilitation. It is driving the Kremlin wild. For the Soviet occupation, meanwhile, has been pursuing an opposite course. In their effort to punish and neutralize Germany, the Russians have been stripping the economy of the Eastern Zone. It is done in the name of reparations but done with a vigor that amounts to plunder.

"The problem was," according to Lord Franks, the British Marshall Planner, "that if Western Germany, which had millions of refugees from Eastern Germany scuttling about in it besides the existing population, if it was to be fed, if it was to have work to do, then the old trade between Western and Eastern Germany had to be resumed; and food and raw materials had to flow from [the East] to Western Germany.

"But the Russians insisted not merely on reparations of capital goods but on taking all the consumer goods, too."

The West was left in the position of having to pour out dollars to keep its zones from starving. The problem was aggravated by a Soviet policy of flooding the country with paper currency, provoking appalling inflation. As a counter-measure, the West implemented a currency reform invalidating the cheap "Occupation marks." The Russians protested. The Allies stood firm.

It was part of a new, positive policy implied by the Marshall Plan. "An orderly, prosperous Europe," said a new directive to the military government, "requires the economic contribution of a stable and prosperous Germany."

That same spring another development had occurred which the Russians viewed with alarm. Encouraged by the progress of the Marshall Plan, Britain's Foreign Minister Bevin was moving on to a more ambitious scheme he had long wanted to pursue: an idea he called "Western European Union," a peacetime alliance which would embrace all of Europe. Eventually, even Germany.

The immediate issue confronting the Russians in Berlin in the spring of 1948 was the Allied currency reform. But it was the specter of a revived Germany within a Western alliance that had sent the Kremlin looking for a button to push, a lever to pull—something to stop the ominous train of events.

On June 24, truck traffic on the *autobahn* connecting the Western occupation zones with Berlin is turned back at a Soviet checkpoint. The explanation: repairs on an overpass. The same thing happens on the rail lines. Even the canal routes are blocked.

The biggest city in Germany, the prewar capital, Berlin sits like an island inside the Soviet Zone. Or more like a gap in the Iron Curtain, where the divided German people can still make contact. Like Germany itself, the city is split into Eastern and Western sectors, but the Western Allies' only access to Berlin is through Russian-occupied East Germany. And now the Russians have slammed the gates shut. Berlin is under a Soviet blockade. The routes along which food, fuel, and raw materials for factories travel from Western Germany to Berlin are blocked—lifelines being squeezed at every vital point.

The Communist move left the Western Allies in a quandary: how to open up the supply routes to beleaguered, isolated Berlin?

The Pentagon received a cable from General Clay warning that the situation was explosive. The armed forces were put on the alert.

STUART SYMINGTON
1948: Secretary of the air force

The question was: should we put American troops on trains and have the trains move into Berlin?

There was a meeting, a large meeting of about twenty of us—the chiefs of staff, State Department people, the secretaries. And at the meeting I think it was about eighteen to three for not putting the troops in. I was for putting them in. I felt certain that we had the Bomb and Stalin didn't and that he would never shoot Americans off the train. General Spaatz, the Chief of Staff of the Air Force, he also felt the same way. We never knew who the third one was that voted with us on it. But we were badly outvoted, and we therefore started the Berlin airlift. It was the only thing we had left when we decided not to challenge them on the ground. I personally thought that was a mistake.

You'll find in Churchill's memoirs that he praised the airlift tremendously; and it was a marvelous technical—technological—development, feat, you might say. But he said in his memoirs that it proved conclusively we could stand on our head indefinitely while the Russians sat in an armchair. I thought that was a pretty good description of what went on. I don't know whether he thought we should have challenged them then when we had the Bomb. But in his memoirs, he says if [they acted that way when] we had the Bomb and they didn't, how would they act when—this is almost a quote—how will they act when we have the Bomb but they have it too?

The epic of the Berlin airlift—officially, "Operation Vittles"—has passed beyond history into folklore. A joint British-American undertaking, its fleet of flying freight trucks fed a city then bigger than Los Angeles and kept it from freezing to death as summer passed and winter came and the blockade stuck.

SIR FREDDY LAKER
Commercial airline operator

I'd been in the airplane business since the end of the war, which, of course, was only two and a half years, and the British government at the time had nationalized air transport, and there was really very little for the rest of us to do. [When] the Russians decided to blockade Berlin, they found the first chink in the nationalization program [because] the British government didn't have enough airplanes to put onto the airlift and keep the Royal Air Force and the British airline—BOAC, as it was in those days—going.

So they had to call upon all of us funny people to fly the materials into Berlin. I happened to have had at the time twelve Halifax bombers, and I sold six to other operators for them to fly; and in conjunction with two friends of mine, we put six of the airplanes on the airlift ourselves. As far as we were concerned, it was a way of earning money, the first real chance we'd had since we started after the war.

But, as the thing went on, we could see the suffering in Berlin and what blockading Berlin meant to us. Oh, the people were shattered, absolutely shattered. They were cold, and, of course, it was a terrible winter, and they were there with sacking on their feet over their shoes, or shoes with great holes in them; their clothes were very tatty.

Whatever hate I had for the Germans because of the war, I can assure you it had disappeared in a few days after going onto the airlift.

It was a very, very rough exercise altogether and very, very dangerous. We were flying converted bombers, some of which had actually been used during the war. We had no deicing equipment on the airplanes at all. And we had literally whisker-type radio sets. We didn't have a radio compass in our airplanes.

There were airplanes all over the sky; the Russians were buzzing us. There was no radar or anything like that. It was a highly hazardous operation. It was almost like having a thousand bombers over Berlin at night during the war, and the only thing that was missing was the flak.

Of course, like everything else, no one thought it was going to go on for very long—it was going to go on for two weeks and then perhaps a month and then perhaps two months. I don't think anyone—or I didn't, anyway—think it would go on for a year.

Air Force Secretary Stuart Symington went over to see how the job was going and flew the airlift himself. "We were putting two planes every three minutes in the worst weather into Berlin. Right into the city, you might say, at Tempelhof, the airport inside of Berlin, you know. When a man missed his landing, he couldn't circle around and land again. He had to go back and get in the chain again in Frankfurt.

"As long as I live, I'll never forget the little German children who'd come out to the airport with flowers, you know, and greet us when we got out of the plane."

"Coal to heat, flour to eat"—the supplies were shuttled in at a rate that for months struggled to reach Berlin's bare subsistence requirement of 4,000 tons a day. By the spring of 1949, it was up to 8,000 tons

—food, fuel, clothing, medicine. Easter Sunday 1949 was the biggest day of all: 1,400 flights carrying a total of 13,000 tons.

The airlift created a heroic image, and it left an impression of American goodwill that registered around the world. Even across the Iron Curtain. The Yugoslav vice-president, Milovan Djilas, recalls that in his Communist country, then in conflict with the U.S. (while also moving toward a conclusive break with Moscow), people identified "with the American struggle against the blockade in Berlin. We felt some solidarity and also some relaxation."

The airlift also left a worldwide impression of American ingenuity and technical skill superior to anything the Russians could muster. The Kremlin found it devastating.

In May 1949, almost a year after it started, the Berlin blockade was quietly lifted. No fanfare, just an informal notice to an American official at the UN over drinks in the delegates' bar. The airlift went on for almost five months after that, helping keep the city supplied while ground traffic was gradually restored. The last flight, on September 30, 1949, was the 277,264th.

The NATO Line

As the cooperation among the countries of Western Europe evolved into a full-fledged military alliance, its prime mover, British Foreign Secretary Bevin, sounded out his American counterpart, Secretary of State Marshall, on the possibility of U.S. participation. Marshall told him, in effect: don't hold your breath. American economic aid was one thing, but an outright military commitment to Europe in peacetime was something else. Marshall doubted that the Congress, reflecting the traditional instincts of the American public, was ready for *that* radical a shift in policy.

Still, Marshall said, he'd see what he could do up on the Hill—he along with his deputy, Dean Acheson, and their increasingly supportive ally on the Republican side of the aisle, a former isolationist from Michigan, Senator Arthur H. Vandenberg.

The American presence in Europe had long since been stripped down to a skeleton force policing the occupation of Germany. Marshall was justified in thinking that the Congress would have no appetite to fill the outbound troopships again.

Furthermore, in 1948, when the alliance was developing, Marshall was part of a lame-duck administration—or, as some wags put it, a "dead-duck administration." In the elections looming that fall, President Truman was an underdog given so little chance that the "Dewey administration" was already discussed as if it were a fact, while headlines reporting a Dewey victory were composed in advance at newspaper plants.

With a late burst of campaigning by railroad, hitting little "whistlestops" as well as the bigger towns, Truman reversed the trend and returned to the White House with his image magnified. He was now ineradicably defined in history as the gritty underdog unfazed by any challenger, urged on by admiring shouts of "Give 'em hell, Harry!"

Among the early fruits of the Truman victory was a treaty signed in Washington in the spring of 1949 and ratified that summer by the Senate. It joined the United States to ten European nations and Canada in an alliance called NATO—the North Atlantic Treaty Organization. It pledged the signatory countries to go to the aid of one another in the event of any attack—an unprecedented peacetime commitment on the part of the United States, even though it did not in itself mean the immediate return of American divisions to Europe alongside the European army. That would have been too much for Congress to swallow and the administration to deliver.

Nor did the alliance then include the Germans. The idea of rearming its traditional antagonist was more than France, among others, could stomach.

But Moscow could see both these eventualities in Europe's future. It now could envision a future Germany not as a harmless buffer zone —a sanitized (that is, communized) strip down the middle of Europe —but as a fortress armed by the West, defended by the most powerful opponent of all, the United States.

Late in 1949 President Truman appointed a civilian high commissioner for Germany, John J. McCloy, to replace the military government. "My job," McCloy recalls, "as I considered it to be and [as] confirmed to me by President Truman, was to preside over a transition of Germany from a conquered power into a partner."

In free elections limited to the Western zones, Germany proceeded to form its first postwar government under an elderly conservative politician with an anti-Nazi record: Konrad Adenauer.

The conflicting occupation policies of the two superpowers had run their course, the rehabilitation of Germany was complete, and the division of Europe was fixed for decades to come.

·5·

SETBACKS

Nations at war, even vast and disparate nations like America, are unified by resistance to a common enemy. The trouble with cold war was that it was sometimes hard for Americans to agree on who or what the enemy was.

The Truman administration defined the threat not as an ideology but a political–military force. The enemy was Soviet expansion, illegitimately imposing its system on countries that would not have adopted it willingly. But there were substantial numbers of Americans, vigorously represented in Congress, who saw the enemy as the system itself. The threat was communism, wherever and however it appeared. For any nation to go Communist would be an added danger to the national security and a moral defeat for American power.

That is why the stakes were so high, toward the end of the 1940s, as the Red tide surged down the map of China, the most populous country in the world. Every new advance widened a rift in American society. The question of "who lost China?" became one of the bitter themes in an unhappy period of the national life.

The China Issue

The postwar collision between the Nationalist and Communist armies in Manchuria had exploded into all-out civil war. It fell like a death blow on a disorganized country that had always had trouble feeding its millions. The economy, milked by Japan during the war, was in worse shape than ever. Hunger was epidemic. Inflation was approaching the classic proportions of Germany's after World War I.

In moving into Manchuria—an area of coal, iron, and, uniquely, of agricultural surplus—the Nationalists were challenging the Communists on the Reds' home grounds. Almost immediately the Communists gained the upper hand, pushing the Government troops back with a combination of guerrilla tactics practiced in the war against Japan, numbers that grew with success, and an arsenal that also kept growing. It was made up first of Japanese arms surrendered to the Russians in Manchuria and handed on by them to their Chinese protégés . . . then American weapons—tanks, trucks, small arms, artillery —given to the Nationalists and abandoned in retreat, sometimes in division quantities.

The collapse of General Marshall's mediation efforts left the United States torn between two hopes, both faint. One was that Chiang Kai-shek's government could somehow be propped up. The other was that the leaders of the opposition—Mao Zedong, its militant philosopher, and Zhou En-lai, his political organizer—would turn out to be moderate, to be reformers rather than revolutionaries.

In trying to assess the Nationalists' prospects, the Truman administration had the testimony of expert witnesses with experience in China during or just after World War II. From outside the administration came a chorus of voices expressing the views of the so-called "China lobby," an alliance of groups and individuals with business interests or bonds of experience linking them to Nationalist China. Some had lived in prewar China, like Henry Luce, the publisher of *Time* magazine, whose parents were missionaries in the Orient.

Almost all Americans who had come in contact with Chiang Kai-shek had been charmed by him and had found him personally upright. But the government of his Nationalist party, the Kuomintang, was described by most witnesses as a kind of feudal system of loosely joined provinces controlled by warlords.

STUART SYMINGTON
1947–50: Secretary of the air force

I remember Mayor LaGuardia [Fiorello H. LaGuardia of New York, then serving as administrator of the United Nations Relief and Rehabilitation Agency] was a great friend of mine, and I was a great admirer of his. And I was going to China when I was assistant secretary of war, and he asked me to look into the amount of graft at UNRRA. And I went to China and looked into it in 1946, and I found out that the standard graft was 20 percent of everything went to the warlords—you know, the Chiang Kai-shek regime. But people were upset around Shanghai because the warlords were taking *80* percent, and only 20 percent was going to the masses or to help the hungry.

LIEUTENANT GENERAL ALBERT WEDEMEYER
Retired business executive
1947: Army commander, special envoy for President Truman

The general was very loyal to these warlords, who had supported him on his way up the ladder. And he was very loyal to friends; and often I, as a Westerner, could observe they were taking advantage of him; but his loyalty always ruled me down. [During the war, as U.S. commander in China] I would want to put another officer in charge of some big area; but he was very loyal to these friends; and I think that was his greatest weakness. It should be a strength but, in this case, it proved to be a weakness.

I did discuss the Chinese Communists [with Chiang]; and [Mao and Zhou En-lai] on occasion had visited me. They'd stayed with me overnight, and after dinner in the evening we'd sit there talking, and I was able to determine that the two Chinese Communist leaders were really honestly believers in marxism, but they did not understand all of the implications of marxism. I had read *Das Kapital* in German when I was in Germany, in school. And so I had some idea of the dialectics, as they say, of the principles of communism and what the Communists visualized doing if and when they gained power.

They—the two Chinese Communist leaders, Mao Zedong and Zhou En-lai—did not understand that very thoroughly. But they were determined to get the power and they were not particularly scrupulous about their plans of how to get the power. And they were doing everything they possibly could to undermine the confidence of the people in the leadership of Chiang Kai-shek.

WALTER JUDD
Physician, former medical missionary
1948: Republican congressman from Minnesota

I was under the Communists. They worked hard. When they came into a place, they didn't have to deal with the country as a whole. They'd improve the agriculture, they'd improve the schools, and they appeared to be a good outfit. And they did, when they were the underdog. When they became the upper dog, they just ditched all that. That was their way of getting support and a good reputation. And they do this in almost every country they take over until they feel they're secure. Then they clamp down the Communist program, and you find it's all a charade. A Communist is first a Communist. I don't care whether he was born an American or an Englishman or a Russian or a Chinese or a whatever it may be—Pole, Greek—a Communist is first a Communist.

Anna Chan Chennault, a vocal China-born advocate of the Nationalist cause, says the administration was judging Chiang's government by unrealistic standards—"When people do not have enough to eat, what do they care about what is democracy?"

Walter Judd points out that the administration's relay team of mediators and fact finders were looking at a country still staggering under the effects of a decade of Japanese occupation. ("What did Georgia look like after one year of Sherman and his troops?") Judd made his own visit to Chiang at the nationalist capital, Nanking, on behalf of the House Foreign Affairs Committee. They discussed the Marshall Plan and the Greek-Turkish aid program.

WALTER JUDD

He said, "Why does your government have opposite policies with respect to our government from that which it has in Europe? You say to countries over there, 'You must keep the Communists out of your government.' Then you come to me and tell me you won't give to our government unless we take the Communists in. It's hard to understand why America has opposite policies in two parts of the world with respect to the Communists. Is that because we're a different race from the white people of Europe?"

I said, "No, sir, I'm sure that's not it. It's [because] you've got ancient struggles going on, warlords, conflicts all these years; and people haven't waked up to the view that I have."

And then he looked up at the ceiling and said, "Well, if your country continues to follow the opposite policy in China from the one in Europe, within a hundred years, you will know you are mistaken."

It would have taken more than the kind of aid being poured into Europe to save the Nationalist cause. Even direct military intervention, Pentagon planners figured, couldn't do it. By remobilizing one million men, the U.S. might succeed only in occupying some coastal ports. A risky operation, ultimately useless.

The course Washington chose to follow was a purely negative one. It shut down the flow of aid to the government and waited to let the revolution take its course.

In January 1949, the Communists captured the ancient capital, Peking (now known as Beijing), and that spring the decisive military campaign began. Along a 400-mile front, Mao's armies breached the government's last defense line, the Yangtze River. Meeting little resistance, they swept on to Nanking, Shanghai, and other great cities.

Chiang's government, in headlong retreat, prepared to withdraw from the mainland to a refuge on the large island of Taiwan (then widely known by its European name, Formosa).

SHEN DAI-CHU
Senior adviser, government of Taiwan
1949: Member of Chinese Nationalist government

I remember talking to Layton Stewart, a former educational missionary, then ambassador to China, on one occasion in Nanking in 1948. He was a dedicated missionary, believing in the innate goodness of all men. Including the Communists. He said to me if he could keep Nanking University—he was chancellor for many, many years—could keep the university open during the Japanese invasion, he could persuade the Chinese Communists to behave. Evidently, Ambassador Stewart was too naive and had little experience with politics or the Chinese Communists.

I can never forget his voice of conviction and his look of innocence, speaking about the Chinese Communists. His judgments certainly had an impact on U.S.-China policy. Later on, when Ambassador Stewart found out about the Chinese Communists, he became a very bitter man unable to forgive himself.

The fatal blow came with the publication of a [State Department] White Paper on August 5, 1949, which virtually wrote off the survival of the National government. In a word, United States foreign policy of cutting off aid, especially economic aid, at a crucial time and then openly supporting the Chinese Communists contributed to the demoralization of the government and the army.

The "support" of the Communists consisted mainly of statements from individuals criticizing Chiang or doubting his prospects. Officially, there was no contact with the Reds.

A few months before the publication of the White Paper, soon after the start of the Communists' spring offensive, the American consul general in Manchuria, a man with the precise, formal style of a career Foreign Service officer, named O. Edmund Clubb, received a message transmitted most informally and indirectly. It came through an Australian news correspondent, and it purported to express Zhou En-lai's interest in exploring the possibility of establishing relations with the United States as well as with the Soviet Union.

Clubb discussed the message with his colleague, the consul general in Shanghai, John Cabot, and their superior, Ambassador J. Layton Stewart. It was transmitted to Washington along with Clubb's theories that it might be "an advance expression, let us say, of 'Chinese Titoism,' or more likely an admission of Chinese need for economic assistance where the Soviets were not in a position to do so." Clubb was instructed to reply—"by direct contact"—that the United States was "desirous of seeing the Chinese sentiments translated into action" (Clubb's paraphrase). The action suggested was an end to the vicious anti-American propaganda then blasting out of Peking.

Following instructions from Washington, Clubb tried to get word to Zhou through Communist channels instead of retracing the original unofficial route. He was rebuffed.

In September 1949, Mao proclaimed total victory and the sovereignty of Communist China. In a sentence echoing Winston Churchill's Iron Curtain alarm, Henry Luce's *Time* reported: "From Bering Strait to the Gulf of Tonkin, Communism was now the major force."

Within six months, China and the Soviet Union signed a treaty linking the two massive Communist nations, whose borders now enclosed more than one-fourth of the human race.

The Red Bomb

The shock waves emanating from events in China were reinforced by another jolt that same September. An American B-29 flying a reconnaisance mission off the Siberian coast returned to base with some ominous air samples. The air force chief of staff, General Lauris Norstad, reported the findings to his civilian chief.

STUART SYMINGTON

I'll never forget the morning that General Norstad came in and said to me, "I have bad news for you. The Soviets have just exploded an atomic weapon." And I said, "Laurie, that can't be true. It's impossible. They couldn't have done it based on what everybody says." And he said, "Well, they've done it."

So we immediately reported it to the Secretary of Defense, Louis Johnson, and to the President. And then we got some scientists, one of whom —I won't mention him because he was wrong on so many things and he thought he was always right—but he said, "This is impossible!" And we said, "Well, come down and look."

So they came into Washington; and they said, "There's no question about it—they've got it."

As soon as we knew that they had the Bomb, we also knew that they were a great new military superpower.

There had never been any doubt the Russians would eventually develop an A-bomb. Their scientists had the theoretical knowledge, supplemented by the captured secrets of German scientists working on nuclear development as the war ended.

But the administration had been assured by its experts (including J. Robert Oppenheimer, chief scientist of the Manhattan Project, the atomic-bomb development program) that the Russians would need seven to ten years to perfect the technology. Now they had done it in less than five.

Driven by a sense of crisis, Truman ordered his National Security Council into action with a massive, top-secret review of America's position in the world. The NSC's report, submitted to the President in the spring of 1950, was a hard-nosed warning—a blueprint for coping with "an indefinite period of tension and danger."

In the strategy proposed by National Security Document 68 the key word was a rather mild one: "containment." That was a policy first enunciated several years earlier by a Soviet-affairs expert, the former U.S. embassy counselor in Moscow, George Kennan. He defined communism as an inherently expansionist system that must be viewed "as a rival not a partner." He proposed that America accept the Iron Curtain as a *fait accompli* but firmly resist any further extension of Soviet power beyond its current boundaries.

The NSC gave "containment" a new hard edge. Kennan had portrayed the Soviet leadership as insecure and flexible, susceptible to influence. The NSC characterized America's rival as a force fanatically bent on world conquest as a constant objective. The threat to America's interests was viewed as nothing less than global.

The President's advisers—Dean Acheson and Paul Nitze were instrumental in the framing of the report—recommended containment by diplomacy wherever possible, but emphasized that the United States must always be prepared for war. And that, the report concluded, meant the rearming of a nation that had been busy stripping off its wartime armor for the last five years. The defense budget (including foreign-aid programs), which stood at about $13 billion, was projected steeply upward, leaping to $22 billion in a year and on up to $50 billion by 1953.

NSC-68 is to the secret history of the cold war what Churchill's Iron Curtain speech is to its public literature—a landmark document. By embracing the recommendations of the report, Harry Truman completed the framework of America's cold-war policy. To commitment —the promise to help other nations that found themselves in danger —he was adding containment—an attitude of alertness and resistance that *defined* the danger in almost limitless terms and, ultimately, in military form. The policy viewed the Soviet Union not just as a rival but as an implacably belligerent one. And it took a belligerent attitude in opposition.

This policy was an extraordinary development—on one hand, generous and courageous; on the other, risky and officious—an astonishing undertaking for a nation traditionally antimilitarist and also isolationist as far as Europe is concerned.

Yet this would be the basic policy of the United States during the next four decades. Presidents during that time would pursue it, expand it, redefine it, or try to reverse it. But in the end the policy stood fast.

·6·

COLD WAR AT HOME

It took detectives, not scientists, to explain the Soviets' speedy development of an atomic bomb. The shortcut was espionage. An investigative trail, first opened up by a Soviet defector in Canada, led to the arrest of a pair of scientists living in England, Allen Nunn May and Klaus Fuchs. By late 1950, the picture of Communist penetration of the wartime nuclear establishment was rounded out. It had reached all the way into the atomic workshops of Los Alamos; from there, blueprints of the bomb itself had been fed by a GI technician to his relatives in New York, a couple of Marxist idealists named Julius and Ethel Rosenberg.

The revelations fitted into an even broader picture that was being presented to the American public by a congressional investigative group, the House Un-American Activities Committee (HUAC). It was an image of the U.S. government—of American society itself—being undermined by forces secretly at work in the interests of a hostile system.

Steered by its ultraconservative leadership, HUAC had set out a few years earlier to expose Communist influence in labor organizations and had discovered a headline-grabbing target in the glamorous precincts of Hollywood. When HUAC summoned a group of suspects from two movie industry unions, the Writers' Guild and the Directors' Guild, headline names rose as if on cue. They organized a Committee for the First Amendment to fly to the defense of the Hollywood Ten.

LAUREN BACALL
Actress
1947: Hollywood ingenue

There was a meeting in Ira Gershwin's house. Everyone—Burt Lancaster and Judy Garland and whoever. There was quite a dazzling array of names.

We had our meeting at Chasen's the night before we left, in which Willie Wyler gave us instructions on how we were to dress—that we would not dress to look like these casual California slobs, that we would get ourselves together like we were real people—you know?

Gene Kelly, who had broken his ankle or something, came on with a cast, on the plane. Danny [Kaye]. I mean, it was quite a wonderful group.

We were really dupes. I mean, dupes and dopes is what we were. I mean, I think our reasoning was absolutely right. I'm sure I would do the same thing again, and I think most of us probably would. But we didn't know the machinations of Washington. We didn't really realize that communism was involved, although communism was legal at that time. The party was not outlawed then. So actually it was not against the law, even. But that wasn't our crusade. I mean it wasn't to do with communism. It was to do with the right to say what you think and to believe what you wanted to believe politically without being censored.

This pig, J. Parnell Thomas, Congressman, who was a real monster, was sitting up there with his gavel and not letting anyone speak! As they started to open their mouths—gavel! "Are you now or have you ever been a member of the Communist party?"

You know, it was unbelievable to be exposed to that for the first time. It was quite extraordinary. And he was so self-righteous and, of course, using Hollywood to make a name for himself.

It was exciting to be in the middle of it, but it was very scary. Because suddenly you felt that you were in jeopardy, and suddenly actually having to face the fact that maybe you were not free to believe as you always thought you were was very frightening. And that you suddenly had to worry about, my God, some of these people will never work again!

We got a lot of press attention. But I think probably we did not accomplish anything. Except that we let it be known where we stood. Some of the people that were on the plane with us were blacklisted. A lot of people had difficulty getting jobs. Bogey [Humphrey Bogart the actor, Bacall's husband] had to make some kind of statement. Not about communism, because he refused to do that, but he was finally convinced six months later that he had to make his position clear. He was convinced of that and regretted always that he ever did it. I mean it wasn't a *mea culpa* apology. But it was the fact that he had to do anything that infuriated him. And Danny had to. And Gene. Everyone had to make some kind of compromise.

In a less anxious time, an individual's political beliefs would have been considered beyond the reach of government. But world events were playing into a streak of narrow-mindedness in the American character that tends to be suspicious of differentness and has trouble distinguishing between disloyalty and dissent.

The imprisonment of the Hollywood Ten; the radio and television blacklist wielded by vigilantes who pressured the networks by pressuring the sponsors; the sudden removal of faces from the tube or voices from the air, sometimes on the flimsiest of "evidence"—a name on the letterhead of some do-good cause, a brief forgotten fling with radical ideas. If this situation had the makings of a witch hunt, then it was worsened by the presence of witches. Atomic espionage was not a right-wing hallucination. The Hollywood ranks did indeed include Communists (though their real offense was not their political convictions; it was their own self-righteousness in publicly presenting themselves as spokesmen for liberty while privately embracing a system that restricted it).

Above all, the United States government was shown to have harbored agents of the Communist cause. And it was HUAC that helped to expose them, largely through the persistence of one committee member, Congressman Richard M. Nixon of California, in pursuing the charges brought by Whittaker Chambers against a former State Department official, Alger Hiss.

Chambers was a *Time* editor, a pudgy, off-putting neurotic. Hiss was an aging preppy reeking of decency with excellent references from Washington and Wall Street—from former colleagues in government like Dean Acheson and current ones in the world of the big corporate foundations like John Foster Dulles, the New York lawyer. Hiss had served as an adviser to Roosevelt at Yalta and as secretary general *pro tem* of the UN in its organizational phase. The idea that he had once been feeding classified State Department documents to Chambers, a confessed former courier for the Soviet, was wildly implausible. So was the melodrama with which Chambers, when challenged by the threat of a law suit, produced his evidence. Documents were retrieved from the dumbwaiter of a relative's New York apartment in an envelope covered with ten years' dust. Microfilm emerged from a hollowed-out pumpkin on Chambers's Maryland farm.

Nixon stuck with the case as it ran its outlandish course. Hiss was protected against espionage charges by the statute of limitations. Perjury charges against him resulted in a trial that ended in a hung jury.

But in a second trial the image of liberal decency collapsed. It was not so much the weight of the evidence that brought Hiss down as the strain on human credulity.

For to maintain faith in Alger Hiss's innocence would have required explaining away Whittaker Chambers's presence in the personal life of a man who claimed to have trouble remembering him. Chambers knew such details about Hiss as his penchant for bird watching and the pet names he and his wife had for each other. The Hisses had turned over their apartment for a while to this supposed near-stranger with a bad credit rating and had given him their old car. There was even some indication that they had given him $400 to buy another car, all but depleting a savings account to do it—this in the middle of the Depression.

To believe Hiss's denial of Chambers's charges, the jury would have had to believe that the FBI had forged documents that appeared to incriminate the former State Department official; that the FBI had also planted an incriminating typewriter for the defense to find and misguidedly bring into the courtroom on its own behalf.

The jury would also have had to discount the confession of one Julian Wadleigh, also ex-State Department, whom Chambers named as another of his sources. The jury would have had to resist the impact of other cases, going on at the same time, which clearly established the reality of Communist espionage. And it would have had to resist the pressure of world events—the shock of the Soviet A-bomb and the Chinese Communist offensive, which was driving the Nationalists back from the Yangtze as the Hiss case unfolded.

When, in January 1950, the second jury convicted Alger Hiss of perjury—in effect, of having been a Communist agent—the verdict fell with devastating effect upon the liberal community and upon whatever illusions may have remained about the good faith of America's wartime ally. For Hiss personified the liberals' vision of a postwar community built on international trust and cooperation. To the hardliners, Hiss's guilt confirmed what they had long believed about Communist "treachery" at Yalta and about the subversion of American interests under the conservatives' arch-villain FDR.

The controversy surrounding the Hiss case died hard, but most of the testimony that drifted in over the ensuing years was damaging to him. More than two years after the verdict, for example, a former U.S. ambassador to Russia and to France, William C. Bullitt, disclosed that as far back as 1939 the French premier, Edouard Daladier, had mentioned an American named Alger Hiss as a Soviet agent. The information came from French intelligence.

At the time, Bullitt said, he had never heard of Hiss and had no idea he was in the State Department. Bullitt had shrugged the story off.

Enter McCarthy

The tragedy of the Hiss case is that it was ancient history widely misread as the latest news. The case was about events that had taken place in the fading time of the thirties, about attitudes—illusions—shaped by the ideas of that decade and the experience of hard times. It illuminated a past danger but at the cost of creating a new one.

There were thirty-seven names altogether delivered to the FBI by Chambers and another admitted one-time Communist agent. None of the thirty-seven was still in the State Department. Several confessed to having been Communists but denied espionage. Others claimed the right to say nothing under the Fifth Amendment. Several were removed from the scene by death, at least one in ambiguous circumstances suggesting suicide—fearing exposure? despairing of justice? It was impossible to tell.

Meanwhile, the Truman administration, yielding to the incipient paranoia and also sharing it, was pursuing a vigorous program of loyalty and security checks on government employees. ("Security risks" could be dismissed for various reasons like personal associations, homosexuality, and so on.) In five years of FBI screenings covering more than three million employees, not a single case of espionage was turned up.

If there was any doubt about the administration's awareness of the *external* threat, then it should have been dispelled within ten days of the Hiss verdict when the President announced he had given the go-ahead on a nuclear weapon that would leapfrog the Soviet A-bomb. He was proceeding with development of a fusion-process hydrogen bomb—the "hell weapon." He was proceeding against the advice of J. Robert Oppenheimer and in spite of a public appeal on television by the patron saint of the atom bomb, Albert Einstein.

But if the Hiss case was to some small degree responsible for this build-up of American military defenses, then it also exposed the country to a destructive internal force, the phenomenon that would come to be known as McCarthyism.

RICHARD M. NIXON

McCarthy, from a personal standpoint, was very attractive. He could be very captivating. He had a lot of charisma. He was a fine speaker. But he was just a loose cannon. He was totally uncontrollable.

What we have to remember is that McCarthy did not—was not one who from the beginning of his career understood the Communist threat and wanted to deal with it. He sort of *discovered* it. He wasn't around when I investigated the Hiss case. He was in the Senate, but he didn't have any interest in it. It was only after Hiss was convicted that he decided to make a speech in West Virginia, and I remember he made the speech without consulting anybody and said there were sixty card-carrying Communists in the State Department.

I immediately got a hold of him in his office and said, "Joe, change that." I said, "If there are Communists in the State Department, they aren't going to be card-carrying." I said, "Hiss didn't carry a card. They don't work that way."

He listened and then went ahead and said in the next speech, he said there are 250 in the State Department. There was no way to control him.

Joe McCarthy came on late, but he came on strong. Anticommunism in the United States had already advanced from a policy to a mission. McCarthy made it a national obsession—and a personal profession.

With his sure feel for the headline phrase, with his nasal church-pulpit voice sometimes sounding slightly slurred by drink, like an alcoholic priest, the first-term Republican senator from Wisconsin led the pursuit of Communists and Communist sympathizers into all the institutions of American life—colleges, schools, libraries, public and private organizations. The press served him by covering him like a movie star, responding to his news conferences, reporting every women's club speech and wild harangue on the Senate floor, validating his wild statistics by printing them without challenge or analysis. Some of his slippery figures on State Department "Reds" actually represented not confirmed security risks, not even people who were under suspicion, but employees whose credentials were being screened for any reason whatsoever, like applying for a government job or being transferred from one agency to another.

With every new headline—every new evidence of political success —McCarthy's position in the Congress became further entrenched. Important Republicans, frustrated by the party's 1948 defeat and desperate for issues for '52, rallied to McCarthy's banner. Mostly, they were midwestern Senate conservatives like Mundt of Minnesota, Hickenlooper of Iowa, Jenner of Indiana. And all over the country, vigilantes rose up in his wake carrying the cause of anticommunism into the classrooms, the city halls, the American Legion halls, purging the local bookshelves of "subversive" literature and the payrolls of wrong thinkers.

While preaching anticommunism as a life-and-death issue, McCarthy played it like a game. Joe McCarthy was so politically motivated that he couldn't even help glad-handing his own victims. A very junior faculty member in Harvard's department of psychology, released from a Senate committee witness stand after hours of being grilled by McCarthy as a menace to American institutions (he had attended a couple of Young Communist League meetings in high school out of curiosity), was bemused to find the inquisitor's arm around his shoulder. "C'mon, Leon," said the dark-jowled watchdog of America's security, "let's go have coffee."

If McCarthy, privately, didn't really take the internal threat to this country as seriously as he seemed to, his followers did and the administration had to—as Democratic foreign policy "disasters" from Yalta to China were raked over almost daily on the Senate floor and in statements duly reported in the media.

"Who lost China?" Dean Rusk, a State Department veteran of that stormy period, asks rhetorically in retrospect. "It wasn't ours to lose. The 'mandate of heaven,' as the Chinese put it, was simply transferred because the Nationalist government had lost the power to govern effectively."

That answer would not have satisfied McCarthy and his cohorts as they sought out the culprits who had, in their view, sided with the Communists and sold out America's candidate, Chiang Kai-shek. The State Department careers of J. Layton Stewart, O. Edmund Clubb, and John Cabot were brought to a halt. General Marshall's undersecretary of state, Dean Acheson, who took over when Marshall resigned because of ill health, was portrayed as "the Red Dean."

Democrats as well as Republicans got in on the kill. Young Congressman John F. Kennedy of Massachusetts joined the chorus deploring

Yalta as an FDR giveaway and blamed China on Truman's policy makers.

It was a cold war being waged at home. Mostly against a nonexistent enemy.

Perhaps the bottom-line statement was made by one Hollywood witness who cooperated with the investigating committee, admitted he had been a Communist party member, and spilled the names of some fellow cell members. "Within that whole group," he said, "there might have been five or six people who, in a crisis, might be influenced to commit an act against our country. But I would have no idea who that five or six might be except that I knew I wouldn't be one of them."

Did that constitute a "clear and present danger"—enough to warrant the restrictions and inquisitions of the McCarthy period? It seems doubtful.

In the record of that grim and bitter episode in American life, only a few moments of levity survive. One occurred during a meeting of Actors' Equity, the Broadway union, at which political accusations were being hurled around between members. A chubby comedian named Hiram Sherman, trying to play mediator, was confronted by a fellow member, who asked him the Awful Question: "Are you, or have you ever been, a Communist?"

Sherman thought it over. "We're not allowed to tell," he said.

·7·

SHOOTING WAR

Under the policy of containment, the United States stood pledged to resist the spread of communism beyond existing boundaries. But did that really mean everywhere in the world? "We were not nominating ourselves to be the world's policeman," one former secretary of state, Dean Rusk, says flatly. But if not, then where was the line to be drawn?

The pledge did not seem to apply to the Asian mainland, where the Americans had stood by and watched as China went Red. It did not seem likely they would choose to defend a much lesser piece of Asian real estate on the Korean peninsula, which had been divided up between American and Soviet occupation forces at the end of the war.

From the very act of liberating and dividing Korea—an ancient nation buffeted between waves of Chinese and Japanese invaders—Washington seemed to be backing away from its stake in that country. Originally, the American military didn't want to occupy Korea at all —didn't want troops stuck on the Asian continent. But the State Department was reluctant to leave it to the Soviets. After V-J Day, a U.S. army team was assigned to work out a compromise with the Russians.

DEAN RUSK
1945: Member of U.S. Army boundary team

One night another colonel and I were sent in to an adjoining room to propose a specific line; and we looked at a map of Korea, thought it would be good if the capital, Seoul, were in our sector, so called. So we looked

67

north of Seoul, and there were no clear distinguishing geographic features, but there was the 38th parallel. And so we recommended the 38th parallel, and the Russians accepted that with alacrity, somewhat to our surprise. And that was the reason for the selection of that line. It was a compromise between the State Department and the army.

Neither the State Department nor military people that were present at that meeting knew that at the beginning of this century the Russians and Japanese had been negotiating about spheres of influence in Korea along the 38th parallel. Had we known that, we would have selected any other line, because that undoubtedly meant to the Russians that we were accepting their sphere of influence north of the 38th parallel and that any talk about the unification of Korea was just froth.

So it turned out to have been a mistake, partly through the ignorance of those present about the earlier history of the 38th parallel in Korea.

In 1949, the Truman administration reduced its occupation of South Korea to a skeleton force by withdrawing the last detachment of combat troops from that country. In doing so it was following the advice of the Joint Chiefs of Staff (as the combined military leadership was now called). As the world situation deteriorated, they were becoming worried about leaving GIs on the Asian mainland for fear they might become hostages in the event of a general war. The Russians similarly withdrew from their sector but left behind them a well-trained North Korean army of 120,000 with a cadre of Korean Communists. They were equipped with up-to-date Soviet tanks and antiaircraft guns and an air force of Soviet Yak and Stormovik fighter planes. The United States, by contrast, was keeping South Korea's militant president, Syngman Rhee, on a short tether with half as many troops, equipped with only a modest arsenal. Washington was hoping to restrain Rhee's professed ambitions to unify his divided country.

Finally, early in 1950, the new secretary of state, Dean Acheson, gave a speech before the National Press Club in Washington, in which he defined the American defense line in the Far East. He left Korea outside it. That could be interpreted as a signal the United States was willing to let events in Korea take their course—as in neighboring China.

Fire fights between North and South Korean soldiers were a way of life along the 38th parallel. But on June 24, 1950, the State Department in Washington received a cablegram from the embassy in Seoul reporting incidents of a more ominous dimension. The whole boundary seemed to be aflame, with North Korean tanks and infantry on the move. Now an assistant secretary of state under Acheson, Dean Rusk was summoned from a dinner table in Georgetown, where he was a guest of the columnist Joseph Alsop, along with Frank Pace, the secretary of the army, and Justice Felix Frankfurter of the Supreme Court, among others. The Truman family was back home in Independence, visiting the President's mother. The first thing Rusk did—in consultation with his boss Dean Acheson and the President—was to start the machinery that would bring the UN into the situation.

The next day, in a Sunday emergency session, the Security Council approved an American resolution calling upon the North Koreans to halt and also calling on all UN members to join in opposing their aggression. The resolution could have been blocked by the Soviet veto, but the Russians had previously walked out of the Security Council in protest over that body's refusal to admit Communist China to the world organization. Dean Rusk was later told by a high Soviet official that Joseph Stalin had personally telephoned his representative at the UN instructing him not to go back into the Security Council to exercise the veto. "Apparently," Rusk speculates, "the Chinese-seat issue was more important to him than whatever the Security Council might do about Korea. As a matter of fact, I don't think the Russians expected us to resist in Korea with our own armed forces."

But Truman was ready to act—and without waiting for Congress to exercise its exclusive constitutional mandate to declare war. Equipped only with the UN resolution and his powers as commander in chief of the armed forces, Truman immediately ordered General MacArthur in Tokyo to supply American air and naval support to the South Koreans. Within a few days, acting as an arm of the UN, American ground troops were thrown into the battle. They could do no more than join a massive retreat by the Republic of (South) Korea army. It did not stop until the UN forces were nearly driven into the sea at the port of Pusan.

The Pusan bridgehead held; reinforcements were quickly poured in. Mostly American GIs, they eventually included troops from sixteen nations. Among them were units from such disparate sources as Britain, France, Luxembourg, Ethiopia, the Philippines, and South Africa, as well as particularly savage fighters from Turkey. Five other nations sent medical units.

A two-month buildup and then, in a brilliant stroke, delivered in spite of the qualms of the Joint Chiefs, Macarthur broke the war wide open by an audacious landing at Inchon, 150 miles behind the enemy lines. In two weeks he all but crushed the North Korean army with its cadre of Chinese Communist "volunteers." Breaking across the 38th parallel, his forces drove northward through the peninsula. At the far edge of their tactical maps lay the Yalu River, and across that boundary lay the territory of Communist China.

HAN XU
Ambassador to the U.S. from the People's Republic of China
1950: Staff member, Peking Ministry of Foreign Affairs

We repeatedly gave warning to the United States not to cross the 38th parallel and not to approach our border. One specific case was [the time] Premier Zhou En-lai told the Indian ambassador, Pannikar, that if the United States crossed the 38th parallel and tried to extend the war, China would not sit back with folded hands. This message was immediately passed on to the United States government. But it was simply written off as a Communist bluff and all propaganda and ignored. It turned out it was not a bluff.

Reports that Communist divisions were massing in Manchuria just beyond the Yalu held no terror for General MacArthur. Nor did the risk of a confrontation with the Russians, who, according to Han Xu, were supplying most of the military equipment for the war "though not without cost."

Douglas MacArthur was a man of commanding—even theatrical— presence: a matinee idol in uniform. His charm was legendary. His use of language was stylish and persuasive. He had repeatedly assured associates he could completely cut off Russia's one Far Eastern supply route by wrecking the Trans-Siberian Railroad from the air. As to the Chinese, privately and publicly MacArthur discounted the likelihood they would intervene and predicted that if they dared to, they would be slaughtered. As if emboldened by his military successes, MacArthur invaded politics with public declarations favoring the "unleashing" of Chiang Kai-shek to reconquer his lost domain on the Chinese mainland. (The two Chinas were then being buffered by the U.S. Seventh Fleet patrolling the Straits of Formosa in an effort both to protect Chiang and to restrain him from any such ambitions.)

Harry Truman was not nearly so sanguine about American capabilities in the Far East as his field commander. The demobilization frenzy had reduced the United States army to about 600,000 men, less than half its strength at the time of Pearl Harbor and only about a fourth the size of the Russians'. The remobilization policy contemplated by NSC-68 had not yet taken hold. There was only one operative tank division against the Soviets' thirty. And in the developing mind-set of the cold war, every Communist action anywhere in the world was assumed to be part of a master plan, with force lines running all over the map. Korea might be only a cover for some more serious move by the Russians themselves in Iran or elsewhere in the Middle East. Possibly even Europe. The United States no longer had a nuclear monopoly to count on as a restraining factor.

Summoned to a meeting at Wake Island with his commander in chief, MacArthur promised to cool his provocative political statements and repeated his assurances about the Chinese. The end of the Korean War was in sight; he would have the boys home by Thanksgiving. Later the promised date was postponed to Christmas.

MacArthur launched his end-of-the-war offensive in November, aiming toward the Yalu. But the holiday hopes barely lasted through Thanksgiving. On the following Sunday, the Chinese struck with 300,000 men, reinforced by more than half a million in Manchuria. Their strength was almost three times MacArthur's estimate. The UN front collapsed. Whole divisions broke up, back-pedaling in trucks to keep from being overrun. Casualties were terrible. A *Time* magazine report evoked images of "Bataan . . . Anzio . . . Valley Forge." The Pentagon drew up plans for rescuing the UN force by withdrawing it to Japan.

In retreat, MacArthur grew bolder than ever in the recommendations he kept firing off to the Pentagon: Bomb the Yalu bridges. Strike at the "Chinese sanctuary" by invading Manchuria with a force composed of half a million Chinese Nationalists from Taiwan and two divisions of U.S. marines. And there was more: Drop thirty to fifty atomic bombs in Manchuria and "sanitize" the China-Korea border by laying down a belt of radioactive cobalt all along the Yalu.

Without resorting to any such draconian strategy, the UN front braced and held in miserable winter weather. But the American military establishment was shrinking from its former hero. MacArthur had dazzled them at Inchon. But lately the Joint Chiefs were losing confidence in him as a tactician—his deployment of troops on the peninsula had left them vulnerable to the Chinese blow.

Now MacArthur, in an apparent act of presidential ambition, resumed his political free-lancing. When President Truman launched a peace message at the enemy, MacArthur sabotaged it by offering terms of his own: surrender or be annihilated. He ingratiated himself with the conservative Republican leadership in Congress—and outraged his commander in chief, Harry Truman—with a letter resuming his public advocacy for bringing the Chinese Nationalists into the Korean War.

It was the last straw. On April 11, 1951, Truman fired MacArthur and took his lumps in the barrage of White House mail and public opinion polls overwhelmingly in the general's favor. The hero of the Pacific war came home to a cross-country triumphal procession ending with a speech before a joint session of Congress, one of the great public events in Washington's history. It was also a national television event commanding almost unparalleled interest. But if MacArthur had a message for the country, it somehow failed to register. The only line history would remember was the closing, a vapid sentiment from an old army ballad: "Old soldiers never die; they just fade away."

Stalemate

Meanwhile, the UN troops in Korea managed to regain the offensive, recapturing the capital, Seoul. One of MacArthur's field generals, Matthew B. Ridgway, took over as UN commander; and by April 1951, the map of the peninsula looked pretty much as it had before the war started: The two armies faced each other again roughly along the 38th parallel—except that now they were not just North and South Koreans but also Chinese and Americans along with their UN allies.

The two opposing forces dug in along the line, and the Korean War settled into a pattern of attrition much like the Western front in World War I. Instead of the Argonne Forest and Chateau-Thierry, the battlegrounds were given homey American names like Porkchop Hill and the Punch Bowl.

The icy deadlock seemed to be breaking up when, that summer, George Kennan of the State Department engaged Jacob Malik, the Soviet representative at the UN, in a series of conversations, which soon produced a glimmer of hope. The focus now shifted from the battlefield to a negotiating site in a bleak field along the 38th parallel at Panmunjom—but the talks dragged on like the war. They began to seem, in fact, like just another form of warfare.

GENERAL WILLIAM K. HARRISON
Retired army officer
1952: Chief UN negotiator in Korea

The Communists had tried several tricks for propaganda purposes—all this happened before I got there. They had suggested we have a cease-fire for a month, and during that time they would delineate the line that separated the two sides. The demarcation line, they called it. By the end of that month, the Commies were so well dug in and were so well resupplied that it would cost the lives of thousands of young Americans [to roll them back].

Now, I joined it towards the end of January 1952. And they were up there meeting every day to no point at all. It was just a waste of time. When Nam II [North Korean general; Harrison's opposite number] had something to say, he just pulled one of his ancient speeches out of his briefcase and read it again. It was just a complete stalemate.

Now, we were in a situation where we couldn't give in any more than we had. Because we had about 14,000 Chinese Communists prisoners of war. And they said they would not go back to China. So we had a choice of either holding on to 'em or sending them back at the point of a bayonet. And our government refused to do that.

Now, I don't know this for a fact, but I was told that at the end of World War II we sent some Russian soldiers back to the Soviet Union, men who had been drafted into the German army. Join or off with your head! And when they [went back] and got out of the [railroad cars], the Russians lined them up and shot them all.

Now, I forget who told me that; but, anyway, our government was not going to give back these Chinese by forcing them to go back. And yet the Communists couldn't admit that any Chinaman wouldn't go back to his own country. So nothing was happening at all. Neither side would give. And they just kept talking.

Time for a Change

The Korean War slogged on without ever really engaging American emotions in spite of the fact that it became the first television war. Edward R. Murrow went to the scene with camera crews late in 1952 for a report on Christmas along the 38th parallel. He found that the occupants of the foxholes hadn't a clue as to what they were doing there. The home front absorbed the shock of casualties and the economy absorbed the jolt of inflation from increased defense spending without sacrifice in the way of tax increases or economic controls. The public accepted the Korean War—or tolerated it—with a sense of duty but little sense of mission, and tolerated it with growing impatience.

But the Korean War was having a kind of ricochet effect all over the world, including the United States. If the Soviet Union had permitted —probably encouraged—its Asian allies to shoot their way across a border when the opportunity was tempting, then might not the Communists be similarly tempted in Europe, where they had overwhelming superiority on the ground? The commander of the newly organized NATO ground forces, Britain's prickly Field Marshal Sir Bernard L. Montgomery, had been given the commission of defending the Elbe, with a fallback position on the Rhine. Monty told his political superiors, in almost so many words: "With the forces you're giving me, I'd be lucky if I can defend Brittany." Another British skeptic said all the Russians needed to get to the Atlantic was boots. Which was probably true. The strongest military forces on the Continent outside the Soviet Union at that time were the Swedes, the Swiss, and the Yugoslavs, none of them in NATO.

Alarmed at that situation, European leaders agreed that NATO would have to be built up from an alliance mainly on paper to a military force in the field. There were only two potential sources for the buildup. First, Germany would have to be rearmed—contrary to the wartime aims of the allies, to Soviet fears, and to historic French forebodings. Second, United States troops would have to be brought back to the Continent—contrary to the whole thrust of American sentiment at the end of the war and to historic precedent in peacetime.

In the "great debate" (as the media called it) in Washington over sending troops to NATO, a fundamental split was revealed in the American outlook toward the world. It was not really a matter of "isolationism" versus "internationalism"—both sides favored American involvement but in different areas of the world. Liberals in both parties, based primarily in the East, had a special interest in Europe. Conservatives, whose strength was mainly in the Midwest and West, tended to look toward the Orient and Latin America.

Possibly there was a cultural component in this schism: conservatives sometimes seemed to feel uneasy dealing with established societies; they preferred the open frontiers of less developed countries, which were more susceptible to American power.

"The commitment of a land army to Europe is a program . . . into which we should not drift," declared the principal conservative spokesman. Ohio's powerful Republican Senator Robert A. Taft. But he and his colleagues regarded Japan, Korea, and the Philippines as vital to American interests, and their voices were the loudest in decrying the "loss of China."

But the most influential voice on the opposite side was another Midwestern Republican, General Dwight D. Eisenhower. The debate ended with Congress voting to send four American divisions to Europe as part of the NATO defense force under Eisenhower's overall command.

When the GOP looked for a standard bearer in the 1952 presidential election, the possibilities included Taft, Eisenhower, and General MacArthur, who threw his visored, gold-braided old soldier's cap into the ring. The '52 convention in Chicago was a struggle for the soul of the Republican party. In choosing Eisenhower as their candidate, the Republicans were confirming the American commitment to NATO and Europe.

The Democrats, behind Harry Truman's hand-picked candidate, Governor Adlai E. Stevenson of Illinois, struggled under the burden of "the mess in Washington." Headlines about Washington scandals and a drumfire of McCarthyite speeches left an impression of an administration riddled with "influence peddling" and undermined by Communist "dupes" and "subversives." It was "time for a change," the Republicans declared. The Democrats had run the country for twenty years, through two wars. And this one was one too many. Eisenhower's campaign promise that if elected, "I shall go to Korea," probably ended whatever slim hopes the Democrats may have had.

But Eisenhower's election as thirty-fourth President of the United States carried with it a guarantee that the Truman policies of containment and commitment would continue.

High point of U.S.–Soviet alliance in World War II came in linkup of GIs and Red Army troops on a wrecked bridge over the Elbe River in Germany, in April 1945. *(UPI/Bettmann Newsphotos)*

At Potsdam conference in defeated Germany, Allied leaders agreed on framework for occupation of country and joint administration of Berlin. Britain's Churchill (left) was replaced in mid-conference as new prime minister, Attlee, joined President Truman and Soviet leader Stalin. *(AP/Wide World Photos)*

When World War II victory celebration jammed New York's Times Square with its largest crowd, on August 14, 1945, the shooting was over, but conflicts that led to the Cold War were already emerging in Europe and Middle East. *(AP/Wide World Photos)*

Battered Berlin, stirring back to life in 1945, would soon become a battleground of East-West policy conflicts. *(AP/Wide World Photos)*

Japanese cooperation with U.S. occupiers was symbolized by the 1945 visit of Emperor Hirohito to American commander, General Douglas MacArthur, at the U.S. embassy in Tokyo—a gesture that shocked many of the emperor's subjects. *(AP/Wide World Photos)*

President Truman and Winston Churchill, flanked by Secret Service agents, en route from Washington to Fulton, Missouri, in 1946. In a speech warning of the Soviet threat, former British prime minister originated the term "Iron Curtain." *(Terry Savage/Harry S Truman Library)*

A-bomb test at Bikini atoll in the Pacific in July 1946 signaled America's monopoly of nuclear power. It would be three years before the Soviet Union tested its first nuclear weapon. *(AP/Wide World Photos)*

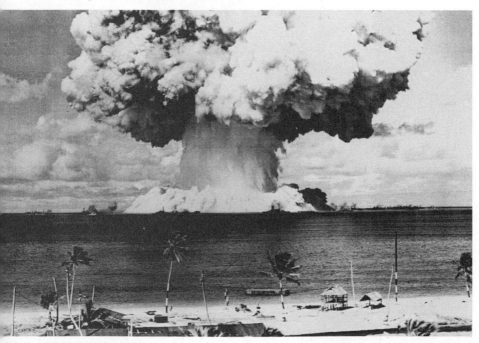

Home front of the Cold War: 1947 hearings on Communist influence in film industry drew Hollywood stars including Lauren Bacall (second row, far right) and her husband, Humphrey Bogart. House Un-American Activities Committee (HUAC) proceedings led to controversial trial of "Hollywood Ten." *(UPI/Bettmann Newsphotos)*

Congressman Richard M. Nixon (right) views microfilmed "Pumpkin Papers" delivered by confessed Communist agent Whittaker Chambers as evidence to support his espionage charges against Alger Hiss, former State Department official. With Nixon is Robert L. Stripling, chief investigator for HUAC. *(AP/Wide World Photos)*

Allied planes were a welcome sight in 1948 to the people of war-ravaged West Berlin. Airlift was the city's lifeline during year-long Communist blockade. *(Walter Sanders, Life Magazine © Time Inc.)*

Czech factory workers were mobilized by Communists in support of 1948 coup, ending the last democratic government behind the Iron Curtain. *(AP/Wide World Photos)*

Greek children line up for distribution of bread baked with Marshall Plan flour, shipped from Higginsville, Missouri, late in 1949. *(UPI/Bettmann Newsphotos)*

British troops remove Jewish refugees from the ship *Exodus* in 1947. Masses of Jewish refugees attempted "illegal" immigration to Palestine before formation of an independent Jewish state. *(UPI/Bettmann Newsphotos)*

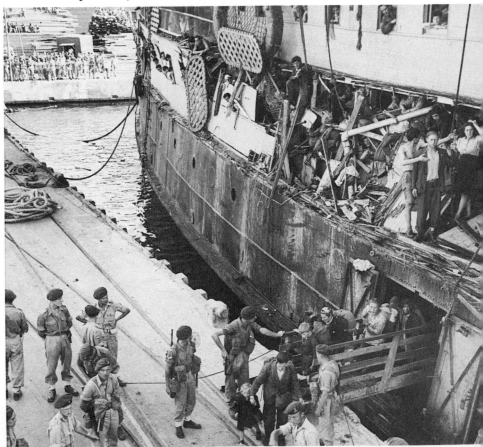

Creation of Israel by the UN in 1948 was signaled by this flag flown from the office of the new government's representative in New York. His 14-year-old son watches well-wishers celebrating by dancing the *hora* in the street below. *(AP/Wide World Photos)*

In homage to Mao Zedong, crowds filled streets of China's cities in 1949, celebrating the triumph of the Communist revolution. *(AP/Wide World Photos)*

As UN commander in Korea, General MacArthur (gesturing, in characteristic dark glasses) followed his troops ashore soon after the 1950 invasion at Inchon, behind Communist lines. *(AP/Wide World Photos)*

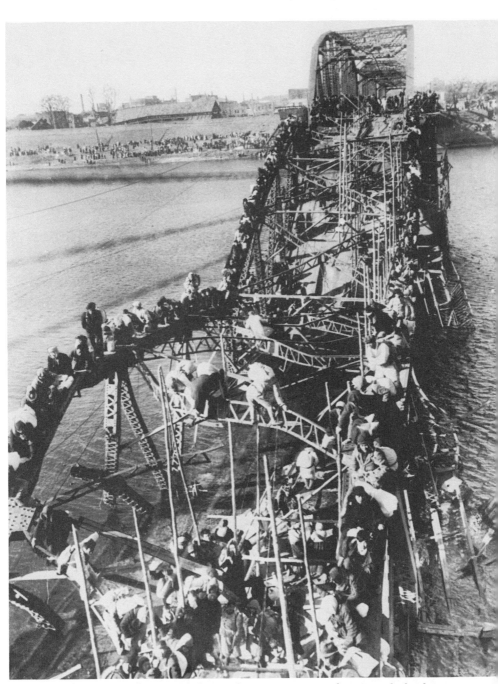

North Korean refugees crawl toward sanctuary across the ruins of a bridge spanning the icy Taedong River in the winter of 1950. Their flight was prompted by advance of Chinese armies entering the war and driving the UN forces south. *(AP/Wide World Photos)*

·PART II·

THE SHADOW OF THE BOMB
Eisenhower and Khrushchev

1953-60

·8·

REVIEWING THE ODDS

Painted over with the soft pastels of nostalgia, the 1950s have receded into the common memory as "Happy Days"—a kind of endless high school term unburdened by books. Its main forms of activity (according to that image) were sock hops and drag races. To the extent that elders come into the picture at all, they are college students without political passions—members of a "silent generation"—and success-oriented parents oblivious to all concerns except getting, spending, and commuting.

The picture is rooted in certain undeniable facts of social history. The decade of the fifties was the period in which adolescents as a group first detached themselves from their families and formed a community of their own as teen-agers (a term that didn't even exist before World War II). The American economy was shifting into high gear. A vast range of new products entered the market, especially household appliances and other electrical gadgets. Installment credit and an ingenious new form of currency called the credit card had the miraculous, if somewhat illusory, effect of spreading the wealth while spurring business growth. The combination of easy money and favorable new union contracts had delivered a middle-class standard of living to the families of American working men and women. Affluence as a general condition of life and consumption as a social value were symbolized by the automobile culture. Once the American goal had been a car in every garage; now it was *two* . . . plus Junior's deuce coupe or his sister's convertible in the driveway.

Political ideas were muted by a growing middle-class consensus.

The American ideal of working for yourself—the ideal historically represented by the farmer or small businessman—was being sold out for the security of a slot in a big corporation. The man in the gray flannel suit was a commuter with a strong stake in the status quo, whose children's instinct for youthful experiment was expressed mostly in a suggestive form of music, a derivative of blues, called rock and roll. The company the breadwinner worked for was rapidly outgrowing its domestic boundaries. American brand names—Ford, General Motors, IBM, and especially Coca-Cola—were following the path of American power and prestige, establishing themselves in overseas markets.

"Happy days," no doubt.

But where in this expansive picture is the constrictive effect of McCarthyism, which reached its zenith in the fifties, sapping much of the political energy of the United States in the process? Where is the continuing debate over America's relationship to the rest of the world —a debate that persisted in spasms of isolationism even after the issue had really been settled, as far as the American majority was concerned, by the Eisenhower election?

And where is the tension that lay close to the surface of American life—even in those supposedly carefree high school corridors—as the Bomb occupied more and more space in the headlines and on the TV screens?

The 1950s was the decade in which the cold war became increasingly militarized.

Understanding Ike

Like the '50s decade itself, the American leader who presided over this era was far more complex than his standard image. With his Kansas farmboy grin, Dwight David Eisenhower radiated friendliness as he inspired confidence. His public manner was rarely anything but unflappably benign. Only intimates were familiar with his explosive temper, sometimes expressed in army-barracks language.

Ike had had a frugal boyhood, and the life of a professional soldier between wars wasn't exactly luxurious. As aide to the army chief of staff, General MacArthur, in the Depression thirties, Major Eisenhower traveled around Washington by streetcar and had to sign chits for the tokens. As President Eisenhower, he worried about the size of the defense budgets the way he worried about spending his own pocket money—worried about it for humanitarian reasons as well as economic reasons.

Ike respected money, and he worshiped rich men, as if unaware that he was a hero to them. Shortly after he entered the White House, he had a dinner for a dozen or so business leaders. Afterwards, he confided to an associate how moved he'd been when, individually, they told him they were flattered to have been invited to share his table.

"And you know," Ike said in a voice filled with awe, "every one of those men was worth at least five million dollars!"

The cabinet that President Eisenhower appointed was described as "eight millionaires and a plumber." (The secretary of labor, Martin P. Durkin, was a steamfitters' union official.) There was a general impression that the President deferred to them—even was manipulated by them. Partly because of his convoluted speech pattern and his often hazy way with details, Ike himself was widely thought to be ill-informed or little interested in ideas. That did him an injustice.

It was true enough that, in the traditional style of military command, he usually left details—especially unpleasant or burdensome ones—to his underlings. But on the big issues Ike was very much his own man.

ROBERT BOWIE
Washington lawyer, university professor, author
1953–55: Director of policy planning
for the State Department

I remember they were discussing a paper dealing with economic assistance to India. It called for quite a large sum of money.

George Humphrey, who was the secretary of the treasury, was finding it very hard to get a balanced budget. So, essentially, why should we be charging the American taxpayer in a free-enterprise society in order to support socialist India?

And Eisenhower leaned back and said, "George, you really don't understand the situation." He said, "India isn't the United States. They can't possibly run a free-enterprise economy as ours might be. If I were running India, I would have to do many of the things that you consider socialist."

Now, where he got his understanding about the Indian situation, I don't know. But he saw a fairly large number of people who went through and talked to them and so on. He picked things up rather quickly. It was pretty clear that he had a very definite picture of the problems of anyone trying to govern India.

It was widely believed that in foreign policy the dour, conservative Wall Street lawyer John Foster Dulles played Svengali to Eisenhower's Trilby. But there were issues on which Ike ignored his secretary of state and some on which he "out-Fostered Foster."

SIR ANTHONY NUTTING
Author and politician
1951–54: British foreign ministry official

They [a British envoy and Eisenhower) were discussing Communist China and the need for America really to accept the fact, the existence, of Communist China. And it wasn't Foster, it was Eisenhower who virtually exploded on the subject of Communist China. He was far more opposed to the recognition of Peking than Foster Dulles. And his reasons for this were largely—you might almost call them—evangelical. For decades, churches in America had been collecting money for little missions and so on, and all this had been "thrown back at them" and they had been "kicked in the teeth" and so on by these Communists. Ike would simply not accept the idea of recognition. Absolutely adamant he was. Far more so than Foster. It was interesting because Foster was always supposed to be the one who was adamantly opposed to recognizing China.

From the beginning of his administration, Eisenhower was under pressure from conservatives both in his cabinet and in the Congress. The powerful Old Guard in the Senate—its principals were Taft and Bricker of Ohio, Jenner of Indiana, Knowland of California, and Dirksen of Illinois—tried to seize control of foreign policy. Bricker's proposed amendment to the Constitution would have seriously restricted the administration's power to make treaties with foreign governments. Ostensibly aimed at those old ghosts, FDR and Yalta, it would, more significantly, have undermined the administration's commitments to NATO. Eisenhower, enraged at the cabal operating within his own party, gladly accepted the support of the Democratic minority in the Senate under the leadership of Lyndon Baines Johnson of Texas to beat the measure down.

The Republican electoral victory had been interpreted by the McCarthyites as a mandate to pursue their hunt for "subversives," both in the pages of recent history and on the current scene. Truman's tough internal security program for screening government employees was further stiffened by Eisenhower. The best-known victim of the program was J. Robert Oppenheimer, the scientific chief of the Manhattan Project, the wartime A-bomb program. Oppenheimer's security clearance was withdrawn by the Atomic Energy Commission. In an appeal hearing, Oppenheimer's loyalty was upheld but so was the AEC action, which was based on his early associations with left-wing friends and relatives. Those associations were an old story, well known to government investigators. Oppie's real offense was that he was the champion of an unpopular cause—opposition to the H-bomb, the weapon that was becoming the cornerstone of American strategy.

The McCarthyites weren't to be bought off with a few victories, however. They seemed to be insisting on total public surrender to their phobic view of the world. His influence and prestige still on the rise, Senator McCarthy himself was off on a wild free-lance campaign, attacking Eisenhower's foreign policy because it embraced Britain, which had recognized Red China, and pursuing "hidden enemies" in Eisenhower's government as energetically as in Truman's.

McCarthy had already invoked Ike's considerable wrath by dubbing General Marshall "a traitor." Ike, one of Marshall's many admirers, chose not to take on McCarthy personally but, in his usual style of command, delegated his vice-president, Richard Nixon, to check the senator's excesses. By his own account, Nixon didn't have much luck trying to reason with McCarthy privately. And publicly, Nixon's handling of the issue was gingerly at best. Nixon's own example: "There is a very famous speech—I think I'm recalling now precisely what I said—'When you shoot rats, you gotta shoot straight, or otherwise you're going to kill some innocents in addition who happen to be around.' That was directly aimed at McCarthy, and it was interpreted that way broadly in the press."

It took Joe McCarthy himself to solve the administration's McCarthy problem. He was asking for trouble when he widened his search for "subversives" from the State Department to a more formidable institution, the United States army. He came a cropper when he used his badgering techniques on Defense Department officials and on one of their generals, Ralph Zwicker, a hero of the Bulge, whom McCarthy accused of being the patron of a left-wing dentist serving in uniform on the general's army base, Camp Kilmer, New Jersey. (The case, which was to prove McCarthy's downfall, sounded like a parody of McCarthyism.)

The Pentagon finally dug in. The conflict with McCarthy led to televised hearings in which the senator's brutalizing style was exposed to a broad public. Anti-McCarthy elements in American public life, rallied by an Ed Murrow television broadcast, were galvanized by the impact of the Army–McCarthy hearings early in 1954. Opponents in the Senate mounted a censure motion. It was watered down to a motion to "condemn" him—not for his dubious investigations but for insulting the censure panel. The motion was delayed until after the congressional elections that November. Then it passed by a vote of sixty-seven to twenty-two.

Mild as that rebuff was, McCarthy's personal influence began to wane, but Ed Murrow's colleague, Eric Sevareid, may have been over-optimistic when he reported some months later that McCarthyism had become a "wasm."

Joe McCarthy died an alcoholic has-been in 1957. But the suspicion he had cultivated in his countrymen was slow to wither. And the damage to America's interests abroad was long-lasting.

The Allies' trust in America's judgment was shaken. Europe worried, recalls Britain's Lord Franks, "that emotion and not reason might dictate American policy—it didn't but it might." Communist governments regarded the phenomenon of McCarthyism much the same as U.S. administrations regarded the anti-American propaganda emanating from Moscow and Peking: as a hostile act—in the words of one Soviet official, "a kind of ideological preparation for war."

McCarthyism, supposedly alerting the country to danger, had made the danger worse.

Secret Policy

To chart a course for dealing with the Soviet Union, Eisenhower ordered a thoroughgoing review of the containment policy he had inherited from the Truman administration. But to this he added two other, tougher options for possible consideration. One was to draw a hard line and, in effect, challenge the Russians to cross it at the risk of meeting major military force. The second was to actually "roll back" the Iron Curtain as some anti-Communist firebrands had urged during the '52 political campaign.

Called the Solarium Project, this three-way debate turned into a six-month operation conducted in the style of a military staff analysis by about thirty high-ranking presidential advisers—conducted in such tight secrecy that even three decades later few other surviving members of the Eisenhower administration were even aware it had gone on. It was a real-life strategy game played for high stakes. The players were considering, in just so many words and numbers, the risks, the costs, and consequences of World War III.

There was a scary paradox about this exercise—a kind of deadly version of Alice in Wonderland, which characterized much of the cold-war strategy on both sides. For it dealt in military terms with a situation from which the military option had been dismissed to begin with.

"Foster and I had come to the conviction that the last thing the Russians wanted was a global war," Eisenhower said in a reminiscent interview after he had left the presidency. He went on to elaborate: "Every place they were in, were threatening in, the Communists were making noises, the Russians were always very careful not to use their own troops. So we were just perfectly certain that they didn't want to go to war. Of course, neither did we. But we were not the ones making threats around the world, and so we just told 'em really it'd be global war if they started—that's all. We were very prompt to warn them that their threats would be met with whatever was necessary to stop them."

That was Ike's interpretation, in hindsight, of the relatively moderate policy that emerged from the crucible of debate in the Solarium Project.

RICHARD M. NIXON
1953–61: Eisenhower's vice-president

Eisenhower considered all the options and finally decided we had to continue with the policy of what was called "containment"—that we could not roll back. But in terms of containment, Eisenhower thought we should do it from a position of enormous, overwhelming military strength. He also decided at that time that it was very important for us to recognize that we would not fight a land war in Europe and that we would not fight a land war in Asia. And that meant maintaining nuclear superiority over the Soviet Union whatever the cost might be. And that was a guiding principle of his policy all the time he was in the White House.

The Eisenhower strategy, with its increased emphasis on nuclear weapons, was translated into a reduced defense budget and a cut of at least 15 percent in the recently built-up armed forces. The policy was summarized in the administration's slogan: "A bigger bang for the buck." The money saved on armed forces, the President argued, could be more usefully spent on a new interstate highway program. This use, he pointed out, would have a not incidental advantage: It would "facilitate the evacuation of large cities in case of an enemy attack."

Kremlin Requiem

One of the factors that prompted the foreign policy review, aside from the White House changeover itself, was a piece of dramatic news that emerged from the Kremlin in the early months of the new administration. Joseph Stalin was dead of a cerebral hemorrhage. The man who had ruled the Communist world for three decades, who had engineered its bloody repressions and its postwar expansion, was gone from the scene. The change in Soviet leadership seemed to suggest an opportunity to reexamine the basic assumption of the containment policy—that the Soviet Union must inevitably be regarded as a "rival, not a partner." Eisenhower's old comrade and critic, Winston Churchill, had been returned to power in the British elections of 1951, and in a private meeting with Eisenhower, Churchill suggested a "New Look." (The term was being widely borrowed from the fashion world —Christian Dior had introduced it in breaking away from wartime austerity with his extravagantly long hemlines and full skirts.)

Eisenhower's response shocked Churchill and his aides, who were used to hearing diplomatic issues discussed in the language of diplomacy. "New look or old look," Ike said, "all I can say is that Russia is the same old whore underneath, and the sooner we can drive her back into the back streets she came from, the better!"

Ike was not as adamant as his language suggested. Soon afterwards, in a speech testing the international waters for a change of temperature, he suggested troop withdrawals in Europe and other conciliatory moves under UN auspices. The proposal stirred little interest in the Kremlin, which was preoccupied with the problems of transition. Stalin's mantle of leadership had passed shakily to a pudgy virtual unknown named Georgi Malenkov (challenged by the steely-eyed secret police chief, Lavrenti Beria). It would soon settle onto not one but two pair of shoulders: the duumvirate of Nikolai Bulganin and Nikita Khrushchev.

Ignored by Moscow, the conciliatory signal flashed by Eisenhower was picked up by the Chinese Communists and their North Korean allies. Ike's postelection visit to Korea had produced no concrete result, but now the truce negotiations at Panmunjom sprang back to life . . . only to run into more stumbling blocks. China, in another one of its venomous anti-American propaganda campaigns, accused the United States of using germ warfare in Korea—a charge that was accepted with exasperating credulity by left-wing elements in Europe. On the South Korean side, President Syngman Rhee threw a monkey wrench into the negotiations by releasing 25,000 North Korean POWs who had chosen to defect but whose fate was supposed to be decided by a UN commission. The Communist army retaliated by launching a major offensive.

What finally put the truce negotiations back on track was a United States move that remained secret for years. Nixon refers to it as "typical of Eisenhower." It was a message privately confided by Secretary of State Dulles to India's UN ambassador, Krishna Menon, well known both for his disdain of the U.S. and his propensity for gossip. The message, in Eisenhower's own paraphrase: "Either this armistice had to be signed and without any further dillydallying, or I was no longer going to be bound by the so-called 'gentlemen's agreement,' and I was going to use whatever was necessary to win."

The "gentlemen's agreement" referred to the Yalu River boundary, between North Korea and China, which Truman had declined to cross. And the rest of that sentence meant only one thing: the Bomb.

As fully expected, Krishna Menon told the Chinese Communists. Soon after, in July 1953, an armistice agreement was signed at Panmunjom, ending a war that had lasted for three frustrating years and taken almost 35,000 American lives.

GENERAL WILLIAM K. HARRISON

We negotiated in tents. Had one tent where we met together. Then there was a tent where I met with my staff. Then we had another tent where the clerks and people were. And when it came time for the signing of the armistice, they built a wooden building. And I never went in it until I went in to sign the armistice.

But I made a point never to go into the negotiating tent until after Nam II [the North Korean general] had started in. I wasn't going to go in and wait for him.

So on this occasion [the armistice signing], I went in, and they had people gathered there—the British commander and commanders of all the other UN units like the Turks and so on. And there were a lot of Commies on the other end. They were all dressed up in their best uniforms. But I didn't believe in bowing and scraping to Communists, so I just went in my old suntans, and there was no exchange between Nam II and me. It was strictly businesslike. And I didn't make any ceremony out of it at all. I just wasn't going to do it. Because, after all, it didn't end the war; it just ended the fighting. And we still got 40,000 troops over there.

The result of the Korean War: in effect, a stalemate. American troops and Communist troops would continue to face each other decades later along the 38th parallel. With minor exceptions, the armistice line was pretty much the original boundary line between North and South Korea.

The Democrats pointed out that Harry Truman would have been crucified if he'd settled for that arrangement. Hard-liners in Eisenhower's own party were outraged at the settlement. That was the trouble with containment. It didn't satisfy the appetite for victories.

·9·

PORTENTS

If the United States had not nominated itself to be the world's policeman, it was nonetheless gradually taking on just such a role. The position of superpower seemed to make it possible; the policy of containment seemed to make it inevitable. But there were cases in which history would argue whether intervention was really justified or wise in the long run.

One was Iran, where the Soviets' continued troublesome presence in the border area made Allied officials nervous. They were also nervous about the Iranian Communists, the Tudeh party, though it seemed to be under control. The supposed threat of subversion, however, became a convenient excuse for American involvement when a nationalist government headed by Premier Muhammad Mossadegh took over the productive Iranian oil fields, shouldering foreign interests—primarily British—out of the picture.

America's Shah

In August 1953, a political coup unseated Mossadegh and restored the Iranian monarchy under Shah Reza Pahlevi.

MANSOUR FARHANG
Former Iranian government official living in the U.S.
1953: Student and political activist in Teheran

On the day of the coup, I was standing in the street arguing politics with some leftist students. And I remember very vividly that about 400 to 500 *lumpen*—thuggish individuals with clubs in their hands—were attacking the stores, certain buildings used by the supporters of Mossadegh. I followed them for about three hours, and I was a witness to the indiscriminate violence against individuals they considered pro-Mossadegh.

I connect that to what I read in the American academic as well as journalistic literature when I came here—that the event in 1953 in Iran was a "national uprising" to support the "tradition of kingdom" in Iran; that the Iranians "worshiped" their king and they rose up against Mossadegh and his supporters in order to bring the king back.

But I think the overwhelming majority of American people, even many policy makers, many journalists, did not really know that they were describing some *lumpen* criminals who had been paid to burn homes and attack individuals. It was a well-organized, well-financed event by the United States and certain religious elements.

Engineered by the CIA, the coup not only restored a ruler whose claims to the throne were flimsy, but it also brought the United States into Iran as the real new power in the Middle East oil picture.

MANSOUR FARHANG

The ironies of the situation are numerous and immense. We must remember that during this period Mossadegh was portrayed by the Soviet Union and its fifth column in Iran, the Tudeh party, as an agent of American imperialism. You see, in those days the world was divided for the Soviet Union as well as for the United States between good and evil. Except that each side thought the other represented the evil.

But it's fascinating, also, to know that someone like the Ayatollah Khomeini was very much in favor of the 1953 coup, not because he supported the Shah or because he had any kind of progressive, democratic inclination but because he saw from the very beginning the liberal, nationalist forces [of Mossadegh] to be a greater threat to traditional mores, traditional customs, and traditional education and so forth than the pro-Western, upper-class elites.

And in my view, the seeds of anti-Americanism, which led to the seizure of the U.S. embassy in Teheran and the repugnant act of taking diplomats as hostage [in 1979] were actually planted on that fateful day in August 1953.

Image of Vietnam

It was early in the Eisenhower era that another distant place name first intruded itself on the American consciousness in an event foreshadowing headlines of the 1960s and 1970s. The place was Vietnam, one of three states (the other two were Laos and Cambodia) carved out of France's old Southeast Asian colony of Indochina. Statehood was a sop the French had thrown to the nationalist movements in the colonies in an effort to hold them within the empire. But in Vietnam especially, where the movement was headed by a European-educated Marxist named Ho Chi Minh, the drive for independence persisted in a widening campaign of guerilla warfare. The French, frustrated and gradually being worn down, tried to draw Ho's forces, commanded by General Vo Nguyen Giap, into a pitched battle. The site chosen by the French generals was Dien Bien Phu, a town on a jungle-covered plain shaped like a fat French sausage. The plain was bordered by peaks.

In the autumn of 1953, the French committed 15,000 paratroops to Dien Bien Phu, baiting a trap for the Vietnamese. They did not worry about the surrounding crests because it was clear the Viet Minh—as Ho's nationalist movement was called—wouldn't be able to drag artillery up to those commanding positions through the surrounding jungle countryside.

They were wrong. For months, an anthill of 90,000 peasants dragged caissons through the jungles to the heights around Dien Bien Phu. And in mid-March 1954, the artillery opened up on the French, beginning the ordeal called the siege of Dien Bien Phu. In the coming months, the place was turned into a kind of tropical mini-Verdun, the site of the quintessential World War I battle, in which French armies (along with their German attackers) were called upon to suffer beyond endurance.

PIERRE SCHOENDOERFER
French film journalist
1954: Combat photographer at Dien Bien Phu

The flies! The bzzzz of a fly is the sound of death. The stink! The stink that a body, alive or dead, can produce. The thirst! At the end, we were hungry. And we were not sleeping enough. And we had to stay—I'm talking not of me, I'm talking about the people I was with. And then to die in a trench full of shit and bodies for many weeks was worse.

It was so hot, and we were always in the mud at the end. For the last months of Dien Bien Phu, we were in the mud and cold by night, and we were too hot by day.

I don't think we were expecting the arrival of American forces directly, no. We just wanted the destructive power that the French air force did not have at the time—the capacity to destroy the artillery positions.

The idea of sending American air support to the beleaguered French at Dien Bien Phu was seriously debated within the Eisenhower administration, though it went against the grain of America's traditional anticolonial policy. FDR had tried to persuade the French to give up their claims in Southeast Asia. Truman and Eisenhower and Ike's secretary of state, John Foster Dulles, all shared the same anticolonial instincts. But support of the French in their doomed efforts to hang on to the shreds of empire was the price of alliance. America was already footing one-third of the bill for French defense efforts in Indochina.

When Eisenhower backed off the idea of going directly to the rescue of the French garrison at Dien Bien Phu, it was mainly because of unmistakable signals from Capitol Hill that the Congress, representing the American public, would not stand for it. Especially not so soon after the sacrifice and frustration of Korea.

American involvement in Southeast Asia continued, however, outlasting the French. The guidepost of American policy in that area was fixed by President Eisenhower in an image forecasting the fall of one country after another if the Communists were not checked: "You have a row of dominoes, and you knock over the first one, and what will happen to the last one is the certainty that it will go over very quickly."

Dien Bien Phu fell, with the wholesale surrender of the French garrison, on May 7, 1954. In a peace conference at Geneva, Switzerland, the French signed an agreement turning over the northern half of Vietnam to the Viet Minh while a French-sponsored regime controlled the south. The country was to be reunited under free elections in 1956—elections the revolutionaries were convinced they would win. The United States attended the conference but did not sign the agreement. Neither did South Vietnam.

Russia and China took an active role in the agreement. At one point in the fighting, Ho Chi Minh had appealed to China—Vietnam's northern neighbor and historic enemy—to send in troops, as in Korea. China, still bleeding from its losses in Korea, was in no position to do so. But Zhou En-lai was persuaded by Khrushchev to "tell [Ho] a white lie. Let the Vietnamese believe that you'll help them if necessary, and this will be a source of inspiration for the Vietnamese partisans to resist the French"—so Khrushchev recalled in memoirs he dictated secretly after his retirement.

Apparently, Khrushchev's tactic worked.

The reunion of Vietnam, north and south, contemplated by the Geneva agreement did not happen in two years—it took two decades. And then it came about not by elections but by violence—violence directly shared by Americans.

But for now there was little premonition of the role that Vietnam would play in the life of America. The country's attention was fixed on the present, the American mind and spirit absorbed in stirrings of profound social change at home.

·10·

WORLD IN CRISIS

The words that opened the drama of social change in America in the mid-fifties were contained in a decision of the United States Supreme Court written by Chief Justice Earl Warren. It was in May 1954, in the case of *Brown* vs. *Board of Education* of Topeka, Kansas, that the court struck down racial segregation in the public schools. The long-accepted practice was found invalid on the grounds that "separate educational facilities are inherently unequal." Lower courts and school districts were charged to carry out the desegregation process "with all deliberate speed."

The ruling proved to be precisely what segregationists feared: the thin end of the wedge of a movement that would eventually roll back the color line in all areas of public life. Local schools began to struggle with the new legalities—at first in the South, soon everywhere. A civil-rights movement was now in gear. Its first great engagement—a bus boycott in Montgomery, Alabama, led by a young black minister, Martin Luther King, Jr.—began in December 1955. As the country approached the presidential election of 1956, the major preoccupations were race (there were billboards and bumper stickers urging "Impeach Earl Warren!") and the President's health (Ike had suffered a serious heart attack). It was an uneventful campaign.

But just two weeks before Election Day, headlines began exploding abroad, and American policies and politics became entwined with incredible events in two remote places: Hungary and Suez.

94

Revolt Behind the Iron Curtain

Budapest, Hungary. October 23, 1956. On this chilly gray Tuesday, a silent demonstration turned into a national revolution, the most ambitious gesture of independence behind the Iron Curtain since the defection of Tito's Yugoslavia. It was one of several signs of instability in the Soviet empire since the death of Stalin.

In June 1953, workers' riots in East Berlin had been put down by Soviet-backed German troops, killing 38 Berliners and injuring almost 300. In the summer of 1956, an uprising of 30,000 Poles in the city of Poznan had also been crushed by force. Death toll: 200 to 300.

The events in Budapest that autumn began with a symbolic public expression of sympathy for the Polish victims, which sharpened into a protest against persistent food shortages and low wages in Hungary. There was no objective beyond that protest. But dissent, once brought together in the streets, proved to have a life of its own.

ENDRE MARTON
University professor and author, Washington, D.C.
1956: Associated Press reporter, Budapest

It was a peaceful demonstration when it started. In hours, it became a revolution; and in two days, it became a war. It was not planned—it was not organized. Indeed, it had no organization at all. It spread like a forest fire. The Hungarians got no assistance from the outside world. It was not an ideological revolution, primarily—and I know this won't please Hungarian emigrés outside of the country—because it was fomented by disillusioned Communists. You know, the peculiar aspect of the Hungarian revolution was that the privileged, the darlings of the regime, the workers, the young people, the students who knew nothing else but life under communism, the privileged like the writers, the journalists, they wouldn't have dared to revolt before '53 and Stalin's death.

When Stalin died, the "God" fell, and there was nobody to replace him. There was "liberalization" in Hungary and in other countries in the Communist orbit. There was a loosening of control.

But, you know, when a dictatorship loosens control, sooner or later it *loses* control. And that's what happened with Hungary. The Communist system collapsed. The party and its organs—I'm thinking primarily about the omnipotent and dreaded secret police—disintegrated in two days.

In two days, defying Soviet tanks, the crowd brought down Hungary's puppet government. It was replaced by a new regime headed by a Communist with nationalist policies, Imre Nagy.

While the bodies of AVO agents—the secret police—swung from lamp posts in a wave of public vengeance and their files were emptied and burned on the sidewalks, the Soviet tanks withdrew to the countryside. Hungary celebrated an unexpected liberation whose fate, meanwhile, was being debated by Khrushchev and his military advisers a thousand miles away in the Kremlin. For the Russians the most ominous signal from Budapest was information that the new leadership of Hungary was seriously discussing applying for membership in NATO.

"If the counterrevolution did succeed," Khrushchev later noted in his secret memoir, "and NATO took root in the midst of the Socialist countries, it would pose a serious threat to Czechoslovakia, Yugoslavia, and Rumania, not to mention the Soviet Union itself."

The Soviet debate—and Soviet military restraint—lasted just eight days.

ENDRE MARTON

On November 4, they came back in force, adding to the 80,000 Russian soldiers [who were stationed in Hungary] a whole army coming from Asia —from the Asian part of the Soviet Union.

It was still dark—three, four in the morning—when they started to shell Budapest. We were at home. I ran to the telephone to call the Associated Press in London. I reached the operator, and I said, "Connect me with London—this number." She was crying on the telephone, "I can't connect you! I can't!"

I had a little Volkswagen from our Vienna office in Budapest with me. So we decided—my wife, my two small daughters, nine and ten—to join the other newsmen in an old fleabag hotel on the Danube where all the correspondents stayed. We drove to the closest bridge. It was already occupied by Russian tanks. They waved us away. Finally, on the last bridge, we could go over. Five minutes later the bridge was closed.

Hundreds of Russian tanks—the most modern they had in those times, the T-52s—hundreds of them were destroyed by the kids using Molotov cocktails, which they learned from the Communist Pioneer organizations to use against the capitalists [if they should ever] invade Hungary.

According to moderate American estimates, 13,000 Hungarians were killed.

When I came out, the question I heard time and again from people in all walks of life, from the secretary of state to—I mean it—the mailman who came to my front door, was one question: What could [the United States] have done? I have only a simple answer: *something!*

"It was a tragedy," says Richard Nixon in hindsight, "and a tragedy to which we contributed." Broadcasts over the American-operated Radio Free Europe, beamed at Hungary from transmitters in Germany, had encouraged the Hungarians in their resistance—encouraged them to hope the United States would come to their rescue in one way or another. The messages apparently were the personal statements of Hungarian emigré announcers, carried away on the tide of emotion and speaking in a language hard for American supervisors to monitor. It may have seemed to be the moment of "rollback," when the United States would start liberating the Iron Curtain countries. Rejected as a policy by Eisenhower's Solarium panel, the inflammatory word was still part of the cold-war rhetoric in America.

But—again, Richard Nixon: "The situation was that the Soviet Union had overwhelming conventional superiority in the area. So what is our answer? To bomb Moscow?"

Eisenhower's answer did not even pretend to pressure the Russians into relaxing their grip on Budapest. "The United States," he declared, "does not now, and never has, advocated open rebellion by an undefended populace against force over which they could not possibly prevail."

It was not a propitious moment for taking on the Russians in Central Europe, even by diplomatic means. For at the very peak of the Budapest crisis, while "freedom fighters"—as they began calling themselves—were battling Soviet tanks in the streets, the United States—now a global fireman as well as policeman—was frantically trying to put out a four-alarm blaze in the Middle East . . . trying to cool off a crisis in Suez before the Russians leaped in.

Debacle in Suez

Suez was an implausible adventure in which friends and allies of the United States tried to seize control of the canal from Egypt by naked force draped with the scantiest figleaf of pretext.

The canal, slicing through the desert of Egypt's Sinai Peninsula, served as a lifeline for Western Europe. One and a half million barrels of oil a day moved through the desert locks.

The company that built and operated the Suez Canal was a consortium, mainly British and French. They protected their stake with troops based in Egypt. But as the tide of imperialism receded in the early 1950s and the tide of nationalism advanced, Britain and France were forced to withdraw their troops.

Early in 1956, an assertive new leadership in Egypt, the government of President Gamal Abdel Nasser, wrested control of its most valuable resource from the Europeans. Nasser nationalized the Suez Canal company, leaving the British and French out in the cold, fuming with frustration. The United States and the Soviet Union—the two great anticolonial powers—meanwhile were jockeying for position to replace them as Egypt's patrons. Secretary Dulles had negotiated a loan to Nasser for the building of a huge dam on the Nile at Aswan. When Nasser persisted in dealing with the Communists as well, Dulles reneged on the deal.

All these balls were in the air at the time of the Budapest crisis. That moment of compelling drama in Europe seemed to give Britain and France the chance they'd been waiting for—a chance to hit the start button on a wild scheme engineered by French Premier Guy Mollet and Britain's new Prime Minister, Sir Anthony Eden. A veteran Conservative diplomat long in the shadow of Winston Churchill, Eden had recently succeeded to the leadership when Churchill resigned at the age of eighty. But Eden's health at fifty-nine was a problem that would prove to have a serious impact on his judgment—and therefore on his country's fortunes.

More than just an issue, Nasser was becoming an obsession to the head of Her Majesty's Government.

SIR ANTHONY NUTTING
1956: British foreign secretary

I picked the telephone up, and the voice on the other end said, "It's me." And I recognized in a flash it was Anthony Eden. Well, I had sent him that day a memorandum suggesting various lines of policy on how to "quarantine"—I think was the word I used—or neutralize Nasser and Egypt. And he screamed over the telephone at me, "What's this poppycock you sent me about neutralizing and quarantining Nasser? Can't you understand I want Nasser"—the word he actually used was—"murdered?"

Which is an indication of just what a very sick man he was at the time, because I am convinced he would never have been party to a plot to murder another statesman [no matter] how bitterly he felt against him. And if he had been, I'm equally certain that, although he was pretty dotty at the time, he would not have screamed on the telephone that he wanted him murdered.

It was just an indication of a mind that was at times really quite deranged. And this was simply because the surgical accident which he had suffered when he had had the gall-bladder operation in 1953 resulted in the bile duct being severed. And the poison from the injured bile duct was just circulating through the system.

It was the French who finally dreamed the idea of getting Israel to make a move and using the Israelis as a stalking horse so that the Israelis would act towards the Suez Canal through the Sinai Peninsula, and we and the French would go in and stop the war, put out the fire, and—here we are on the Suez Canal! How extraordinary! British and French troops in occupation!

Israel had its own interest in "liberating" the Suez Canal: Nasser had closed it to Israeli shipping. Furthermore, to seize the Sinai Peninsula would relieve Israel of a threat it had lived with ever since independence—repeated border raids from Egypt.

For Israel, an invasion of Egypt would be in the nature of a preemptive strike. For the European allies, it would be an excuse to intervene —supposedly to save the canal for Egypt.

As soon as Eisenhower got wind of this incredible scheme, he sent his foreign-policy point man into action. The first objective: keep the Israelis from stepping off.

Eisenhower, in a postpresidential interview, in 1964: "I said, 'All right, Foster, you tell 'em that, goddamn, we're going to apply sanctions, we're going to the United Nations, we're gonna do everything we can to stop this thing!'

"I got calls from New York City and from some of my friends: 'Well, you've lost New York!' [The election was less than two weeks away.] And I said, 'I don't give a goddamn!' We said we thought the American Jew was an American before he was a Jew, so we'll just take a chance thataway."

Foster Dulles, at that point, was not at his most effective. Within days he was to be hospitalized for cancer surgery.

On October 29, 1956, an Israeli armored force struck across the Sinai Peninsula and advanced rapidly toward the Suez Canal. Britain and France immediately leaped into the crisis they had created, launching a joint invasion of Suez.

SIR ANTHONY NUTTING

Meanwhile, we had been bombing Egyptian airfields, which was rather a strange thing to do, considering the Egyptians were the victim of aggression and not the aggressors. Why didn't we bomb the aggressors—namely, the Israelis?

And the other ridiculous thing, of course, was the ultimatum which told everybody to get ten miles on either side of the canal—the Egyptians ten miles their side and Israelis ten miles on the eastern side. Well, at that particular point, the Israelis were about seventy miles from the canal. So the effect of the ultimatum was to tell the Israelis to advance and the Egyptians to retire. The whole thing was so cocked up as well as being so grossly dishonest.

I expected the American reaction to be more or less what it was. I thought it might not be quite as severe as it was. But Eisenhower and Cabot Lodge [Dulles's stand-in] between them were really very, very angry indeed. And when I saw both of them after the event, I was still slightly surprised that they were quite so angry. But it was the deception by their closest ally—that was what hurt and what hit home.

The [British] government certainly didn't believe the United States would support us, but I think they hoped that the Americans would, as it were, turn a bit of a blind eye. They'd say, "Well, we can't support this." But what we did not expect was that the Americans would come out as strongly as they did. After we had vetoed the resolution in the Security Council telling us to get the hell out and withdraw our forces, then they [the U.S.] insisted on calling a meeting of the Assembly, where the veto, of course, did not apply. We were totally outnumbered. And not only that, but, of course, when we needed to borrow the dollars to replace our oil supplies when the canal was blocked as a result of the fighting, they refused.

And it had just happened coincidentally that the Russians were beating the bejesus out of the Hungarians at that point. And so Eisenhower felt that he couldn't condemn the Russians for an act of aggression in Hungary and condone an act of aggression by Britain, France, and Israel in the Middle East.

I think Eisenhower's handling of the episode was pretty straightforward. And what you would expect of a man who had very clear, if you like, simple —some people would call it simplistic, but I think they were clear and simple —standards of international behavior.

Eisenhower believed in the United Nations. Other people believed in it for what they could get out of it, but Eisenhower believed in it as a principle.

And, after all, he had commanded the forces of the Allies in the Second World War whose victory led to setting up the United Nations so that there would be no more wars and people would not do the sort of thing that we had done at Suez—in breach, I might add, of an agreement which I had signed myself on behalf of the British government two years before saying that we would not do precisely what we did, which was to send armed forces back into Egyptian territory without an invitation to do so.

The wild adventure in Suez ended on the day of Eisenhower's landslide election victory over Adlai Stevenson. Ike carried New York by a record margin.

The Israelis and their backers, the British and French, that day accepted the UN General Assembly's call for a cease-fire. To that very moment the administration was desperately fending off a Soviet threat to land "volunteers" in support of the beleaguered Egyptians.

The Suez crisis was over, but it had long and dramatic repercussions, international and personal. Anthony Nutting resigned from the British cabinet rather than join his colleagues in "telling lies through their teeth to the House of Commons, to the French Parliament, to the United Nations, and to the Americans." His last meeting with his old colleague Anthony Eden was a sad one: "He said—he used a French expression—'Tout casse sauf l'amitié': Everything breaks except friendship. 'My hope is we will see something of each other in the future.' And I never saw him again."

Eden himself resigned a few months later, citing reasons of health, his career ineradicably blighted by the debacle of Suez.

That episode had brought the Russians into a part of the world they had been trying to crash for generations. It ended, as Khrushchev noted, the time when "the Soviet Union—and Imperial Russia before it—. . . treated the Near East as belonging to England and France."

As for the British and the French, they were now finished as world powers. For the British people, Suez was nothing less than a national trauma, a shock to the common ego—the people's sense of themselves built up over generations of preeminence.

It was just such a shock that Americans would experience almost precisely one year later.

·11·

A LEAP INTO SPACE

Early on the morning of October 5, 1957, a British scientist named Bernard Lovell was wakened by a telephone call from a London newspaper asking him to comment on a news development he had not yet heard about. Lovell's field was astronomy, an abstruse and—in more ways than one—unworldly specialty, and astronomers were not then accustomed to being consulted about current affairs. But this was clearly an event whose impact transcended the bounds of science. The Soviet news agency, Tass, had just announced that the world's "first artificial earth satellite . . . was successfully launched in the USSR."

It was a Saturday morning. As director of the Jodrell Bank observatory in the northwest of England, Lovell had worked late the previous evening tinkering with his brand-new, expensive, and thus controversial new "toy," a powerful radiotelescope. Designed for tracking meteors, it was the most advanced instrument then available to world science for investigating celestial phenomena.

Lovell had left the observatory that night thinking that it must be "the most wonderful place on earth." The news he wakened to the next morning told him he'd been wrong—"the most wonderful place on earth at that moment was in the Soviet Union, where Sputnik was being launched."

In Moscow that morning, there may have been many Soviet citizens who felt just that way. One of them was a twenty-seven-year-old junior diplomat, who some years later was to defect to the United States.

102

ARKADY SHEVCHENKO
U.S. intelligence consultant,
former UN Assistant Secretary General
1957: Junior staff member,
Soviet Foreign Affairs Ministry

Let me tell you that we thought that the Soviet Union really achieved something. We had always been behind the West in almost everything. In standards of living, whatever it was—especially technology. And this was the first time [involving] such a highly sophisticated technology that the Soviet Union became ahead.

You know, I never had a hatred of the United States, frankly speaking. I was a good Communist and defended the interest of the Soviet Union. But, you know, I didn't think in terms of what kind of threat [something] could be for the United States. I was proud—this was the feeling—proud of the achievement for my country, that my country achieved something which the United States could not achieve.

Sputnik Shock

The United States, meanwhile, was waking up to a world that seemed to have turned upside-down overnight. James Killian, the president of Massachusetts Institute of Technology and a White House scientific consultant, was summoned to a meeting with President Eisenhower. He found Ike calm, but concerned about the military implications of the Soviet feat, and feeling a need to reassure the American public, which was in the throes of humiliation and self-doubt. Sputnik, as the historian William Manchester observes, was "a shock on the order of the [1929 Wall Street] Crash."

In spite of a speech by the President, the country went into a tailspin—a kind of psychic depression, a period of gloomy self-examination in which things once hailed as uniquely American were called into question: the American economy, its wastefulness symbolized by the chrome and tailfins of big, expensive autos, the American educational system, with its emphasis on social adjustment rather than academic excellence. A television documentary compared the Soviet educational system, engaged in turning out battalions of scientists and engineers, with a U.S. suburban high school where boys and girls goofed their way through elective courses like Coeducational Cooking.

The object of all the consternation was a steel sphere about the size of a beach ball, weighing about 185 pounds. Sputnik—the name is the

Russian word for "companion" or, in a more apt translation, "fellow traveler"—was at least eight times heavier than an object the United States was planning to launch into orbit a couple of months later.

Visible through binoculars, emitting triumphant bleeps from its radio transmitter as it circled the globe every 96 minutes at a speed of 18,000 miles per hour, Sputnik was both a marvel and a taunt to Americans, who followed its progress, along with the rest of the world. The experts, meanwhile, were paying closer attention to the vehicle that launched the tiny satellite and was now trailing in its wake, carrying a message of profound military significance.

SIR BERNARD LOVELL
Professor emeritus, University of Manchester (England)
1951–81: Director of Nuffield Radioastronomy Laboratories,
Jodrell Bank

You could pick up the bleep-bleep from the Sputnik by a simple receiver. But the strength of our position [at Jodrell Bank observatory] was that we could give information about this rocket, which was an intercontinental missile, hurtling around in space. And I think it was the lack of information from the Soviet Union about this and the fact that they themselves did not know where the rocket was that caused this tremendous interest.

And after a few nights, it was with this device that we succeeded in locating the carrier rocket. It was a tremendous sighting. Nobody—certainly *we* had never seen what an echo from a missile looked like. And I very much doubt if anybody in the world did know what a radar echo from an intercontinental missile in orbit would look like. And it was quite spectacular. The tube was full of the transient-meteor echoes; and then, suddenly, on the cathode-ray tube, the echo from the carrier rocket appeared, a massive echo traveling in range along the orbit—unmistakably something that had never been seen before. It showed us the Soviets could use a missile to land a weapon on the United States from Soviet territory. Just that. And at that time, it would not have been possible for the United States to have replied.

The possibilities of this situation were hardly lost on the Russians themselves.

Khrushchev, in his memoirs: "No longer were we contaminated by Stalin's fear. . . . No longer was the industrial heartland of the United States invulnerable to our counterattack. Of course, we tried to derive maximum political advantage from the fact that we were the first to launch our rockets into space. However, now that we had nuclear bombs and the means to deliver them, we had no intention of starting a war."

One of Arkady Shevchenko's first assignments, when he reported to his office in the Soviet foreign ministry after the historic weekend of the Sputnik launch, was to consider how the new capability in outer space "can be used to pressure the United States in Europe and other Western countries." The "missile gap," it came to be called by critics of the administration.

The Soviet advantage may have been illusory; at worst, it was temporary. The United States was beaten to the draw in space simply because of two factors: economy and complacency.

Although the launching of satellites was part of a worldwide scientific project—the International Geophysical Year—the Russians had been using military rockets to advance their program. The United States had military rockets capable of the feat, but President Eisenhower had opted to keep the American satellite "pure" and also (relatively) cheap by separating it from the missile-development program. In doing so, the administration had disregarded the advice of its leading rocket expert, the former chief of Hitler's V-2 project, Wernher von Braun.

The U.S. had also disregarded the mounting evidence of Soviet capability. The Russians had announced the development of an H-bomb—probably more efficient than the American "hell weapon"—less than a year after America's first H-bomb test. The Russians had announced the development of a long-range rocket. And they had announced plans to put up a satellite—which, if successful, would prove that the rocket was capable of launching a massive payload.

The Americans stuck by their conviction that Soviet technology simply wasn't up to the job—and were stuck *with* it as Sputnik II soon followed—over 1,000 pounds in weight, carrying a dog into orbit as passenger. Meanwhile, America's feeble Vanguard—carrying a tiny payload the size of a basketball—finally staggered into position on the launch pad. As described by a reporter assigned to the new space beat, "it rose less than five feet, toppled over, and exploded."

Introducing the Astronauts

From this humiliating start, the American space program made a remarkable recovery. About two months later, on January 31, 1958, with a Jupiter rocket borrowed from the army, the first American satellite was launched into orbit. The National Aeronautics and Space Administration was organized—with a substantial budget, with foundations planted firmly in the defense establishment, and with an announced goal of putting man into space. In April 1959, the first group of candidates for that mission, the Mercury astronauts, were introduced to the public. They were a crew-cut bunch of seasoned test-pilots, all in the American-hero mold, selected from the military services. Their mission was widely perceived as an extension of the cold war—but not by the astronauts themselves.

ALAN SHEPARD
Houston businessman
1959: Navy pilot selected as Mercury astronaut

I've always been aware of the existence of the Soviet Union. Still am. I mean, that's a powerful consideration in today's environment. And there are going to be confrontations. But not a "race." Certainly not to the point where we would take chances that you wouldn't take otherwise. In other words, you wouldn't make a political decision as opposed to an engineering decision.

At that particular time, we were part of the design process, working with the engineers in trying to learn how to marry the machine and the individual. And so we deliberately chose not to get detailed briefings on where the Soviets stood.

In those days, the major consideration was in the physiological area: what's going to happen to the human body during the forces of acceleration at launch and what's going to happen during reentry—these sort of things. What'll happen to the human under weightless conditions, for even short periods of time? Will there be some psychological changes? Will the mind be able to cope with this tremendous change in flying at high altitude, high speed, and so on?

It seemed to me that the doctors were always around. They were always interested in how you were doing and sort of like looking over your shoulder all the time.

There was a sadistic device which NASA had developed in which we sat in a chair and within a gimbal within a gimbal within a gimbal so we could be spun, pitched, or rolled at fairly high rates. *Ad nauseam.* And that was kind of uncomfortable. But, nonetheless, we went through it, and we all proved that a person can respond.

Of course, we did a lot of survival training. In the jungles. In the ocean. In the desert. I mean, nobody knew where exactly we would come down if there was some kind of serious malfunction, so we did a lot of that sort of thing. Bobbing around in the water and crashing through the jungles.

We were anxious to fly the spacecraft as an airplane. So the only down side, really, of the training, as far as I was concerned, was too much attention to physiological aspects of it.

Alan Shepard would have to sweat out two years of training, with the ubiquitous doctors looking over his shoulder, before he got his chance to fly—the first American in space.

Meanwhile, there were efforts to disengage from the cold war even as the arsenals grew and the potential battlefield was extended—on earth and beyond, into space.

·12·

LOOKING FOR A WAY OUT

Korea, Iran, Indochina, Hungary, Suez . . . the places identified with the cold war in the 1950s, like the battle sites of World War II, were comfortably remote from American shores. And there were no intimations of the global conflict in a scene that took place in Havana, Cuba, just ninety miles off Florida, on January 1, 1959. Thus, many Americans remained incredulous as they watched the connection emerge. They were watching the establishment of nothing less than a Soviet base in the Western Hemisphere.

Conceivably, it might have turned out differently, if not for a historic failure of East-West efforts to reach an overall agreement at the summit.

"Fi-del! Fi-del!"

The New Year's Day event in the Cuban capital was a kind of military parade—a procession of soldiers in GI fatigues riding in U.S. surplus trucks and tanks with the insignia of the Cuban armed forces.

Until that day, the forces had been under the command of Cuba's dictator, Fulgencio Batista. Now Batista was in flight from the island. The army had switched sides, joining a bearded orator named Fidel Castro, whose guerrilla troops numbered a mere two thousand. After three years in the island's mountainous eastern provinces, building his rebel movement, Castro was arriving in triumph to claim the capital, while the crowd along the boulevards roared in approval.

What followed almost immediately was a disillusioning program of drumhead trials and purges that seemed aimed not simply at punishing the crimes of the old regime but also at liquidating Cuba's middle class as a potential source of opposition. The program was accompanied by the expropriation of American business interests on the island. A slogan sprouted on stucco walls: "*Cuba si! Yanqui no!*"

In scenes reminiscent of Hitler's Nuremberg stadium or Mussolini's Piazza Venezia, thousands of *campesinos*—Cuba's peasant masses—were trucked in from the countryside for rallies, where they listened to hours-long anti-*Yanqui* harangues from the leader and responded with orchestrated cheers: "Fi-del! Fi-del!"

For a newly installed autocrat seeking a cause to justify his excesses, anti-Americanism was a natural. American business interests (sugar, rubber, utilities) and Mafia racketeers (dope, gambling, prostitution) were both instrumental in old Cuba's lopsided economy—millions of destitute farm workers supporting a handful of rich families. A current of resentment toward America was traditional, along with an admiration of things American.

But to the volatile chemistry of Latin American politics, Castro was adding a new, incendiary element: communism.

HUBER MATOS
Cuban exile leader in Miami
1959: Castro general and cabinet member

I wanted to go back to my work, to leave the government, because I realized that the course of the revolution was altered. It was not a democratic revolution; but, rather, Fidel was converting himself into a dictator; and, besides, he was naming Communist officers to the armed forces and posts in the administration. So I realized that Raúl [Fidel's brother] and Che [Guevara] were in on this maneuver, penetrating the military setup and even the administrative force with men of the Communist party.

I went to discuss this with Fidel two or three times, and I saw that he was permitting this, that he was playing a double game. On one side, he says: "You know that I am not a Communist and that this revolution is not Communist." I say: "Yes, but you are permitting the Communists to take it over. You are the chief and you permit this. I am leaving; we are on the wrong road, and the revolution is going to fail."

He says, "No, don't go away. I need you, and the revolution is not going to fail."

After I went there two or three times and we talked like that, when I said I was finally going, he took me prisoner and wanted to shoot me. He ac-

cused me of organizing a sedition. It was a lie. I simply wanted to leave
because I was not in agreement with him.

Castro is not a Communist. Castro is an actor and affirms that he is a
Communist and that he has surrendered himself to the Russians and, in
short, that he has a Communist government. But Castro does not believe
in that. He is perhaps more of a Fascist than anything else, because he
wants to rule forever.

For his outspoken criticism of Castro, Huber Matos was to spend
twenty years in prison before he was released and expatriated to
Florida. There he joined thousands of other fugitives from Castro's
revolution.

American officials were slower than Matos to become disillusioned
with the new Cuban leader. When Fidel visited New York for a United
Nations meeting, some months after taking power, the CIA arranged
a secret meeting with him in New York to brief him about the presence of Communists in his inner circle. "We were profoundly naive,"
confesses a CIA official involved in that pointless undertaking.

Even the Russians were unsure about Castro for a while. When the
Soviet premier, Nikita Khrushchev, came to the United States for the
next year's (1960) UN session, he had discussions with his aides on the
trip over and later with his UN ambassador, Andrei Gromyko, centering on Raúl Castro as someone they could count on and speculating
as to whether Fidel shared his brother's political convictions.

Khrushchev soon had a chance to find out for himself. Castro's
rather slovenly entourage was kicked out of a midtown New York
hotel, and he pointedly moved uptown to the Hotel Theresa in Harlem. Khrushchev thereupon decided to do a personal recruiting job
and, at the same time, work in a little anti-American public relations
of his own.

The Soviet leader explained in his memoirs: "I felt it would be better
for me to make the first visit. This would underline our solidarity with
Cuba, especially in light of the indignity and humiliation they were
being subjected to. Secondly, the Cuban delegation was in Harlem,
and the owner of the hotel was a Negro. By going to a hotel in a Negro
district, we would be making a double demonstration—against the
discriminatory policies of the United States toward Negroes as well as
toward Cuba."

The premier of the Soviet Union paid a call on the leader of the little
island revolution at a rather seedy hotel on 125th Street. Whatever

Fidel's personal political convictions, if any, Cuba's role in hemisphere affairs was soon fixed. Soviet aid became the mainstay of Castro's erratic economy. The Communists now had a base only ninety miles from Florida.

And Cuba became a historic oddity: with an American naval base long established at Guantanamo, Fidel's island became—and remained—the only country in the world containing both Soviet *and* American military installations.

A "Psychiatric" Summit

The presence—even the disruptive presence—of a Soviet chief on United States soil was a remarkable occurrence. It suggested at least a glimmer of change in Russia's historic isolation. It was part of the unforseeable aftermath of an extraordinary process in which East and West struggled to find some new basis for dealing with each other in the light of changing political and military realities—the end of Stalinism and the development of the nuclear arms race.

During the decade of the fifties, the cold war had become institutionalized. What had begun as a set of conflicting policies was now organized into a set of hostile alliances openly affirming their opposing interests and arming to defend them. The last major piece had been fitted into the NATO archway in 1955 when West Germany was enlisted in the alliance. Immediately afterwards, the Soviet Union organized its satellites into the alliance known as the Warsaw Pact.

Meanwhile, a contrary process—a process of disengagement—was also under way.

It had proceeded in fits and starts since the summer of 1955 when Eisenhower, along with British and French leaders, met with the Kremlin tandem of Bulganin and Khrushchev in a conference at Geneva. The first reunion of East-West leaders since Potsdam, exactly ten years before, it was referred to as a "meeting at the summit"—the highest level of political power. A "psychiatric summit," it was later called by a political scientist, Henry Kissinger, since it produced nothing but vague feelings of well-being . . . which proved transitory.

Ike scored some public relations points at Geneva with a proposal for an "open skies" agreement that would have laid the defenses of both sides open to each other for aerial surveillance. Spectacularly unrealistic at the time, it was to become a *fait accompli* in the age of space satellites.

The conference represented an effort by the Western Allies to explore the new situation in the Kremlin—the transition from Stalinism to . . . what? The new era had no definable shape, but some sort of lightening of the internal atmosphere seemed to be taking place under the Bulganin–Khrushchev team.

Within a year, Khrushchev eased Bulganin aside and stood on his own at the pinnacle of power in the Kremlin—so well established that he could dare to knock the towering image of Stalin off its pedestal. In a momentous speech to the twentieth party congress, Khrushchev enumerated and condemned the repressive acts of his predecessor.

Meanwhile, as the cold war persisted into the space age heralded by Sputnik, the nuclear shadow lengthened. The two antagonists were arming themselves with intercontinental missiles, and the rest of the world was held hostage to their rivalry.

As nuclear bomb tests proliferated—above ground, underground, underwater—scientists were issuing warnings about the pollution of the atmosphere and the irradiation of a whole generation through milk contaminated by radioactive vegetation ingested by cows. Within a couple of decades, according to one authoritative prediction, the entire population of the planet would be affected if the testing continued at the current rate.

The threat of the Bomb was no longer a mere matter of military strategy. It was a fact of everyday life for every age group. "Fallout" and "strontium-90" (the milk contaminant) became part of the common vocabulary. Civil-defense studies were published that considered the problems of evacuating cities and evaluated chances of survival. To the average citizen, the studies made evacuation sound impossible and survival pointless. The concept of "megadeaths"—civilian casualties in the millions—was introduced into national policy planning.

The reaction to this public dialogue could be characterized as justifiable hysteria. Perfectly reasonable people—if they could afford to—hired contractors to excavate their backyards not for swimming pools but for fallout shelters, to be maintained at all times with a supply of canned food and water. A much-debated public issue was the question of whether it was morally justifiable to shoot a neighbor who tried to force his way into your overcrowded shelter when the deadly crunch came.

Nuclear drill became as routine as fire drill in the schedules of America's public schools, and the Bomb became the bogeyman in the childhood nightmares of the fifties generation. A fifteen-year-old boy in a New York hospital came out of a fevered delirium crying and told his parents, "I pushed a button and blew up the world!"

* * *

The Eisenhower administration clung for a while to its relatively blithe view of the Bomb. The President had not hesitated to flourish it in order to bring the enemy to heel in Korea. And when, some time after that, Eisenhower received a cautionary message from Churchill about nuclear weapons, Ike's response was almost cavalier. He shocked the messenger, the prime minister's private secretary, John Colville, by telling him: "You British look upon the atomic weapon as something totally new. But you've got to remember, throughout history new weapons have in due course become conventional weapons. The atomic bomb will soon become a conventional weapon."

John Foster Dulles declared U.S. foreign policy to be based on a principle of "massive retaliation," meaning that even a slight Communist infringement on the free world would be met by strong measures up to and including the use of the Bomb against Russia. Clearly, however, that was another example of rhetoric outrunning policy, like the notorious "rollback." Eisenhower's low-budget defense program left the country theoretically dependent on the Bomb, but when it came down to cases, reason prevailed and U.S. action was abjured (as in Indochina) or lesser force was applied. In 1958, in Lebanon, Eisenhower used the old-fashioned device of landing the marines in response to a proclaimed threat of Communist subversion by way of neighboring Iraq. That was an application of the so-called Eisenhower Doctrine by which the President had been authorized by Congress to send military and economic aid to any country requesting it in order to ward off "armed aggression by . . . international communism." The marines were withdrawn four months later.

Over time, the administration's attitude toward nuclear weapons was maturing. Dulles himself, by now terminally ill, was becoming concerned about the erosion of America's image as a moral force in the world because of the dangers of nuclear testing.

When that same concern was strongly expressed within the scientific community, a panel of technical experts was assembled under Dr. James Fisk, a prominent physicist and Bell Telephone executive. The Fisk panel began quietly meeting with a group of Russian experts in Geneva to explore the feasibility of putting a halt to bomb testing as a first step toward arms reduction.

Admittedly, it would be a touchy step, because any serious attempt to regulate underground testing would require the kind of on-site monitoring that horrified the Russians, with their passion for secrecy. Incredibly, the two sides began to make progress.

JAMES KILLIAN
Physicist and educator
1958: President of MIT,
Eisenhower's chief scientific adviser

The Soviet attitude was responsive. And that was in many ways the most successful and amicable—not always amicable but the *most* amicable—of all the meetings we had with the Soviets that related to disarmament. And they came out with a report that the Soviets agreed to, that permitted on-site inspection, permitted other things that had been considered to be beyond their willingness to meet; and it was really a triumph, that session.

After the report came out and it was made public, the antidisarmament, anti-stoppage-of-nuclear-tests [interests] went to work. And Edward Teller and Ernest Lawrence and the group representing the Atomic Energy Commission, I think it fair to say, deliberately set out to provide a counter to that. And, in fact, they made technical developments that brought into question the accuracy of the basic data that had been used by the Fisk panel in regard to the detection, the difference between earthquake signals and bomb signals.

What happened later was that these groups who opposed stopping nuclear testing began arguing that we've got to test and test and test in order to develop "clean" bombs. I don't say they weren't sincere, but I can say that they were enormously hurtful and damaging.

The fact that these attacks began on the Fisk report caused the Russians to react violently. They claimed—and there is some justification to this—that we set out to destroy what had been agreed upon in the Geneva technical discussions. And when the meetings were set up for the following diplomatic discussions of how to put the technical results of the Fisk report into operation, the Russians had changed their attitude completely and were ferociously nasty and bad in all that debate.

It's possible that within the Soviet government there had been similar reactions to what had happened in the Fisk study—that there were elements of the military in Russia that decided to oppose the findings. But the main thing was that they said, "We can't trust the Americans any more."

ARKADY SHEVCHENKO
Soviet defector, U.S. intelligence consultant
1958: Member of Arms Control Division,
Soviet Foreign Ministry

It looked sometimes like a propaganda debate, but it was a serious negotiation, because we discussed it with Khrushchev, and we—I don't like to say "we" now because I do not belong to them any more—the Soviet Union was ready to make a very substantial concession as far as control is concerned.

[Detecting tests in] the atmosphere, in outer space—it was no problem. Or underwater. The crux of the matter was the underground tests, and there the Soviet Union was ready at some point to accept quite a substantial inspection in a form of the presence of the international observers in the seismic stations on the territory of the Soviet Union.

I think that partially the United States was responsible [for the failure of negotiations] because they didn't see properly the signals of the Soviets, and some of the requests and some of the arguments about how many inspections they could have in a year were ridiculous. Because Khrushchev wanted it, really.

Return to the Summit

Eisenhower's hands were tied. He sometimes complained about the obstructive attitude of the Atomic Energy Commission group, but he seemed reluctant to override their warnings and make an agreement on nuclear testing with the Russians.

Approaching the end of his presidency, Ike's sense of mission as a peacemaker grew more intense. It was encouraged by political advisers with an eye to the 1960 election, in which the Republican presidential candidate would need a healthy legacy from the outgoing administration. There were not many issues accessible to peacemaking efforts, however. The disarmament negotiations in Geneva were snagged, and their technical nature was not the stuff to seize the popular imagination.

No problem. The Russians provided a crisis that people could understand and that would show Ike at his best as the charismatic man of good will. Khrushchev delivered it, almost obligingly, in mid-1959 in the form of a fierce-sounding ultimatum to the Western Allies: get out of Berlin in six months.

It was a demand Khrushchev had raised before and one he would issue again to put pressure on the Western Allies—and take pressure *off* the Communists.

The Allied sectors of the city, sharing the so-called economic miracle of West Germany, were alight with prosperity, while the eastern neighborhoods (except for an avenue of huge, forbidding "model" apartment buildings) still looked like postwar rubble fields, still bore that telltale smell of stagnation. The disparity was driving East Berliners across the boundary by the thousands.

Eisenhower's response to the ultimatum was to invite Khrushchev to visit the United States en route to a later summit meeting at which Berlin, arms control and other East–West issues would be laid on the table. That invitation, in the summer of 1959, was the beginning of one of the most extraordinary chapters in the history of diplomacy. For the next nine months, international relations—traditionally arranged in secret by foreign-affairs specialists—were conducted by the world leaders themselves in the limelight of unprecedented media coverage.

President Eisenhower made a preparatory trip of his own to Europe to consult with Britain's Prime Minister Macmillan, French President de Gaulle, and German Chancellor Adenauer. In later swings, Ike would visit such lesser capitals as Rome, Delhi, Karachi, and Lisbon, as if embracing nations all over the world in his campaign for peace. And his vice-president, Richard Nixon, paid a kind of warm-up visit to Moscow, where the United States was participating in a vast trade fair. There Nixon and Khrushchev engaged in an impromptu debate—on capitalism versus communism—in the model kitchen of the American exhibit.

On September 15, 1959, the Chairman of the Soviet Presidium and First Secretary of the Communist party, Nikita Sergeievich Khrushchev, landed in the United States. From the moment of his arrival ("I come with an open heart and good intentions"), the round little Communist leader demonstrated a talent for performance that would have stood him well in a Chekhov play.

For the next two weeks, there was perhaps no more compelling theater in the United States than Khrushchev's coast-to-coast tour, in which, constantly in view of television cameras and troops of reporters, he tramped through an Iowa cornfield, ate hot dogs, put on a ten-gallon hat, watched can-can dancers on a movie set (and expressed puritanical distaste at what he saw) . . . and engaged in slanging matches with the immigrant head of a movie studio, Spyros Skouras, with various local officials, and with his guide, UN Ambassador Henry Cabot Lodge.

The Soviet leader was plagued throughout the trip by a statement he had made, speaking in behalf of communism and rhetorically addressing the capitalist system: "We shall bury you!" It was meant as a boast that communism would *outlast* capitalism, but it was persistently interpreted as a threat to *destroy* the West.

In the meetings between Khrushchev and Eisenhower, the two leaders rubbed each other the wrong way. Several years after leaving office, Ike was asked by an interviewer, curious about the atmosphere of those meetings, how he and Khrushchev had addressed each other.

Did they use first names? Last names? Did they call each other "Mr. President" and "Mr. Chairman"?

Ike, who had as much trouble with foreign names as he did with "nuclear" (he made it "nu-cu-lar"), replied: "Well, mostly I just said, 'Now, goddamn it, Crook-shoff!' Of course," Ike added, "they [Communists] are *trained* to be bad-mannered in the presence of capitalists."

In meetings at Camp David, the rustic presidential retreat in the Catoctin Mountains of Maryland, the two leaders put aside their antipathy and agreed to join French and British chiefs of state in a four-power summit conference the next year. Ike accepted the chairman's invitation to return the social call with a visit to Moscow after the summit. And, under pressure, Khrushchev agreed to postpone his ultimatum on Berlin.

Eisenhower recalled: "I told him, 'Well, the hell with it! Goddamn it, if that's the way it's going to be, then the hell with the summit meeting! I told him I simply wouldn't go. So, of course, he finally agreed and said he hadn't meant it to be a deadline at all."

For months the world basked in the promise of the busy diplomatic calendar.

The Crash of the U-2

The summit site was picked. Auspiciously, it would be Paris in the spring: May 16, 1960.

On May 1, while the French presidential residence, the Palais de l'Elysée, was being freshened up for the arrival of its distinguished guests, President Eisenhower received a piece of news that dismayed him: a U-2 reconnaisance plane operated by a civilian pilot named Francis Gary Powers as an employee of the CIA was missing on a flight over the Soviet Union.

U-2 flights had been going on for four years—an espionage operation so sensitive that no plane ever left the ground without specific authorization from the White House. Everything, including the uniquely designed high-altitude aircraft itself—light, quiet, with a vast wing surface—had been developed under the CIA because Ike had been reluctant to put vital intelligence about Russia in the hands of the air force. Its leaders might be tempted to exploit the information or distort it in order to support air force budget requests.

From the beginning, Ike had had forebodings about the operation.

The United States, he said, would never have tolerated any such flights by a Russian plane. If a U-2 ever went down over Soviet territory, he told an aide, "the world would be in a terrible mess." But he had authorized the program out of concern about the possibility of a surprise attack.

So far the gamble had paid off handsomely. It was the U-2s that had provided the administration with reassurance in the wake of the Sputnik—evidence that the Soviet missile capability was not an immediate threat to the United States. And it was the U-2s that had kept the administration abreast of the Soviet missile program ever since.

Operating out of a base in Pakistan (one of forty-two countries now linked to the United States by an ever-lengthening chain of defense treaties), the U-2s flew above the reach of Soviet radar and fighter planes. Until now they had flown without mishap.

RICHARD BISSELL
Washington consultant
1960: Deputy director of the CIA

We'd had a lot of training flights over the U.S., and I'd seen a lot of the photography. And it's absolutely astounding. Anyone who hasn't seen modern high-altitude reconnaissance photography really has a stunning surprise coming to them. One I saw was of a high school football game in Butte, Montana, taken from 100,000 feet up, and you could see the football.

I remember all too vividly [the day of the U-2 incident]. I had come back from being away for a day. I came back on a Sunday afternoon. I immediately had a call from the office and had to go down there. And I was told that Powers had been—his flight had not arrived. And he presumably was down and lost.

We scrambled around that afternoon and evening on a cover story. That turned out to be a mistake. We, of course, assumed that he was dead. Whether of the crash—whether he'd been shot down—or whether it was a malfunction of the system, we suspected that he would not have survived.

So we had what we thought was a nice, plausible cover story. And as everyone remembers, within a day or so that was shot out of the water when the Russians announced that they had the pilot alive.

That was one of the more traumatic episodes in the intelligence business during those years.

The cover story, issued over Ike's misgivings, said that a "weather research plane" was missing on a flight over Turkey, having presumably strayed off course. Khrushchev pounced on it with a counterstatement of his own, delivered dramatically before the Supreme Soviet. The aircraft, he revealed, had been shot down by improved Soviet weapons over the city of Sverdlovsk, some 1,200 miles inside the Soviet border: the pilot had confessed to espionage as his mission. Its broader purpose, the chairman fumed, was to sabotage the summit conference—an aim he attributed to "Pentagon militarists."

Carefully giving Eisenhower an out, Khrushchev said, "I am quite willing to grant that the President knew nothing" about the flights.

Eisenhower declined to use the escape hatch, not only assuming responsibility for the flights but defending them as necessary to America's security because of the threat of Soviet aggression. Privately, Ike fumed at the problem created by "this goddamned plane!"

The Big Four assembled at the Elysée Palace as scheduled but in an atmosphere charged with recrimination. Khrushchev, in a kind of bellicose appeal for help in defending himself against Kremlin hardliners, demanded an apology from America for "past acts of aggression." Eisenhower assured him the flights had been stopped but refused to apologize. Khrushchev thereupon proposed that the summit be postponed until after Eisenhower left office and canceled the invitation to Ike for a visit to Russia. The Russian leader then drove away from the Elysée, looking apoplectic with rage. Ike left, equally furious at what he regarded as an "ultimatum."

After a two-day standoff the Soviet chairman gave the summit the *coup de grâce*. In a melodramatic press conference at the Palais de Chaillot, flanked by a stony-faced general, he issued a vitriolic denunciation of the United States and its leaders. The Soviet Union, he said, having come to the summit in hopes of resolving the Berlin issue by agreement, would now do so its own way—by signing a peace treaty with East Germany and turning the future of the city over to the government of the People's Republic.

ARKADY SHEVCHENKO

I never at that time understood why Khrushchev reacted in that way—such an absolutely incredible reaction, canceling the Paris summit, canceling something on which I myself had been personally involved in preparing the instructions for the Soviet Foreign Ministry. We thought that it would be going on as serious negotiations on arms control and on many other things. All the things had been prepared in the Foreign Ministry, went to the Politburo, approved by the Politburo. And, all of a sudden, because of the incident, which, you know, was not unusual because there were flights going on all the time—why had it happened?

Only later, when I had more access to the more important people in the Soviet Union and talked within the circles of the leadership of the Soviet Union or looked at some of the documents, did I find the answer.

The answer was that at this period of time Khrushchev had antagonized the military by reducing very substantially the armed forces of the Soviet Union and by reducing the production of the conventional weapons like tanks and placing everything on the strategic force. Before that, he had antagonized the KGB by downgrading the role of the KGB, or security apparatus of the Soviet Union.

[The U-2 incident] was an internal political move in which Khrushchev wanted to show that he was really defending the interests of the Soviet Union in the military field.

Dwight D. Eisenhower had a different explanation. Khrushchev, he came to believe, wanted above all to find some excuse to renege on the Moscow visit. Khrushchev had been shaken by the cool reception he got on a visit to neutralist India, in contrast to that country's overwhelming response to the American leader on his December stopover in New Delhi. Ike's visit had provoked a worshipful stampede of pedestrians, taxis, private autos, and bullock-drawn carts to welcome him at the Delhi airport . . . an unbelievable assemblage of 2.5 million more jamming a fairground a couple of days later when he made a platform appearance with Prime Minister Nehru. Ike suspected that Khrushchev was afraid the Eisenhower magic might even work with the Russians: "He just decided he couldn't afford to have me in Russia, and that was that."

For all his disappointment over the failure of the summit, Ike continued to defend the U-2: "There's nobody I know of regrets our getting that amount of information, because in those days we had all sort of talk and uninformed yakking and demagoging about 'bomber gaps' and then 'missile gaps.' Well, we knew. We had to keep still, but we knew what they were doing."

The whole chapter of "personal diplomacy" left Ike with a keen sense of disgust—about Russian deceitfulness in general and Khrushchev in particular.

A year or so before his death (in 1969), Ike sat in a cottage provided for him on a California ranch each winter by one of his rich admirers

—sat reminiscing about the aborted summit with a visitor from back East. The subject immediately reminded Ike about gratuitous lies he had been told by Russian officials going back to his postwar visits to the Soviet Union. They had lied to him, he said, about such simple matters as the population of their cities. They claimed to have manufactured machinery on which he could read the stamp, "Made in the U.S.A."

As for Khrushchev: during the chairman's visit to the United States, Ike gave him a personal gift—a Black Angus heifer from the herd on his farm in Gettysburg, Pennsylvania. Ike got his friend and neighbor, Admiral Lewis Strauss, the AEC chairman, to contribute a bull. "They were fine animals," Ike recalled. "The heifer was worth at least a thousand dollars. I thought Khrushchev would use them to start a nice little herd of his own. It could be the beginnings of a Soviet beef-cattle industry—they were having a hard time feeding their people in the Soviet Union. The Black Angus are fond of cold climates, you know.

"Khrushchev seemed terribly pleased but wondered how he'd get the animals home. I knew they didn't have the transport, so I told him, 'Don't worry, I'll get 'em there.' And I did."

In return, Ike went on, Khrushchev presented him with a shotgun. "Beautifully tooled piece. Hand-carved stock and everything. First thing I did, I sent it over to our ordnance people and had it appraised. They called it the best they'd ever seen in their lives. The rifling was as close to perfection as it could possibly be. Every part just machined to unbelievable tolerances.

"Well, after the summit blew up and everything and I left the presidency—it must have been a year or two later—I wondered how those Black Angus were doing. I asked the Pentagon to see what they could find out. Well, there wasn't a trace of them. No herd, no beef-cattle industry—they'd just disappeared! I don't know, I suppose they ate 'em.

"Well, I was so disgusted I gave away the shotgun. I don't even remember who I gave it to."

It was in September 1960—four months after the aborted summit —that Khrushchev paid a second visit to the United States for the UN session—the visit in which he struck his alliance with Fidel Castro. He also scandalized the General Assembly by taking off his shoe and rapping his desk to command attention. The flamboyant Soviet chairman came and went without any significant contact with U.S. officials.

The cold-war temperature stayed down. East–West relations were on hold.

In the presidential elections that fall, the Democratic standard bearer, Senator John F. Kennedy of Massachusetts, edged out Ike's vice-president, Richard Nixon, whose campaign was a sequence of mishaps: a knee banged on a car door, sidelining him at a crucial moment; an ill-timed hospitalization that left him looking pallid and peaked; a bad makeup job done to his own specifications for a television debate against a fit-looking, media-wise antagonist.

Even so, the election was a squeaker, decided only the morning after Election Day by the seesaw count in a few big states—decided by little more than one-tenth of one percent of the voters. The final margin was less than 113,000 out of a record total of nearly 69 million.

Economics—a flattening out of the business curve—was probably a factor, but the election most likely was decided on the basis of personal image: Kennedy, the handsome and dynamic young hero, still in his early forties, squarely facing up to public doubts and prejudices about his Catholic background; Nixon, less than four years older but with a saturnine look and a reputation as "Tricky Dick" from his early political career.

In foreign policy, the Democratic campaign made some effort to exploit the supposed "missile gap," calling for an effort to "restore our national strength," but also urging renewed efforts toward disarmament. The Republican platform seemed to reflect Eisenhower's frustration about a disengagement with the Russians by its emphasis on "our military might . . . second to none" and the need to "perfect the new generations of weapons [to] arm ourselves effectively and without delay."

The departing Republican President was not content, however, to risk leaving the disarmament issue in bad repute. In a farewell address, broadcast to the American public three days before he left office, Eisenhower confessed a "definite sense of disappointment." But to this he added a warning against "the unwarranted influence . . . [of] the military-industrial complex" in the United States as a potential danger of the arms race. "Disarmament," he declared, ". . . is a continuing imperative."

McCarthyism personified: Senator Joseph McCarthy, the powerful voice of unbridled anticommunism in the early 1950s, confronts one of his few outspoken critics in Congress, Republican Senator Ralph Flanders of Vermont (standing). Seated between them is McCarthy's investigating committee counsel, Roy Cohn. *(AP/ Wide World Photos)*

Death of Stalin in 1953—commemorated by wreaths at Soviet war memorial in Berlin—shook Moscow's grip on satellite countries. *(UPI/Bettmann Newsphotos)*

The head of toppled statue of late Soviet leader Stalin sits on Budapest pavement while citizens of Hungary enjoy their moment of freedom after 1956 revolution. A few days after this, Russian tanks reoccupied the city. *(UPI/Bettman Newsphotos)*

Jeeps of the UN Emergency Force move into position between British troops and Egyptian defenders along the Suez Canal during the ill-fated 1956 invasion. *(UPI/ Bettman Newsphotos)*

Coup in Iran, engineered and financed by the CIA, led to installation of pro-Western Shah in 1953. Playing to crowd of Shah supporters at gates of the Majlis (parliament), officer is parodying the leftist prime minister, Muhammad Mossadegh, as a dictator. *(AP/Wide World Photos)*

Reinforcement of French troops by air at Dien Bien Phu in 1954 failed to stave off bitter defeat by nationalist insurgents, the Viet Minh. America's support of French efforts led to involvement in Vietnam. *(UPI/Bettmann Newsphotos)*

Man's first, sketchy mark in outer space—October 1957. It was the trail left by the Russian Sputnik's carrier rocket, following along in orbit after separation of the payload and recorded in a time exposure by a *Life* photographer. *(Robert Kelly, Life Magazine © Time Inc.)*

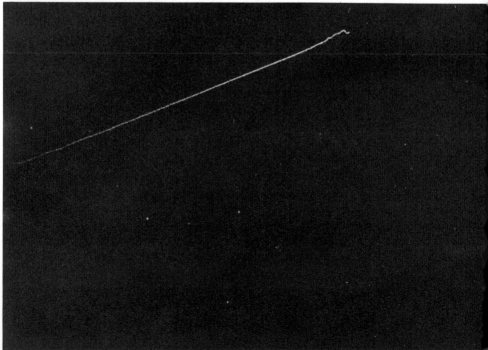

Soviet leader Nikita Khrushchev engaged Vice-President Richard Nixon in impromptu debate—communism versus capitalism—at model kitchen display in 1959 American exhibition in Moscow. At right is Politburo member Leonid Brezhnev, who succeeded Khrushchev as Communist party chief five years later. *(AP/ Wide World Photos)*

Colorful Soviet leader Khrushchev commanded attention and stirred controversy everywhere he went on 1959 tour of the U.S.A. UN Ambassador Henry Cabot Lodge (left), his official guide, accompanied him on tour of San Francisco supermarket. *(UPI/Bettmann Newsphotos)*

His car swamped by idolatrous crowds, President Eisenhower is welcomed to India in a storm of flower petals. Visit was part of Ike's preparations for 1960 summit conference. At right (in white hat) is his host in New Delhi, Prime Minister Nehru. *(UPI/Bettmann Newsphotos)*

In bombastic Paris press conference after breakup of 1960 summit, Khrushchev —with Defense Minister Rodion Malinovsky at his side—denounces President Eisenhower and proclaims Soviet determination to resolve Berlin issue on its own terms. *(AP/Wide World Photos)*

Fidel Castro, aboard a tank, leads his bearded revolutionaries in triumphal entry into Havana on New Year's Day 1959. Revolution, at first welcomed by U.S., soon took an anti-American course. *(UPI/Bettmann Newsphotos)*

Soviet Union embraced Cuba as an ally when Khrushchev met with Castro in New York during 1960 UN session. Moscow proceeded to establish a Western Hemisphere base on Castro's island. *(AP/Wide World Photos)*

· PART III ·

THE AGE
OF AQUARIUS
Cuba to Saigon

1961-75

·13·

"LET THE WORD GO FORTH"

A former British cabinet minister once complained that American cold-war leaders had one-track minds—they seemed to feel "that the only thing that mattered in the world was the military relationship between the Soviet Union and the West."

Men charged with the responsibility for keeping the power to destroy the world in check might have been excused for failing to pay enough attention to some of the forces at work in society during the 1960s and 1970s. Global television, emergent feminism, "recreational" drugs, the Pill and sexual freedom—all these social phenomena had a life apart from the cold war and may in the end have affected the world more profoundly than the ratios of missiles and warheads. But there were two other forces that *converged* with the cold war to shape world events. In principle, they were benign, progressive, full of promise. But sometimes their effects were horrendous.

One of these forces was nationalism. The other was its natural ally, youth. This was a period when subordinate groups of people all over the world were asserting themselves against traditional authority— against colonial bureaucracies, racist institutions, establishments of all kinds, including family and school.

"Here comes the newest of the emerging peoples," said a State Department wit as he watched a parade of blue-jeaned demonstrators displaying the banners of various causes. "Here comes the undeveloped nation of Youth."

No sudden eruptions, these two historic movements were foreshadowed by developments of the fifties.

With the breakup of colonial empires, nationhood was becoming a contagion. The United Nations, which admitted just twenty new members in the decade following World War II, took in more than twice that number during the sixties. Lesotho, Botswana, Burundi, Gabon . . . the unfamiliar names of new countries sprang onto the world map like new suburbs in the American countryside.

Cold-war interests gave the United States a stake in many of these remote places. East and West were competing for influence in the so-called Third World and for the globe's declining supply of strategic resources like oil, bauxite (for aluminum), tungsten (steel), and cobalt (nuclear devices, military and otherwise). As had happened in Britain's old stamping grounds, Iran, and in France's old colonial outpost, Indochina, America's ties to NATO allies sometimes put Washington and its massive aid programs on the side of the old order.

Not necessarily so at the unofficial level. Visceral bonds of sympathy linked American youth to nationalist independence movements—both had an interest in experiment and change. The vibrant young American lifestyle, with its emphasis on abundance and freedom, set an international standard.

The influence wasn't all one way. African independence was an inspiration to America's black minority, which was straining toward the full rights of citizenship.

ANDREW YOUNG
Mayor of Atlanta, former UN ambassador
1960s: Civil rights activist

I think that to some extent the civil rights movement came to us in the overall movement of the world against colonialism, starting with the Indian independence in 1948.

After the Second World War and the horror of the holocaust and the events in Nazi Germany, there was a new respect and demand for human rights. We encouraged England and France to decolonize and to allow their colonies to become independent. And suddenly we found ourselves in the same situation—many of the people who had fought against the Germans went back home and found that they were still in a subservient position.

Well, you don't risk your life in Europe for democracy and come back home and be denied it yourself.

Civil rights was not just a dream of repressed American blacks. It was also the first great cause of white middle-class American youth—

the first serious issue to engage the group consciousness developed in the teen-agers of the 1950s. When the SDS (Students for a Democratic Society) was organized in 1962 at a convention in Port Huron, Michigan, its manifesto identified "the degradation of racism" as one of the two overriding concerns of the college generation. The second was "the enclosing fact of the cold war."

John Fitzgerald Kennedy was the generation's first political hero. Slow to join in the civil rights issue, when he did take the plunge it was on the side of the young and the black, and it was with the power of the federal government behind him. On the cold war, his pronouncements, first as a candidate and then as President, suggested a new sort of spirit, which the young found congenial and inspiring. It carried the promise of a break in the oppressive deadlock that had gone on as long as some of them could remember.

To describe the mood of the new administration, a history-conscious observer might have invoked the presidency of an earlier young hero, Theodore Roosevelt, with his confidence, vitality, and love of muscular sport.

But in this generation there were many who disdained history as irrelevant. Looking for examples and explanations in nonrational sources, they communed with occult religions, consulted swamis, threw I-ching sticks, and dealt themselves Tarot cards. Their basic science was astrology.

In 1962 a particularly bright star would be visible in the constellation of Aquarius, "the water carrier," which believers associated with calm and peaceful temperaments. Taking it as an omen, the young looked forward to "the age of Aquarius."

Generation Gap

"Let the word go forth from this time and place . . . that the torch has been passed to a new generation of Americans. . . ."

Standing coatless and hatless in the midwinter cold of his Inauguration Day, Jack Kennedy presented himself to the world as the representative of a vigorous new breed. It was more than just a pose. At forty-three, he was the youngest man ever elected President (Teddy Roosevelt was a forty-two-year-old vice-president when the death of McKinley elevated him to the office but forty-six when elected in his own right) and the first President born in the twentieth century. Historically, the age difference from one chief executive to the next had usually been a matter of five to ten years; never before had the country elected a leader more than eighteen years younger than his predecessor (the spread between young Lincoln and old Buchanan). Kennedy, however, was Eisenhower's junior by all of twenty-seven years. For the first time, in inaugurating a new President, the country was leaping a whole generation.

The change could be seen and felt in a number of superficial ways. Where Ike, in his hospital bed, had amused himself reading Western novels by Zane Grey, Kennedy was an early fan of James Bond, the jet-age hero. Jack and his glamorous young wife, née Jacqueline Bouvier, caught the latest Broadway musicals. *Camelot,* based on the King Arthur legend, was their favorite. On the White House guest list, Ike's aging millionaires were replaced by Kennedy's young Harvard scholars, who found themselves rubbing elbows with names from the arts and show business.

If Jackie Kennedy had an instinct for chic, then Jack was compulsively—voraciously—*au courant.* On the Kennedy plane during the presidential campaign, no newspaper or magazine left on a seat was safe from his grasp. He loved to walk back and gossip with the reporters, talking in their informal style, with a touch of underplayed, deprecatory (often *self*-deprecatory) humor—the style of the World War II generation.

He was at home in the age of media. His presidential press conferences, unprecedentedly frequent and—also without precedent—carried live on television, made him not just a leader but a star. He was well-prepared, unflappable, good-humored. At the beginning, in the glare of early foreign policy disasters, he was subjected to merciless grillings before nationwide audiences. Asked how he now felt about these media rituals, Kennedy told the questioner and the viewing electorate, with a pained smile, "Well, I like them. Sort of." (LAUGHTER).

In his approach to the cold war, Kennedy's stance not only appealed to the liberal young but also encouraged more conservative elements.

The generation that was growing up in the fifties had escaped Korea; but every crisis since then—Hungary, Suez, the U-2—carried the risk of a direct collision between the superpowers. And repeated crisis had created a suffocating atmosphere of tension that was repugnant to the very spirit of youth.

Technology had robbed war of its romantic appeal. Now it carried only a threat of extinction—at best, disruption to young lives. But there were altruistic motives too. For all Eisenhower's worries and warnings about overblown military budgets, clearly it was becoming harder and harder to avoid the high cost of competing with the Communist world. And more money for the arms race meant less for socially oriented programs like public housing for the poor.

More money for missiles also meant less of a chance for aid to the public schools, which were widely deplored as overcrowded and understaffed—ill-equipped to meet the post-Sputnik demand for "excellence." Federal aid to build new school buildings and raise teachers' pay was an insistent cause among young suburban families.

For these young liberal constituencies, the one best hope was a negotiated end to the arms race.

There were millions of other Americans—many blue-collar families, for example, and older citizens of all classes—who were not interested in ambitious social programs but who were restive about the Soviet challenge. There were many among them who would have distrusted any agreement signed by the Russians and felt the only security was in outrunning and outgunning them.

So, faced with that "enclosing fact of the cold war," Americans either wanted the competition defused, or they wanted to recover the superiority that had insulated them before the jolt of Sputnik.

The repeated theme of Kennedy's election campaign had been an injunction to "get America moving again." In that single expression, he at once addressed a recent slowdown of the economy, the prevalent feeling of losing ground in the global competition, and the collapse of efforts to check the arms race. Whatever the interest of the listener, the tone of youthful confidence and dynamism sounded reassuring.

The tone rang even more vigorously in President Kennedy's inaugural address on that cold, snow-speckled January afternoon:

". . . We shall pay any price, bear any burden, meet any hardship, support any friend, oppose any foe to assure the survival and the success of liberty." In some ears, that may have sounded like the ultimate challenge—the battle cry of a confirmed cold warrior. But it was followed by a conciliatory message—expressed just as forcefully: "Let us never negotiate out of fear. But let us never fear to negotiate."

Indeed, what was most striking about those now-familiar passages was the particular way they departed from the traditions of cold-war rhetoric. It was not so much a matter of substance—no new policies were being staked out—as of style. But style is character, and character sometimes shapes events. Where the traditional anti-Communist posture emphasized the menace and exuded an aura of fearfulness, Kennedy was emphasizing possibilities and encouraging optimism. The defensive, often phobic attitude with which America had come to view the world was to be dispelled, like a healed patient shaking off the habits of illness. The nation was being rallied to go on the attack —not so much *against* an enemy as *for* objectives of its own, shared with free peoples everywhere: "My fellow citizens of the world: ask not what America will do for you but what together we can do for the freedom of man."

Jack Kennedy's anti-Communist credentials were in perfectly good order. In the Senate he had participated in criticism of the Truman State Department for the "loss" of China; his brother Robert had served as an attorney for Joe McCarthy's investigating committee. But on assuming the presidency, Jack Kennedy took a stance that was not so much anti-Communist as it was aggressively *American.* It was patriotic without being jingoistic, moral but not moralistic.

Whether calculated or not, the message did not fail to register on the young, who took it as a hopeful sign of change. The signal was picked up by members of the new Kennedy administration, which was being assembled largely from his Ivy League brain trust, his old navy buddies, and progressive young leaders of industry.

ROBERT S. McNAMARA
Retired head of the World Bank
1961: President of Ford Motor Company,
appointed JFK's defense secretary

I tried very hard to reduce the emotionalism associated with the quote "Red threat" unquote, and I insisted we strike out of speeches and language and statements from the Defense Department such words as "Red" and "communism" and talk about "the Soviets" because it was the Soviets we had to consider. And I tried to, in a sense, reduce the hysteria that came out of the McCarthy period and was still widely prevalent at the time.

"It was a time," recalls JFK's secretary of state, Dean Rusk, "when we thought we could take a good many new looks at long-standing questions to see if we might find any new solutions." Still in his early fifties, Rusk found himself one of the graybeards of an administration

whose spirit combined the verve of a college varsity with the dedica-
tion of the Manhattan Project. Even this professional diplomat, distinguished for his low-key temperament in a field where cool is the norm,
was not immune to Kennedy's inspirational charm: "He tended to set
everyone around him on fire a bit."

The atmosphere of White House meetings—informal, slightly disor-
derly; views expressed freely, often vehemently—contrasted remarkably with the highly regulated bureaucratic style of the Eisenhower
presidency.

There seemed to be hardly any limit to the new leader's appetite
for information—to his capacity for assimilating it and his facility for
dealing it out at news conferences: current facts and figures on shares
of the federal budget for various categories of expenditures, growth
rates of the gross national product . . . even such recondite matters as
China's population increase and historical statistics like the GNP of
Czarist Russia as compared with the U.S. economy in that pre–World
War I era.

When appointed chairman of the Council of Economic Advisers,
Walter Heller was counseled by Kennedy's long-time economic guru,
John Kenneth Galbraith of Harvard: "Don't be afraid to write him
lengthy memos. [Eisenhower, like many executives, had wanted everything reduced to a single page.] Just be sure to put a little humor
in it."

For old navy cronies like Dave Powers (a Massachusetts compatriot
as well), being part of the team that got Jack Kennedy elected President would have been satisfying enough. Going to the White House
with him was "like dying and going to heaven." There was an inside
joke, shared by the President and his personal staff, that originated on
the day after the Inauguration, when Kennedy asked Powers, "Well,
Dave, how do you like it so far?"

"Best White House I ever worked in," said Powers.

Kennedy picked that up as his own motto, adding: "And I can walk
home to lunch."

In its energetic style, the new administration immediately tore into
an ambitious agenda: in foreign affairs, those "many new looks at
long-standing questions"; on the domestic front, a range of emerging
issues barely recognized by previous administrations—consumer
rights, women's rights, the environment—as well as ongoing controversies like health insurance and aid to schools. The White House was
setting an example of activism for the youth of America.

There were a couple of faint discordant notes. One holdover from the previous administration, Richard Bissell of the CIA, found the informal, unregulated style of the White House meetings "very appealing [but] it had its bad side in that there were misunderstandings." And one highly qualified observer had forebodings about the new spirit in the administration. That was Clark Clifford, Jack Kennedy's personal attorney, who had his own experience in the Truman White House to go by. He was bothered, in the early weeks of the new regime, by the muscular attitude of the Kennedy crowd—by "a false sense of overweening confidence on the part of his staff. I wondered when something might happen. Well, it didn't take long."

·14·

FLASHPOINTS

When John F. Kennedy, the day before he was sworn in as thirty-fifth President, got a foreign affairs briefing from the outgoing chief, Dwight D. Eisenhower, the subject Ike spent most of his time on was Indochina. Specifically Laos.

The Geneva agreement ending France's travails in the mid-fifties, while dividing Vietnam, north and south, had certified the independence and neutrality of the two neighboring states, Laos and Cambodia. Now the integrity of Laos was being sabotaged by a Marxist rebellion, armed and supplied by Moscow and Beijing. Ike told Kennedy he'd have to send in American troops. The Joint Chiefs of Staff offered the same advice. Kennedy demurred. He needed more time for a decision like that.

There was another situation Kennedy was inheriting from the Eisenhower administration on which events were already in motion, though by no means irreversibly. That lesser, but much closer, hot spot was Cuba.

Only a matter of weeks before the presidential transition, Eisenhower had taken a drastic step against the increasingly obnoxious Castro regime, breaking off diplomatic relations. That was in reprisal for the latest act in Castro's "mini-cold war" with the United States: an order requiring the U.S. to reduce its embassy staff in Havana on the grounds (undoubtedly accurate) that many of its members were engaged in espionage.

As the incoming President, Kennedy had been invited to share in the Eisenhower decision, but he declined, feeling it would tie his hands unnecessarily.

As soon as Kennedy took office, however, he found that for Cuba as for Laos there was an intervention plan afoot. This one didn't come from the Pentagon, though it had the Joint Chiefs' stamp of approval. It had been developed by the Central Intelligence Agency and reflected an aspect of CIA activity that had been given increased emphasis, back in the early fifties, by Eisenhower's hush-hush Solarium Project. In renouncing outright measures like a "rollback," Solarium prescribed "covert measures designed to create and exploit troublesome problems" for the Communist side.

The original idea of the CIA's Cuba plan, as approved by Eisenhower in 1960, had been for the agency to train a kind of anti-Castro resistance cadre of perhaps two hundred Cuban exiles—train them at a base in Central America, since by its charter the CIA was prohibited from operating inside United States territory. This cadre would be infiltrated into Cuba to develop an underground movement aimed at unseating the pro-Soviet Castro regime.

Somehow the original idea ballooned. Now, in early April 1961, with a ten-week-old administration still finding its way around the White House, there was an armed force of 1,300 anti-Castro Cubans—Brigade 2506—trained at camps in Florida and Louisiana and supported by a little air force of eighteen American surplus B-26 bombers. The brigade was waiting to be launched on a military invasion of the Cuban homeland.

Only about two hundred of the troops were really soldiers; the rest were doctors, accountants, store clerks, farmers—all newly trained by CIA instructors. With what now seems like insane bravado, they would be challenging an army that Castro had built up to perhaps 200,000.

But, Kennedy was assured, Cuba was like a wax candle; the landing needed to do no more than light the wick. Castro's support would "melt away" at the first sign of opposition. Hadn't Fidel himself taken over Cuba with a rebel force of fewer than two thousand men?

Having set events in motion, all the United States needed to do was to exploit the landing by flying in a group of exiled political leaders to form the counterrevolutionary government—which would be reinforced by immediate diplomatic recognition by the United States and its Latin American allies. Just to make sure the invaders had a chance to establish themselves on the island, the nighttime landing was to be covered by an American naval air strike the next morning.

The young new President agonized over the plan for weeks, troubled by its flimsiness and by the diplomatic risks of U.S. involvement. The CIA director, Foster Dulles's brother Allen, advised him that it would be embarrassing to call the exiles off. And the Joint Chiefs were astonishingly optimistic about their prospects. The Pentagon's assurances seemed to sweep away any possible doubts. Kennedy told his personal aide and confidant Dave Powers afterwards: "I was a lieutenant junior grade on a seventy-eight-foot PT boat when Arleigh Burke was the commanding admiral of the Pacific fleet. And when Arleigh Burke [now Kennedy's subordinate as Chief of Naval Operations) said to me, 'It's a good plan, Mr. President,' I'm thinking of this great naval hero. He has to know more about it than I do."

Kennedy's advisers seemed similarly dazzled by the brass. Few raised any objections to the plan.

DEAN RUSK
1961: Secretary of state

We were all very new to each other. We were strangers. The tendency was for each one of us to sit over in our own little chair of responsibility and not look at this problem from the broad point of view. As a colonel of infantry, I knew this operation did not have any chance of success. But in the spring of '61, I was not a colonel of infantry; I was the secretary of state. And the Joint Chiefs of Staff are sitting there . . .

I think I badly served President Kennedy in not pressing him to ask a question which he did not ask. He should have turned to our Joint Chiefs of Staff and said to them, "Now, gentlemen, I may call upon you to do this with American forces, so you come in here by noon tomorrow and tell me what you would need for this operation."

Well, the Joint Chiefs would have come in with plans involving systematic bombing of Cuba ahead of time, with the landing of at least two divisions, backed up by the army and navy and air force and everybody else. And the contrast between what our Joint Chiefs thought they would need and this tiny little brigade in Central America would have been so startling that I think President Kennedy would have seen that this brigade had no chance.

D-Day was scheduled for early morning of Monday, April 17. All week before, Washington buzzed with rumors of some impending action in Cuba. The President complained that "Castro doesn't need any spies over here—all he has to do is read the papers." At his news conference, he was obliged to issue a disclaimer: "There will not be under any circumstances any intervention in Cuba by United States forces." He was still nursing his doubts about the landing.

RICHARD BISSELL

I told him that he had until noon on Sunday to call it off, but that was absolutely [the deadline]. I was obviously sitting at the end of a telephone in my office, and the telephone didn't ring at noon, and it didn't ring at one o'clock.

And then I tried to call him. He was in Virginia, in the country. I think I finally got him around two o'clock, and he said he knew he was a little late, but it was okay to go ahead.

Then later Sunday afternoon I got the call from McGeorge Bundy [the President's special assistant for national security affairs] that the Monday morning air attack, on which we heavily relied to neutralize Castro's air force, had been canceled. My immediate boss, the deputy director of Central Intelligence, and I went to Rusk's office. Rusk said, after listening to us himself: "My judgment is that although that air strike would be valuable to you, it is not really essential. And I see it as having a grave political cost."

With perhaps misdirected concern for political cost, the operation proceeded. The brigade's little war-surplus air force was sent into action on its own, disguised with Cuban air force markings in order to suggest that the planes were being flown by defectors coming in from Castro's own airfields. One of the planes was even shot full of holes on the ground in Guatemala and then flown up to Miami for a "forced" landing.

A preliminary air raid on Cuba by the old B-26s knocked out half of Castro's scant air force of about twenty planes—destroyed them on the ground. When Cuba complained before the UN, laying responsibility for the attacks on the United States, America's UN Ambassador Adlai Stevenson responded with utter conviction, "These charges are totally false, and I deny them categorically."

What Stevenson did not know was that the pilots were mostly Americans. About a hundred good ol' boys from the Alabama Air National Guard had been recruited by the CIA as crews and instructors, their unit having been one of the last in the armed forces to fly the old B-26. Four Americans were killed in the Cuba operation, and several others were captured after being shot down.

Meanwhile, the invasion troops were under way across the Caribbean in five leaky old freighters—an expedition so seedily mounted that an observer might well have doubted its sponsor was the world's richest country. In the overnight darkness, they were off-loaded in fourteen-foot open boats pushed by outboard motors. Their objective: a dismally swampy stretch of Cuba's southeast shoreline called Girón Beach, in the Bahía de Cochinos, the Bay of Pigs.

The execution was almost as bad as the plan.

The element of surprise was immediately lost when frogmen planting beacons on the beach were spotted well before the first troops came ashore. They were commanded by a Cuban exile, José Pérez San Román, but the point man was an American, CIA agent Grayston Lynch, who fired the first shots.

Castro had 20,000 troops in the area, a fact unforeseen by the plan, which was based on inadequate information and outdated maps. The maps didn't show that the once-isolated beach area was being developed as a workers resort by the Cuban government. A new highway therefore made it possible for the defenders to move tanks and other equipment swiftly to the spot.

Radios didn't work, leaving the brigade—strung out along fourteen miles of coastline—dependent on couriers for the most routine messages.

Bringing only one day's supply of ammunition ashore, the brigade quickly ran out of firepower.

Despite all this sheer fecklessness, the exiles actually managed to establish their beachhead. Not only that, but they were inflicting heavy casualties on the defenders.

MARIO CABELLO
Miami attorney
1961: Member of Brigade 2506

We were *there!* And all we needed was a little push. I'm not saying that 1,300 men would have defeated the whole army. But the conditions were right inside Cuba. There was a vast net of underground forces. Castro's army was not prepared. That's why we were able to hold the ground so well, because they didn't know how to fight a war. They would come in bunches of a hundred or so at a time, crying and shouting. They were easy prey to our fifty-calibre machine guns. And we didn't even have to aim our rifles.

The anti-Castro underground was no myth. But the signal that was supposed to rouse them to action never reached them. Meanwhile, the brigade's military success proved short-lived.

In the morning, Fidel got the surviving half of his air force into the skies over Girón Beach. That included two T-33 jet trainers armed for combat. Without help from U.S. navy fighter planes, the lumbering propeller-driven B-26s were no match for them. The invaders were pinned down on the beach; their supply ship was blasted out of the water, leaving the troops on shore empty-handed. The rest of the creaky old flotilla turned tail and steamed away, leaving the brigade to an inescapable doom.

To the Cuban exiles the absence of American airpower was nothing short of a betrayal. Mario Cabello: "We were promised—and I was witness to that—the American trainers promised us that the air would be ours."

Brigade commander Pérez San Román surveyed the predicament of his troops and clutched at a straw of trust: "I never saw the U.S. lose a war, so I thought some mistake had happened and they were going to land later on. I thought they were going to come in and give us a hand until we were strong enough to continue by ourselves."

It was the Hungarian uprising all over again. A counterrevolutionary force had been given an unwarranted belief in American omnipotence and American intentions—in this case by the CIA recruiters. "At no time," according to Dean Rusk, "did President Kennedy ever give any thought to the use of American forces in this operation, but apparently the brigade thought that if they got ashore and got into trouble that the army and the marines and the navy and everybody else would be in behind them."

The ultimate disappointment was still to come. With the plan in tatters and the brigade itself in jeopardy, the President was prevailed upon to authorize a navy carrier to fly one hour of air cover on Wednesday morning—long enough for the freighters to return on a rescue operation.

It never happened—apparently for the most banal of reasons. According to the CIA's operation planner, Richard Bissell, in the navy chain of command "somebody was on daylight saving time, and somebody was on standard." Before the confusion could be straightened out, it was too late. The expedition was finished. In the scant three-day adventure, the brigade had lost 114 dead; a handful of its members escaped into the Cuban countryside; the rest—well over a thousand —were captured, subjected to a humiliating trial in a sports arena, and imprisoned (to be ransomed by the U.S. government two years later for $53 million worth of baby food and medical supplies).

If the exiles' disappointment evoked memories of Budapest, then the net result seemed more like an American Suez—a symbol of disgraceful failure. Communist spokesmen exploited the issue in the UN; their propagandists had a field day. NATO Allies were doubly shocked: first, because the American involvement violated the UN Charter, and, second, as a British MP said, "because it was carried out with supreme incompetence on the basis of very bad intelligence."

Like Suez, the plan had backfired. Castro now had all the justification he needed to repress his opposition and renounce all pretext of democratic procedures. Vaguely promised free elections were indefinitely postponed. The anti-Castro resistance was dead, and Fidel himself had gained credibility throughout Latin America. His fulminations against the Yanqui threat had proved to be justified, and he had stood up to it and survived.

There was no lack of postmortems in the United States. Richard Bissell, the CIA's chief planner of the operation, concluded that the big mistakes were all at the policy level: he should have been given thirty-five B-26s instead of eighteen and twenty American air crews instead of six. Washington's official "hands-off" posture, Bissell decided, was wasted: "We should have known that disclaimability was not very important because everybody in the world was going to attribute this operation to the United States whether we could disclaim responsibility for particular actions or not."

The original sponsor of the CIA's counterrevolution, ex-President Eisenhower, never uttered a word of public criticism but in private he was vehement. Gritting his teeth in a typical Ike expression of deep feeling, he told his former vice-president, "You know, Dick, I would never have approved a plan without air cover!"

In a speech barely twenty-four hours after the expedition was abandoned, President Kennedy's tone was far from defensive:

Cuba, he said, while hardly "a threat to our survival," remained as "a base for the subverting of other free nations throughout the hemisphere." The use of American military force in support of the invasion "would have been contrary to our traditions. . . . But let the record show that our restraint is not inexhaustible." And should the time ever come, "we do not intend to be lectured on 'intervention' by those whose character was stamped for all time on the bloody streets of Budapest!"

As far as public discussion was concerned, Kennedy tried to put the mortifying affair behind him as quickly as possible by taking full blame for what he grimly conceded to have been a bad decision. Privately, he felt he had been betrayed by bad advice, the product of that "very bad intelligence" about such basic matters as Cuba's strength and troop dispositions. A thoroughgoing review of the government's intelligence operations was ordered under Kennedy's adviser/attorney, Clark Clifford. "I cannot take a chance on this happening again," Kennedy told him. "If it did, I would be driven from office." When one of the President's colleagues called his attention to a Gallup poll that (as often happens when a President comes under attack by foreign enemies or allies, even for good reason) showed public approval of Kennedy on the *upgrade* after the Bay of Pigs, he said wryly, "I hope I don't have to keep making stupid mistakes like that to keep my popularity up."

Six months later, the President was able to talk about the affair almost philosophically. It was probably a good thing the Bay of Pigs happened when it did, he told his special counsel and speech writer, Theodore Sorenson. "Otherwise, we'd be deep into Laos by now."

Instead, having learned a lesson from his first foreign policy disaster, the President convened his military advisers and told them to put their recommendations for sending troops to Indochina in writing—individually—including what they each thought the action would accomplish, what the Communists' response would be, and when and where it would all end. The reports proved so disparate and unconvincing that the President dismissed the idea of armed intervention.

Meanwhile, the Kremlin was making its own assessment of the Bay of Pigs and the young new President who was responsible for it.

FYODOR BURLATSKY
Soviet writer on military affairs
1961: Khrushchev's speech writer

To my mind, it [the Bay of Pigs] was the gravest mistake of his political career—first, because he undertook this action, and, second, because he lost it. Some of the specialists [on U.S. affairs in the Kremlin] certainly considered him at that moment to be not very decisive and not a very great President.

That was the assessment Nikita Khrushchev took with him in June of '61 to his first face-to-face meeting with John F. Kennedy.

Khrushchev's Wall

The routine exchange of diplomatic good wishes at the start of the new administration, like the perfunctory greetings of business acquaintances, led to a half-hearted social engagement. Washington and Moscow agreed to renew the summit meetings broken off so brusquely at the time of the U-2 incident the year before. The break had left such raw feelings that neither capital was up to the role of host, however, so in June 1961 the two leaders would make a fresh start at a new, neutral site: Vienna.

Approaching the first one-on-one match with his main antagonist, Khrushchev, after a losing encounter with a warm-up opponent, Castro, Kennedy was anything but casual. In a political career that started relatively soon after a tough Ivy League college education, he had developed assiduous habits of homework. In the non–Ivy League metaphor of Dave Powers: "He prepared for that meeting like Notre Dame prepares for Alabama. Anyone that knew anything about Khrushchev or anyone that knew anything about the Russians he spent hours with. He had a book on that Vienna meeting *that* fat!"

In some respects, the trip was a Kennedy triumph. In side visits to Paris and London, the NATO allies were bowled over by the Kennedy charisma. France's haughty old President, Charles de Gaulle, was impressed by the young American leader and captivated by his elegant wife. A French audience was delighted when the head of the world's most powerful nation introduced himself by saying, "I am the man who accompanied Jacqueline Kennedy to Paris."

Britain's Conservative prime minister, Harold Macmillan, had been concerned about the change in American leadership and what it might mean to the alliance. "You know, I had such a good relationship with President Eisenhower," he had told a visitor some months earlier. "We knew each other during the war. We looked at the world more or less in the same way. We enjoyed each other's company. And now there is this young, cocky Irishman. He belongs to a different generation. How am I going to establish a special relationship with him?"

By the time the presidential entourage left London, Kennedy had established the basis of a relationship with the British prime minister that was close, personal, almost father and son.

Among Macmillan's Labour party opposition there had been some early alarm at the pugnacious tone of the Kennedy oratory and the apparent ineptitude with which the Bay of Pigs had been handled. The Kennedy presence now dispelled those misgivings. "He seemed to represent a new spirit in the world," recalls Labour's Denis Healey, "and people were prepared to forgive what he said and even what he did, certainly for the time being."

Khrushchev and Vienna were another matter.

DEAN RUSK

Secretaries of state are very skeptical about negotiations at the summit. Summits tend to put an undue amount of pressure on an American President because people expect some result. And there are public opinion pressures on a President at a summit meeting which do not apply to the Soviet leader.

But there's something about the chemistry of being President that causes Presidents not to agree with secretaries of state on this matter. They just get the idea that somehow if they can sit down with their opposite number, maybe they can work things out. But it just doesn't work that way.

President Kennedy went to Vienna to meet Khrushchev without an agreed agenda, without prenegotiations that would have opened up the possibility of a serious agreement on any important point, and Kennedy came away with this rather harsh and brutal ultimatum on Berlin that Khrushchev handed him at Vienna.

At one point, Mr. Khrushchev said, "We're going to do the following with regard to East Germany and access routes to Berlin, and if there's any attempt at interference by the West, there will be war!"

I, in diplomacy, never used the word "war." Talk about "the gravest possible circumstances" or something of that sort.

But Kennedy had to look him in the eye and say, "Then, Mr. Chairman, there will be war. It's going to be a very cold winter."

Behind Khrushchev's bluster lay some troublesome statistics. One-third of all university and technical school graduates were leaving the

GDR (the German Democratic Republic, the official name of East Germany) for the West as soon as they finished their studies. From 1949 to 1961, perhaps one-sixth of the whole East German population had "voted with their feet." Berlin was their open gateway to the West. Many other East Germans were "crossing over" just long enough to visit and shop and were spending millions of marks on Western consumer goods. The talent and the currency were drains that the sluggish economy of the East could ill afford.

Agenda or no, Berlin—that perennial sore spot, that "bone in the throat," as Khrushchev once put it—was what the Soviet leader had come to Vienna to talk about. "He went there knowing exactly what he was going to say," Kennedy told his buddy Dave Powers. "Whatever I said didn't make any difference. It was like the transcript was going back to the Kremlin."

Across the dinner table the same evening at Schönbrunn Palace, Vienna's glittering baroque landmark, the mood changed abruptly. Khrushchev was the soul of geniality to Kennedy and his wife, confirming the President's impression that in talking tough Khrushchev once again (as in the U-2 incident) may have been playing to the hard-liners back home.

But the ultimatum was on the record, impossible to ignore for a young leader who knew his nation's resolve was being tested with his own. "He thinks I have no guts," Kennedy said grimly. And the implications of the Berlin pronouncement went right to the heart of the cold war's central issue: Germany. For by his threat to sign a separate peace treaty with East Germany—the threat issued after the aborted U-2 summit in Paris—Khrushchev proposed nothing less than to kick the Western Allies out of Berlin. In relinquishing control of the access routes to the East Germans, Khrushchev claimed, he would nullify the rights that Russia had guaranteed to the Western Allies under the Yalta and Potsdam agreements—rights the West had maintained ever since, at whatever cost.

In Kennedy's scheme of foreign policy absolutes—commitments the United States simply could not back down from—the commitment to West Berlin headed the list. Returning to Washington with a sense of impending crisis, he could see no recourse but to tough it out. Using television and his pipeline to leading journalists, he conveyed his grim reading of the situation to the American public and began mobilizing for "what might be a collision of major proportions between the Soviet Union and the United States in Berlin."

Draft calls were doubled, the armed forces increased by 200,000. An immediate call-up was issued for 76,500 reserves. The Berlin garrison was beefed up. Mothballed ships were recommissioned. Congress was urged to raise the defense budget inherited from the previous administration by some $1.8 billion. Kennedy stopped short of declaring a national emergency because, he told associates, he wanted to *alert* people, not *alarm* them. But that was exactly the unwanted impact of one measure he announced to the television audience. It was a recommendation for a national civil-defense program emphasizing the construction of public fallout shelters.

The program, which soon got under way with bipartisan support, was one Kennedy and his advisers later decided was a serious mistake. It might have alarmed the Russians, they concluded, into thinking the United States was planning a first strike and preparing to protect its population against whatever feeble retaliatory blow the Soviets could deliver.

As to whether the bomb shelters would actually protect the public, former Defense Secretary McNamara says: "Not only did anyone believe it, I'd say essentially everybody believed it. Certainly I believed it. The President believed it. I testified in favor of it. I was totally wrong."

To personalize America's commitment Kennedy dispatched his vice-president, Lyndon B. Johnson, to West Berlin with a message of reassurance to the citizens and their charismatic mayor, Willy Brandt. Johnson found the atmosphere tense but relatively calm. It was on the Communist side of the line that the strain was really showing. The perpetual stream of East Germans fleeing west via Berlin was now reaching flood tide. In July 1961, more than 30,000 crossed over; in early August, they were crossing at an even greater rate.

The crisis escalated, Khrushchev keeping pace with Kennedy step by step: an upward thrust in the Soviet defense budget, a fusillade of bomb tests and space launches, a series of bristling speeches.

Around Berlin itself a noose was being tightened. As if to forestall a reprise of the dramatic 1948 airlift, the Russians began disrupting navigational radar by dropping tinfoil-like streamers of "chaff" in the air corridors. When the Allies responded by increasing their ground traffic, Khrushchev ordered the East Germans to block the highways. Backed up by Macmillan and de Gaulle, Kennedy now put military escorts into the supply convoys. They were halted . . . but then were let through without a shot being fired.

At a diplomatic reception in Moscow, the British ambassador, Sir

Frank Roberts, expressed his concern about the situation to Khrushchev's tough number-two man, Frol Kozlov, who told him blandly, "No, no, you needn't worry. We will make trouble for you on your side of the line, but never at the risk of war. And we would expect you to make trouble for us on our side of the line, but never at the risk of war."

Not long afterwards, Khrushchev himself buttonholed Sir Frank and informed him that he'd just appointed a new troop commander in Berlin—adding pointedly that it was the same general who had put down the Hungarian uprising in 1956. When the ambassador, not knowing what to make of that information, didn't appear sufficiently impressed, Khrushchev went on: "What's more, I could destroy your country with eight bombs!"

The ambassador kept his diplomatic cool. "We're a very small island," he said. "Six would be enough for us. But then, don't forget that with our Royal Air Force we can destroy twenty of your biggest cities, including Moscow, without the help of the Americans. So isn't this rather a foolish conversation?"

"Yes," Khrushchev agreed in his typical hot-and-cold style. "Let's have a drink."

Roberts reported the encounter to the Foreign Office in Whitehall as "a strange conversation," but he didn't know what to make of it until a few days later, on the morning of August 13.

That day, Berliners woke to find their historic city—the capital of a nation and a culture—being cut apart as if by some brutal surgery, being disfigured by a scar of barbed wire and concrete blocks from one end of the East–West sector boundary to the other. Erected by East German workmen under cover of East German guards backed by Russian tanks, an ugly wall, thirteen feet high, was rising between the bleak landscape of East Berlin and the glittering promise of the West. Khrushchev's bomb rattling had presumably been intended as a warning to the West to keep hands off while the builders did their work. Later, in a less incendiary style, he justified the wall as the only way he could stop the "hemorrhage" of East German resources. In a somewhat different metaphor, he once asked a Western diplomat challengingly, "How would you feel if your teeth were being pulled out one by one?"

Berlin is not only a handsome city but an expansive one with a remarkably varied landscape, encompassing apartment-house districts and gardened suburban neighborhoods, business centers, factory zones, forested parks, lakes, and even small farms. Because in some places the boundary ran down the middle of a street or between back yards, the wall separated children from their playmates, neighbors from neighbors, and family members from each other. It separated workers from their jobs, people from their aspirations for a better life.

DR. RAINER HILDEBRANDT
Museum curator, West Berlin
1961: East German journalist, novelist

At the beginning, many thought, dear God, maybe we can flee through the Bernauer Strasse, because over the entire length of that street the walls of the houses are the border, so that when you are in the house you are in the East, but if you jump from the window you are in the West. And it was gripping to see how the people jumped, first from the ground floor, and did not get hurt. But then the ground floor windows were walled up, and then they had to jump from the second floor, and the [West Berlin] firemen came and spread a safety net. Then from the third, fourth, and fifth floors. One whole week long it got higher and higher. Some were killed jumping because they missed the safety net.

In the beginning there was, so to speak, some friendship with the guards at the wall. But then other, stricter people were placed there. And after the first week, of course, the first people were killed.

Die Mauer. The common noun for "wall" in the German language came to acquire a very specific meaning. It came to mean that brutal boundary in Berlin. The Wall acquired a lore of its own: personal stories of ingenious escapes in which heroism was almost routine. In the darkness of the first night after the barbed wire started to go up, a young East Berlin factory worker named Kurt Wiesmach set out with his wife, neither of them taking anything but the clothes on their backs. They spent hours traveling the subway and elevated lines hoping to find an unguarded railway bridge. No exit.

Finally, leaving one station on foot, they brazenly walked through a roadblock into a street as if they lived there—a street bordering the Landwehr Canal. After hiding for some time in a rubble-strewn lot, they stripped down to their underwear, left their clothes tied in a bundle, and plunged into the filthy canal.

Helping his wife across, Wiesmach installed her on the Western bank while he swam back for the clothes, nearly swam right into the arms of a couple of *Vopos* (*Volkspolizei*, the East German People's Police) who had been napping on duty, managed to retrieve the bundle, and then lost it just as he was climbing safely ashore to join his wife in the West.

Now, at two o'clock in the morning, they found themselves in a dreary neighborhood entirely dark except for one dim light behind the door of a neighborhood bar that had just closed. Filthy, wet, and shivering in their underwear, they knocked on the door. The proprietor opened up, looked them over, and said matter-of-factly, "You're the third ones here tonight."

The boundary was soon hardened. In a cleared strip along the eastern side of the Wall, concrete dragon's teeth sprouted alongside steel barricades under the glare of floodlights. It was the landscape of a prison camp under constant surveillance from armed watchtowers. The stream of fugitives was all but shut off—all except for those nervy and ingenious few who would continue to cross over by concealing themselves in the undercarriage of a car or by crashing through a barricade in a specially reinforced vehicle, by tunneling under the Wall or flying over it in one homemade contraption or another. There were just enough dramatic escapes to keep the lore and the hope alive. But in twenty-five years after the building of the Wall, seventy-four people are known to have been killed trying to cross the forbidden boundary.

When the President made a personal visit to Berlin in 1963, the ugly landmark had already taken on the aura of a shrine, and the trip had the air of a pilgrimage. As Kennedy stood on a platform built over the steps of the West Berlin city hall, a tide of faces—perhaps 150,000— lifted to hear him declare his solidarity with the people of the island city: *"Ich bin ein Berliner!"*

"I am a Berliner!" *Everybody* living in freedom was on the side of the people of Berlin, the President was saying.

The cheers mounted to a roar of affirmation such as Berlin had not heard in almost two decades.

The atmosphere was so intense that it worried Kennedy's host, the elderly German chancellor, Konrad Adenauer. The emotional pitch of the crowd, he told Secretary of State Rusk, reminded him too painfully of Nazi rallies.

Kennedy himself worried afterwards that he might have pulled the emotional stops out too far. In building up to that declaration, he had played heavily on the Communist menace; and by that time Khrushchev had once again withdrawn his ultimatum to the Allies. The American President and the Soviet Chairman were well along on an extraordinary secret effort to achieve quietly what they had failed to accomplish in the limelight of summitry. They had begun an exchange of private letters that eventually would lead to improved understanding between the two leaders and produce one of the few concrete agreements between East and West.

But things were to get worse before they got better.

Competitors

In John Fitzgerald Kennedy and Nikita Sergeievitch Khrushchev the cold war had brought together two political leaders of vastly different backgrounds but similarly competitive temperaments. Khrushchev had spent his early boyhood in peasant poverty, working as a cowherd, and his teens working in a mine. With the passion of an ideologue, he was continually urging his countrymen to overtake the capitalist nations in every field—economic, scientific, military. Jack Kennedy of the Boston Irish Kennedys had been brought up in a banker's household—though the family's earlier background was in saloon keeping and ward politics.

If the Kennedys had a crest, the motto would have been that maxim perhaps less known to bankers than to bar fighters and politicians: "Don't get mad, get even!" Norman Mailer, whose Harvard class was between Jack's and his younger brother Robert's, once said of Bobby (at a time before experience had mellowed him) that he was the sort of competitor who would knee you in the groin in an *intramural* football game.

To put the cold war in the past may have been Jack Kennedy's ultimate goal, but as long as there was a race against the Communists going on in any field of activity, he would not settle for second place. Not in missilery, in space, in any significant area of production.

The competitive issue that Kennedy himself had introduced into the political campaign—the so-called missile gap first indicated by the Sputnik launch—was resolved early in his administration.

ROBERT MCNAMARA

The missile gap was not a fabrication. Nobody consciously distorted facts. The missile gap was a reflection of this weakness in our society—a willingness, an obsession if you will, in exaggerating the strength, overestimating the strength of our opponents and underestimating our own.

When I was sworn in as secretary of defense on January 20, 1961, I thought my first responsibility was to determine the extent of the missile gap and the action we should take to overcome it. And my deputy and I spent the first three weeks of our service in the Defense Department investigating the subject, and it took only three weeks for us to determine there was no missile gap.

Well, I shouldn't say that. There was a missile gap, but it was exactly the reverse of what had been alleged. Instead of finding that the Soviets had a strength superior to ours, we found exactly the reverse.

I don't recall the exact number of missiles, but I do recall the number of strategic nuclear warheads at the time, which is even more important. And the ratio was something on the order of 6,000 Western strategic nuclear warheads to 200 Soviet strategic nuclear warheads. That is a rough measure of the relative strategic nuclear strength of the two powers at that time.

In addition to the security offered by those figures, the United States also had the comfort of geography. Insulated by oceans, the U.S. was in a position to threaten the Soviet Union with medium-range Jupiter missiles based just outside the Russian borders in Turkey, a NATO ally.

There were no such favoring facts and figures to be found in the related but separate competition in space. The head start Russia had achieved with the Sputnik had been followed up by further advances in satellites and rockets, and the evidence was right there for the world to see, in the heavens and in the headlines.

Early in April 1961, with the United States poised to launch the first manned space flight, the Russians once again stole a march on their rivals. A Soviet test pilot named Yuri Gagarin hurtled on a complete orbit of the earth in a rocket-launched capsule—one of the spectacular feats of early space exploration.

Gagarin's American counterpart, Alan Shepard—his training finally completed under the inescapable gaze of the doctors—had been primed to go first. Instead he had to watch his vehicle being launched without him for one last unmanned test. It had been ordered by the space program's master mind, Wernher von Braun, to iron out a kink in the separation of spacecraft from escape rocket.

The Soviets played the first orbital flight like a rerun of their Sputnik triumph. Gagarin was proclaimed "the world's first cosmonaut" and his capsule as "the first spaceship." Eastern-bloc schoolchildren were given a holiday to celebrate a new Russian hero. The name Gagarin was attached to streets, buildings, parks.

Jack Kennedy was dismayed but undaunted. The Russian spaceship had barely landed back on earth when he summoned a meeting of science advisers, confronting them with one urgent question: "Can we leapfrog?" He was looking for a project big enough, dramatic enough, to steal the Russians' thunder. How long would it take us to land a man on the moon?

Vice-President Johnson was assigned to explore the possibilities. He came back with an enthusiastic report. It could be done by the end of the decade. The hardware could be built, the astronauts trained. Facilities at Cape Canaveral would have to be vastly expanded. A new mission control center would be established (it wound up in Johnson's home state of Texas, at Houston).

"For God's sake, Lyndon," Kennedy kept interrupting, "how much is this gonna cost?"

The answer: a projected $56 billion. Kennedy gave it the green light.

In the meantime, the United States had to content itself with small, relatively subtle victories. Commander Shepard's flight, a month behind Gagarin's, was not a complete orbit like the Soviet pioneer's 108-minute trip; instead it was a 15-minute trajectory up through the atmosphere and down again. But the American pilot actually flew the spacecraft briefly, working the controls, while Gagarin had been essentially a passenger in free flight. "Boy, what a ride!" Shepard exulted.

Not until the following year, in February 1962, did the United States actually put a man in orbit when John Glenn circled the earth three times in a five-hour mission, with a national television audience listening in on every "Go!" and "A-OK!" exchanged between the astronaut and Mercury control.

With that flight the President's leapfrog campaign was well under way. The Russians were unlikely to match the massive investment. From a purely scientific standpoint the potential rewards were negligible; much the same results could be achieved with unmanned instruments. From a strategic standpoint there was little to be gained. But as a human adventure, as a coup for American prestige, it would be dazzling. If it worked, America would finally overtake the Soviet Union in the competition to be number one not just on earth but also in outer space.

The Missiles of October

Even Cuba goaded Kennedy's fiercely competitive instincts.

After the Bay of Pigs fiasco, many Americans had written off the counterrevolution as a lost cause. There was a general assumption that the administration had, too. But Jack Kennedy had not been brought up to swallow a defeat. Together with his brother Robert, serving in the cabinet as attorney general, he set about getting rid of Castro his own way.

Far from being abandoned, the CIA's anti-Castro campaign simply went back underground. More personnel, more money, more resources were funneled into the anti-Castro effort now than at the height of the Bay of Pigs preparations. The CIA was secretly commissioned to mount a vast program of paramilitary operations and sabotage based in Miami—an outright violation of the law limiting the agency to foreign activities. The largest CIA mission in the world at the time, it consisted at its peak of six hundred to seven hundred "company" officers plus about two thousand Cuban exiles. The strategy was, by attacking such crucial targets as cane fields and power plants, to bring down the Cuban economy and the Castro regime with it. One Cuban agent alone made some three hundred fifty clandestine missions to the island. His name was Rolando Martinez; he, several of his colleagues, and their CIA connections would surface a decade later in the notorious Watergate break-in.

By the summer of 1962, the CIA's range of activities had expanded to include plans (never actually carried out) to use chemical and biological warfare against the Cuban sugar industry and bizarre plots against Castro using the services of American Mafia bosses and their Havana contacts. They would humiliate him by drugging him into incoherence before a speech; they would destroy his image with a substance that would make his beard—his trademark—fall out; they would assassinate him by poisoning his cigars.

The whole campaign was conducted with the standard secrecy of CIA covert operations, and how much of the sordid details the Kennedys themselves knew is a matter of some dispute. But at the level of public policy, meanwhile, the administration was tightening its grip on Castro's economic jugular. The sale of American products to Cuba was embargoed, and some Allied governments were persuaded to institute similar measures. Cuban sugar was boycotted, cutting off Castro's main source of foreign currency.

Russia, meanwhile, had cemented its ties with Castro and was subsidizing the beleaguered island to the extent of $1 million a day, mostly in shipments of oil and machinery.

"The overthrow of Castro," Robert Kennedy told a group of his associates, "has the top priority in the United States government. All else is secondary."

JFK's defense secretary, Robert McNamara, recalls the atmosphere this way: "We were hysterical about Cuba."

By some lights, the administration wasn't doing nearly enough. Firebrands on Capitol Hill were urging outright invasion. At his news conferences in the summer of 1962, the President was called upon repeatedly to respond to these inflammatory demands. He cited America's worldwide commitments, which, he said, mandated caution. The Russians were making curious new moves in Berlin, sending little expeditions of armored personnel carriers into West Berlin daily. It was within their rights, but possibly they were probing for some new opening. The U.S. had to stay ready to handle trouble in the main arena.

But beginning in late August, there were persistent reports of a dangerous escalation in the amount and kind of Soviet aid arriving in Cuban ports: first, groups of military technicians, then troops in substantial numbers, relatively advanced antiaircraft weapons, and, finally, some ominous cargoes unloaded from Soviet freighters—long cylindrical objects looking suspiciously like missiles. That last, most alarming report was confirmed on October 14 when the CIA flew two U-2 reconnaisance planes over Cuba to see what was going on.

When the full scope of Khrushchev's audacity was ultimately revealed, it showed that the Russians were in the process of installing forty-two medium-range (1,100-mile) missiles, twenty-four intermediate-range (2,200-mile) weapons, and forty-eight Ilyushin attack bombers on Cuban soil. All this weaponry was accompanied by no less than 22,000 military "advisers." Khrushchev was establishing a nuclear base just ninety miles off the Florida keys.

The missiles were just starting to arrive; none was yet armed with a nuclear warhead; the launchers were not yet emplaced. But once they were, the Soviets would be in a position to threaten any American city on the Eastern seaboard from Miami to New York—even to strike at Strategic Air Command bases in the Rockies.

When the President was briefed on the U-2 revelations, he asked tersely, "How much time do we have?"

The estimates ranged from ten to fourteen days before the Russians could get the missiles operational.

Already hypersensitive to the Cuba issue, the administration immediately mobilized once again, for a crisis of the gravest proportions. In a style at once grim and calm, the President assembled a group of men whose judgment and experience he trusted most. They included not only his brother Robert, Secretary Rusk, Secretary McNamara, and various other members of the National Security Council but also some elder statesmen from previous Democratic administrations like Dean Acheson and John J. McCloy. Numbering about twenty in all, the group functioned as the executive committee of the National Security Council.

When he assumed office, John F. Kennedy had urged his cabinet and other close associates to read Barbara Tuchman's account of how the nations stumbled into World War I in *The Guns of August*. Now, with gunpowder amplified into nuclear power, they had reason to apply the lessons of restraint as they confronted the missiles of October.

ROBERT MCNAMARA

He instructed us to meet—sometimes with him, sometimes without him —until we had determined on a course of action we were prepared to recommend to him, and not under any circumstances to make public the knowledge we had that these Soviet missiles had been introduced into Cuba until he had made his decision. We took the rest of that week to decide what to recommend.

There was great division as to whether we should essentially follow a military course that would involve an attack on Cuba.

THEODORE SORENSON
New York attorney
1962: JFK's special counsel, chief speech writer

Dean Acheson, the former secretary of state, recommended an air strike against the missiles in Cuba. Someone said to him, "Mr. Secretary, what will the Soviets do in response?"

"Oh, I know the Soviets pretty well," he said, "from dealing with them over the years. I think they will then feel obligated to launch an attack and knock out our missiles in Turkey."

"And what will we do then, Mr. Secretary?"

"Well," he said "under the NATO treaty, we would then be obligated to knock out Soviet missile sites inside the Soviet Union."

"Well, what would *they* do then, Mr. Secretary?"

"Well," he said, "we hope by that time cooler heads will prevail and everybody will sit down and talk."

Fortunately, he [Kennedy] did not take that advice.

For all the risks of escalation, an air strike had considerable support. But Bobby Kennedy deplored the idea of a Pearl Harbor attack that would inevitably kill civilians—and possibly Russians. And even the advocates conceded that the missiles couldn't be taken out "surgically" from the air; the United States would have to follow up the aerial bombing with ground troops to capture and totally neutralize the missile bases. That seemed like the least desirable option.

The most desirable option was, in McNamara's words, "to avoid the necessity of attacking Cuba in the first place, and the way to do that was to move the Soviets to take those launchers and the associated attack aircraft out of Cuba."

While the President made a show of going about his normal routine, the tense debate continued all week behind the scenes. On Saturday, October 20, the President broke off a congressional-campaign trip on the pretext of having caught a cold. Convincingly bundled into an unusual—for him—coat and hat, he returned to Washington, walked into a White House meeting room, looked around the table at the assembled advisers, and said with a tight smile, "Well, gentlemen, today we're going to earn our pay."

The crisis atmosphere was by then inevitably beginning to ooze out of the White House. Navy vessels were being deployed in the Caribbean. B-52s were in the air fully loaded with H-bombs. Washington reporters were getting messages from their editorial desks asking them to check on reports of troop movements from bases in Texas and Florida.

Ex Comm (as the impromptu executive committee was dubbed) was ready with a recommendation. The options had been narrowed down to a single proposal urged by Rusk and McNamara and favored also by Bobby Kennedy: stop the missiles in transit by imposing on Cuba a kind of naval blockade which the proponents referred to as a "quarantine." Rusk's recollection: "Over the centuries the notion of blockade has become very complicated as a matter of international law. We used the concept of quarantine partly because no one knew what quarantine meant."

Adlai Stevenson, the elegant man of reason serving as American ambassador at the UN, suggested accompanying the naval action with a diplomatic offer to Moscow: if Khrushchev pulled his weapons out of Cuba, the United States would dismantle its missiles in Turkey and give up its long-held Guantanamo naval base in Cuba. Guantanamo was a relic of Yankee imperialism dating from the Teddy Roosevelt era. The Jupiter missiles were obsolete—quirky, unreliable, slow to put into the air in a crunch. They wouldn't be much of a sacrifice.

The President, in fact, had already decided to dismantle the bases in Turkey—but he was not about to do it under pressure. Stevenson's bargaining chip was vehemently rejected as a giveaway.

There were no "ifs" attached to the decision which the President took that weekend. A line would be drawn 500 miles off Cuba. At that point, ships would be stopped and searched for offensive weaponry. The Soviet missiles already in Cuba must be removed immediately.

On Monday, October 22, Kennedy turned the crisis loose. Rusk called in the Soviet ambassador, Anatoly Dobrynin, and gave him Kennedy's demands. Adlai Stevenson called for a special meeting of the Security Council. Dean Acheson flew to France and briefed NATO leaders on the ominous situation. In a private conversation with de Gaulle, the French President told him: "I don't believe there will be war. But if I'm wrong, France will be on your side."

The same day President Kennedy went public in a television speech informing Americans that the Kremlin was engaged in developing Cuba into a base whose purpose "can be none other than to provide a nuclear strike capability against the Western Hemisphere."

The only response from the Kremlin was a bland insistence that the weapons were nothing but *defensive;* they were only surface-to-air missiles, antiaircraft rockets shielding Russia's protégé Cuba from the threat of an American invasion. Kennedy was infuriated by the denials. He had the reconaissance photos to disprove them. In his memoirs Khrushchev eventually would admit that "within weeks we had installed enough missiles to destroy New York, Chicago, and other large industrial cities—let alone a little village like Washington."

Twenty-five Soviet ships were spotted en route to the Caribbean, one of them named the *Gagarin* after the space hero. The first American ship to confront them at the quarantine line would be the *Kennedy,* a destroyer named for the President's war-hero brother Joseph. In the Pentagon, admirals crowded into an operations room to watch the plotting board as the two forces converged. "Admirals standing against the walls," their civilian chief, McNamara, recalls. "They couldn't even sit down." Nerves were drum-tight.

Several Soviet ships were stopped, searched, and let through when their cargoes proved innocuous. Others turned back on their own, presumably with weapons aboard. The whole explosive procedure was handled gingerly on McNamara's orders. He insisted that any ship potentially coming into contact with a Soviet vessel must have somebody aboard who spoke Russian, to avoid misunderstandings. When the chief of naval operations, George Anderson, proposed to stop an oncoming tanker by firing a shot through its rudder if necessary, McNamara said testily, "Let me tell you something. You're not gonna fire any shot against that tanker, with the possibility that it'll blow the damn thing up and that this will be the start of war, without my permission; and I'm not gonna give you my permission without the President's permission. Now, do you understand that?"

Anderson assured him, "The navy's been handling quarantines and blockades since John Paul Jones, and if you'll let us handle this one, we'll handle it right."

McNamara turned and walked out of the room.

Meanwhile, in Cuba, missiles and launchers were still being hurriedly assembled. For most of a week, the situation hung somewhere between resolution and explosion. On Friday, the 26th, there was an apparent breakthrough when President Kennedy received a curious message from Khrushchev, proposing to remove the missiles if the United States would pledge not to invade Cuba. The message was in Khrushchev's personal style, by now familiar to Kennedy from his secret correspondence with the Soviet leader; it was free of the stylistic fingerprints of official Soviet communications—the signs of editing by Kremlin colleagues—and it carried a certain undertone of desperation.

"You can be certain," Khrushchev told the American President, "that we are quite sane and understand clearly that if we attack you, you will retaliate. But we will match you blow for blow. . . . Why, then, should we court disaster. . . ? Only a lunatic or suicide would do that. . . ."

Clearly, Khrushchev was feeling the heat. Why he had chosen to embark on such a reckless course in the first place is a question that has never been answered satisfactorily. The most likely explanation is that he was gambling on a kind of shortcut to strategic parity—a move that would, simply and relatively cheaply, balance the American superiority in numbers and the threat of those missiles in Turkey. The vehemence of the American response apparently took him by surprise.

"Khrushchev never anticipated that the Americans would react in such a way, with the blockade," according to the high-level Russian defector, Arkady Shevchenko. "There was no contingency planning for such a situation."

In Dean Rusk's phrase, "Khrushchev simply ran out of scenarios."

Apparently, one was supplied to him by his Kremlin colleagues. For within hours after that first rather conciliatory offer, a second message came in from Moscow—this one in official language with a much tougher tone. It repeated the offer to withdraw the missiles but added a new condition: the United States must dismantle its missiles in Turkey.

Almost simultaneously with the new message came news that a U-2 had been shot down over Cuba.

And that day—"Black Saturday" to the people in the Kennedy administration—the mood in the White House took an awful plunge. There were plans to evacuate the government from Washington. Time was running short. The Joint Chiefs of Staff were urging an immediate air strike against the Cuban bases. Ex Comm, reversing itself, was ready to go along with them and hope for the best.

ROBERT MCNAMARA

It is very unlikely that the political leaders of the Soviet Union would ever have authorized a nuclear response to a U.S. air attack and/or ground attack on Cuba. However, it was highly probable that they would authorize some other form of military response: attacks on the flanks—Norway, Turkey, for example, attacks on the central front of NATO [i.e., Germany].

[And] in the face of an air attack [on Cuba] and in the face of the probability of a ground attack, it was certainly possible, and I would say probable, that a Cuban sergeant or Soviet officer in a missile silo, without authority from Moscow, would have launched one or more of those intermediate-range missiles, equipped with a nuclear warhead, against one or more of the cities on the East Coast of the United States.

They could have hit Miami. They could have hit Washington. They could have hit New York.

DEAN RUSK

When I was a small boy in the Presbyterian church, I memorized the Westminister catechism, and the first question in that catechism is: "What is the chief end of man?"

Well, as I drove through the streets of Washington and saw people on the sidewalks and in their cars, it was sobering to realize that this first of all questions, "What is life all about?" had become an operational question before the governments of the world.

Sander Vanocur, the television correspondent, who was then assigned to the White House beat, recalls being led through the Cabinet Room at some point during that weekend en route to a briefing. (He had been informed that he would accompany the President in the evacuation of the White House.) As Vanocur passed the President's place at the cabinet table, he noticed a lined yellow note pad, and on it in the President's handwriting was "Berlin Berlin Berlin Berlin Berlin—five times and circled every time." That's what was still worrying him—the big target in Europe.

The President himself was resisting the military's pressure for an air strike. His concerns had shifted from the strategic to the simply humane: he was thinking, he said, about "the children of the world."

DAVE POWERS

People that were never afraid were scared [that weekend]. Everything was going wrong. Jackie and the children were at Camp David, and I was having dinner with the President that Saturday night. He had sent Bobby down to talk to Dobrynin to see if there was something they could resolve. I remember that we had chicken and white wine, and the President was having chicken and milk and mashed potatoes. And Bobby came back after seeing the Russian ambassador, and all the news bad. And I continued to eat nervously, unaware that the two brothers had stopped talking.

Then I heard that great voice go, "Dave, you are eating the chicken and drinking the wine like it is your last supper."

And I looked up embarrassed, and I said, "Mr. President, after listening to you and Bobby, I'm not so sure it isn't."

In the morning of Sunday, October 28, the fever suddenly broke. The folklore of the Cuban missile crisis says it was finally resolved that second weekend by an ingenious stroke of diplomacy backed by an adamant American attitude. The record is somewhat ambiguous.

The question was how to deal with Khrushchev's two successive messages—one mild and agreeable, the other tough and unacceptable. The formula that emerged from Ex Comm to break the deadlock couldn't have been simpler: the White House accepted the first proposal and ignored the second.

To his dying day, Nikita Khrushchev insisted that before he made a move to withdraw the missiles from Cuba, he had assurances from Bobby Kennedy (presumably through Ambassador Dobrynin) that the American missiles in Turkey would likewise be removed. Ex-Secretary McNamara insists just as vehemently that "it was not a deal." Only after Khrushchev had *agreed* to defuse the Cuban base did Kennedy instruct the Pentagon to dismantle the offending—and obsolete—weapons in Turkey. "And then," McNamara recalls, "I went to the Defense Department and I spoke to John McNaughton, my assistant secretary, and said, 'John, get those missiles out of Turkey. Take them to Italy. Cut them up. Saw them up. Take photographs of them. Deliver the photographs to me. Don't tell anybody why you're doing it. Do it!' "

No matter what compensation the Kremlin was able to extract from the White House, the Cuban missile crisis was perceived worldwide as an American triumph, a Russian backdown. A test of wills and conflicting aims had brought the two superpowers eyeball to eyeball (the phrase came out of this incident and entered the language), and it was the Soviet that blinked. The humiliation put Khrushchev in a hopelessly vulnerable position against his opponents inside the Kremlin; eventually, they would bring him down.

On the American side, far from trumpeting the victory, Jack Kennedy—wise to the things that drive competitors like himself—cautioned his colleagues not to make any sort of gloating claims that might stir the Soviets to get even. There was good reason to be modest. The missiles were gone from Cuba, but the Communists' ally, Castro, was still there, now protected by an American pledge not to invade. And after this the United States would no longer be able to impose its will on the Soviet Union by sheer nuclear superiority. Khrushchev chose not to get mad *or* get even, after all, but to preclude another such defeat by catching up with the U.S. in missile power.

Both leaders emerged from the crisis with a somber sense of having walked the edge of nuclear catastrophe. They were drawn together, these two curiously matched antagonists, the way soldiers on opposing sides of a war are often drawn together afterwards by the life-and-death experience they have shared.

During the storm over the missiles of October, a U-2 based in the Far East to monitor Soviet H-bomb tests happened to stray over Siberian territory. In remarkable contrast to the mood of conflict over Cuba—and to his own behavior in the U-2 incident with Eisenhower a couple of years earlier—Khrushchev merely registered a rather mild protest. Kennedy apologized.

During the crisis, in his first, personal message offering to remove the missiles, Khrushchev described the two of them as being at opposite ends of a rope that was knotted in the middle. If they kept pulling in opposite directions, he said, the knot would become so tight "we will never be able to undo it."

Once the agreement ending the crisis was reached, the Russians were uncharacteristically cooperative about carrying out the unpalatable terms. They were forthcoming with information about the offending missiles, planes, and troops. And they stood by while the retreating weapons were examined aboard homebound freighters by UN inspectors, most of whom were American engineers.

It was in the immediate aftermath of the Cuban missile crisis that Kennedy and Khrushchev set up a teletype hot line giving the White House and the Kremlin instant contact in the event of some future crisis.

The Defense Department was instructed to leash American nuclear power with a kind of fail-safe program. Robert McNamara, who was charged with carrying it out, describes it as a system making it impossible for "any person on the ground having access to [a nuclear warhead] to fuse it and launch it without an input from the President of the United States. Not all but essentially all of our warheads carry such devices to this day, and we hope that Soviet warheads do likewise."

That was still a long way from security in Kennedy's mind. If he had arrived on the international scene as—in Prime Minister Macmillan's phrase—a "young, cocky Irishman," then his brush with nuclear catastrophe had changed him. He emerged with a diminished confidence in the very future of mankind.

"I believe," he said, when asked to assess prospects for international security, "that sooner or later someone is going to make a mistake."

·15·

A LEGEND WITH
THE WRONG ENDING

The surge of nationalism in the sixties was sometimes hard to distinguish from the thrust of communism. And the opposition sometimes took forms too oppressive to be considered democratic.

France was torn apart by an unrelenting guerrilla war in Algeria, where less than a million French *colons,* some settled there for generations, were trying to hold their ground against a Muslim nationalist majority of nine million. Underground organizations on both sides waged campaigns of terrorism—the rebels with help from East-bloc sources, the *colons* represented by powerful elements within the French military establishment. The government in Paris barely escaped a *coup d'état* before President de Gaulle forced the generals to accept the inescapable trend of history and let Algeria go. Independence followed in 1962.

In the African interior a savage civil war with cold-war overtones broke out in the Belgian Congo with the approach of independence. European interests tried to maintain a foothold in the vast preserve, rich in gold, diamonds, and strategic minerals. A United Nations military force was interposed between rival armies, but the UN secretary general, Dag Hammarskjold, was a committed advocate of third-world interests and leaned over backward to avoid giving any advantage to former colonial powers.

The Soviet protégé, a tribal leader named Patrice Lumumba, was assassinated, possibly with the complicity of the CIA. Hammarskjold himself was killed in an unexplained air crash just outside the borders of the country that—as the new republic of Zaire—would eventually achieve a measure of dubious stability the way many new nations did: under a tough, high-living military regime which called itself socialist but was linked to the West.

The nationalist movement in Indochina was carrying Communist banners and confronting the Kennedy administration with a tough decision.

The situation appeared to have been stabilized in 1961, when Kennedy—resisting Eisenhower's parting advice to send troops to Laos—instead negotiated an East–West agreement reinforcing Laotian neutrality. The agreement came unstuck almost immediately when the Pathet Lao, the Communist rebels, resumed their attacks with the help of their neighbor, North Vietnam. The North Vietnamese were using Laotian territory as a corridor to supply yet another Communist underground movement, the Viet Cong of South Vietnam. A Soviet air lift to Hanoi was feeding this whole network of rebel movements. Khrushchev had made it known that while seeking an accommodation with the West, Russia would feel free to support so-called "wars of national liberation." The gauntlet had been flung down in Southeast Asia.

The United States had a treaty commitment to South Vietnam, and was unrestrained there by any paper neutrality as it was in Laos. President Ngo Dinh Diem of South Vietnam, entertaining a stream of visiting firemen from the Kennedy White House, was sending back requests for American troops. Most of the visitors were favorably impressed, but one—George Ball, the number-two man at the State Department—worried that in five years the United States would have 300,000 men in Vietnam. Kennedy thought Ball's figures were "crazier than hell," but he was leery of escalation himself. If the United States sent in troops, he said, "then we will be told to send in more troops. It's like taking a drink. The effect wears off and you have to take another."

In the end, the administration wound up making a commitment that was less than substantial but more than just symbolic. Military aid to Diem's anti-Communist regime in Saigon was stepped up, and with it Kennedy sent a contingent of uniformed "military advisers" amounting to more than a division's strength—almost 17,000 men. The main cadre was made up of Special Forces, distinguished by their cocky green berets. The headgear marked them as experts in counterinsurgency techniques, designed to fight guerrillas. Kennedy, with his James Bond penchant and his eye for the up to date, was much taken with these tough new operatives.

Somebody asked him how, once involved in Vietnam, he expected to get out. "We will back a government that will ask us to leave," he answered.

It proved a lot more complicated than that, but the issue was one Kennedy never had to face. It became part of his legacy.

The Young Idealists

Elsewhere in the vast expanse of the earth's surface occupied by new and underdeveloped nations, the emphasis was on nonmilitary forms of aid. Kennedy, according to his associate Robert McNamara, genuinely believed that the United States had not only the capacity but also the obligation to help disadvantaged nations improve their social and economic conditions.

It was a kind of idealism expressed in the Alianza para el Progreso —the Alliance for Progress, a $3 billion aid program for Latin America —and in Kennedy's extraordinary Peace Corps, which evoked a tremendous response among young Americans (and many of their elders as well). Twenty thousand volunteered for the first 2,500 jobs. They and a whole generation that followed them served their country abroad by instructing Peruvian villagers in nutrition and infant health problems . . . or helping to bring a water pipeline into a *barrio* in Colombia . . . or pitching in on an irrigation project in Tunisia or Togo . . . even helping women in India construct their own native form of cooking stove. A departure from traditional forms of Western paternalism, the object was not to impose "more advanced" American methods on local populations but to help them make the most of their native traditions and resources.

At the same time, many other young Americans were becoming involved in efforts to raise the status of disadvantaged groups at home —efforts that would inevitably carry echoes abroad.

For more than a year before the Kennedy administration, groups of young blacks had been quietly challenging local segregation ordinances by sitting in at lunch counters traditionally restricted to white customers. In the spring of 1961, a northern-based organization, the Congress of Racial Equality, decided to broaden the attack. CORE began sending mixed busloads of white and black "Freedom Riders" on southern routes to assert a common right to use waiting rooms, rest rooms, and other public facilities under federal laws barring discrimination in interstate travel.

The Freedom Riders were traveling bare-handed in hostile territory. Southern black groups, mostly organized around the churches, rallied to support them and to rescue them when necessary. Leading the regional civil rights forces was the young Atlanta minister, Martin Luther King, Jr.

By 1963, the civil-rights campaign was in full swing, built on models deliberately chosen from the experience of colonial peoples in the Third World. Where the original sit-in protesters, once arrested as lawbreakers, would "bail out"—having made their point—the Freedom Riders and their local supporters adopted a tactic that was explicitly Gandhian: they set out, without using violence, to burden the local communities by filling the jails. In a widely publicized letter written as a kind of manifesto from a jail cell in Birmingham, Alabama, Martin Luther King declared: "The American Negro has been caught up by the Zeitgeist, and with his black brothers of Africa and his brown and yellow brothers of Asia, South America, and the Caribbean, the United States Negro is moving with a sense of great urgency toward the promised land of racial justice."

In King's Atlanta study, the heroes whose photographs hung on the wall were African nationalist leaders: Milton Obote of Uganda, Julius Nyerere of Tanzania, Kenneth Kaunda of Zambia. Martin Luther King was becoming an international hero himself. When one of his associates, a Georgia pastor named Andrew Young, later traveled abroad as President Jimmy Carter's UN ambassador, he was astonished at how many schools and monuments bore the name of the American civil-rights leader, not only in the Third World but even in European countries. And doors were opened to Young "not just because I was appointed by Jimmy Carter but because I had worked with Martin Luther King."

In their own encounters with nationalist movements, the European colonial powers often experienced violent revolution and bloody guerrilla warfare. The civil-rights movement was following a strikingly different course.

HENRY BRANDON
British journalist
1960s: Washington correspondent

I traveled in Mississippi and Georgia and other places, and it was hard to believe that there was this kind of division between whites and blacks. And yet at the same time you had to admire the fact that there was no real warfare between the two and that the two sides were groping for some sort of coexistence. And I think that there is no country in the world that has handled its racial problems better than the United States.

ANDREW YOUNG
Politician, diplomat
1960s: Civil-rights activist

Blacks and whites all had guns, and yet we never turned them on each other. I think part of the reason is the Judaeo-Christian heritage of the South but also the fact that Martin Luther King advocated a means of change that did not destroy either person or property. It was essentially change without violence, even though there was a very aggressive struggle.

If we had not had that nonviolent struggle, we would have some of the same problems that you now see in Lebanon and Ireland.

The record was not *totally* free of violence, even in those first few innocent years of the civil rights movement. White vigilantes operated with the acquiescence and sometimes the active cooperation of local authorities. There were ugly incidents—buses ambushed, passengers pulled out and beaten. Once arrested, riders and local demonstrators were sometimes mistreated and humiliated in the jails. There were shooting incidents, Ku Klux Klan lynchings, a bombing of a black church in Birmingham in which four youngsters were killed.

If these tragedies were relatively few, then it was partly because of the role the federal government came to play in the civil-rights campaign.

Not by instinct a social reformer, Jack Kennedy shared the moderate liberal views of his post-FDR generation. His record on civil rights while in Congress was decent but hardly distinguished. But once federal laws were invoked by the activists, then the government was inevitably drawn in on their side.

The issue crystallized as it moved on from the bus stations to university campuses in the South. When black students (traditionally restricted to separate, lesser institutions for Negroes) tried to register at state universities, the governors—Ross Barnett in Mississippi, George Wallace in Alabama—based their resistance on the theory of states' rights, long discredited in law and by history.

The federal government could hardly let these challenges to its authority go unanswered. In the face of threats to the safety of travelers and of students, Attorney General Robert Kennedy sent federal marshals to the scenes of resistance, and President John F. Kennedy backed them with federal troops when things seemed about to get out of hand.

Aside from the constitutional issues, the administration also had a certain practical foreign-policy interest in the civil-rights issues.

DEAN RUSK

Ambassadors to Washington or to the UN—those of dark color—had great difficulty in knowing where they could have lunch, in finding office space, living quarters for themselves and their staff. An ambassador would drive down to a Maryland beach on a Saturday afternoon and be turned away. His wife would ask a State Department wife to go to the supermarket with her because she was afraid of incidents. This was a very serious problem for us.

On one occasion, an ambassador of dark color from south of the United States was on a plane going to New York, to the United Nations. The plane stopped in Miami for refueling, and just about all the other passengers were taken into the airport lunchroom to have lunch. He was put on a folding canvas stool in a corner of the hangar and brought a sandwich wrapped in wax paper. Then he went on to the United Nations. And we were supposed to get his vote up there.

We organized a social committee in New York City, and the State Department worked very hard in Washington with the realty boards and the hotels. But it soon became evident to us that you cannot solve these problems on the basis of diplomatic passports. You've got to solve them for the community as a whole. And so we in the State Department took a leading part in pressing for the civil-rights laws of the 1960s.

By the summer of 1963, civil rights was a national cause with a constituency that included many middle-class whites. Its new status was demonstrated in a huge rally in Washington, where, the *New York Times* noted, in spite of some forebodings there was no violence, "and an air of hootenanny prevailed." Celebrities from the music world performed for the crowd and led them in civil-rights songs. The Reverend Dr. King moved the American public with a speech in which he shared his dream of racial equality and brotherhood.

MARY TRAVERS
Folk singer, political activist
1963: Member of trio Peter, Paul, and Mary

The march on Washington in 1963 was on a hot day, and a quarter of a million people—men, women and children, white and black—were assembled in the Mall area together. And hope and goodness were palpable. And for me it has served as a touchstone, if you will—a place I can go back to in my mind; and it gives me sustenance when I look at the terrible things, the terrible possibilities, you know—nuclear holocaust, war, all of the dreadful things that seem so out of control. In those moments when I wonder, "Is mankind fated to destroy itself?" I go back in my mind's eye to that moment and say, "Humanity is capable of good."

Committed to civil-rights legislation, President Kennedy was unable to translate the rising spirit into congressional action. The same thing was true of other major domestic issues. The entire Kennedy social program, boldly proclaimed as the "New Frontier," bogged down. Federal aid to education was bungled by overcautiousness: as the first Catholic President, Kennedy shied away from a bill that would have included funds to parochial schools. He had been moved by reading Michael Harrington's book *The Other America*, which analyzed poverty as a separate, self-perpetuating subculture, to declare a "war on poverty," but he was unable to mobilize the congressional forces to carry it out. Nor was he able to muster enough support for a health insurance program designed particularly to protect the elderly against catastrophic costs of illness.

The one substantial achievement Kennedy could point to, as he approached the end of his third year in office, was his success in defusing the cold war.

Banning the Bomb Tests

Practically from the moment the Cuban missile crisis ended in the fall of 1962, Kennedy had engaged Khrushchev in efforts to damp down the nuclear danger. Public awareness of the issue was high; a kind of consensus was building, at least within government circles. "Defense intellectuals" like Secretary McNamara were trying to steer American strategy away from the Dulles concept of "massive retaliation"—away from reliance on nuclear weapons toward an emphasis on conventional arms.

Claude Pepper in the Senate, attending a football game as a member of the presidential party in his home state of Florida, noticed an admiral sitting nearby with a black box between his feet. That, Pepper was informed, was the "football," the President's means of control over nuclear weapons. It accompanied him wherever he went. The senator was horrified at the thought of the President making a decision about using the Bomb between plays of a game.

The President was horrified himself. As a first step back from the nuclear abyss, he proposed that Khrushchev join him in taking one more crack at that elusive ban on nuclear testing. On this issue, there was little of the tentativeness JFK showed in domestic controversies. He took on Eisenhower's old nemesis, the voluble opponent of a test ban, Dr. Edward Teller—took him on publicly.

"I understand Dr. Teller is opposed to it," Kennedy said at a televised news conference. "Every day he is opposed to it." But the President was "haunted," he said, by the trend of nuclear proliferation. "How many weapons do you need, and how many megatons do you need to destroy? . . . What we now have on hand, without any further testing . . . will kill 300 million people in an hour."

Khrushchev had his own gadfly-scientist—but on the opposite side. Andrei D. Sakharov, one of the inventors of the Soviet H-bomb, was finding it hard to live with his "responsibility for the problems caused by radioactive waste," and was urging a halt to testing. "Sakharov is a good scientist," Khrushchev responded, "but he should leave foreign policy to those of us who are specialists in this subtle art."

But the atmosphere of Soviet-American relations was mellowing remarkably. Kennedy had earned the Kremlin's respect by his combination of vigor, toughness, and forbearance. He further impressed Khrushchev and his Kremlin colleagues by a speech at American University in Washington in June 1963, in which he urged his countrymen to "reexamine our attitude toward the cold war" with a view to "a relaxation of tensions." That fall the first sale of surplus wheat to the Soviet Union was initiated, helping to bail Khrushchev out of an agricultural crisis. Between those events, an agreement was reached in Geneva to suspend nuclear tests everywhere except underground (the difficulty of detection would have made that too hard to enforce).

DAVE POWERS

If President Kennedy were here today and we asked what he was most proud of in the two years and ten months and two days he was President, I believe he would say: "The signing of the nuclear test ban treaty." I was with him in Duluth when he got word that the Senate had ratified it. It was September 24 [1963], and I never saw a man so happy.

The Tragic Season

In the fall of 1963, a number of important matters were in flux.

In Vietnam, where optimistic reports earlier in the year had led to a decision to start withdrawing the American soldiers, the situation was turning bad. Instead of implementing promised political reforms, Diem's Catholic regime had undertaken a program of repression against its Buddhist opposition. Disturbed by evidence that the war effort against the Communists was suffering, Washington began to cool on Diem. In the last analysis, President Kennedy said in a televised interview, "it's *their* war." He was determined that Vietnamese, not Americans, should carry the brunt of the fighting.

On November 1, a group of South Vietnamese generals seized the government. They disposed of Diem by murdering him. The coup had the approval of American officials in Saigon—a ranking CIA officer was at the rebel headquarters when it happened. According to Lyndon Johnson, it was okayed in Washington by mid-level State Department officials at a moment when "Jack Kennedy was off in a sailboat at Hyannis and Dean Rusk was away for the weekend."

Kennedy was terribly upset by the news. He may have been disenchanted with Diem, but the outcome repelled him. He reaffirmed as the twin objectives of his policy to "intensify the struggle" and to "bring Americans out of there." Whether he would have been able to reconcile those two aims—whether he would have been able to carry out the troop withdrawals—seems questionable. Like most American policy makers of his time, he was too deeply committed to the cold-war view—to the Eisenhower view—of the world as a row of dominoes.

"Are we going to give up in South Vietnam?" Kennedy asked rhetorically. He had supplied the answer a few months earlier: "For us to withdraw from that effort would mean a collapse not only of South Vietnam but Southeast Asia."

On the domestic front, things were also in transition.

The President's popularity was on the downgrade; from a high of 76 percent it had fallen below 60. His pronouncements on controversial issues had alienated the conservative southern branch of his own party without mobilizing enough liberal support to secure passage through Congress. School aid and health insurance were hopelessly stuck. On civil rights, some harsh new voices were being raised within the black community. Like the man who called himself Malcolm X (rejecting his legal surname, Little, as a "slave name"), they offered no dreams of racial brotherhood and integration, only garish visions of black separatism and liberation from the rule of the "white devil."

In his aspirations for a second term, President Kennedy could anticipate a campaign in which the nation might be polarized by these issues. His Republican opponent—a foregone conclusion—would be Senator Barry Goldwater of Arizona, a conservative ideologist and a champion of old-fashioned "big stick" policies in arenas where American interests were challenged, like Southeast Asia.

In planning for the 1964 campaign, Kennedy was prepared to write off most of the South. But he felt he could offset the losses somewhat by holding its two biggest blocs of electoral votes, Florida and Texas. On November 21, 1963, John F. Kennedy flew to Texas with his wife and his vice-president, a native son, to start raising funds and mobilizing the state's Democratic leadership for next year's big push.

At 12:30 the next afternoon, as the President rode in a motorcade through a Dallas intersection called Dealey Plaza, all the plans came to an appalling end in a volley of rifle shots. John F. Kennedy lay dying on the back seat of an open car, his shattered head cradled in his wife's lap. The awakened spirit of the sixties ebbed away with his life, leaving a space to be filled by shock, by disbelief, by sorrow and suspicion. The nation's self-confidence was shaken by the reminder of that dark side of the American character: its infatuation with violence. Paranoid fears cultivated by two decades of cold-war hostility immediately rose to the surface.

When Lyndon Johnson was told, in a guarded waiting room at Parkland Hospital a scant half hour after the shooting, "He's gone!" the thought uppermost in his mind was "that this might be an international conspiracy of some kind." The new President of the United States was taken to the airport slumped down in the seat of an unmarked car; he was hustled aboard the presidential plane, Air Force One, and flown back to Washington on a zigzag course to elude possible pursuit. Nuclear bombers were put into the air in a condition of alert.

Johnson's fears were amplified by unusual circumstances that fragmented the American government at the very time of the assassination. Not only were both the President and the vice-president absent from Washington, but so were six members of the cabinet, en route to a high-level meeting with Japanese officials in Tokyo. Accompanying them on a scouting mission for Kennedy, who was planning a later Tokyo trip of his own, was the presidential press secretary, Pierre Salinger.

While over the mid-Pacific, the group started getting alarming messages about events in Dallas. Confusion aboard the plane was compounded by the fact that nobody could find the code book translating the names of high government officials. They had turned around and were on their way back when they received a message they couldn't mistake but could hardly believe: "Lancer is dead." Lancer was the code name for President Kennedy.

They arrived back in Washington late at night, just about the time Kennedy's body was brought home to 1600 Pennsylvania Avenue. Salinger, numb with shock and fatigue, spent the night at the White House along with several other members of the Kennedy inner circle.

PIERRE SALINGER
Paris bureau chief, ABC News
1963: John F. Kennedy's press secretary

We talked to—oh, five, five-thirty in the morning, and finally I went to sleep. And at seven o'clock in the morning the phone next to my bed rang. I picked it up, and I heard the operator say, "Mr. Salinger, the President wants to speak to you." And I had that instantaneous thought that I'd just had an awful nightmare.

Then I heard this voice saying, "Pierre, this is Lyndon." And that's when I really recognized that John Kennedy was really dead.

You can hardly find anybody abroad today that believes it was simply the act of a crazy man. From the beginning, in Western Europe it was "a plot." I mean, there were all kinds of theories, but never abroad have they accepted the idea that Kennedy was killed by Lee Harvey Oswald acting alone. That was accepted in the United States for some period of time. Interestingly enough, the major change in that perception in the United States came over Watergate. People saw all kinds of machinations in the government during the Watergate thing, which instilled a spirit of conspiracy in America

which hadn't existed before. So that today in the United States, I'd say 85,
90 percent of the people also believe that it was a conspiracy.

I personally don't. I stay firmly with the idea that Kennedy was killed by
Lee Harvey Oswald [alone] and that he—Oswald—was killed by another
crazy man, Jack Ruby.

The early conspiracy fears were largely dispelled by the report of
the Warren Commission. Headed by the Chief Justice, that blue-rib-
bon panel had been quickly assembled by President Johnson, who was
himself the object of some of the wildest suspicions.

The basic facts of the assassination stood up under every reasonable challenge: the fatal shots were clearly fired from the window of
a book warehouse on Dealey Plaza—fired by Oswald, a twenty-four-
year-old social misfit who had once defected to the Soviet Union
and who was an avowed partisan of Castro's Cuba. The secondary
outrage—the murder of Oswald by Ruby scarcely forty-eight hours
later—was witnessed by millions on live television as the President's
assassin was being transferred from one Dallas police facility to another.

But the man who commissioned the Warren Report was himself
never convinced that Oswald had acted entirely on his own. "He was
quite a mysterious fellow, and he did have connections that bore
examination," Lyndon Johnson told an interviewer more than five
years later. ". . . I don't think they [the Warren Commission] or we or
anyone else is absolutely sure of everything that might have motivated
Oswald or others that could have been involved."

So persistent were the doubts and so strong did they become in the
light of post-Watergate revelations that some members of the Warren
Commission and its staff eventually repudiated the report, and in 1976
the House of Representatives mobilized an independent investigation
of its own—now almost thirteen years after the event.

The findings of that two-year inquiry stood the Warren Commission
verdict on its head. President John F. Kennedy, according to a 1979
report bearing the credentials of a committee of the United States
Congress, "was probably assassinated as the result of a conspiracy."
The plot presumably "originated with members of organized crime"
but also probably involved "anti-Castro Cubans."

In reaching that astonishing conclusion, the House Select Committee on Assassinations had to cut its way through the undergrowth of
suspicious sightings, blurry photographs, and missing files, which by

now covered the landscape of assassination lore. Instead, the investigators' attention was compelled by two secrets of 1960s history that were unavailable to the Warren panel in that pre-Watergate era.

One was the CIA's Mafia-linked plots to assassinate Fidel Castro. (There were meetings between contacts as late as the very day of the President's murder.) The other was the harassment of underworld figures in an FBI program of illegal wiretaps. (It was part of a Kennedy administration campaign against organized crime.)

These revelations seemed to give a sinister new cast to Oswald's unsavory associations in the New Orleans demimonde and his links to *both* sides of the Cuba issue. Likewise Jack Ruby, who lived and operated in a sleazy twilight at the edge of the underworld; he had a Cuba connection of his own that involved one of the CIA's mafiosi, and his testimony to the Warren Commission was riddled with holes. His murder of Oswald, in the description of the House committee's chief counsel, "had the earmarks of a gangland rub-out."

But for all the investigative effort and the congressional credentials, the conspiracy theory remained just that—not a case but a theory, a possible explanation of events too awful to go unexplained. In murdering President Kennedy, Lee Harvey Oswald *may* have been acting on behalf of, or with the encouragement of, vengeful crime figures who thought they'd bought the government's leniency by their deal with the CIA but who instead found themselves under fire from Kennedy and his brother in the Department of Justice. Oswald *may* have had the complicity of some Cuban exiles who felt embittered by Jack Kennedy's apparent abandonment of the anti-Castro cause. And Ruby *may* have been the instrument by which the underworld, in its traditional way, silenced a hit man.

If any of this was true, none of it could be proven. After so many years the trail was cold. Some of the underworld suspects themselves had been violently removed from the scene.

As to those first high-level fears of an *international* conspiracy, the House Committee agreed with the Warren Commission that Jack Kennedy's foreign antagonists had little to gain and much to lose by his death.

Fidel Castro pointed out that for him to engineer Kennedy's assassination, even in reprisal for the CIA plots, would have exposed Cuba to the American invasion it had so far been lucky to avoid. The Soviet government was quick to express its horror at the Dallas events and turned over a mass of documents pertaining to Oswald's three years in Russia. Within months, a defector named Yuri Nosenko showed up with KGB credentials to reinforce the official disclaimer of any link between Soviet officials and Oswald.

The defector's story had some flaws. Suspected by some American officials of being a KGB plant, he was treated harshly. His auspices continued to be argued—inconclusively—in U.S. intelligence circles for years. But there was no evidence to shake the belief that chaos was as contrary to Soviet interests as it was to America's and that in his brief time on the international stage Jack Kennedy had won not the enmity but the goodwill of most reasonable people on both sides of the cold war.

He had won considerably more than that.

MELOR STURUA
Soviet journalist
1963: Chief of *Izvestia*'s Washington bureau

I was taking a shower, and my wife called me. "Somebody's calling you," she told me, "from *Izvestia*. Somebody shot Kennedy."

I went immediately back [to the bureau], and everybody was in such a mood as if we lost our good friend despite the fact that, before, we knew that we were adversaries, and we knew that he was a very strong defender of the American way of life.

Everybody was in a very tragic mood. And I remember afterwards, after our [Soviet] television showed the burial of Kennedy and John-John going like that [Kennedy's four-year-old son saluting the funeral cortege], we started to receive letters with money from our readers: "Please send this money to the children of Kennedy." And we had to answer all those letters and send the money back saying "They are well provided and they don't need your rubles," et cetera.

But still we thanked them for this affection, which shows, by the way, the soul of Russia. Some of [the letters] were written by quite illiterate people, but still their feeling was so pure, so fine.

BERNARD-HENRI LÉVY
French philosopher and writer, ex-radical leader
1963: High school student

I knew his life by heart—the relationship to the parents, the story of the three brothers and how they were brought up . . . the making of a presidency and so on. We had the stories in the French newspapers. It was a sort of modern legend. We could not imagine that there would not be a happy end to this modern legend.

After Kennedy, each time there was a new politician in France, a man with esteem, we always said, "He's the French Kennedy."

DAVE POWERS

They all loved the President like a son—world leaders at that time: de Gaulle, who was old enough to be his father, and Adenauer and DeValera. But what I remember mostly is that after the funeral President DeValera came back to the White House and talked to Jackie, and then I sat with him in the Cabinet Room. This wonderful man that represented so much of Ireland's history and loved President Kennedy said, "In Ireland, they will compare him to one of Ireland's own great liberators, Owen Will O'Neill, of whom Thomas Davis wrote, 'We're sheep without a shepherd when the snow shuts out the sky. Oh, why did you leave us? Why did you die?' "
And he had tears in his eyes.
But watching the world leaders in the room with Jackie that day was— they just showed their love and respect for this young man that went out in the twilight of his career. But what we lost more than that is the hope and confidence that he had spread not only here but around the world.

With the shocking loss of its hero, the youthful spirit of the 1960s turned inside out. The new mood converged with cold-war events, and the age of Aquarius became a period of hostility and violence.

·16·

LYNDON JOHNSON'S WARS

"We were not like brothers," Lyndon Baines Johnson once said about the man he replaced in the White House. "We were not constant companions."

The institution of the American presidency, for all its many virtues, does not lend itself to sudden transitions. Vice-presidents have rarely been chosen because they were intimates or replicas of the chief executive but almost for opposite reasons, in order to balance the ticket. A VP who succeeds his leader in midterm is likely to bring to the office a contrasting background and style, different experience, and even different interests. All this may give policies a jolt of new emphasis if not a change in direction.

The regional differences between Johnson and Kennedy were as sharp as the generational contrasts between Kennedy and his Republican predecessor, Eisenhower. Kennedy's urbane Ivy League manner belonged to the atmosphere of the corporate executive suite and the country-club locker room. Johnson, the rangy small-town Texan, reflected the political tradition of the courthouse steps. Lyndon was a kind of frontier character, bigger than life and twice as coarse. Even his tall-tale habits of speech, his loose way with facts in the interests of making a point, contrasted with Jack Kennedy's style of subtle understatement.

After the heady experience of power as Senate Majority Leader, Lyndon had found the vice-presidency a frustrating job. "The vice-president has no troops," he pointed out. "He has no power." But his long service in the ranks of the party and the congressional power structure had taught him to be a good soldier as well as a commander. And in fact his relationship with John F. Kennedy—uncompanionable as it may have been—was closer than that between many Presidents and their potential successors. Truman had been largely ignored by FDR. Eisenhower never quite cottoned to Dick Nixon and all but withheld his endorsement of the Nixon candidacy in 1960. Johnson was an outsider to the Kennedy circle of fraternity-house brothers, but he had JFK's personal respect and got a reasonable apprenticeship for the presidency. Aside from goodwill missions to Berlin and Asia and the fact-finding assignment on the space program, Johnson had had the instructive experience of hunkering down in the White House Cabinet Room with Ex Comm through the trials of the Cuban missile crisis.

LBJ's frustration didn't end when he inherited Kennedy's constitutional power. He still envied Kennedy's personal appeal; his influence with the Eastern liberal establishment, which dominated the Democratic party; his Boston and Harvard credentials, which made Johnson all the more painfully conscious of his farmhouse background and his teacher's college diploma. And once he'd inherited Kennedy's troops, he found that many of them—cabinet members, White House aides and advisers—resented him as a usurper occupying the place that belonged to their hero.

But Lyndon Johnson shared their sense of tragic loss—the nation's —and on assuming the presidency his compelling objective was to build a political memorial to the man in whose shadow he had served for three years. It was not just an expression of personal grief; it was also a way to take control, assume command of a demoralized country, and prove his right to the office. He would build where Kennedy himself had tried and failed—on the domestic front. For that was where, by background and preference, Lyndon Johnson operated best: not in the cool diplomatic atmosphere of foreign affairs but in the hurly-burly of congressional politics, where allies and antagonists alike engaged each other in blunt talk, with arms around shoulders or lapels clutched between fingers like reins as they jockeyed toward some inevitable compromise.

Where Kennedy had made his mark as a cold-war leader, from the very beginning domestic issues were uppermost in Johnson's mind.

JACK VALENTI
President, Motion Picture Association of America
1963: Texas political public-relations specialist

I was in the motorcade in Dallas when Kennedy was murdered; I was hired by Johnson that very hour, shortly after 1 P.M. [as a White House special assistant]. I was on Air Force One with him in that bleak homecoming, with the flag-draped coffin of the thirty-fifth President in the after-portion of Air Force One. And that night, November 22, Bill Moyers and myself and the late Cliff Carter spent the night with Lyndon Johnson on the very first night of his Presidency. [Moyers, then a Peace Corps official, became LBJ's press secretary; Carter, as aide to LBJ as vice-president, joined his White House staff.]

I remember we were in his bedroom. He was sprawled out on a vast bed. He had his pajamas on. And that night Johnson painted on a canvas the "Great Society," though that night we didn't know it had a name.

He talked at length about how he was going to make it possible for every boy and girl in America to get "all the education they could take"—by loan, scholarship, or grant. Well, that's the Elementary and Secondary Education Act.

He said to me, "Now, Jack, I want to talk to Dick Russell"—Senator Richard Russell [Georgia Democrat], the leader of the Southern forces, the patriarch of the Senate. He said, "I gotta tell Dick that we're gonna have that civil rights bill that's been languishing in the Senate. We're gonna get it with no quarter given and no quarter asked."

And then he said, "We're gonna do something that Harry Truman tried to do and every President's tried to do: we're gonna get Medicare. We're gonna have medical care for the old and the sick in this country who can't afford it."

And to my bewilderment and puzzlement and surprise, he made it all come true. I might add as an aside—ironic: he never mentioned Vietnam.

I think most professional observers would count the Great Society to be the most revolutionary upheaval in social legislation that this country's ever seen—and not only proposed but, more importantly, passed.

But keep in mind that the whole rostrum of his presidency rested on continuing the Kennedy legacy. In his first joint-session speech, five days after he was President, he said, "John Kennedy said, 'Let us begin.' I say, 'Let us continue.' "

Much of the legislative firepower for the Johnson program was supplied by young northern liberals in the Senate—Hubert Humphrey and Eugene McCarthy of Minnesota, Philip Hart of Michigan, George McGovern of South Dakota, Edmund Muskie of Maine. But Johnson was also able to cash in his credit as a born-and-raised southerner with conservatives like his friend Dick Russell of Georgia.

There was a mood of reconciliation in Washington and an impulse to deliver on promises long withheld . . . as if good deeds might wash away the country's sin of violence.

There was also very real pressure building up in the cauldrons of chronic poverty that Kennedy had read about and worried about: the urban racial ghettoes of the North. Here a population of black migrants forced off the land in the South during the postwar decades was living in a state of permanent dislocation and producing a new generation of young militants, little employed and without much of a stake in either past or future. Here the civil-rights issue was taking on a more volatile, more ominous shape than in the South, where, for better or for worse, people and patterns were well established. This was civil rights with a detonator cap attached to it.

In the summer of 1964, a kind of warning explosion was heard: riots broke out in the streets of half a dozen northern communities. In the South, in the earlier stages of the civil-rights campaign, the only violence had come from whites resisting change; now, in northern city streets young blacks were throwing bottles at police and wrecking the shops of neighborhood merchants.

His good offices established by his civil-rights legislation, Johnson was able to call on elders from the more conservative black organizations like the NAACP and the Urban League to help damp down the fires of the "long hot summer." For the time being.

The ghetto disturbances were not the only sign of a disruptive new spirit abroad among the young. That same year, 1964, the University of California at Berkeley was thrown into a noisy turmoil of sit-ins and demonstrations. The original cause was the students' right to solicit contributions on campus for civil-rights campaigns. It broadened into the right to express their views freely on various subjects (including the quality of the university's administration) in behalf of various viewpoints (Maoist, Zen, Goldwaterite) and in language unrestricted by conventional standards of decency. Officially, it was the Free Speech Movement; more colloquially, the Filthy Speech Movement.

By late 1964, the Johnson legislative program was in gear and picking up speed: the Great Society—that vision shaped in the great liberal tradition extending from FDR's New Deal and Harry Truman's Fair Deal to Jack Kennedy's hardly explored New Frontier.

Or was it something more than that?

The Johnson program was in fact so far-reaching as to be almost a *departure* from the liberal past. Besides the basic legislation for voting rights and other civil rights, for health and school aid, eventually there would be programs like Head Start (classes for disadvantaged pre-school tots and their mothers); VISTA—for Volunteers in Service to America (a domestic Peace Corps); federal aid to underdeveloped Appalachia; and Community Action Programs giving the poor deci-sion-making experience on local issues (and paychecks for getting the experience).

Not only was government moving into new social areas but even in the economic field there was a radical new canon whose implications only gradually emerged. The New Deal, with programs like the Works Progress Administration and the Civilian Conservation Corps, only made government a provider of *jobs*—a guarantor of the chance to work. By the time of the Great Society, government was guaranteeing *income*. The "right to earn a living" was being short-cut to "the right to a living." The work ethic was replaced by the welfare principle.

The historic change could be traced by the evolution of rhetoric. "Relief" was a New Deal *benefit*; "welfare" was an entitlement. This represented a new mind-set toward the individual's relationship to government—or government's "obligations" to the individual. It also represented an ambitious undertaking by the federal bureaucracy— and an expensive one.

When Johnson eventually tried to undertake an ambitious program in foreign policy as well, his war against poverty came into conflict with the cold war.

"The Bloc! The Bloc!"

For more than a year President Johnson had the luxury of concen-trating on his cherished domestic programs because of an almost un-precedented lull in the cold war. An era of relative good feeling between Moscow and Washington had been ushered in by the nu-clear-test-ban treaty. It was reinforced by the saddening impact of Kennedy's death. And it was also helped by monumental develop-ments inside the Communist bloc. The alliance between the Soviet Union and China, the two largest countries in the world, had come apart, and so had Khrushchev's political power.

The schism with China had taken place over a period of years, a result of various factors—economic, strategic, even personal. A Chi-nese economic mobilization—Mao's frenzied "Great Leap Forward," involving backyard steel smelters, forced collectivizing of farms, mass population shifts—proved to be a disastrous misstep, and the failure was blamed partly on the tighfistedness of Soviet economic aid. Beijing was also disappointed when Moscow declined to take China's side outright in a boundary war against India. Khrushchev seemed as eager to avoid alienating India's Prime Minister Nehru as to placate his own ornery ally, Mao Zedong.

There was a lot of truth to that impression. The patron saint of China's revolution had taken on a kind of diabolical image in Khrushchev's eyes, an aura of irresponsibility that hardly suited the realities of the nuclear age. Cavalier about the prospects of atomic war—convinced that it would blow world capitalism away while the populous Socialist societies survived—Mao pressed the Kremlin for aid in developing a bomb of his own. He deplored Khrushchev's retreat in the Cuban missile crisis. "The East wind now prevails over the West," in Mao's poetic language—now was the time to press forward with world revolution. The nuclear-test-ban treaty was regarded as a mistake if not a betrayal, in which Beijing refused to participate. Meetings between Chinese and Soviet leaders turned into contests of Marxist-Leninist dialectic which turned into slanging matches.

Finally, Russia and China became engaged in a serious boundary dispute of their own. By 1961 the alliance was barely functioning; by the end of 1964 the two great Socialist nations were separated by an open breach. Russian loans were canceled, engineers and technicians withdrawn. Hostile divisions faced each other along a stretch of the Sino-Siberian border.

Foreign policy failures—the loss of China, the Cuban missile fiasco —eroded Khrushchev's standing in the Politburo, but his main problems were economic. The leader who was determined to challenge the capitalist countries in production had been forced to admit to ghastly shortages of consumer goods. The large-scale importation of grain reflected a 10 percent decline in agricultural output. Meat and butter prices had to be raised so drastically that the usually passive Russian public broke out in protest demonstrations. Khrushchev's pet program—developing new agricultural sources on virgin lands—was a disaster.

Meanwhile, the crazy mechanism of the centrally managed economy was churning out warehouses full of unsalable cameras, books, clocks, sewing machines.

Khrushchev hardly helped his own cause by an attitude of short-tempered arrogance toward his critics inside the Kremlin. Finally, in October 1964, while he was on vacation at his Black Sea villa, the Praesidium of the party's central committee voted to remove him from office, dividing his powers between Leonid Brezhnev as party chief and Aleksei Kosygin as premier.

Confronted with dismissal, Khrushchev went home and broke the news to his wife, telling her that he took some satisfaction in knowing that "they were able to get rid of me simply by voting—Stalin would have had them all arrested." He was retired to a house in the country with a modest pension, medical insurance, a second-hand car, and the use of an apartment in Moscow.

The gentle transition was a measure of the influence ascribed to Khrushchev by his one-time debating opponent, Richard Nixon: "He was, to the extent it was possible in the Soviet Union, a liberating force."

For a decade Khrushchev had also been a dynamic force behind international crises. He left Berlin and Cuba in a state of relative calm. The American secret war against Castro—the campaign of commando raids and sabotage—had faded out with the death of President Kennedy, although the CIA's Miami station was not actually closed down until 1967.

So far as the third cold-war trouble spot was concerned, Lyndon Johnson was unhappy about the situation he had inherited in Vietnam, but he had no great impulse to change it. The violent removal of Ngo Dinh Diem troubled LBJ as it did LBJ's predecessor. Johnson had been one of Kennedy's emissaries to Saigon and came away describing Diem as "the Winston Churchill of Southeast Asia." That was one of Lyndon's exaggerations, but the fact remained that Diem's successors proved hardly more reform-minded and much less capable of leadership. There were three changes of government in a matter of months. The legitimate political opposition remained intractable, while the Communist Viet Cong underground kept growing more powerful. A steady trickle of desertions sapped the strength of the South Vietnamese army.

The situation might have prompted American leaders to reconsider whether the United States had any valid interest in Vietnam. *Was* this a cold-war situation, an example of Communist aggression from outside? Wasn't it really an internal problem, a continuation of the Vietnamese national revolution against French colonial rule, part of a historical process that Diem had merely obstructed by resisting elections leading to reunification with the north?

The ultimate result of reunification might be an all-Communist Vietnam under Ho Chi Minh. But if that was the country's will—if Ho was the definitive expression of Vietnamese nationalism—was there any point in trying to stand in its way?

Critics of the administration's policy tried to put the issue on a *moral* basis—to identify Ho's revolution with the advance of liberty. But there was hardly any greater virtue on the Communist side, with its purges and its conversions by terror, than there was on the side of the authoritarian Saigon government. In between the two extremes, there should have been some middle ground—a benevolent non-Communist nationalist element that Washington could support—for most politically aware Vietnamese in the south did not want to go the way of their brothers in the north. "There was *life* there," one French observer remarked sadly, "but no force"—no political organization.

Someone in the administration might have remembered what Jack Kennedy had been told by Charles de Gaulle when they met in Paris before the 1961 Vienna summit. Reflecting France's bitter experience in Indochina, de Gaulle warned JFK not to get into a war in Vietnam because even the United States couldn't win it. "You can defeat an army," he said, "but you cannot defeat a country." Vietnam was in the process of becoming a country.

The reasoning in the Johnson White House rarely got to that point because, as in all administrations since the 1940s, the cold-war view of the world shaped and colored everything. It was like one of those distorted cartoon maps, a New Yorker's view of the United States, which shows everything between the coasts in relation to Manhattan. Whatever took place on the far side of the Iron Curtain was seen as linked to a central plan and motivated by a single purpose, which was hostile to the United States.

Lyndon Johnson, characteristically, put the issue in the homiest of terms. "Give up Vietnam," he once said over a drink during a quiet moment among friends in Texas, "and you wind up losing India, with six hundred million people, and then you lose oh, so much more! That is the plain truth of it—they're out to get us, and don't you think they're not! If you let a bully pick on your helpless neighbor today, why tomorrow he'll kick you out of your own front yard. And if you let him do that, why the next day he'll kick you out of your living room. And"

—he suddenly stiffened and glared around the circle of listeners—"the day after that he'll be upstairs raping your wife in your own bed!"

The geopolitics of Southeast Asia had been defined for subsequent administrations by John Foster Dulles when he declared that North Vietnam was merely a surrogate for Communist China and China a surrogate for the Soviet Union. "Essentially," the military historian Harry Summers observes, "we had bought the Communist myth that communism transcends nationalism, that suddenly, because they had become Communist, all the realities of history and culture and everything else were no longer meaningful—they'd been subsumed by a new force called communism."

It was a peculiarly American fallacy.

MAURICE COUVE DE MURVILLE
Former premier of France
1958–68: Foreign minister

I remember Dean Rusk, when we spoke of Vietnam, always repeated, "The bloc! The bloc!" That meant they were waging a war against the Communist bloc, which meant not only the Soviet Union but China. In other words, they [U.S. policy makers] still believed there was a Communist bloc in the world which was waging a war against the free world—not having even considered that China and Russia at the time were becoming the worst enemies in the world.

Edging into Vietnam

Preoccupied as they were, Moscow and Beijing were by no means divorced from the revolution in Vietnam. Separately, they were supporting the North Vietnamese (and through them the Viet Cong in the south) with supplies and advisers. In retrospect, Dean Rusk sees the two great Communist powers as jockeying for position with Hanoi. But at the time the Vietnam issue began rising to the surface of concern in the Johnson administration, in the summer of 1964, the official view was that the enemy's success represented a single will and a monolithic effort.

Appointed commander of American forces in Vietnam that year, General William C. Westmoreland delivered a gloomy situation report to his civilian superior: "I told Mr. McNamara, 'Mr. Secretary, we have a formidable task here. It's very difficult to see the end of it. I think it's going to try the patience of the American people, and I just wonder if they've got the staying power.' "

In the face of advice from McNamara, from Rusk and other Kennedy holdovers to start turning up the heat in Vietnam, the President remained unengaged. "I don't know anything to do except more of the same," he told a Senate ally, William Fulbright of Arkansas, the Foreign Relations Committee chairman.

Johnson's lengthy holiday from foreign affairs might have gone on even longer but for the fact that 1964 was a presidential election year.

Democratic Presidents had learned the axiom that "you had to be conservative abroad in order to be liberal at home." That is, if you wanted support for your domestic programs, you couldn't expose yourself to the charge of being soft on communism. As if Lyndon Johnson needed any reminder of that historic lesson, he had the conservative ideologue, Barry Goldwater, running against him. The air during that campaign summer crackled with references to "pushing the button" and landing the marines and with Goldwater's most memorable statement—that "extremism in the defense of liberty is no vice."

Johnson was running not as a war candidate but as the heir of Kennedy's policy of resolve balanced with restraint. He still had no plans for any new course of action in Vietnam—certainly not for the use of American troops. He pledged he would not "send American boys nine or ten thousand miles away from home to do what Asian boys ought to be doing for themselves." But he had to look tough and he had to get ready to *be* tough. His advisers had persuaded him that some drastic measures were inevitable, and he wanted to be armed for the moment when it came. Above all, he wanted to be sure he had a President's closest potential ally and most troublesome potential enemy, the United States Congress, on his side.

"When the incident occurred," recalls LBJ's hired hand, Jack Valenti, "we had a resolution already prepared."

The incident occurred in the first week of August 1964.

Brandishing a report that American destroyers had been attacked twice by North Vietnamese torpedo boats in the Gulf of Tonkin, the President called upon Congress to back him up in taking "all necessary measures to repel any further armed attack against the forces of the United States to prevent further aggression." He had already ordered American bombers to retaliate with a raid on North Vietnam.

COLONEL HARRY SUMMERS
Military affairs writer, *U.S. News and World Report*
1964: U.S. infantry officer in Korea

The idea that this was made out of whole cloth I think is not really fair. I think the evidence today is that the first attack probably took place. The second attack probably didn't. But we see [in later international incidents] the same kind of reports—[evidence] of sonar men being very nervous, as you can imagine, being under enemy attack. And they misread these instruments—they're not infallible. So what many people have seen as a conspiracy I think is more than likely just people overexcited and overreporting at a particular time.

There was overreaction on the part of the White House as well since the attack in any case was hardly unprovoked. The destroyers were operating in support of South Vietnamese commando raiders in the gulf. But the Vietnam issue was charged up by politics. It was ready to be ignited.

August 6, the day Johnson sent his precooked resolution up to Capitol Hill, is a day that has stayed in the memory of Pierre Salinger. He had just recently become a senator from California, having resigned from the Johnson White House to run for a vacated seat. He was assigned a desk next to Wayne Morse, a maverick veteran senator from Oregon, who kept prodding him about the resolution: "What are you going to do on this?"

"Well," Salinger said, "I'm going to follow the majority and vote for it."

Morse shook his head. "It's the biggest mistake you'll ever make in your life."

The mistake was shared by nearly all of Salinger's more experienced colleagues. The only nays cast in the Senate were by Morse and Ernest Gruening of Alaska. There was not a single negative vote in the House.

GEORGE MCGOVERN
Washington attorney, public-cause lobbyist
1964: Democratic senator from South Dakota

In my own case, I saw it not as an extension of the war in Vietnam but simply as an affirmation of the retaliation the President had ordered against what I honestly believed had been an attack on two American destroyers.

The other thing that was in my mind as a Democrat is that Goldwater was running on a platform that [the U.S.] needed to show some muscle out there in Vietnam, and I thought this was one way to do that that would be comparatively harmless.

But I don't know of a single member of Congress who really believed that [the resolution] would extend the war except Morse and Gruening, who saw that potential in it, and they turned out to be right. Later on it was cited as an indication that the President's expansion of the war had previously been endorsed by the Congress.

The Goldwater challenge proved surprisingly ineffectual. Lyndon Johnson was elected President in his own right (with Hubert Humphrey as his running mate) by a huge national consensus, giving him every state except five in the Deep South and Goldwater's own Arizona. For his campaign to extend the boundaries of the Great Society he really had the troops now—a Democratic majority of more than two-thirds in both houses of Congress.

The expansion of the war did not come at once. There was no immediate follow-up to the reprisals after Tonkin Gulf. But Johnson's sense of the national honor—and his own—was being goaded by events in Vietnam. In November, five American uniformed advisers were killed and seventy-six wounded in a Viet Cong mortar attack on a South Vietnamese army base at Bien Hoa, just north of Saigon. On Christmas Eve, two more Americans were killed and fifty-eight wounded by a bomb planted at an officers' billet in Saigon.

Then, on February 7, 1965, guerrillas zeroed in on an American barracks at Pleiku. Eight GIs were killed. Six planes and sixteen helicopters were blown up.

That was the moment of truth, as Johnson saw it. Now, armed with his congressional warrant, he initiated a program of massive, continuous bombing of the north. And now began the process of gradual, inescapable escalation that became the path of disaster for United States policy in Vietnam. For the American commitment had outgrown the limits of mere "military advisers." The presence of American bombers required the presence of American crews to fly them and service them, American troops to protect the air bases.

A contingent of 3,500 marines was shipped over to defend the air base at Da Nang, way up the coast near the DMZ—the demilitarized boundary zone between north and south. Within weeks, there were more than 80,000 American soldiers in Vietnam. Lyndon Johnson saw this not as a violation of his campaign pledge but a fulfillment of his congressional mandate. He wasn't sending those American boys to do Asian boys' dirty work but to protect the lives of other American boys. A fine and legalistic distinction. It was all but erased when General Westmoreland began sending U.S. paratroopers into battle alongside South Vietnamese units in order to stiffen them in search-and-destroy missions. In July the President began sending ground troops in substantial numbers.

The change in the American role was not brought to the notice of the American public, which was starting to pay attention to the escalating war in Vietnam.

The President would have preferred to keep it a low-profile operation, though his advisers were urging him to go all-out—put the country on a war footing, with a tax increase and a call-up of reserves. The Joint Chiefs projected that it might ultimately take a million men to fight the war in Vietnam. Westmoreland urged LBJ to start whipping up public emotion behind the effort; he proposed, for example, that American cities be encouraged to "adopt" South Vietnamese communities.

Whipping up emotion was the last thing LBJ wanted to do—next to going to the Hill for a tax hike. That would have put the war in Vietnam in competition with the war against poverty. And that, says Jack Valenti, "would have meant that the Great Society which he had so carefully planned and had for so long dreamed about to lift the quality of life in this country—as we were wont to say in those days —would have collapsed."

Rather than face that loss, Johnson preferred to camouflage the war costs, which amounted to $8 billion in 1966. He preferred to live with a budget deficit that tripled the next year—then tripled again, reaching the astonishing level of $25 billion in 1968. That figure was unprecedented in peacetime.

The problem wasn't economics or manpower; it was strategy. Or more to the point, it was the foreign policy *underlying* military strategy. If a war was to be fought in Vietnam at all—if it was to be fought successfully—it would have had to begin by shooting down some of the conventional wisdom that had prevailed through two decades of cold war.

It was clear by the end of 1965 that Vietnam was too much for the limited sort of counterinsurgency operations contemplated by Jack

Kennedy with his Green Berets. The image of the enemy as "elusive guerrillas clad in black pajamas" was only part of the story.

The guerrilla threat was still there and getting worse. At first there had been no safe roads out of Saigon beyond Tan Son Nhut airport; then the road to the airport became unsafe; now there were hand-made bombs exploding in the Saigon cafés, especially the ones with American uniforms at the tables. But at the same time a "real" war was shaping up—a war of battle formations.

The Americans had started out talking about "combating Communist subversion" to "win the hearts and minds of the people." Now they were faced with fighting a war to keep from losing territory.

In the fall of 1965, in the Ia Drang valley, American troops began to encounter North Vietnamese in units of regimental size—up to 2,500 men equipped for field operations. The troops and their equipment were being infiltrated down the thousand-mile Ho Chi Minh trail through Laos and Cambodia; arms were also coming in by sea at Cambodian ports and trucked up from there. The American bombing of the north was doing little to stop the traffic. Probably nothing could shut it down short of a massive extension of the war on the ground. It could go in either of two directions: an invasion of North Vietnam to capture the source; or a westward strike across Laos and/or Cambodia to cut off the supply channels.

Neither of these offensive strategies was about to happen. They were prohibited by the cold-war perspective in which Hanoi, Moscow, and Beijing were all linked in a monolithic plan.

GENERAL ALEXANDER M. HAIG
International business consultant
1964: Deputy secretary of defense

The perception that the People's Republic of China was perhaps the culprit in Vietnam also led to the other conclusion, and that was that if we ever conducted that conflict with the demeanor that we intended to win— that we took the battle, for example, to North Vietnam, which was the agent of the Soviet Union—that somehow we would see a repeat of the debacle of Korea, where hordes of Chinese forces could cross the northern borders of Vietnam and engage our people there. This was a very erroneous and self-defeating misjudgment of the realities of the Chinese attitude at that time.

The Chinese attitude was, of course, that the greatest threat to them was not the "imperialist American," which had given them such difficulty in the revolution in the late forties, but rather the growing threat from the Soviet Union, which even at that early date had some forty divisions poised on the Chinese border. They could see a containment of the Chinese mainland by a Soviet Union on the border and Hanoi—dominated and controlled by the Soviet Union on another—which was also poised to overrun all of Southeast Asia.

China's apprehensions were presumably sharpened by centuries of enmity with their neighbors the Vietnamese.

Whether the war could actually have been "won"—that is, the Communist takeover of the south stopped—by an offensive strategy was a matter of conjecture that could not be tested. President Johnson would not countenance the risks. He was reluctant to cross a boundary for the same reason he had declined to declare war: "I didn't know what treaty China might have with North Vietnam or Russia might have with North Vietnam—the Communists have these agreements among themselves." He was afraid he might "trigger the thing." He was also convinced that the gradually increasing pressure of the bombing would achieve the same result sooner or later. It would bring the enemy to the negotiating table; and there, at close range, Johnson would be able to turn on him the weapons in which he himself was skilled. In the end, it would come down to politics.

"I always believed," LBJ once told his biographer Doris Kearns, "that as long as I could take someone into a room with me, I could make him my friend, and that included anybody, even Nikita Khrushchev. . . . I believed that if I handled him right, he would go along with me. Deep down, hidden way below, he too wanted what was good."

That also included Ho Chi Minh, the leader of North Vietnam, whom Johnson, while pressuring him with bombs, also tried to entice into the room with the offer of something good: a Mekong River valley development project to benefit both populations, north and south. Surely, the leader of a country would not be able to resist the chance to have a Great Society program of his own.

It was a source of unending frustration to LBJ that "one time, two times, a dozen times we made substantial offers to Ho Chi Minh to go anywhere, any time, talk about anything—'just please, let's talk instead of fight!' And in not one single instance, not one, did we get anything but an arrogant, tough, unyielding rebuff!"

* * *

The bombings were massive. In some weeks more explosive power was dropped on the tropical countryside of Vietnam than had been delivered against the industrialized landscape of Germany during all of World War II. But the bombings were also inconsistent, alternating with peace feelers delivered through various international channels. There were repeated offers to halt the bombing—on condition the other side agree to some conciliatory gesture.

The Communists were not disposed to accept any conditions. They seemed unmoved by either the carrot or the stick. And during the bombing pauses, they were able to repair the damage to their relatively simple war machine.

Meanwhile, the stakes in the war kept rising. There were 450,000 Americans in Vietnam by the end of 1966. They were fighting a demoralizing kind of war in which progress was hard to see on the war maps, and they were surrounded by visible evidence that the Vietnamese themselves were something less than wholehearted about the cause.

Supplies delivered to the Saigon government by grace of the American taxpayer were peddled in the flourishing black market. ARVN (the Army of the Republic of Vietnam) remained an uninspired fighting force. Desertion rates rose as high as 15 percent. The enemy formations proved to be adept at melting back into Communist-held territory or into sanctuaries in Laos and Cambodia.

American successes were measured in atrocious terms—in "body counts" of VC killed or wounded, among whom the distinction between military and civilian personnel was often too hard to define. The slightly built enemy in black pajamas sometimes turned out to be a woman or a child—possibly innocent, possibly carrying a grenade. Villagers living in thatched "hootches" were repeatedly caught in the crossfire of ground troops or under the indiscriminate rain of destruction from the air. Of all the war deaths in Vietnam, at least 50 percent were civilian.

It was a war that disgusted almost everyone who went near it.

GEORGE MCGOVERN

I remember going to a hospital in Da Nang. I had asked one of the officers there about the civilian casualties from what was called "harassment and interdiction," where you'd just fire heavy shells off into the jungles; and he said, "Well, we always give warnings, and we think the civilian casualties are small."

Nonetheless, I asked to go to a civilian hospital in Da Nang the next day, and I'll never forget that scene. As we approached the hospital, there were people lying on every available inch of ground for maybe a hundred yards all around the hospital. You went up on a little veranda—they were lying on the veranda, usually two people in each little cot. Then I walked into the main hospital, and there was a room there about the size of a basketball gymnasium in a small school. It was filled with the most savagely wounded people. People with arms gone, legs gone, their faces blown off—terribly mangled. They were the worst cases.

I remember one mother who had a little child—his head was all wrapped in bandages. One little eye you could see peeking through a hole in the bandage. And what struck me was that there wasn't a sound.

I remember seeing a wounded deer one time that looked that way—just sort of frightened. The deer couldn't move—just looking at me.

I just couldn't support the war after that. Just couldn't do it.

A Nation Torn Apart

The number of Americans who could not support the war remained remarkably low for a long time. Even a dubious military cause, once undertaken, can go a long way on a combination of patriotism, inertia, and abhorrence of failure.

Vietnam had grown too big for the President to keep in the closet. The continuous draft calls and increasing troop shipments and lengthening casualty lists couldn't be overridden by optimistic reports from the military command and the embassy in Saigon. By the end of 1967, the Communists still held the initiative on the ground. Dissidence plagued the latest in the line of Saigon governments—the sixth since Diem. It was a military regime headed by Air Marshal Nguyen Cao Ky as premier and General Nguyen Van Thieu as his deputy. The war was being shown nightly in living color on the news programs in America's living rooms, and it was not a heartwarming picture. Among its scenes were indelible images like one of a "Zippo squad" in action—marines setting fire to the hootches of a village with their cigarette lighters. In military terms, the village was a suspected hideout for VC, but in human terms, it was the home of poor people defenseless against the engines of war.

Perhaps even more shocking than these images to millions of American viewers was the unfamiliar experience of seeing and hearing their favorite television correspondents and anchor men—traditionally pillars of neutrality—begin to express their personal disillusionment with the war. The growing estrangement of press from government was only one of many rents opening up in the fabric of American society.

Opposition to the war centered on the college campuses, where protest demonstrations had become a collegiate way of life in the three years since the free-speech bust-out at Berkeley. By now, protest was replacing panty raids and ritual spring "riots" as a release for pent-up youthful energies.

In the sixties, the campuses were ripe for rebellion. Like the inner cities, they had undergone an unsettling population explosion since World War II. The GI Bill of Rights, affluence, and rising expectations among minorities had conspired to drive kids en masse into academe. In one generation, the number of college-age Americans enrolled as students had risen from 15 percent to a remarkable 40. The college population was now a burgeoning, jostling 5 million.

No longer the ivory tower, the typical institution of higher education was an overcrowded, depersonalized community tense with competition. In the first experience away from home and family, a youngster was most likely unknown to professors, and the "family tie" to the university was a computer in which his or her ID was registered and grades recorded.

No wonder so many students attached themselves to nonestablishment movements. First it was civil rights; then it was the antiwar campaign. Total, unconditional opposition to the American presence in Vietnam became the preoccupation of the American higher-educational system.

In both movements, the young people had the leadership of their generational heroes from the special world of their music—rock and the emerging substrains of folk and country. The very popularity of those earthy forms was a rejection of the complex, urban society most of these young people were born into; it was a way of identifying with the society's underdogs. The sons and daughters of the gray-flannel generation adopted faded jeans and torn overalls as *their* uniform and sang songs extolling the life of fieldhands, jailbirds, and drivers of big highway rigs.

With their music and by their example as activists, popular singers like Joan Baez, Bob Dylan, and the trio Peter, Paul, and Mary dramatized social issues of the day: race, unionism, world peace. And some musicians popularized another cause: the use of mood-altering drugs like marijuana and LSD. Even better than meditating, chanting, or charting the signs of the zodiac, "doing drugs" was the ultimate gesture against the rationalist tradition of the established culture. Make way for the *counterculture.*

Heeding the injunction to "tune in, turn on, and drop out," many young people abandoned any attempt at structure in their lives and lapsed into the squalid, shoeless life-style of hippies. In urban slums or rural retreats, they reinforced each other by adopting a communal pattern of living. The contraceptive pill, the aspirin of their generation, gave them some measure of protection against the sexual consequences of their undisciplined lives.

In 1967, there was a massive rally of 55,000 antiwar protesters around the Lincoln Memorial in Washington. The atmosphere was a long way from the hootenanny spirit of the gathering on the Mall four years earlier when Martin Luther King made his "I have a dream" speech.

MARY TRAVERS

I think there was a feeling of resolve there—a feeling that they just weren't gonna give up. There was anger and disappointment, and there wasn't that sense of joy that was present at the '63 march. '67 was about grim business, and it was about people dying.

Fundamentally, the civil-rights movement was an altruistic movement— hopeful, positive. "We can make things better." The antiwar movement very quickly slid into a sense of cynicism and anger.

A Freudian-oriented observer might have speculated that the anger was partly a manifestation of guilt. Students were deferred from the draft. Their places were being filled to a large extent by the sons of poor families, the same people whose interests middle-class white youth was supposedly defending in the civil-rights movement. According to one postwar study, blacks accounted for nearly one-fourth of the combat deaths—twice their percentage in the U.S. population.

Instead of simply taking cover behind their deferments, the students challenged the draft in a drumfire of moral outrage. Defiantly, dramatically, they burned their draft cards in public ceremonies. With a lot of help from sympathetic professors, they openly offered their peers counseling in draft evasion. Perhaps as many as ten thousand dodged their Selective Service boards by going across the border to Canada, whether with the help of their parents or in defiance of their elders' sense of duty and democratic process.

COLONEL HARRY SUMMERS

One of the things that was strange about the Vietnam War was that the antiwar movement attacked the soldiers who were fighting the war directly, and it said to them, "You shouldn't obey your orders; you shouldn't fight in the illegal war in Vietnam."

I don't think they understood what they were saying. They were challenging one of the foundations of our democracy, that is, civilian control of the military. I went out on the campuses during that period, and I would say to them, "You know, I was sent to Vietnam by the person you elected to be the President of the United States. The Congress that you elected bought me a gun and bought me ammunition and bought me a ticket to Vietnam and sent me to Vietnam. And the Supreme Court has not ruled that it's illegal."

But the only people that disturbed me were the people carrying the North Vietnamese flags [in antiwar marches]. As the aftermath of the war has shown—with ten thousand people in gulags and concentration camps, with literally millions of people killed—if we were not right, that didn't mean that the North Vietnamese and the Viet Cong were. And I took great offense at that, when American soldiers were being killed. That went beyond legitimate dissent.

The American military establishment came to feel isolated from a large segment of the American public, and the public itself was torn apart by the argument between so-called patriotism and the so-called higher morality. To some eyes the protesters were aiding and abetting the enemy—but legally there was no enemy in an undeclared war. Was it subversive or was it humane when antiwar demonstrators set up blood-donor stations on behalf of the Viet Cong? Or was it mainly just another way of shocking your elders—another way of saying, in the phrase that the free-speech movement brought into what used to be called polite society, "Fuck the Establishment." (The euphemistic form of the verb—"off"—was also used as a synonym for "kill.")

There were other phrases just as intemperate. In a costly war that was remarkable for the absence of territorial ambitions, U.S. policies were denounced as "imperialist." Professors of history and political science, who should have known better, explained the war as a search for markets by big business and for bases by the military. (Indochina was one place in which corporate America showed little if any interest, and the Joint Chiefs had written the area off back in the Eisenhower administration as possessing no intrinsic strategic value.) Crowds of young people gathered in the street and chanted in unison, "Hey, hey, LBJ! How many kids did you kill today?" Their placards and speeches compared the President to Hitler and the United States army to Nazi storm troopers.

The administration was certainly guilty of arrogance in its war policies. Late in 1967, LBJ sent Clark Clifford, the workhorse of several Democratic Presidents, on a tour of Pacific and Asian capitals in an effort to round up troops to take the load off the United States. One by one, the Allied countries turned him down: Australia, New Zealand, Thailand, the Philippines. Not one government, Clifford discovered, viewed the conflict in Vietnam "in the same light that we did. They did not see it as an expansion of Soviet or Chinese communism [but] more as a civil war." Clifford was shaken but did not give up his support of the war.

Until much too late, American leaders seemed undeflected either by the mounting criticism or by their policies' apparent lack of success. And it was hard to escape a certain air of callousness on their part toward the deaths and mutilations of so many "little brown people."

But it was not the administration, it was the protesters who sometimes conducted themselves like Hitler's brownshirts.

Not content to resist a draft that had, after all, the sanction of law, they sought to disrupt it by breaking into Selective Service offices and destroying files. Even moderate spokesmen for the war were rarely given a chance to speak; they were hounded off the platform. Personnel recruiters for companies that did business with the war effort, like Dow Chemical and Union Carbide, were driven off the campus. ROTC programs were forcibly closed down. The universities themselves, with research programs subsidized by federal grants, were under assault as branches of the hated establishment. Offices of deans and presidents were occupied in sit-ins that in some cases developed into rampages of vandalism. From Columbia and Harvard to San Jose and San Francisco State, students were deprived of education by their classmates as the educational process was brought to a halt by riots.

Though the cause transcended political ideology, the leadership was often from the politically aware left, and some students took themselves quite seriously as "Marxist-Leninists," as "Maoists," as members of one revolutionary faction or another. But the guiding spirit of the protest movement wasn't communism, it was anarchy—rejection of authority in almost any form.

What saved the antiwar cause, kept it from simply blowing apart of its own disorder, was the fact that it had a legitimate political wing. Serious, outspoken opposition to the war was taken up by energetic members of Congress. Some of the same young liberals who had hauled the water and driven the wagons for Lyndon Johnson's Great Society program—people like George McGovern and Gene McCarthy —were joining William Fulbright in renouncing the Tonkin Gulf resolution as a deception and denouncing the administration's war policies. The conflict between hawks and doves—between supporters and opponents of the Vietnam War—became the fundamental division in American political life.

Meanwhile, the establishment came under a more violent form of attack from another quarter.

Ghetto after urban ghetto exploded in an annual wave of self-destructive anger, each explosion set off by some conflict with the police—in black rhetoric, the "occupation force" or the "pigs." The Watts community in Los Angeles, Bedford-Stuyvesant in Brooklyn, Roxbury in Boston, Hough in Cleveland . . . black neighborhoods of Chicago, Rochester, Newark . . . smaller communities like Grand Rapids, Michigan, and New Haven, Connecticut—all became fiery battlefields.

The worst in terms of "war damage" was Detroit, where in the summer of 1967 a total of 15,000 local police, national guardsmen, and federal troops were engaged, and where wholesale arson, looting, and killing went on for a week. The casualty list showed 41 dead and 347 injured. There were 3,800 arrests. Five thousand persons were burned out of their own homes, and 2,700 businesses were looted. Damage came to something like half a billion dollars. *Time* magazine called this "the most sensational expression of an ugly mood of nihilism and anarchy that has ever gripped a small but significant segment of America's Negro minority."

Perhaps the most *explicit* form of nihilism came that year in the town of Cambridge, Maryland, where a militant black crowd responded to a speech by a twenty-three-year-old orator named H. Rap Brown urging them to burn down a black school building as a firetrap and to "get yourself some guns" because "violence is as American as cherry pie." The crowd rioted and burned down the school.

"I think the civil-rights movement began to lose its credibility with the violence," observes the moderate black spokesman Andrew Young. "Nothing much changed after 1965—there was no civil-rights legislation. Essentially, the issue then became the violence rather than the problems of the society."

When a federal commission finished investigating the urban riots in 1968, it identified the underlying cause as "white racism." But the electorate wasn't ready to let the rioters off the hook quite that easily. Chaos in the streets and on the campuses had produced a backlash in the mid-term elections of 1966. Among the results was the installation of a remarkably articulate conservative spokesman, a former actor named Ronald Reagan, in his first public office as governor of California.

With the waves of urban violence the Great Society was losing its spirit and its impetus. The domestic budget came under heavy pressure. With the unremitting war in Vietnam the President was losing his magic. The hallmark of his style became the "credibility gap." He was routinely described by the press as lying about the war, lying about his objectives, even lying about such petty matters as how fast he drove his big white Lincoln convertible on the roads around the LBJ ranch in Texas on his occasional retreats from the turmoil of Washington.

In the Oval Office he worked in a state of embittered isolation. The drowning out of all prowar voices by the dissenters appalled him. "I don't understand that kind of behavior," he said. The revolt of young blacks "almost tore his heart apart," according to Jack Valenti. It did not seem to count that in 1965 LBJ had staked his popularity as President and his heritage as a southerner by sending federal troops to protect Martin Luther King and his marchers in Selma, Alabama, when they were threatened by the brutality of local authorities; that he had gone to Congress in person to ask for a law to secure the voting rights sought by the Selma demonstrators—the first President to identify himself so aggressively with the black minority cause. He was dismayed that he was being forced to choose, finally, between the Vietnam War and his dream of ending poverty and injustice in America.

The President and his inner circle were often portrayed as obsessively, even demonically, bent on a military victory. In a phrase he had sometimes used in the early stages of the war, he was seen as willing to settle for nothing less than "nailing the coonskins to the wall."

Johnson saw himself, on the other hand, as a force of moderation and restraint, saving the country from the wilder demands of the extreme hawks, some of whom talked about "nuking the Cong" and "bombing their country back to the Stone Age."

Shadings between adherents of the war were lost in the domestic strife.

DEAN RUSK

In retrospect it seems to me that the leaders in North Vietnam never had any incentive to negotiate. I think up until 1966 they thought they could accomplish their objective by military means. But by that time it was clear that we had established with the South Vietnamese and our own forces and allies a position in South Vietnam which they could not possibly have over-run. But then in '67 and '68 they began to hear a lot of voices from this country.

If we had seen 50,000 people demonstrating around the headquarters in Hanoi, calling for peace, we would have thought the war was over. Well, they could see 50,000 people demonstrating around the Pentagon. So I think that those dissenters in this country, whatever their motivations, in effect said to Hanoi, "Just hang in there, gentlemen, and you will win politically what you could not win militarily."

·17·

ZENITH OF A SUPERPOWER

In the spring of 1967, while the American spirit was being tried by Vietnam, Lyndon Johnson received a White House visitor carrying a message from the president of France, Charles de Gaulle. It was a proposal that "the four great powers should get together" to head off a crisis that was building up in the Middle East.

"What do you mean 'the four great powers?'" Johnson answered disdainfully. "Who the hell are the other two?"

The role that Johnson played on the sidelines of the conflict deepened America's involvement in that part of the world. A dramatically brief episode, its echoes would continue to be heard in the following decades.

The Six-Day War

The crisis began when the president of Egypt, Gamal Abdel Nasser, in a bid for leadership of the Arab world, turned up the pressure against the Arabs' designated enemy, the young and still wobbly state of Israel. Nasser had the backing of the Soviet Union, with its unslaked appetite for mischief in the Middle East.

In a grandstand gesture, Nasser demanded the removal of the United Nations troops that had served as a buffer between Egypt and Israel ever since the 1956 Suez invasion. Probably to Nasser's surprise as much as anybody's, the UN secretary general, U Thant of Burma, docilely complied.

That put it up to the Egyptians to follow through—which they did by moving their own troops into the abandoned UN positions on the

Red Sea coast and closing off the Gulf of Aqaba. Israel's only southern port, Eilat, was blockaded.

With each step in this escalation, Nasser pulled Syria, Jordan, and Iraq along with him. Joined in an alliance, with a unified military command, the Arab leaders reviewed troops together, joined each other in fiery statements—though they did not all share Nasser's enthusiasm.

HUSSEIN I, KING OF JORDAN

I said, "We have reached the point where I believe a war is inevitable. Can we discuss and see what can be done to minimize the danger?" He [Nasser] appeared to be overly confident that either a war was not going to take place or that, if it did take place, that there wasn't any real serious danger.

As far as I was concerned, that didn't make sense. One knew that Israel was going to lash out and that we had nowhere near prepared for the consequences. We were in a trap.

Nasser was undeterred—caught up, apparently, by his own momentum. Speechmakers and cheerleaders were sent into the streets of Cairo to drum up the war spirit; the city's vast squares rang with rhythmic chants of revenge against the Zionists and their friends, the imperialists of the West.

Hemmed in by this rising menace, the Israelis decided to strike first. Vastly outnumbered, they had the advantage of a superbly trained air force, flying French jets (their only American equipment being some defensive weapons supplied by the Kennedy administration), and a remarkable intelligence service, which had penetrated the Egyptian high command. They knew the Egyptian army's daily schedule to the minute. The Israelis had intentionally developed a fixed routine of their own.

On a June morning, Israeli crews took their jets into the air on what appeared to be a routine patrol. But as they approached Egyptian territory, they didn't make their usual turn out over the Mediterranean. Flying low over the desert, they came in under Nasser's radar, arriving over Egypt just at the defenders' breakfast hour. Not one of Nasser's Russian MIGs got off the ground to meet them. The Egyptian air force was knocked out on the spot. That same day the Israelis made similar runs against the other three Arab allies, destroying a total of 410 aircraft at a cost of nineteen of their own.

With the air in their control, the Israelis sent tank columns rumbling across the Egyptian border through the Sinai peninsula, overrunning Egypt's defenses and sweeping up whole formations of troops and their equipment.

After six devastating days of war, the desert was littered with the debris of the Egyptian military force—with Communist-built tanks, trucks, artillery, complete field kitchens, stacks of ammunition, piles of boots . . . all abandoned in the cataclysm of defeat. And Israeli military power was clamped down on Egypt's vital artery, the Suez Canal.

Meanwhile, when Nasser's allies, rejecting appeals from Tel Aviv, opened fire on Israel's other borders, they were not only stopped but rolled back. The Syrians were dislodged from the Golan Heights, where their artillery positions had dominated Israeli settlements for twenty years. Israeli armored columns rolled toward Damascus. Jordanian troops trying to seize the Israeli half of Jerusalem (the modern part of the city) were forced out of their own sector, with its ancient sites sacred to Jews, Christians, and Muslims. Jordanian guns on the west bank of the Jordan had threatened to cut Israel's narrow territory in half; within days, those positions were taken over by Israeli forces.

The response of the Western world was one of overwhelming sympathy for Israel as the underdog. In mass rallies, American Jews raised $100 million within three weeks to underwrite the cost of war and rehabilitation. The Teamsters Union donated its services to deliver supplies for Israel to the airports. A German bank subscribed to nearly a million dollars worth of Israeli bonds, and the Frankfurt airport was jammed with young volunteers—of various faiths, from many nations —rushing to the Israeli cause.

ABBA EBAN
Israeli scholar and politician
1967: Foreign minister

We must remember that a few weeks, even a few days before the war, there was a lot of talk about whether Israel would survive. We were pictured as building air raid shelters, preparing hospital beds, vainly appealing for external assistance. And here, within a few days, there was this dramatic transition from the image of Israel, as it were, cowering on the brink of destruction to an Israel which had removed all its enemies from any proximity to its populated centers and which, in six days, had made Nasser's boasts look ridiculous and made his speeches look absurd.

All that week American and Soviet fleets were eyeballing each other in the eastern Mediterranean. There was one tense moment when an American electronic surveillance ship, the *Liberty*, was hit by bombs from the air, with a loss of thirty-four dead and seventy-five wounded. The attackers might have been Russian, might have been Egyptian.

Just as the President was alerting his flagship, a message of apology came from the Israelis. It was *their* bombs that had hit the *Liberty*. How and why the incident occurred has remained a matter of controversy ever since; but a former Israeli general once explained it privately as the accidental work of Israeli pilots, emotionally pumped up by their successes, who thought they were hitting a *Russian* ship.

Johnson had made a last-minute effort to stave off the war before the shooting started by trying to organize a "Red Sea regatta"—a UN fleet to run the Egyptian blockade on behalf of Israel. When he failed to get enough takers and was informed the Israelis were about to jump off, he braced for his first confrontation with the Soviets. It turned out to be the first conducted via the recently installed hot line. By telex— with a machine in the White House basement clattering out letters in the Cyrillic alphabet and its counterpart in the Kremlin clattering in English—Johnson managed to fend off Premier Kosygin's demands, at first for an immediate cease-fire and then for an Israeli withdrawal from the captured territories.

ABBA EBAN

We followed our victory with extremely conciliatory political statements. My prime minister at the time, Levi Eshkol, authorized me to say to Egypt and to Syria, through the United States, that we were prepared to give up Sinai and give up the Golan Heights in return for a peace agreement with Egypt and with Syria. We offered [Jordan] what we call the Alon Plan, which meant that they would get a majority of the [West Bank] territory and nearly all the people.

We believed that because we had won the war we were bound to get peace. What we didn't understand was the extraordinary capacity of the

Arab world, even in defeat, to deny us peace. And it took a long time for the Israelis to understand that the Six-Day War was not such a revolutionary change in Middle Eastern history as we might have hoped.

First of all, we had the paradox of victory. Okay, we had now got this territory. But we had a million people more—what were we going to do with them? If we gave up the territory, we would lose strategic depth. If we kept the territory, we would confuse our internal structure by exercising coercive jurisdiction over a foreign people.

And in Israel the psychological effects were not good. There was a glorification of the military element of our power. It is an important element but it does not basically change the fact that the Arab states are bigger than we are in territory, in population, in money, in oil, in their command of international voting systems. And, therefore, the belief that the military victory meant that you are basically stronger was an illusion.

Far from crushing Arab will, Israel had only stung Arab pride. The speaker of the Egyptian Parliament, a former military officer named Anwar el-Sadat, was so devastated by the scope of his country's defeat that he went into seclusion for several weeks at his home in the desert near Cairo. But almost at once, with a new infusion of Soviet aid, the Egyptian government began planning a campaign to retrieve the Sinai and redeem the national honor.

Israel was now completely cut off from the Communist world. Moscow broke diplomatic relations with Tel Aviv and took the other Warsaw Pact governments along with it. Israel soon began to receive shipments of tanks and guns from the Johnson administration; by the end of the year, the U.S. was also shipping Skyhawk and Phantom jets.

The dividing lines were deepening in the Middle East, and the arsenals on both sides were growing.

New Jersey Summit

One immediate result of the Middle East crisis was to bring Johnson and Kosygin face to face. The Soviet premier visited the UN to bring his personal weight to bear against the Israeli "aggression." The American leadership had been trying for months to pin Kosygin down to a meeting in which they hoped to dissuade him from taking an ominous new step in the arms race. The issue was the ABM, or anti-ballistic-missile defense, forerunner of the concept that would come to be known in a later decade as "Star Wars." The concerns were much like those that had arisen belatedly about civil defense.

ROBERT MCNAMARA
1967: Secretary of defense

They had begun to deploy an ABM system. We knew they were doing it around Moscow. We had satellite photographs of it. And here is where we may have misjudged their intentions. We assumed they wouldn't be so silly as to put it only around Moscow—what good would a defense of one spot in the Soviet Union be?—but rather that this was the beginning of a defensive system to extend across the Soviet Union. This was a very dangerous situation for us.

We sought to initiate what later became the SALT discussions. We tried very hard to do that over a period of time. We finally got to the point where Kosygin came to this country to go to the UN. He and the President were finally persuaded to meet at a point halfway between the UN in New York and the capital of the United States, Washington. Somebody put a compass on the UN and drew a circle, and put a compass on Washington and drew a circle. They intersected at Glassboro [New Jersey]. That's where we met.

At lunch, we were seated at a table that seated perhaps eight or ten. On one side was Kosygin, Gromyko [the Soviet foreign minister], Dobrynin [Soviet ambassador to Washington], two or three others. On the other side was the President, Dean Rusk, Tommy Thompson [U.S. ambassador to Moscow, Averell Harriman [ex-ambassador to Moscow], myself. And I was seated on the President's right, and opposite the President was Kosygin.

And part way through the lunch, the President got completely frustrated by his inability to persuade Kosygin that what he was doing was contrary to his interests and ours, and he turned to me and he said, "Bob, you tell Kosygin why you persuaded me it is absolutely wrong for the Soviets to go ahead with their ABM."

So I said, "Mr. Prime Minister, you don't seem to understand—when you go ahead with those defensive systems, we must expand our offense. We believe our security depends on our ability to deter you from ever launching an offensive strike against us. The only way we can be certain of deterring you from that is to confront you with a force so strong that you recognize when you launch against us, a sufficient portion of our force will survive so we'll be able to launch it against you and inflict unacceptable damage on you. And, therefore, I tell you today: you proceed with that ABM, we're gonna expand our offensive force!"

He damn near exploded. His face got red. The veins in his neck expanded. He pounded on the table. And he said, "Defense is moral! Offense is immoral!"

The ABM issue remained on the table unresolved for several years. Johnson was just as adamant in refusing to concede on Israel's need to stand firm in the Middle East.

In spite of those deadlocks, the overall atmosphere at the weekend-long summit was cordial. Kosygin even volunteered a piece of helpful information on the Vietnam War: Hanoi was ready to negotiate if the United States would stop the bombing. Before the weekend was over, Johnson gave him a studied response: the United States was willing to halt the bombing on the understanding that Ho Chi Minh would not take advantage of the hiatus to build up for an offensive. Not exactly unconditional but a definite step-down from Washington's earlier preconditions for a bombing halt.

Kosygin, in LBJ's account of the conversation, said he thought "Ho could live with that formula." U.S. code breakers soon informed the White House that Kosygin had transmitted the offer. But that was the end of it. The White House never heard another word. Unofficially, however, Kosygin was later reported to have told a British official: "The North Vietnamese are too stubborn to be swerved from their course."

The American Image

At that critical point in time, mid-1967, a great many Americans would have found no argument with Lyndon Johnson's view that there were only two powers in the world that really counted. And there was still plenty of evidence to support the belief that the United States was still securely number one—a nation at the peak of its strength—in spite of the growing frustrations over Vietnam.

The alarm over the supposed missile gap had long since died down. The ambitious space program—undeflected by a recent tragedy in which three astronauts died in a fire on the launch pad—was on course and on schedule.

As an economic power, the United States had no visible challenger. On any list of the world's largest industrial firms, at least half would be American; the ten biggest banks in the world all were American.

What was harder to define but at least equally impressive was the sheer intensity of the American image around the world.

The emanations of American pop culture crossed the oceans with the speed, if not of light, then of sound—arriving with such an impact they sometimes bounced back. Elvis Presley begat the Beatles (their

"Sgt. Pepper" album was one of the social phenomena of 1967), who spawned a whole generation of electronically amplified performers, who likewise proceeded to engage the enthusiasm of young crowds all over the world. Rock became something as close to a universal language as the world has ever heard. With its black origins and its percussive beat, its success in crossing third-world frontiers was not surprising. What was harder to comprehend was how effectively it penetrated the Iron Curtain as well.

In third-world capitals, a television channel was invariably one of the first institutions to be established by a newly independent government. Almost as invariably, the programming would be launched with imports like "Gunsmoke," the Western series, and "Mr. Ed," a sitcom about the adventures of a talking horse in an idyllic American suburb. That was America's secret weapon: the lowest common denominator.

Even the mounting criticism of the United States around the world was a kind of love-hate expression. Vietnam was becoming a worldwide cause. But in almost any city—European, Asian, African—the ranks of the protesters with their anti-American banners would be filled with young people dressed in that quintessentially American uniform, blue jeans. Some would be wearing cowboy-style boots and hats. They would be marching to the beat of a Dixieland band or rock group. And when the musicians took a break, the marchers would more than likely fill in with a chorus of "We Shall Overcome!" or some other American civil-rights anthem.

That was 1967. Within a year, the adulation could scarcely be seen or heard through the hostility; American self-esteem was shaken to its roots, and the American leadership seemed powerless against the chaos in the streets.

The focal point of this agony was, of course, Vietnam.

·18·

YEARS OF ANGER

There were really two Vietnam debates.

There was the noisy public controversy between hawks and doves as to whether the war was morally right or wrong. But the more decisive conflict in the end was a more subdued one going on within the ranks of the administration's hawks. The issue there was whether the war effort was working or not.

Believers like Dean Rusk were convinced by the end of 1967 that South Vietnam was saved—though the situation was a long way from a victory celebration. It was defined in terms of cautious optimism by General Westmoreland when he was brought home by the President in November of that year to deliver his appraisal in person.

Westmoreland declared that "the enemy is certainly losing"; he described the outlook as "very, very encouraging." In briefing his commander in chief and the armed forces committees of the House and Senate, he said that he foresaw no early termination of the war, but there was a likelihood that American troops could be pulled out in two years as the South Vietnamese army took over the defense of the country.

At a news conference the President reported that Westmoreland "anticipates no increase" in American troops for Vietnam above previously authorized levels.

One significant piece of intelligence LBJ chose *not* to pass on was the warning of an anticipated "major effort" by the NVA—the North Vietnamese army.

Something was lost in the translation of all this data. The optimism came through, all right, but not the cautions. Administration spokesmen summarized the prospects in a catchy phrase: there was finally "light at the end of the tunnel." (The phrase, ominously, was one that French generals had used during the siege of Dien Bien Phu.)

That prospect took some of the bitterness out of a series of high-level defections that had riddled the administration. White House aide Jack Valenti, national security adviser McGeorge Bundy, even the staunch defense secretary, Robert McNamara all left because they could not share Rusk's confidence. They had come to regard the war as hopeless. Those nonbelievers felt it couldn't possibly succeed. South Vietnam could *not* be saved, not at any price that would be acceptable to the American public.

To fill the vacated defense post in his cabinet, the President appointed that foreign-affairs veteran of several Democratic administrations, Clark Clifford. The choice proved fateful.

After his recent unsuccessful trip to round up Allied support for Vietnam, Clifford had repressed his concern "because all of the reports coming from Vietnam were so optimistic. Perhaps we were going to have our men back by Christmas, there was going to be a victory for our arms, and it was all going to turn out well. But that was all exploded when the Tet offensive began in early '68."

The Trauma of Tet

Tet, the three-day Buddhist New Year, is customarily celebrated by the Vietnamese—like the Chinese—with the gladsome noise of firecrackers. That year, when Tet fell on January 31, more menacing noises were heard inside a huge concrete building in downtown Saigon, which stood like a symbol of American invulnerability. It was the headquarters of the United States ambassador to South Vietnam, Ellsworth Bunker—the six-story embassy, surrounded by a ten-foot wall, that was sometimes known as "Bunker's bunker." It was guarded by a handful of marines.

ALLAN WENDT
State Department officer
1968: Embassy official in Saigon

It was about 2:30 in the morning, I think, in this little room on the fourth floor [quarters of the officer on duty overnight], when all of a sudden there was a loud explosion—so loud that it literally shook everything that was in the room. Of course, I knew a war was going on, but up until then I hadn't really gotten caught up in the middle of any fire. I didn't know what had happened.

And then I heard the crinkling of masonry all around me. I dove under the bed simply because we had all been taught that in the event of an explosion, get under something to protect yourself from flying glass and falling debris. Then I immediately heard machine gun fire, automatic weapons fire, more explosions. Rockets started butting into the building. I just could not imagine what was going on. But I quickly realized that we were being attacked.

I was so overwhelmed at what was going on that I didn't, in the beginning, have time to sit down and call Washington, but I got a call from Phil Habib, who was on duty in the White House situation room. And he said to me, "Allan, what the hell's going on out there?" And I held up the phone and said, "Phil, listen to it!" And just when I did that, another rocket butted into the building.

What I learned from the marine on duty on the ground floor was that the Viet Cong had gotten into the compound but hadn't penetrated into the embassy building itself. They had blown a hole in the perimeter wall and had poured through that wall—we didn't at the time know how many of them there were—and were just shooting up the place. And they had every imaginable weapon. They had hand grenades, rocket launchers, AK-47 assault rifles. And we assumed that they had explosive charges and that their objective, obviously, was to get inside the embassy and . . . heaven knows what! Blow the place up if they had the capability of doing that.

There were twenty of them, and we learned they did have explosive charges, and for reasons that have never been fully explained, they never succeeded in planting those charges and blowing open the doors and getting into the building.

The compound was a mess. It was strewn with bodies of dead Viet Cong sappers. There was debris everywhere. I remember one thing in particular. And that was General Westmoreland advising me to get the embassy cleaned up as quickly as possible and get people back to work by noon.

The Viet Cong attack on Bunker's bunker ended only after a six-and-a-half hour battle with marine guards helped by fire from adjoining buildings. It was put down when American paratroopers landed by helicopter on the roof pad. Five Americans were killed.

That was only one symbolic blow in a Viet Cong offensive that set the whole 500-mile length of South Vietnam afire—a hundred towns and cities from the DMZ south to the Mekong River delta. General Westmoreland describes it as a "last gasp" by the losing side to change the course of the war, like Hitler's futile offensive in the Bulge or Lee's northward foray into Gettysburg. It cost the Communist forces 40,000 deaths—a loss that shattered the Viet Cong organization and put the main burden of the war on their allies, the North Vietnamese. In purely military terms, it was an outright failure.

NGUYEN CO THACH
Foreign minister of the Socialist Republic of Vietnam
1968: Deputy foreign minister, North Vietnam

I think in the Tet offensive we could not succeed in our military targets. Capturing Saigon, for instance. But we did succeed in showing to our people and to our army and to the American army and to the whole world that the defense of the U.S. Army was vulnerable. It was very important strategically.

If Tet was a setback for the Communist side, it didn't look that way in the headlines or on the evening news. The big story, as reported by the media, was that an enemy recently believed to be hanging on the ropes had managed to mount a well-organized, well-supplied major offensive.

BOB JORDAN
Retired marine major, editor of navy publication
1968: Marine officer in Vietnam

Tet had been reported as a military failure in the press, and yet we were getting reports of how we had destroyed complete NVA [North Vietnamese army] units and totally decimated the VC infrastructure. Then we discovered all the bodies in Hue that the VC and NVA had assassinated and put in mass graves. And, strangely, that was not being reported back to the American public with the enthusiasm that our failures—or so-called failures—were being reported.

HARRY MCPHERSON
Washington lawyer
1968: Special counsel to the President

Like every other American, I was dismayed by the Tet offensive. I'd gone to Vietnam the summer before to see what it was like. So I had a sense of what was happening and in what villages—I'd been in many of them.

I went down to see Walt Rostow [Mac Bundy's replacement as national security adviser] in the White House basement, and he was reporting that we had clobbered the enemy and that we were going to rebuild—the South Vietnamese army had really shown itself to have a lot of guts and a lot of fighting power—and that this had been a disaster for the North.

And it was one of those really curious things about the impact of television. Seeing the American embassy under attack, of seeing Hue, the queen city up the coast, under siege, seeing such terrible devastation wrought by both ourselves and North Vietnam and the guerrillas, the Viet Cong—the impact of seeing that on television was greater on me than the intelligence information I was getting in the White House basement.

I was two or three rooms away from the cables and had been in Vietnam myself and had been dealing with the issue, but I was still more persuaded by those pictures and by the image of General Loan [the South Vietnamese national police chief] firing his pistol into the head of that Viet Cong guerrilla —I was more moved by that and appalled and depressed by it than I was strengthened and encouraged by what was coming from Saigon from our side.

The difference between the official view of Tet (Rostow's and the military's) and the view presented by the media recalled Charles de Gaulle's maxim about fighting colonial wars. What the Pentagon saw in the liberated ruins of Hue was the track of a defeated army; what the media saw was the path of an undefeated country.

The shock of Tet was soon followed by another piece of Vietnam news, also far from bullish. The Joint Chiefs were reported to be asking the White House for an additional 206,000 men for the armed forces, an expansion required primarily by the demands of the ongoing war. There were howls of disbelief on the Hill and in the press. There seemed to be no bottom to the pit called Vietnam.

The first assignment of President Johnson's new defense secretary was to chair a study of the controversial troop request.

CLARK CLIFFORD
1968: Secretary of defense

What that request did was bring into sharp focus all of the problems in Vietnam. That indicated that the military was saying, "We're not winning" —that we *can't* start to withdraw men. Do we *need* 206,000 more men? The public outcry was substantial.

I came to the inescapable conclusion that we were not going to win, that we ought to get out. And I spent the rest of the time that I was in the

Pentagon trying to convince President Johnson to that effect—and other government leaders both in the executive branch and in the legislative branch.

Behind the scenes in the White House, a struggle was under way for the conscience of the administration.

For his self-appointed mission, Clifford sought reinforcement from the President's own group of so-called wise men—fourteen individuals distinguished by long experience in national security matters whose advice LBJ had solicited before. They included Johnson idols and intimates like Supreme Court Justice Abe Fortas, World War II General Omar Bradley, Korean War General Matthew B. Ridgway, ex-Secretary of State Dean Acheson, and former presidential troubleshooter John J. McCloy. When previously assembled in the fall of 1967, the wise men had responded by telling the President his Vietnam policy was working and the United States was on its way to wrapping up the war successfully. Now, summoned again in March 1968, they came to an opposite consensus. Johnson was shaken.

From the domestic front, meanwhile, election-year politics were converging on him. Senator Gene McCarthy, the darling of the doves, made a surprisingly strong showing in the New Hampshire Democratic primary with the help of a corps of collegiate volunteers. Bobby Kennedy, by now acquiring statesmanly status as a senator from New York, tried to pressure the President into a kind of public trial of his Vietnam policy. When Johnson refused ("a very firm answer and a quick one," as LBJ described it, his eyes narrowing meaningfully), Kennedy threw his own hat into the ring as an antiwar candidate, drawing cheers from his large and powerful constituency of urban liberals.

It was perhaps less than an even-money bet that either challenger would be able to wrest the nomination from the incumbent President. But the prospect of having to *fight* for a nomination that belonged to him by rights didn't please LBJ, a politician who lived for consensus and seemed to have an inordinate appetite for the voters' *love*.

March 31, 1968, was a date heavily circled on the White House calendar. By LBJ's reckoning, it was the deadline for launching a primary campaign. It was also the date he was scheduled to make a major television speech on Vietnam. The speech had been in the works since before Tet. In the established White House process, draft after draft was checked out with the top national security officials, including the secretary of state and the secretary of defense. But it wasn't until the final rewrite, a day or two before the delivery date, that Clark Clifford could be sure his mission had been accomplished and the struggle for the heart and mind of Lyndon Johnson had been won.

A speech that had once read "Tonight I want to speak to you about the war in Vietnam" now began "Tonight I want to speak to you of peace in Vietnam." Originally, its tone was one of determination to hold firm to the existing course. Now its whole thrust was to begin winding down a war that until that moment had known no trend but escalation. Its central idea was a halt in the bombing of the north— this time with *no* conditions. That decision was accompanied by an invitation, once more, to the Communist leaders to sit down at the negotiating table.

The peace offer was linked to another piece of big news. In place of an ending that the speech writer, Harry McPherson, had scissored off because it seemed out of character with the new policy—"too bellicose"—Johnson supplied one of his own. He had hinted at it to several members of the White House circle but had shown it to none of them:

". . . With our hopes and the world's hopes for peace in the balance every day, I do not believe that I should devote an hour or a day of my time to any personal partisan causes or to any duties other than the awesome duties of this office. . . . Accordingly, I shall not seek, and I will not accept, the nomination of my party for another term as your President."

One of the leading doves in the Senate, George McGovern, went to visit Lyndon Johnson in retirement on the LBJ ranch four years later when McGovern became the Democrats' presidential candidate. What struck the visitor as the President came to greet him at the ramp of the arriving plane was that "his hair was down to his shoulders— he'd let it grow just like the hippie kids. I don't know how a psychologist would explain that," McGovern muses, "but I explain it as an effort on his part to try and heal the wounds, to show that he wasn't entirely out of step with the youthful mood of the country.

"But I think the war in Vietnam and the political reaction to it broke Johnson's heart. I think that's what drove him from the White House."

LBJ himself would have objected to that definition of the event. "I was not driven from the presidency," he said to another visitor, a journalist who was trying to reconstruct the decisions of 1968. "I was not driven from office. There is no doubt that I would have won the nomination. And I would have defeated Nixon and been confirmed in the presidency."

Another time, on the same subject: "You can say what you want about the Johnson administration, but there's one thing you'd better understand: nobody ever forced me to do *anything*. I was nobody's captive—neither the JCS [Joint Chiefs of Staff] nor Dean Rusk, not Fulbright or Bobby Kennedy or anyone else on *that* side. I had my advisers. I listened to advice. But *I* made the decisions, and nobody pressured me into *anything*."

In leaving the White House, under his own power or otherwise, Johnson made one final gesture—typically large, like everything about the man, untypically private. He sent out a personal farewell greeting expressing goodwill—sent it to the head of every single government in the world, accompanied by a photograph of the planet Earth as seen from outer space. He liked to show visitors to the ranch one of the thank-you notes he received in return. It was from Ho Chi Minh, the antagonist he had often addressed but had never been able to bring within his embrace.

Season of Violence

With LBJ's unconditional bombing halt, the course of American policy had been reversed. Still the agony of Vietnam went on. The Communists were responsive, but they were far from ready to leap to the negotiating table. The South Vietnamese government—now headed by General Thieu as president with Marshal Ky as vice-president—also dragged its feet. Saigon's leaders had been persuaded by the Republican presidential candidate—according to noncandidate Johnson—"that they would get a better deal" from a Republican administration if they held out until after the election.

Nor did the wave of protest abate. The chaotic week-long takeover of Columbia University by students occurred that spring; the same week a million college and high school students boycotted classes for a day. Then the ugly pool of violence that seemed to lie just below the surface of American life was stirred by two isolated, crazed acts. In Memphis, the Rev. Martin Luther King, Jr., standing on a motel balcony, was shot to death by a white sniper aiming from a rooming-house window. That turned loose a rampage of black anger expressed in rioting, looting, and arson in 125 cities and towns across the country. The outbreak in Washington was the most vivid. "From the air," wrote one reporter, "the capital looked like a bombed city." Upon the President's proclamation of "a condition of domestic violence and disorder," a brigade of the Eighty-second Airborne Division was brought in from Fort Bragg, North Carolina, to put their new antiriot training to use.

Only two months later, as Robert Kennedy was winding up his California primary campaign in quest of the Democratic nomination, he was shot to death by a Palestinian nationalist—an adherent of a cause that seemed absurdly remote from the issues of that moment in American life.

The Democratic convention met in Chicago that summer in an atmosphere charged with tension worsened by the presence of several thousand young dissidents in the streets and parks—hippies, yippies (from "Youth International Party"), devotees of pot, along with serious critics of the war, sympathizers with the poor, earnest left-wing agitators, and put-on artists dedicated to nothing so much as baiting their elders, the "Establishment." A battle in the streets on the night of the climactic nominating session became the enduring televised image of that convention. The violence was later defined by an official board of inquiry as a "police riot," resulting from the failure of Chicago's uniformed force to exercise self-restraint in the face of provocations by the city's unwanted guests.

The Transatlantic Wind

Violence may have been—in the words of the black militant, H. Rap Brown—"as American as cherry pie," but protest by now was international, sweeping across oceans like so many other American influences. A French journalist, returning home in the spring of 1968 from a series of assignments in Asia and Africa, found Paris like "another third-world capital," brought to a standstill by a daily outpouring of students and intellectuals. The air was drugged with "poetry and mad politics."

The European left had its own agenda, but the emotional links to the American protest movement were strong.

BERNARD-HENRI LÉVY
1968: French radical student leader

I remember that we were very moved by what happened in America. On the one hand, we thought and said that America was the fatherland of fascism, imperialism, racism, and so on, and we were demonstrating in Paris streets against America—"Yankee, go home!" "Ho-Ho-Ho Chi Minh! North Vietnam is going to win!" and so on. All this was our very strong anti-Americanist protest.

But, on the other hand, we had the strong feeling, which was contradictory to the first one, that the truest revolution in the world at this period, the truest inspiration of our revolutionary spirit, was located in America. We were strongly convinced that the revolutionary wind was not coming from Cuba, which we loved, was not coming from Ho Chi Minh, who was to us like a sort of God, but we knew without really saying it, that the true revolution was coming from America. So, of course, we were watching what happened in the [American] university campuses.

I, like all the Marxist-Leninist revolutionary students and individuals at that time, thought that America was leaving the last stage of the capitalistic contradiction, that it was like the last days of the Roman Empire, the last days of Constantinople, the last days of the Mongol Empire in China. My conviction was that the new barbarians—the Cambodians, Vietnamese, and so on—were bringing down Imperial America.

Observers in the Kremlin apparently had no such interpretation of the turbulence within the United States.

ARKADY SHEVCHENKO
1968: Soviet foreign ministry official

As Andropov [later Premier] once mentioned at a Politburo meeting at which I was present, the war would be won not in Vietnam but in the streets of American cities.

But my feeling is that Soviet leadership never lost the opinion that the country [the U.S.] is a strong one militarily, a country which can stop the Soviet expansion anywhere. It was understood that there were internal troubles in the United States, but let me tell you that the Soviets had a long memory and they understood history well. And there was the feeling that something had been lost for one or two years, but the United States still was the United States.

The wind that blew across the Atlantic and through the streets of Paris in 1968 swept on across Germany and did not stop at the Iron Curtain. Czechoslovakia experienced a euphoric season known as the "Prague spring," in which censorship was abolished by a new party leadership headed by Anton Dubcek. Intellectuals began to speak out boldly in the press, films, and theater. By no means anti-Communist, they were proponents of "socialism with a human face"—a relaxation of the centrally managed economy, more decisions left to the workers in the plants, more emphasis on consumer goods. But along with this came demands for political reforms, greater religious freedom, an opening up of the marketplace of ideas.

The noise of even that much freedom grated on the Kremlin's ears. In late August, Warsaw Pact tanks on maneuvers outside the Czech borders suddenly crossed and rumbled on into Prague. Dubcek and his associates were arrested and quickly flown to Moscow.

In Washington, President Lyndon Johnson, receiving Soviet Ambassador Dobrynin at the White House, was expecting the visitor to deliver a piece of good news, which Johnson would be able to relay to the Democratic national convention, then about to open in the chaos of Chicago. Moscow, LBJ thought, was informing him of its agreement to start negotiating a disarmament treaty.

Instead, what Dobrynin had come to announce was the Soviet occupation of Czechoslovakia, necessitated by what was described as "complete chaos" in Prague.

Dobrynin *read* the announcement to Johnson from a prepared document, keeping his eyes fixed on the paper and never looking up until he'd finished.

The President was appalled.

The negotiations for SALT—the Strategic Arms Limitation Treaty —were put off for a whole year, until after the Johnson administration had left the White House.

·19·

NAM AND THE WORLD

The politics of 1968 contained a number of apparent clues to the changing mind-set of the American public toward the Vietnam War, but the evidence was hard to sort out.

A Harris poll on the eve of Tet had shown 52 percent of the people would prefer to spend money on that remote and unproductive war rather than on improving their own slums—against only 32 percent favoring domestic programs. After Tet, about three out of four Americans (74 percent) were still in favor of the war.

On the other hand, by early March 1968, almost half the people (49 percent) felt the United States had made a mistake in sending troops to Vietnam. And the Democratic candidate who emerged from the chaos of Chicago as expected—Vice-President Hubert Humphrey—began to gain on his Republican opponent, Richard Nixon, only after a speech in Salt Lake City in which Humphrey put a little distance between himself and the Johnson war policies.

One reasonable interpretation of those disparate facts: there was an increasing revulsion from the war, but many Americans were even more repelled by the conduct of the "peaceniks." In the minds of some, the protest movements were all lumped together—draft resisters, political radicals, black militants—and all were vaguely identified with the "permissiveness" of liberal Democratic policies.

This complex of attitudes produced a presidential election in which the incumbent Democratic party—the leadership of an ongoing war —was removed from office, though by the thinnest of margins, less than one-half of one percentage point. And an avowedly reactionary third party, headed by Alabama Governor George Wallace, got almost one-third as many votes as either major candidate.

Nixon, a phoenix who had publicly buried his own political career six years before, had revived himself with a new image. From the combative, somewhat underhanded anti-Communist of the McCarthy era, he had transformed himself into a healer who would make a divided nation whole again. His campaign also had a kind of underground theme—the persistent report of a secret plan to end the war.

RICHARD M. NIXON

That was one of those figments of the imagination that always comes up in a campaign. I made it clear during the campaign that I had some definite ideas about what to do once I came into office. I believed that what was important was to de-Americanize the war by training more effectively the Vietnamese troops—Vietnamization, as it was called.

The only way you could really win the war would be for the South Vietnamese to develop the capability of winning themselves, so that they could defend [their country] once we left.

Vietnamizing Vietnam

When the Nixon administration took over in January 1969, there were some 550,000 American troops in Vietnam, almost twice as many as the forecast JFK called "crazier than hell." In June of that year, the President announced that the quality of the South Vietnam army and its American weaponry had been upgraded sufficiently to permit the beginning of U.S. troop withdrawals in stages. Preliminary peace talks with the North Vietnamese got under way in Paris.

The withdrawals proceeded smoothly, but the negotiations bogged down. And even though, under a new commander, General Creighton Abrams, the American role was technically shifted from offense to defense, there was no end to the casualties in a war that now seemed to have no purpose but survival against the odds.

In his book *Dispatches,* war correspondent Michael Herr described the peculiarly poisonous atmosphere of Vietnam in this period when the war was supposedly being wound down:

The roads were mined, the trails booby-trapped, satchel charges and grenades blew up jeeps and movie theaters. The VC got work inside all the camps as shoeshine boys and laundresses and honey-dippers, they'd starch your fatigues and burn your shit and then go home and mortar your area. Saigon and Cholon held such hostile vibes that you felt you were being dry-sniped every time someone looked at you, and choppers fell out of the sky like fat poisoned birds a hundred times a day.

Even the language of the Vietnam war was dehumanizing. No more jaunty "doughboys" as in World War I or official-sounding "GIs" as in World War II, the foot soldiers of Nam were mere "grunts."

Any war is a filthy business, but this one seemed to have no redeeming social virtues. Any war is fought with an attitude compounded largely of cynicism, but the spirit of Vietnam was sheer decadence. Grunts routinely carried their marijuana pipes and their little sacks of grass as part of their field kit. They went on patrol fortified by uppers or downers prescribed by the medics, and they went their way stoned through the war.

Increasingly they felt themselves resented by the people they were supposed to be defending in Vietnam and unappreciated by the people back home. There were anti-American demonstrations in Saigon, and humiliating experiences awaited soldiers when they returned to "the world." Officers were by no means immune to the insults. Major Bob Jordan, briefly stationed in New York, sometimes came in from the street with spittle on his dress blues. Colonel Charles Beckwith, who later commanded the Iran hostage rescue attempt, once had "perfectly good whiskey poured all over me" while walking through the San Francisco airport terminal in uniform.

Atrocities are part of the lore of warfare in this century, but never before had there been such horror stories from the American side. There were soldiers who professed pleasure in the experience of killing. There were grunts who carried sacks of ears cut off VC bodies as trophies. In a place called My Lai, a village where the Viet Cong was understood to be active, 347 South Vietnamese civilians were massacred on a day in May 1968—an incident that did not come to light until 1971. The victims included women and children. The day-long bloodbath was carried out by a platoon that had taken savage losses from the guerrillas and their booby traps.

The endless tragedy of the Vietnamese people reached many Americans in a single excruciating news photograph. It showed an eight-year-old girl, the victim of an errant napalm bomb, running naked and screaming down a road. The bomb had been dropped by a South Vietnamese pilot flying an American plane.

PHAN THI KIM PHUC
College student, Vietnam
1972: Grade-school pupil

I remember that, as a whole bunch of people ran out the gate of the schoolyard, the airplane came in and dropped a bomb, and I was wounded. There was no one at all around me, and my clothes had completely burned. At that point, I was terrified, but I continued to run on for about another kilometer. At that point, I passed out, and people took me to the hospital.

I continue to suffer from headaches a great deal, and when the weather changes, the scars are very painful, so my health continues to threaten my studies. But I try hard to overcome this.

I feel that we should forget the war now.

Cambodian Incursion

In April 1970, the war assumed a whole new dimension. In terms of pure geography, the key word was Cambodia. That small country, bordering South Vietnam on the west, was inhabited by a race with a gentle tradition, the Khmers.

By the spring of 1970, the North Vietnamese infiltration of Cambodia had gone so far that they, along with their local Communist protégés, the Khmer Rouge, controlled one-fourth of the country. Their supply corridors and sanctuaries—a source of irritation and frustration to the Americans throughout the Johnson administration—had by now been consolidated into what the Communists called a "liberated zone."

Cambodia was an issue in the Paris peace talks, in which Nixon's national security adviser, Henry Kissinger, was deadlocked with his Hanoi counterpart, Le Duc Tho. Cambodia, Le Duc Tho insisted, was an integral part of the struggle of the people of Indochina for independence.

For more than a year the Nixon administration had been conducting a secret program of bombing targets inside Cambodia. It was accepted by the country's leader, Prince Norodom Sihanouk, with the same compliance he showed toward the Communists; when Sihanouk's government was overthrown by a coup from the right, the bombing had the more active assent of his successor, Lon Nol.

On April 20, 1970, Nixon announced that, in keeping with his policy of Vietnamization, a withdrawal of 150,000 American troops would be carried out during the next year. On April 30, he took an action which Westmoreland and other military advisers had urged on the Johnson administration but which LBJ had firmly resisted. That crucial move: an "incursion" across the Cambodian border by American troops and the army of South Vietnam. It was perhaps the single most controversial act of the Vietnam War.

The term "incursion" in place of "invasion" was a calculated one.

RICHARD M. NIXON

Now to say that the United States "invaded" Cambodia is just like saying Eisenhower "invaded" France when he went in to drive the Germans away from the French-occupied territory. What happened was, as far as Cambodia was concerned, the areas that we went into were completely controlled by the North Vietnamese. They were making hit-and-run attacks upon American forces. Thousands of casualties were being suffered. We had to stop that. So we went in to clean out those sanctuaries.

There were two purposes. One: to save American lives, which was my responsibility as commander in chief. And two: to shorten the war by stepping up our own Vietnamization.

It served both purposes. Our casualties went down. There was no Tet offensive that year. We were able to increase the withdrawals that we were making.

The administration thought it had anticipated every criticism.

An "extension of the war?" The war had already been extended into Cambodia by the North Vietnamese.

An "obstruction to the peace negotiations?" A "nullification of the U.S. withdrawal policy?" If the Communists were allowed to remain entrenched in Cambodia, they would be in a position to swarm over South Vietnam as soon as the Americans pulled out. As Kissinger wrote later, the issue as the administration saw it was "whether Vietnamization was to be merely an alibi for an American collapse or a serious strategy to achieve an honorable peace." A peace, that is, that would leave South Vietnam capable of resisting a Communist takeover.

The arguments only poured fuel on flames of protest that had been spreading all spring—flames fed by leaks to the press about the Cambodia operation in advance of the Nixon announcement. In college communities Cambodia instantly became a buzz word signifying the worst sort of betrayal—a reescalation of the Vietnam War. There were demands for the impeachment of the President. The editors of eleven major campus newspapers ran a common editorial urging a nationwide student strike. The presidents of thirty-seven institutions joined in a letter to the White House warning of "an unprecedented alienation of America's youth."

There was a surge of campus violence. The ROTC building at the University of Maryland was ransacked. And a five-day sequence of events in the college town of Kent, Ohio, ended in a national tragedy. First, a student beer bust overflowed into an antiwar riot. The town cut off the local beer supply. A retaliatory spree of "trashing" culminated in a fire that burned an ROTC building to the ground.

Governor James Rhodes had been obliged to call out the National Guard when a black-minority action and an anti-ROTC demonstration at Ohio State University converged in a six-hour battle with police. Now he sent the guard in to occupy the campus at Kent State.

DEAN KAHLER
County commissioner, Athens County, Ohio
1970: Kent State University freshman

I was real aware of what was going on with the Vietnam War. My church started sending me literature about the war in Vietnam when I was fourteen or sixteen years old—about alternatives to the draft—and I was a conscientious objector at the time.

I hadn't really been to any antiwar demonstrations. I went there out of curiosity, having read all the things in the newspapers and the magazine articles—about the presidents of universities coming out and talking to the students and giving them an outlet for the type of things they wanted to express.

And with Nixon's announcement that he was invading Cambodia, it seemed like he was flying in the face of all his campaign promises, that he was lying to the American public all through that campaign. And we had had a year and five months of his administration where nothing had changed. We were still seeing the body counts, and my friends were coming home with wounds, and some of them weren't coming home at all.

I became a little angry and a little frustrated because we had, I thought, a First Amendment right to assemble and address our grievances against our country, and all we were getting was the military pointing their guns at us. And they kept shooting tear gas at us and chasing us and shooting more tear gas at us and chasing us. And I remember picking up some stones and throwing them in the direction of the National Guard a hundred yards away. I threw them more out of frustration than I did out of anger, because I wanted them to get away and leave so we could go back to school.

I was at the bottom of Blanket Hill. The guardsmen worked their way up from the practice football field, and when they reached the top of the hill, I was about a hundred yards away from them, following them along. I was gonna divert and go over to the Student Union and get a cup of coffee and get ready to go to my one o'clock class.

When they reached the top of the hill, they turned and fired. I couldn't believe that they were actually firing toward us, the students. So when they started firing, I jumped on the ground and laid there and covered my head and said, "Oh, my God, I hope I don't get hit." About that time I got hit.

And then I heard all the chaos and all the craziness going on around me —people screaming and hollering. There were still bullets zinging past me, and you could hear them cutting through the grass and bouncing off the blacktop. And people just crying. And it was just really, really horrible, really horrible. And then the shooting stopped, and there was a real eerie silence. And then someone came to me and said, "Who are you and how can we reach your parents?"

In thirteen seconds of trigger-happy insanity, sixty-seven shots were fired; thirteen students were hit. Four of them died. Eighteen-year-old Dean Kahler, partially paralyzed by a spinal-cord injury, was consigned to life in a wheelchair.

In the outburst of emotion that followed Kent State, 448 colleges were closed by sympathetic administrations or by student and faculty strikes; antiwar marchers and a counterforce of hard-hatted construction workers clashed in New York's financial district; in Washington, upwards of 75,000 people gathered in sadness and anger in the Ellipse, a park within view of the President's windows, while a barricade of buses was drawn up as a shield between the crowd and the White House grounds. A procession of symbolic coffins moved toward Arlington National Cemetery.

Nixon had enflamed the young opposition by referring to campus arsonists as "bums." It was heard as an epithet for the whole antiwar movement. The President, in what seemed like a desperate effort to "relate," as he later explained, to his young critics, made an abrupt appearance at 5 A.M. among a startled group of demonstrators sleeping on the steps of the Lincoln Memorial. Looking haggard, accompanied only by a valet and a single Secret Service man, he tried to engage the young people in conversation, but succeeded only in making himself sound trivial and incoherent. Football and surfing weren't the subjects uppermost in these students' minds.

The barricade at the White House grounds suggested the state of siege that was enveloping the Nixon presidency as it had his predecessor's. His personal security was a constant concern. Fears of some ugly incident forced changes in White House travel plans, including the cancellation of a visit to the Smith College campus in Massachusetts for the graduation of his daughter Julie.

Nixon anticipated the possibility of being forced out of politics like Lyndon Johnson, and hinted that he might throw the 1972 nomination to Chief Justice Warren Burger.

Incensed by the press leaks about the military operations in Cambodia, Nixon went on a fateful tear, telephoning his national security adviser, Henry Kissinger, at least ten times one evening (by Kissinger's account), interrupting him first at home and then at a dinner party . . . hanging up on him several times . . . and then ordering wiretaps installed on the phones of staff members in Kissinger's office as the suspected source of the news leaks.

Richard Nixon, feeling threatened both personally and politically, was lashing out. The momentum would carry him from here to the brink of the abyss called Watergate.

·20·

NEW DIRECTIONS

On a July weekend in 1969, the nation's attention had been riveted by an event that combined exhilarating drama with the epic qualities of a great adventure. It took place 250,000 miles away in space, and to a public frustrated by failure in Vietnam it was a welcome reminder of America's capacity for achievement.

With half a billion people around the world as witnesses by way of television, a pair of astronauts stepped from the ladder of a spiderlike *Apollo II* landing module onto the powdery black surface of the moon. "That's one small step for man," astronaut Neil Armstrong declared to perhaps the largest audience any man ever addressed, "one giant leap for mankind."

The sense of historic moment was inescapable. "After centuries of dreams and prophecies," *Time* commented, ". . . man had broken his terrestrial shackles and set foot on another world." This was the payoff of the Kennedy administration's expensive gamble, delivered ahead of the end-of-the-decade deadline and within minutes of the landing time scheduled months before.

Coming exactly six months into the Nixon administration and four years into America's ground war in Southeast Asia, the spectacle of the moon landing was only a diversion from the realities of life among the nations of the earth. According to one highly placed British observer —James Callaghan, soon to become a Labour foreign minister and then prime minister—Vietnam was destroying "any illusion that might have remained of America's superior wisdom and its omnipotence, its capacity to do what it said it wanted to do."

227

In this country, Vietnam was causing a massive reappraisal of the cold-war experience and its meaning.

LESLIE GELB
News executive, *New York Times*
1969: Defense Department policy planner

I came out of a background very typical of people who held high office in American foreign policy since World War II, and it was a background that pretty much accepted the Truman containment doctrine toward the Soviet Union. This was revealed scripture. What Vietnam began to do, kind of artichoke leaf by artichoke leaf, was to cause people like me to begin to question some of the fundamental working assumptions about foreign policy.

The philosophy of the cold war said in effect that the world strategically is an interconnected whole, that an attack, a challenge to Western interests anywhere was a threat to us everywhere. [The intervention in] Vietnam represented the culmination of that thought.

The other philosophy that came in said, "The world is not one chunk, and Moscow doesn't pull the strings on what goes on in Vietnam or Africa as a puppeteer"—that each country or region has a life of its own that we have to deal with in its own terms. It was not realistic, so the proponents of this view argued, to go in and try to change nature and history with American military force; there were limits to American power, and in Vietnam we had reached them.

The thirty-seventh President of the United States was one of the participants in that great reappraisal.

RICHARD M. NIXON

One of the advantages of coming into office in 1969 was, first, I had been vice-president for eight years and had a pretty good teacher in President Eisenhower. Second, I had the advantage of being out of office for eight years—as de Gaulle and Churchill would put it, "in the wilderness"; a chance to think.

I had traveled around the world. I had met most of the world leaders, had gotten their views about the world, which differed from mine. It brought me along in my own thinking.

So, consequently, when I came in, I was not just thinking of the immediate issue. The immediate issue was the war—get the war over with. But I wrote a piece for *Foreign Affairs,* the magazine, which came out the year before I came into office, in which I surprised many people by coming out for a new relationship with the People's Republic of China.

I thought that Vietnam had tended to blind many American policy makers to the broader responsibilities and dangers that we faced in the world, that we needed to reevaluate our relationship with China, with the Soviet Union, and everyone else.

When I came into office, everything was in place. The Sino-Soviet split was very clear; they were at each other's throats, so to speak, on the borders in several instances. Second, the Chinese no longer were an expansionist power; they were looking inward; they no longer threatened their neighbors. And, third—and this was a secondary reason—they were in Vietnam.

The Opening to China

Internal developments inside China had been commanding the interest of American policy makers for several years, beginning with the breakdown of the economic folly called the Great Leap Forward. At first, the tremors emanating from the vast, crowded Asian mainland were all but incomprehensible to the West. They were the vibrations of an epic struggle by Mao Zedong to keep control of China's destiny by restarting his vaunted revolution. This time it was in the form of a "Cultural Revolution," carried into the streets by daily waves of chanting marchers and troops of fanatical Red Guards. Starting in 1965, the convulsions seized and held the country for three terrible years.

LIANG HENG
Writer and editor
1966: Member of the Red Guards

The Cultural Revolution gradually, day by day, became crazy. Nobody really understood what was happening. I saw people use machine guns to shoot each other in the streets. Today this faction was wrong but tomorrow maybe they are right. Today you were right; maybe tomorrow you become a counterrevolutionary.

Chairman Mao treated Chinese people as soldiers—all China as an army. He broke into the family structure. At that time, nobody went to school or college to study. Why? Because the slogan was very popular: "The more education and knowledge that you have, the more reactionary you are." So, no books, only Chairman Mao's books! The library was closed also. We had no school, and we were wandering the streets.

My father, as editor, worked at the newspaper. When the Cultural Revolution happened, all the journalists were beaten by the Red Guards. My father, who loved Chairman Mao and supported the Communist party, became the "enemy of the party," became the "counterrevolutionary."

My father, like most intellectuals, was sent into the countryside to do hard jobs, so I went to the countryside with my father. We often had no food. I was so hungry at night I went to the field to steal sweet potatoes.

We didn't know what happened outside of China. We only concerned ourselves with ourselves as a great people. Chairman Mao said the Chinese system was the number-one system in the world.

By the early 1970s, China had emerged from its convulsions with Mao entrenched in power but a more rational view taking hold of China's fortunes. Within a few years, the recent experience would be seen as a catastrophic mistake. "I think no one wants to repeat the Cultural Revolution," says Han Xu of the Chinese ambassadorial corps, with careful understatement. "We hope it will never happen again."

Meanwhile, a kind of ground swell favoring some new approach to Communist China had been rising in the United States—rising, curiously, from the more conservative reaches of the political map. Its spokesmen included not just Nixon but also his chief rival for leadership of the Republican party, Governor Nelson Rockefeller of New York. Rockefeller reflected a growing interest in China among American business and banking leaders. The strategist behind his China position—Henry Kissinger of Harvard, the principal proponent of a new pragmatic, or "power-realist," school of foreign policy—became national security adviser in the Nixon White House. The Nixon and Kissinger viewpoints converged to destroy one of the most forbidding taboos of American foreign policy and revolutionze the approach to the cold war.

Developments followed a straight course from the trivial to the historic. In the spring of 1971, a United States table tennis team was invited to compete in Red China (where the sport is immensely popular). The United States government lifted its restrictions against travel to China by its citizens, as well as a trade embargo against China that had been in effect since the Truman years. And Washington withdrew its implacable resistance to seating Communist China in the UN—

something a generation of congressional stalwarts had declared would happen only over their dead bodies.

In the summer of 1971, during a carefully staged trip to Pakistan, Kissinger eluded the corps of reporters accompanying him and made a secret flight to Beijing to meet with Premier Zhou En-lai and arrange a visit by President Nixon the following February.

In the numbing cold of China's winter, the American President walked the Great Wall, spent hours at a time in earnest conversation with Zhou, sat in the benign presence of the revolution's sainted Mao Zedong. In a sitting room that was also his bedroom, its floor strewn with books, Mao received the President in oracular style, asking questions and commenting cryptically on the answers. At one point, Nixon remarked that the chairman's teachings had transformed China and affected the whole world. "No," said Mao Zedong with some accuracy, "all I have done is change Beijing and a few of its suburbs."

The ceremonies and discussions went on for almost a week, but the real significance of that trip was compressed in the single moment when Nixon first stepped off the ramp of "The Spirit of '76" (the former Air Force One) at Hung Chiao airport in Beijing—met by no crowds, no banners or bunting, only a military guard of honor and the outstretched hand of Zhou En-lai.

With that greeting the two leaders rejected more than two decades of cold-war history. Ever since the revolution in the late 1940s, Chinese propaganda had portrayed Uncle Sam in classic terms as the "foreign devil." And in American political life, reconciliation with Communist China was long regarded as unthinkable. Nixon's own mentor, President Eisenhower, had in effect forbidden it. The platform Nixon first ran on for the presidency, in 1960, declared that his party remained "firmly opposed" to it.

Jack Kennedy once told an associate that he intended to "do something with China but not until the second term." The subject was so touchy that his secretary of state, Dean Rusk, says he had to "play the role of the village idiot" whenever anyone so much as brought up the subject of Communist China. The Democrats, he points out, were saddled with Nationalist China and "their myth that they were the government of all of China and that some day they would go back to the mainland." In exile at his Texas ranch, former President Lyndon Johnson said about that historic handshake, with undisguised bitterness: "No Democrat would have been allowed to do it. Only Republicans are allowed to 'surrender to the Communists.'"

RICHARD M. NIXON

I had been a strong anti-Communist all of my political life. I had been strong against recognizing China and admitting it to the United Nations during my service in the Eisenhower administration and in my years out of office. It had taken three years for us to have this initiative come to fruition. And I felt, as our two hands came together, that we were changing the world.

Now, they will say, "That's Nixon, overstating it again as he usually does." And it's true we all do that in politics. But if I look back on the period that I was in office, there was no event that perhaps had a greater significance and in the longer term a greater effect on the whole situation in the world, the geopolitical balance, than the new relationship between the U.S. and China.

My judgment of a leader is: did he make a difference? And the China initiative was one of the few cases where I did something that others might not have been able to do. Not then.

I suppose all these things must have gone through my mind, but when I first came off [the plane], I noticed that—well, that it was very cold, that Zhou wasn't wearing a coat even though he was very frail—I wasn't wearing one either—and his hands were cold and mine were warm. [Note: photos of the event show both men wearing coats.]

Many people have never forgiven me—many of my closest friends and supporters—for going to China. They think I went to China because I finally had found that the Chinese weren't all that Communist. That wasn't the reason. I knew that the Chinese were Communist. They were then; they still are. They will continue to be.

But they are there! We have to deal with them.

I could see China, with a fourth of all the people in the world, potentially among the most capable people in the world, as an enormous force in the next century. And as President de Gaulle once said to me, "Better to recognize China now, when they need you, than wait until later when their strength forces you to do so."

Truce at Last

As some of its proponents had dared to hope, the "opening to China" became a gateway to much more.

The new Beijing connection was bound to make an impression on Moscow, where Nixon was also determined to establish a new relationship. Almost at once, Moscow, which had been cool to Nixon's earlier advances, became interested in a meeting at the summit. As with China, it was something demanded by the long view of history—"it would have happened," according to Richard Nixon, "whether there was a war in Vietnam or not." But now the Russia policy and the China policy became interlinked parts of the machinery that was grinding on toward a Vietnam truce—a process slow and frustrating, like the war itself.

"The Vietnamese are really hard cases," says Henry Kissinger, recalling his three and a half years of Paris negotiations with his Hanoi counterpart, Le Duc Tho. "I mean they are really tough customers. I think what shocked them—the first, really overwhelming shock to them—was my secret trip to China."

Hanoi had a shock of its own to deliver. In the spring of 1972—just weeks after Nixon's visit to Beijing, just weeks before his scheduled trip to the summit in Moscow—the North Vietnamese launched a massive offensive. Unlike Tet four years learlier, this was no guerilla infiltration. It was an outright invasion, spearheaded by Soviet-built tanks, across the DMZ, the boundary line recognized for almost two decades. That was followed by another invasion from the sanctuaries in Cambodia. Both offensives resulted in the capture of provincial capitals; South Vietnam was nearly severed at its narrow waist.

Washington was confronted once again with a crisis of decision. Nixon's response was a calculated risk: to resume the policy of massive punishment against the north—the policy that Lyndon Johnson had brought to a dramatic halt in 1968. Nixon considers this his "toughest decision" in Vietnam, even tougher than Cambodia, even harder to justify."

RICHARD M. NIXON

I made the decision over the objections and concerns of many of my advisers that we would bomb [Hanoi] and mine [the port of Haiphong]. Many thought it would ruin the chance for a summit. But I knew this: we couldn't go to the summit with Soviet tanks in Saigon. If we did, we'd be in an incredibly poor position to bargain with them. I felt, therefore, that if we had to take the choice of letting the Soviet proxies overrun South Vietnam and the choice of stopping that or of stopping the summit, we'd have to stop the summit.

I frankly was not surprised, however, that the Soviet Union did go forward. After our visit with China, the Soviet Union particularly felt very strongly that they had to go forward with the summit. And also they were interested in arms control; they were interested in trade. We had a lot of very positive inducements for them to come to the summit.

VADIM ZAGLADIN
Member of Central Committee, Communist party, USSR
1972: Soviet government official

It was definitely not a simple decision. You might know that a special session of the Central Committee was called to decide whether to go to the summit or not. And we consulted our allies and our Vietnamese friends as well. And we considered the summit to be more important, to give more to our relations, than, well, not going to it.

Not only did the Moscow summit proceed on schedule in May, but the Paris truce talks got back on the rails. With the 1972 presidential election campaign warming up, it began to appear that the incumbent would have an invaluable asset tied up by Election Day.

HENRY KISSINGER
International consultant
1972: Nixon's national security adviser for foreign affairs

When the Communists, especially the Vietnamese Communists, want to settle, you couldn't drive them away from the conference table with an elephant gun. And if they don't want to settle, you couldn't get them *to* the conference table with an elephant gun.

The Vietnamese were always extremely polite but obnoxious in the sense they'd repeat the same speech over and over again—word for word, the same speech in order to wear us down. But they began to make subtle changes. I formed the opinion in July that if President Nixon was five points or more ahead [in the election polls] by the middle of September, they'd give in to our major demands.

We had taken the position for four years that we would under no circumstances make an agreement in which we were required to overthrow a government which had been allied to the United States for ten years, whose soldiers had fought side by side with us. Secondly, we would not settle unless Vietnamese infiltration into South Vietnam stopped and no additional supplies were sent into South Vietnam. We thought that the two conditions we had put—no infiltration and no resupply—would lead to the atrophy of North Vietnamese forces in South Vietnam.

On a Sunday afternoon [in October] Le Duc Tho suddenly tabled a document—in fact, a peace agreement—which granted us those essential conditions.

LE DUC THO
Former member of the Vietnam Politburo
1972: Chief negotiator for North Vietnam

The reason for allowing Thieu to stay was because we felt that if Thieu had to leave, the Americans would bring in another lackey who would be no different than Thieu.

But with those Paris accords we won a very fundamental victory. The entire American army and the American satellites had to withdraw completely from South Vietnam. That was a most fundamental victory for us because once the American army had completely withdrawn from South Vietnam, it would be very difficult for the Americans to return.

In the light of that "fundamental victory," the military conditions —no infiltration or resupply—apparently presented no problem to Hanoi. Those terms could be circumvented all too easily.

With an agreement on the table, Kissinger reported on the eve of the presidential election: "Peace is at hand." Once again American hopes were being raised only to be dashed. For the South Vietnamese, faced with the reality of being left on their own, seemed to panic; Kissinger and Thieu, by one insider's account, nearly came to blows over the document the American negotiator brought from Paris. Then Hanoi turned recalcitrant.

The White House issued a warning that unless North Vietnam came to terms, the bombing of Hanoi and mining of Haiphong harbor, suspended during the latest stage of negotiations, would be resumed once more. The North Vietnamese did not budge.

In mid-December 1972, American B-52s began an eleven-day blitz of the North Vietnamese capital—the so-called "Christmas bombing." It concentrated on shipyards, factories, antiaircraft missile sites, transportation links. But civilian neighborhoods also suffered. And fifteen of the American bombers were brought down by the improved Communist defenses, with the loss of ninety-three crewmen.

HENRY KISSINGER

There are certain American perceptions that are totally wrong when you are dealing with revolutionary Communists. One of these perceptions is that you gain goodwill by not bringing pressure on them. Usually, when you don't bring pressure on them, they see no reason to settle, and, therefore, they are very tough.

Now, conversely, the American perception is that when we bombed them they were extremely angry at us and very hostile. And there had been the Christmas bombing, which was egregiously misreported in the American press because it cost very few civilian casualties in Vietnam.

The Vietnamese publicly played this game of being very mad at us. They wouldn't greet me at the door; they wouldn't shake hands with me in public. But, inside, they were exuberantly friendly, and I thought Le Duc Tho had discovered some hidden physical attraction in me. He couldn't keep his hands off me. And it was an extremely friendly atmosphere, and it was absolutely clear that they had come to settle.

The civilian death toll of 2,000 in the Christmas bombing may have been low by the standards of modern warfare. But to opponents of the war, this was the final affront, the ultimate expression of a cynical policy.

GEORGE MCGOVERN
1972: Democratic presidential candidate

That was really rubbing salt in the wounds—to win an election after needlessly continuing a war for four years, announce a week before the election that the war is over, and then pick it up with the most murderous aerial raids of the war. I think the reason they quit those raids is not that they were killing people in Hanoi and in North Vietnam but because we lost so many bombers. If we had continued those raids for another thirty days, our entire Pacific bomber fleet would have been gone.

I can't complain about the fact that we negotiated a treaty to end the war. What distresses me is that so many people died needlessly when that same treaty could have been negotiated many years before it was.

We could have stayed there. We had the physical power to stay there. We could still be there, holding the fort in Saigon. It would still be called Saigon. We'd probably have lost another 150- or 200,000 Americans by now, but Saigon would probably still be Saigon.

The question is: what led us to believe that we have that kind of obligation? We never did have a national interest in Vietnam that justified the kind of commitment we made there.

On January 20 in Washington, there were more protesters than celebrants gathered for the inauguration of Richard Nixon's second term. Federal troops stood guard through the day's festivities.

Exactly one week later, under an ornate crystal chandelier at the Hotel Majestic in Paris, Kissinger and Le Duc Tho put their signatures to the document that ended America's nine years of warfare in the remote jungle country of Vietnam. By one unofficial estimate, it had cost $165 billion. Over 3 million Americans had served in Southeast Asia, and 58,000 lost their lives there. There were more than two thousand names on a heartbreaking list headed "MIA"—missing in action.

The country of Vietnam—north and south—suffered an estimated 4 million deaths in the war. Those casualties, soldiers and civilians, amounted to 10 percent of the population.

The American agony was not really ended by the truce. There was still a humiliating epilogue to be experienced and a lasting impact on the American spirit to be endured.

·21·

THE WATERGATE ERA

RICHARD M. NIXON

During the Eisenhower years, the United States had unquestioned nuclear superiority. Sputnik began to raise doubts, but it wasn't until much later that the Soviet Union caught up.

When I became President, the situation had changed. We were still ahead in some areas, like under the sea and in the air, but they had moved ahead in strategic ground-based missiles and also in intermediate ground-based missiles. So the power balance had changed. It was not a question of the United States being number one, but of both the Soviet Union *and* the United States being number one.

It was also a time when Americans were terribly disillusioned by the war in Vietnam. And so, under the circumstances, it was not an easy time to be President—not only because of the international problems, the war, but also because of the social problems at home. There was unrest—the bombings, the violence. People forget: it was a rather rough period then.

Nuclear superiority had been the touchstone of American policy since the mid-forties. With the seventies, nuclear parity became the basic new fact of international life. Nixon's way of dealing with it was by replacing the historic policy of containment with a policy of détente (in French, the traditional language of diplomacy, the term for a relaxation of tensions). Both Eisenhower and Kennedy had made moves in that direction, responding to Khrushchev's call for "peaceful coexistence." But it remained for Nixon, the well-known anti-Commu-

238

nist, to pursue détente systematically and make it the very basis of America's relationship with the Communist powers.

GEORGI ARBATOV
Director, U.S. and Canadian Studies Institute, USSR

You know, we Marxists give only a limited place in history to individuals. We think actually the policy of a country is more determined by economic, political, social, and other factors. And I remember very well that I had to explain just this question to my countrymen, and I told them that actually Nixon hadn't changed. He strove for one thing—and one only: for power to become a President and to remain a President. To get into history.

Several years earlier, to achieve this goal he had to be a Communist-baiter, a staunch anti-Communist. [Now], to get power he had to speak out for dialogue, for turning from confrontation to negotiations. And this just shows how the situation can change some men.

This was actually one of the brightest periods, or maybe the brightest period, in postwar relations between the Soviet Union and the United States. A lot of things looked very possible at this time.

The possibilities began to open up with Nixon's 1972 trip to Moscow —the first by an American President since the cold war began. It expanded into an exchange of visits with Leonid Brezhnev (who had emerged as the dominant member of the Brezhnev–Kosygin tandem) in which the two superpowers reached a historic agreement on arms control. Called SALT (for Strategic Arms Limitation Treaty), it checked the growth of the nuclear arsenals for the first time. And it halted that worrisome development of antimissile defenses.

The treaty, the *New York Times* pointed out, "involves no disarmament. Its purpose is to freeze the balance of terrifying weapons and to make sure the terror works by preventing any effective defense against them . . . [But] it is a beginning."

"A great victory for the Soviet and American peoples," Brezhnev called it, "in . . . easing international tensions."

In the new spirit of détente, the leaders went on to sign agreements in other fields, including trade, and to draw plans for joint ventures in space and medical research.

One barely noticed development of this "brightest period" in East-West relations was a four-power agreement that finally laid the Berlin issue to rest. It assured the U.S., France, and Britain access to West Berlin.

The Watergate Path

Nixon's response to the domestic troubles confronting him was much less sure-handed than his treatment of foreign affairs.

The last gasp of the Aquarian spirit had occurred during his first year in office, 1969, at the Woodstock rock festival in upstate New York, in which a self-proclaimed "nation" of 400,000 young people communed in the noise and mud. The event was a mess but a benign one.

After that final, fading summer of the sixties, the antisocial forces turned loose during the decade assumed their most destructive form. In the course of Nixon's first term, the once-moderate student organization called SDS became radicalized; an underground group called the Weathermen dedicated itself expressly to violence as a form of protest; and the activist role in the black community was preempted by extremist groups like the Black Panthers.

Shock followed shock in daily headlines about antiestablishment activities:

BOMB FACTORY SUSPECTED IN TOWNHOUSE EXPLOSION . . .
UNIVERSITY BLAST KILLS RESEARCHER . . .
PATTY HEARST KIDNAPPED BY RADICAL GANG . . .
RADICAL PROF SOUGHT IN COURTROOM SHOOTOUT . . .
MANSON "FAMILY" HELD IN HOLLYWOOD MURDER.

Many Americans felt threatened by the pervasiveness of political violence; as President, Richard Nixon was hardly less vulnerable than the ordinary citizen. During a 1970 congressional campaign trip, the President's car was assaulted with stones and eggs in an incident scarily reminiscent of an occurrence in South America during his vice-presidency, in which the lives of Nixon and his wife Pat were endangered.

If the President felt tremors of political insecurity from the Cambodia press leaks in 1970, then he was really shaken a year later when the *New York Times* began running the Pentagon Papers, a massive collection of classified documents from the Defense Department's Vietnam files—7,000 pages of documents and analysis, thirty-nine book-length volumes. The memos, cables, and reports all dated from the Johnson administration; they contained few actual revelations as they traced the escalation of the Vietnam War. What was shockingly disclosed was a massive hole in the government's ability to protect its secrets.

For this was no mere leak. The Pentagon Papers amounted, literally, to a truckload. And, according to a Nixon White House source, the truck had delivered copies not only to the *Times* but also to the Soviet embassy in Washington and (for unexplained reasons) to the Japanese embassy as well.

Richard Nixon was by nature a defensive person. In the course of his controversial career he had learned not to expect people to like him or trust him. He was accustomed to exercising power without popularity. In his executive style he combined traits of the emperor and the hermit. He had cultivated a taste for expensive living, was given to impenetrable rages, and was essentially a loner, tending to brood his way to solitary decisions behind the protective barrier of his staff.

In the current atmosphere of violence and lawlessness, it was not necessarily irrational to look for enemies instead of mere critics. But Nixon's way of dealing with the threats that he felt converging on him was to make vehement demands (for identifying culprits, punishing misdeeds, defending against recurrences) which his staff tried to satisfy by excessive means, with or without his knowledge. The ill-fated process had been set in motion with the efforts to trace the Cambodia leaks by wiretaps; it continued with an effort to trace the Pentagon Papers by using former CIA agents and a team of their Cuban-exile protégés—nicknamed the "plumbers unit"—to break into a psychiatrist's office in search of confidential data on one of his patients, the leading suspect, a former Pentagon consultant named Daniel Ellsberg.

There soon followed a whole sequence of operations, some appalling, some merely comic, whose purpose was to protect the Nixon administration against its supposed enemies and assure its continuation in office. Phony information was systematically planted about political opponents. The FBI was used to investigate reporters considered to be unfriendly to the administration, and the power of the White House was used to intercede with their bosses in an effort to intimidate them. In June 1972, with the presidential campaign in the offing, the plumbers unit was sent into the field once again, this time to burglarize offices of the Democratic National Committee in Washington's Watergate building complex. The main object was to try to find out how much the Democrats knew about some millions of dollars in questionable political contributions collected from big corporations (mainly oil companies and airlines), lobbies (the dairy industry, for example), and individuals (the secretive billionaire Howard Hughes, the fugitive financier Robert Vesco) on behalf of Nixon and his reelection campaign.

The arrest of the Watergate burglars nearly escaped notice. And later that summer, when reporters at the GOP national convention in Miami picked up rumors that anti-Nixon demonstrations in the streets were being prompted by *agents provocateurs* of the White House, the stories were dismissed at the time as implausible.

But Nixon was right in believing his enemies in politics and the press were out to get him. There were many who had never forgiven him for the excesses of his early years as an ambitious young congressman playing politics with the anti-Communist issue. Once they picked up the trail, they did not stop until they had followed it all the way from break-ins and laundered funds to dirty tricks and enemies lists—acts shielded from prosecution by an elaborate White House cover-up. Twenty-five well-connected people ended up in prison, including the President's counsel (John Dean), special counsel (Charles Colson), chief of staff (H. R. Haldeman), chief domestic adviser (John Erlichman), and two cabinet members (John Mitchell, Maurice Stans). In a separate, parallel case, Vice-President Spiro Agnew was forced to resign under fire for tax evasion.

The ultimate question was tersely put by one of the administration's own allies in the Senate, Republican spokesman Howard Baker of Tennessee: "What did the President know and when did he know it?"

The answer began to emerge from the tapes of Oval Office conversations which Nixon himself had secretly recorded: he knew quite a bit and he knew it quite early. A President who had been reelected by an overwhelming majority of 61 percent was in retreat. Supposedly conducting an investigation of Watergate, he was its prime target— the ultimate Watergate defendant.

HENRY KISSINGER

The impact of Watergate on foreign policy was a disaster. We were in an almost unique position, partly due to circumstance, partly due to Nixon's skill and toughness. We were closer to Peking and Moscow than they were to each other. We had isolated Vietnam. We had good relations with Europe. We had a lot of options open to us. You cannot, however, exercise your options if you have no authority, and Watergate gradually diminished the authority of the President.

The Yom Kippur War

In October 1973, Nixon had to summon up all his failing authority in order to deal with a new crisis in the Middle East.

The leading activist among Arab leaders in the fifties and sixties, Gamal Abdel Nasser of Egypt, was now dead; his political heir was the parliamentary leader, Anwar el-Sadat. With an armed force almost 100 percent Soviet-equipped, Sadat undertook a mission that had preoccupied him ever since the disgrace of the Six-Day War: the redemption of the Arabs' damaged honor.

Reversing the events of 1967, Sadat launched a stunning surprise attack across the Suez Canal. He timed it, as calculatingly as the Israelis had timed their 1967 blow, for a moment when the enemy was particularly vulnerable. The Egyptians attacked on Yom Kippur, the Jewish holiday devoted to solemn introspection.

Striking deep into Israeli-held Sinai, the Egyptian columns inflicted heavy casualties on the Israelis and huge losses in matériel, while Egypt's ally, Syria, attacked from the north. The Jewish state reeled. But in just over a week aid arrived that enabled the Israeli army to right itself and take the offensive.

RICHARD M. NIXON

We had a situation where, through our airlift, the Israelis turned the tide and surrounded the Egyptian Third Army. The Soviet Union changed its tune and, having before opposed a cease-fire when their clients, the Egyptians, were ahead, now supported one. They then urged that we, the United States, join them in sending a conventional peacekeeping force into the area. Well, I wasn't about to buy that.

Then Brezhnev sent a very tough message indicating that in the event we did not agree to go in together with him, he unilaterally was going to send forces into the area to impose peace—on Israel, of course. Under those circumstances, we had to react.

We did it in two ways. One, we sent a message in which we indicated to Brezhnev that in the event that he did take unilateral action it would jeopar-

244 ·   JOHN SHARNIK

dize our détente relationship and probably totally destroy it. And then we took an action which we thought would emphasize those words by calling an alert of our forces, which included nuclear forces.

Many observers believe that Brezhnev played the hard line that he did in the Yom Kippur War because he thought that I was wounded and that I would not react.

At the time Nixon acted, Brezhnev's paratroopers were already assembled at staging areas in the Soviet Union, possibly ready to move, more likely as a *coup de théâtre*, a dramatic bluff. Nixon himself was at bay politically. It was the week after the "Saturday Night Massacre," in which the President fired the Watergate special investigator Archibald Cox—and Attorney General Elliott Richardson and his deputy resigned—in a dispute over whether the Oval Office would have to surrender the telltale tapes.

Nixon won the showdown with Brezhnev but lost the battle over the Watergate tapes. Step by step the President was being pushed out of power in a constitutional process that astonished both the allies and the antagonists of the United States.

ARKADY SHEVCHENKO
Soviet defector; U.S. intelligence consultant
1974: UN undersecretary general

Initially in Moscow, they just ignored Watergate. When it developed into a major crisis in the United States, they were surprised. At the time of Watergate, let me tell you, there was much less understanding of the American political system and distribution of power between the President, Congress, public opinion, and so on than now. At the time, they thought the President of the United States was a king, and no one could do anything against him.

GENERAL ALEXANDER HAIG
1974: White House chief of staff

[The NATO Allies] were totally befuddled by it all, and as a matter of fact, shortly after I arrived in Europe as the Supreme Allied Commander, almost every head of state sought me out and in private conversations said, "What in God's name have you American people done to one of the most effective leaders of this generation?"

DENIS HEALEY
1974: Chancellor of the exchequer

I think the first thing to be said [about Watergate] is that many people in Europe, of all parties and all countries, regard the Nixon–Kissinger period of Soviet-American relations as a golden age which we would desperately like to restore. So the Greek tragedy of Watergate and Nixon's downfall were regretted to that extent.

Now, American politics has never been regarded as being totally free from behavior of which saints wouldn't approve. And the concentration on the lying was regarded as a little hypocritical.

People were very down on Nixon. I was down on him myself. There were things one didn't like about him. But again, there was great gratitude to him, I think, in much of the world for a serious attempt both to control the arms race and to reach an understanding with the Soviet Union.

What I think shocked people very much were the tapes and the revelation of the sort of people who worked for him in the White House. But people wrongly believed that there's a good deal of corruption and dishonesty in American politics. I don't think we realize that, in fact, it is the nearest thing to heaven which has ever been seen on this earth.

For much of two years the Nixon administration was consumed by the agony of Watergate as its predecessor, the Johnson administration, had been consumed by Vietnam. What was going on in the White House was only a charade of government, which continued until reality finally caught up with the President in the first week of August 1974. That was when a federal court ordered the White House to release the crucial tape recordings of conversations in the Oval Office. Among the tapes was a so-called smoking gun—a piece of conclusive evidence. It showed that the President had personally directed efforts to conceal evidence and buy the silence of witnesses.

HENRY KISSINGER
1974: Secretary of state

It's so strange about Watergate—I've actually forgotten what was on that tape. But at any rate, when that tape appeared, it was generally assumed that that was it.

That came out on a Monday; there was a cabinet meeting on Tuesday morning; and Nixon began it, for some inscrutable reason, as if that tape hadn't appeared, and began to talk about inflation control. And he came as close to getting a cabinet rebellion as I ever hope to see in the American system, where one after another of the cabinet members were saying that the problem was how to continue government and it couldn't go on like that. And I finally said, [as] the most senior of the government members, we were here to do the nation's business and we weren't here to say what couldn't be done but to try to do what was necessary. And that sort of calmed things down in the cabinet.

When the cabinet broke up, I stepped out and told the press that foreign policy would be conducted with regard to the national interest and would not be affected by whatever crisis they might perceive—which had to be done to discourage any adventurous designs. And then I went back to the Oval Office and told President Nixon that what I said publicly, in the Cabinet Room, was one thing because I did not believe that the cabinet appointed by the President should, as a body, stand against him; but as a friend, I had to tell him that it seemed to me time had run out, and I thought he should consider resigning.

But I did it with great pain, and I think that President Nixon deserved well of the country. I told him then—and I still believe it—that history would treat him much better than his contemporaries, whatever mistakes he made.

On August 9, 1974, with articles of impeachment proceeding through the House of Representatives, the thirty-seventh President removed himself from office in a one-sentence note hand-delivered to the Secretary of State by the White House chief of staff, General Alexander Haig. The note read simply: "Dear Mr. Secretary, I hereby resign the office of the President of the United States. Sincerely, Richard Nixon."

Excluded from the inauguration of his successor, Vice-President Gerald R. Ford, Nixon and his wife left the White House by helicopter a half hour in advance of the swearing in.

GERALD R. FORD

When you walked out to see them off on their helicopter, it was very difficult. You didn't know what to say. You wanted to say good-bye and add whatever you could, but words weren't easy to come by. And then, when we came back into the White House, I then had to think about my speech to be given after I took the oath of office.

Gerald Ford, a longtime spokesman for the solid midwestern center of the Republican party, had arrived in the vice presidency less than a year before. He had been appointed by Nixon as a replacement when Spiro Agnew resigned under a cloud. In becoming the thirty-eighth President of the United States, Ford also became the first un-elected President.

"My fellow Americans," President Ford announced, "our long national nightmare is over."

Extending Détente

The outside world's bafflement at the Watergate drama and its consequences produced some poignant moments. The day after Nixon's departure, a group of journalists was shown through the White House, some of them foreigners and some, like Anthony Sampson, the British writer, seeing the place for the first time. Sampson's most vivid reaction was one of surprise—surprise to find that it was like "an ordinary house instead of a bunker," surprise to see Jerry Ford "just sitting there as President as if nothing much had happened, this normal man, relaxed, apparently perfectly casually running the country after that amazing period of doubt."

The Russians' misunderstanding of Watergate and its outcome could have presented serious problems to the new President. For there were some in the Kremlin who, like Vadim Zagladin of the Politburo, believed then—and remained convinced afterwards—that "it was a successful attempt to eliminate a President whose political course was not to the liking of some forces." In other words, a coup against the policy of détente.

Ford and his secretary of state, Kissinger, took action to assure the Soviet leadership of the continuity of Nixon's policy. Extending a presidential trip to the Far East that autumn, Ford met with Brezhnev in the Siberian port of Vladivostok to lay the base for a second stage of SALT agreements.

It was a complicated negotiation, one that would spill over into later presidential administrations. It involved protracted haggling over the offsetting values of various sizes of ballistic missiles and launchers, of "throw weight" and "MIRV capacity" (for Multiple Independently targeted Reentry Vehicles—multiple warheads launched from one rocket). Two nonballistic weapons were introduced into the debate that would plague negotiators for years to come: America's low-flying engine-propelled cruise missiles and Russia's long-range Backfire bombers. While accepting a lid on their stockpile of missiles, both sides were trying to maintain unrestricted freedom to deliver the H-bomb by other vehicles.

The net effect of the Vladivostok summit meeting, nevertheless, was reassuring.

GERALD R. FORD

After we had negotiated the first night until about two or three in the morning and followed up with the negotiations later that morning and then with a luncheon, Mr. Brezhnev asked me if I would like to go and see the city of Vladivostok. I was very anxious to do it because I had heard so much about Vladivostok, so we got in a Soviet limousine with a driver, an interpreter, and a security man.

It's a big country. Vladivostok's a long way away from Moscow. But, anyhow, as we drove around—and it was a sightseeing tour with the head of the Soviet Union as my guide . . . I'm sitting on this side with Mr. Brezhnev, when all of a sudden he grabs my left hand.

I'm not really accustomed to holding hands with men in the back seat, but it was an interesting experience, because he immediately started talking about our mutual responsibility to prevent the nuclear holocaust.

He started out this way. He said, "Mr. President, both of us were in World War II. My country lost millions and millions of our citizens in that war. You in the United States lost thousands." Mr. Brezhnev said, "If we have a nuclear confrontation and a war develops, millions and millions of people not only in your country but in my country and elsewhere will be killed. It would have a devastating impact on mankind."

This was a very impressive, I think, real expression of concern on his part. I felt it was a different person than the individual I had negotiated with through the previous two days. But he was, in my judgment, speaking truly from his heart and from his own experience.

Saigon: Indecent Interval

If the long national nightmare of Watergate had ended with Nixon's departure from Washington, a much longer nightmare was only drawing to a close in the first year of the Ford administration. It was happening half a world away, but Watergate proved a factor in the outcome.

The Vietnam truce agreement signed in Paris early in 1973 was conceived by its American architects (primarily Henry Kissinger) as a livable stalemate—the best the U.S. could hope for. The arrangement was premised on the idea of keeping Saigon strong enough to discourage the North Vietnamese from attempting a military conquest. Economic aid to both sides presumably would help stabilize the situation.

Cynics saw it as providing nothing more than a "decent interval" between the American withdrawal and whatever resolution the two sides worked out—more likely fought out—between themselves.

The treaty required the United States to withdraw the last of its troops but acknowledged the Americans' right to maintain aircraft carriers in nearby waters and air bases in nearby Thailand as a guard against truce violations.

The right proved to be meaningless. The United States Congress, incensed at Nixon's aggressive war policies and in full cry against the President over Watergate, had passed legislation precluding the use of funds for United States military operations in Southeast Asia. At the same time, the Congress successively chopped down the yearly appropriations of military aid to South Vietnam, thereby neutralizing the policy of Vietnamization. General Alexander Haig, White House chief of staff in the last months of the Nixon administration, calls that congressional conduct "an act of legislative masochism that defies parallel in recent history."

Exploiting the situation in Washington and the declining morale in Saigon, the North Vietnamese began violating the truce with wholesale infusions of troops and equipment. By January 1975, a massive Communist offensive was under way and a massive retreat of the South Vietnamese army was pushing a wave of refugees before it toward the overburdened capital, Saigon. President Ford's appeal to Congress to relent on its strictures was rebuffed.

The *coup de grace* was a stroke of ineptitude on the part of Saigon's military command. In March, the South Vietnamese army was withdrawn from its defense lines in the central highlands and the northern provinces bordering the DMZ. That pulled the plug, and the Communists came flooding in.

During the last week in April, Saigon went to bed to the nightly sound of enemy artillery as approaching armies encircled the capital. Among the inhabitants were about five thousand Americans—government officials, civilian employees, uniformed embassy guards— and two to three hundred Western journalists. There were also perhaps 45,000 South Vietnamese employees of the U.S. government agencies—everything from clerks and drivers to propagandists and spies—whose jobs left them vulnerable to Communist reprisals. They and their families were, in effect, wards of the United States embassy.

The Americans had been briefed on plans for an evacuation from designated assembly points around the capital. The signal they were told to listen for was the playing of the song "White Christmas" on the American FM radio station. As the sound of approaching guns grew louder, the American ambassador, Graham Martin, procrastinated, thinking the front would hold. At the end he was still delaying the destruction of embassy files—apparently out of some misguided sense of orderly procedure.

When the FM station finally spun its Christmas recording on the morning of April 29, it was too late for procedure. The mood was one of panic. The final images of America's long and painful involvement in Vietnam came from the ensuing scenes of pandemonium and disgrace.

JIM LAURIE
Tokyo bureau chief, ABC News
1975: ABC News correspondent in Saigon

My intention was not to leave but to stay and report the evacuation and then presumably the Communist victory, which we knew to be imminent. So I simply came to this location, which was the former United States Information Service headquarters of the U.S. embassy just to watch my colleagues leave and see what the atmosphere was.

There were perhaps two or three hundred journalists and others here at this site. Army buses pulled up, driven by U.S. marines fully armed; and each bus was packed with Americans. Not only Americans, but as many Vietnamese that could cram aboard did so.

It was a scene of panic as Vietnamese tried to push their way onto these buses. The buses went off toward Tan Son Nhut air base, where there were fixed-wing aircraft and helicopters waiting to take the people to the aircraft carriers in the South China Sea.

I got in a small car and followed the buses to the airport, and all along the way there were hundreds of Vietnamese following the army buses shouting at the marines. "Please, let us aboard! Take us out of this country! We're afraid!" And this went on, it seemed to me, for hours. People just desperate to get out of the country, trying to get aboard these buses.

KEN KASHIWAHARA
ABC News San Francisco correspondent
1975: ABC News correspondent in Saigon

Our bus, when it got to the Tan Son Nhut gate, was stopped by South Vietnamese soldiers. They fired at our embassy escort and turned away the bus. From that point on, we drove around Saigon for four or five hours. The evacuation plan, in effect, simply broke down. Our bus driver, who was from the embassy, simply didn't know what to do.

We drove around. Vietnamese on the streets were shouting anti-American epithets at us. We went to the port, hoping that we could find a boat that we could get onto. There were mobs of Vietnamese just pouring onto the boats and barges.

We had to get back on the bus. I, unfortunately, was caught outside the bus and was attacked by the mob. They grabbed all the bags I had and started pulling me back, and I simply let the bags go and ran for the bus and got on.

As the bus was pulling out of the port, this Vietnamese man came running alongside the open door yelling, "Take my baby! Take my baby!" At that point, he tripped and fell, and the bus ran over the baby.

Finally, out of desperation, we decided to go to the embassy. There were thousands around the embassy trying to get in.

ALAN CARTER
Cultural exchange director, U.S. State Department
1975: U.S. Information Service officer in Saigon

At 11 A.M. on the morning of the 29th, I was called to a meeting at the embassy. When I got to the embassy, I realized that I wasn't being called over for a meeting—something else was going on. They were shredding documents, obviously throwing stuff out of files and safes, and so I finally cornered the deputy chief of mission, and I said, "Wolf, what in the hell is going on?"

He said, "We're leaving." And I said, "But, my God, you called me over, and I've got three other Americans on my staff plus another 120 Vietnamese in the compound!"—about whom he'd forgotten. Those things happen in that kind of pressure point.

We sent a car back to get the other three Americans over. We couldn't get the Vietnamese. We tried all day long—we just couldn't get them over. Remember that there was chaos going on in the streets at this time.

I went up to the roof of the embassy with my American colleagues, and when they were on the helicopter, I refused to go. I decided that I needed to try to do more about my Vietnamese staff. So I went back down to an office in the embassy and tried to reestablish phone contact with them. I couldn't. They had panicked. More than that, they felt that I had deserted them.

I waited, frantically trying to establish contact with them till finally—I think it was 11:30 at night—I was told that the second-last of the helicopters that would take the civilians out [was leaving]. There would be several coming to move the marine security detachment after that.

And so I stood in line with a lot of others up the long stairway leading to the roof, with my attaché case and what I had on my back, and finally crowded into this helicopter. And as we took off, you can imagine the scene: An embassy that was under siege, if you will, by tens of thousands of Vietnamese—many inside the compound, many desperately trying to get inside, get over those gates. And it had the look of a Roman carnival, because the streets were well lit; there were thousands of people milling around in the street; two ammunition dumps were exploding, one at either end of the city, so that you had a skyrocket effect. If you looked down and didn't know, you would think you were looking at a carnival. But we knew what we were looking at.

And I turned to one of my helicopter companions and said, "There they are, the hearts and minds that we won."

I think the end was inevitable. If we *had* given them a decent interval of one or two years after we actually left, the North would still have come in. That's my own personal conviction. It was the manner in which we acted that I think disturbed so many of us who were involved. It wasn't getting out —that was bad enough—but the *way* we got out, the bad faith.

JIM LAURIE

I returned to the U.S. embassy at about eight in the morning on the 30th of April and saw the last U.S. marine helicopter taking off from the roof.

The smell of tear gas was very thick in the air. The marines, in the attempt to make their escape, had been throwing tear gas canisters down the stairwell in a desperate effort to keep the Vietnamese back.

As I came into the embassy, I saw Vietnamese clambering all through the compound, clambering into the embassy building. Many had reached the top of the embassy and were on the helicopter pad. They were waiting for more American helicopters to come and pick them up. However, we had seen the last chopper leave.

At that point, the mood of the crowd seemed to change from one of expectation to one of vengefulness. The people—and there were thousands—started to go through the embassy, floor by floor, looting everything they could find. Photographs of President Ford were dragged from the building. The American flag was dragged from the building and lit on fire right in front of the embassy.

I was standing there long after the last helicopter had left, and now some Vietnamese rushed up to me and showed me their ID cards, ID cards that had been given to them years before by the U.S. government. They had been U.S. government employees, or they had worked for the U.S. army in the PX or in restaurants or somewhere, and each and every one of them thought that these ID cards entitled them to get out of the country.

Two hours after the last American choppers left the embassy roof, a column of Communist tanks rolled into the grounds of the presidential palace, occupied by the latest—and last—leader of independent South Vietnam, Duong Van Minh.

BUI TIN
Editor, North Vietnamese newspaper, *The People*
1975: North Vietnamese army colonel, deputy editor of NVA newspaper

We accompanied the first tanks to enter the palace grounds, and I saw that twenty-four people of the puppet government had assembled in a large reception room. When I stepped into the room, I was introduced as a high-ranking officer of the liberation army who had come to meet with them. And they all stood up when I got into the room.

Then Duong Van Minh clasped his hands to greet me and said, "We have been waiting for you gentlemen since early morning to turn over governmental authority."

I said right away, "There is no issue of turning over governmental authority. Your administration has completely collapsed in the general uprising and general offensive. There is only the issue of surrendering. One cannot hand over something that he does not have."

At that moment, all of them became extremely sad.

In the final accounting of America's two-decade episode in Vietnam, most of the footnotes are sad ones. In the Communists' advance to Saigon, which they renamed Ho Chi Minh City, they swept up $5 billion in American military equipment. Only about 30 percent of the U.S. embassy employees got out. "We could never have taken them all out," according to Alan Carter. "But 30 percent could have been 50 percent, or 55 percent."

The United States would have a chance to redeem that painful memory. In the following years, many thousands of Vietnamese made their own way out of the country, mostly at great risk and in hardship, traveling to safety by boat. At least 125,000 of these refugees were given sanctuary in the United States.

The Communist victory in Saigon had horrifying echoes in neighboring Cambodia. As the North Vietnamese were advancing on Saigon, their allies, the Khmer Rouge, seized control of the government in Phnom Penh under the leadership of a Maoist general named Pol Pot. There ensued one of the most barbaric episodes in recent history as the revolutionaries sought to destroy the old order in one swift wave of violence.

In scenes recalling China's catastrophic Cultural Revolution, much of the urban population was literally stampeded out of the overcrowded cities to new villages in the collectivized countryside —driven by armed squads of Khmer Rouge in an orgy of killings and beatings that had no purpose beyond demonstrating the new regime's authority. Brutal executions were staged in public. Well over a million people—perhaps one-fifth of the population—were murdered or died of hardship in the forced exodus to the countryside during Cambodia's two-year transition into the People's Republic of Kampuchea.

The Khmer holocaust happened too far from America to stir deep emotions, and it happened in an area that American history had now left behind. But the event was not without its impact in parts of the world inhabited by enthusiasts of the revolution from the left. There—at least among some individuals—it had the kind of effect on this generation of the left that Stalin's purges had in the 1930s and Hungary in the 1950s. It was the great disenchantment.

BERNARD-HENRI LÉVY

The Khmer Rouge had pushed the revolutionary process as far as it could be pushed. They had emptied the cities. They had destroyed the difference between individual and manual tasks. So we discovered that the most genuine revolution in the world was the most horrible black bloodbath in the world, too. We had pure revolution producing pure barbarity.

In the following decade, the situation in Southeast Asia was to undergo a kind of crazy fragmentation, as unified Vietnam—still the most restless force in the region—occupied Kampuchea, displacing the Khmer Rouge government, and China briefly invaded Vietnam. The new leftist regime in Phnom Penh was supported by Hanoi and

Moscow while the United States joined China in recognizing the radical Marxist, Pol Pot.

Irony? Anomaly? Paradox of détente? The new reality in Southeast Asia was all those things, but after the shattering conclusion to two decades of American effort in the region, there was still vast disagreement about the meaning of the costly experience. Experts who approached Vietnam from the same vantage point sometimes came away with opposite lessons.

"Those who opposed the war," says Dean Rusk, "can now see in South Vietnam, in Cambodia, in Laos a pretty clear picture of what we were trying to prevent. And I regret the outcome of that struggle more than I can say."

The premise of American intervention, his colleague in the Johnson cabinet, Clark Clifford, points out, was the threat of a takeover by Russia and China. "If that [threat] had existed, then after our withdrawal they would have gone ahead and engulfed that whole part of the world. That didn't take place at all. Laos is perfectly all right. Burma is perfectly all right. Cambodia and Vietnam are in that age-old problem that they're always in. So what has happened ever since the end of the war there clearly confirms that we made a miscalculation to go in there at all."

Yet there was one lesson that did seem unarguable. What Vietnam had demonstrated beyond disagreement was the limits to America's power. Even if the destructive force of the American arsenal was, to all intents and purposes, boundless, then there were restraints of politics, economics, morality, public opinion that in the end could prove just as effective as military weapons.

Five days before the fall of Saigon, Col. Harry Summers was in Hanoi as a U.S. military cease-fire negotiator, and he remarked to his North Vietnamese counterpart, "You know, you never beat us on a battlefield."

The Communist colonel thought it over for a moment. "That may be so," he conceded, "but it's also irrelevant."

The military postmortem went on. The revolution, Summers declared, was not all-powerful or inexorable—"we could have destroyed North Vietnam any time we wanted to with nuclear weapons."

"We knew you had that capability," said the Vietnamese. "We also knew you'd never use it."

Jack Kennedy may have been telling the truth as he saw it when he

said the United States was willing to go anywhere in the world—
"support any friend, oppose any foe"—in defense of liberty. But that
would be less true after the mid-seventies.

And Lyndon Johnson may have been accurate in his time in believing, as he said, that the world belonged to just two nuclear superpowers. But that, too, would be challenged—by economic,
political, and religious forces—in the post-Vietnam, post-Watergate
world.

President Kennedy sought guidance from his predecessor, General Eisenhower, in meeting at Camp David after 1961 Bay of Pigs fiasco. *(AP/Wide World Photos)*

Summit sidelight: Vienna meeting with Khrushchev (left) in 1961 was a diplomatic trial for new President John F. Kennedy but a social triumph for his wife, Jacqueline. *(UPI/Bettmann Newsphotos)*

A woman in East Berlin (background, facing camera) and her daughter in the West are still able to make contact through a chink in the Communist wall, erected only days before, in August 1961. The barrier was soon heightened and sealed. *(UPI/ Bettmann Newsphotos)*

Somber moment during the Cuban missile crisis of 1962. Clockwise, from left, President Kennedy, Secretary of State Dean Rusk, presidential press secretary Pierre Salinger (background), Defense Secretary Robert McNamara. *(John F. Kennedy Library)*

Berlin wall, blocking escape route to the West, was a two-year-old landmark when Kennedy visited the city in June 1963. *(AP/Wide World Photos)*

Death of John F. Kennedy—the lost commander symbolized in military funeral by riderless horse at lower right—interrupted détente process initiated by JFK and Khrushchev. *(UPI/Bettmann Newsphotos)*

Pondering foreign policy. President Johnson (right), with Secretary of State Rusk (center), and national security advisor Walt W. Rostow at a moment in 1966 when internal political situation in South Vietnam was a matter of deep concern. *(Okamoto Photos/Lyndon Baines Johnson Library)*

On 1966 visit to Vietnam, President Johnson visits wounded GIs. At left, the U.S. military commander in Vietnam, General William C. Westmoreland. *(Lyndon Baines Johnson Library)*

An impromptu 1967 summit meeting in Glassboro, New Jersey. Soviet Prime Minister Kosygin brought LBJ conciliatory message from Communist leadership of North Vietnam. But follow-up peace efforts came up empty. *(Lyndon Baines Johnson Library)*

Egyptians on banks of Suez Canal shake their shoes in a derogatory gesture as U.S. navy aircraft carrier *Intrepid* steams by. Gesture expresses displeasure at American support of Israel in crisis that led, only days later, to outbreak of the Six-Day War in 1967. *(UPI/Bettmann Newsphotos)*

Americans in Vietnam, 1967. *(UPI/Bettmann Newsphotos)*

Antiwar demonstrators confronted military police with "flower power" in 1967 march on the Pentagon. *(Bernie Boston)*

Execution of a Viet Cong guerrilla, captured in Saigon during Communists' 1968 Tet offensive, was carried out on the spot by South Vietnam's national police chief, Brig. Gen. Nguyen Ngoc Loan. *(AP/Wide World Photos)*

Alone in the White House Cabinet Room, Lyndon Johnson gives in to fatigue. At this point in the summer of 1968, U.S. bombing halt in Vietnam seemed to be producing no results, and Communist forces were reportedly building up for a new offensive. *(Jack Kightlinger/ Lyndon Baines Johnson Library)*

In retirement at LBJ ranch in Texas, Lyndon Johnson let his hair grow in the style of his young antiwar detractors. *(Frank Wolfe/Lyndon Baines Johnson Library)*

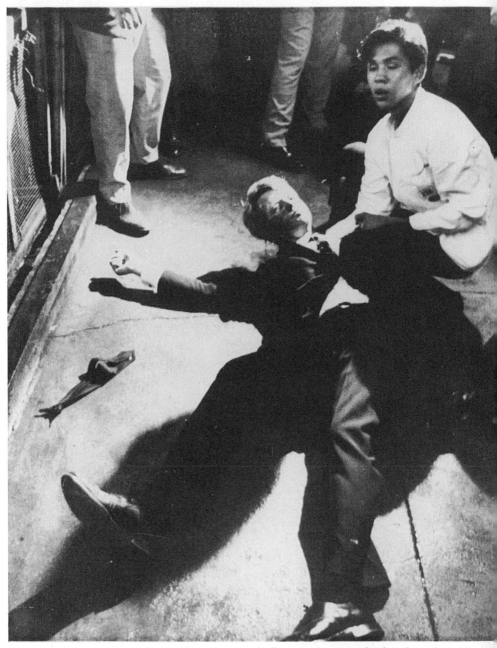

Robert Kennedy dying of an assassin's bullet in a Los Angeles hotel in 1968. He had just completed his campaign for the Democratic presidential nomination as an antiwar candidate. *(AP/Wide World Photos)*

The battle of Chicago: Police and protesters clashed near the site of the 1968 Democratic National Convention. Democrats' Vietnam war policies were the demonstrators' main target. *(UPI/Bettmann Newsphotos)*

After the Prague spring: Graffiti on a fence in Prague equates the Soviet (CCCP) occupation of Czechoslovakia (CSSR) with American war in Vietnam—and links both with Nazis, symbolized by swastika inside star. In background: a Soviet soldier on gun mount—part of the force that moved in when Czechs instituted liberal reforms in the spring of 1968. *(UPI/Bettmann Newsphotos)*

Jungle war: After a firefight with Viet Cong guerrillas, a GI guides a medical evacuation helicopter into a jungle clearing to remove the casualties. *(AP/Wide World Photos)*

Tragedy on Kent State campus occurred when Ohio National Guard opened fire on students protesting extension of Vietnam War into Cambodia in the spring of 1970. Student waving flag, Alan Canfora—struck as he was photographed—was among 13 wounded. Four students were killed. *(John Paul Filo)*

A South Vietnamese mother and her children wade to safety in flight from their bombed village during 1965 fighting. *(UPI/Bettmann Newsphotos)*

Horrors of war in Vietnam were symbolized by 8-year-old napalm victim, Kim Phuc. She had ripped off her burning clothes in flight from accidental bombing near her village school. INSET: Kim Phuc as a college student in 1984. *(AP/ Wide World Photos)*

Nixon's host on historic 1972 trip to China was Premier Zhou En-lai (left). Joining them at elaborate lunch in Shanghai was regional Communist party leader Chang Chun-chiao. *(UPI/Bettmann Newsphotos)*

On the verge of a Vietnam truce agreement, U.S. representative Henry Kissinger and North Vietnam's negotiator Le Duc Tho emerge from a session in Paris, in January 1973. *(UPI/Bettmann Newsphotos)*

Homecoming from Vietnam. This jubilant family reunion was one of the personal sequels to the Vietnam truce of 1973. Lt. Col. Robert Stirm, greeted here by his wife and children at Travis Air Force Base in California, had spent five years in a North Vietnam prison camp. *(AP/Wide World Photos)*

At ease at the summit: President Nixon and Soviet leader Brezhnev developed close working relationship in pursuit of détente. They are shown here in 1973 at the President's home in San Clemente, California. *(AP/Wide World Photos)*

The flight from Vietnam: Crowd fights for space aboard an overloaded American plane departing from an airstrip in South Vietnam as Communist armies advance on Saigon in April 1975. *(UPI/Bettmann Newsphotos)*

·PART IV·

DECADE OF DISILLUSIONMENT
Iran to Iceland

1976-86

·22·

AMERICAN MYTH
MEETS NEW REALITIES

The United States had emerged from the double disaster of Vietnam and Watergate like a movie star coming out of a car crash—with an understandable concern about the damage to its looks.

For three decades following the Second World War, Uncle Sam had kept a semblance of order in the world by projecting a towering image of leadership—moral, economic, military. It was that aura defined by James Callaghan, Britain's prime minister in the mid-seventies: that illusion of "America's superior wisdom and omnipotence—its capacity to do what it said it wanted to do."

No nation could have lived up to that myth indefinitely; history would have caught up with it sooner or later. The misadventures in Indochina and at home were tragic and costly, but they didn't destroy the American image; they merely cut it down to a more realistic size. Even the Kremlin recognized that "the United States is still the United States."

But to a nation grown accustomed to almost unlimited power—or the illusion of it—reality wasn't good enough. Americans were reluctant to give up their national myth, and the nation's leaders helped keep it alive for its irresistible political value. A substantial segment of the American public seemed to require constant reassurance, like fans at a ball game, that "we're number one!"

Nixon reassured them, in the face of imminent failure in Vietnam, by his muscular actions against Cambodia. The United States, he said (invoking that traditional image of an outsize Uncle Sam), would not acquiesce to the threat from Cambodia like some "pitiful, helpless giant."

His successor, Gerald Ford, used a relatively minor challenge to demonstrate that American military might was alive and well.

The two Presidents who led the country in the decade after the fall of Saigon both tried to reinflate the American image—Jimmy Carter by reclaiming America's moral leadership and Ronald Reagan by turning back the pages of history to an earlier era of cold-war confrontations.

The Mayaguez *Incident*

Ford's challenge came in May 1975, only weeks after the last helicopters cleared the rooftop pad of the Saigon embassy.

An American ship, the *Mayaguez,* was seized in the Gulf of Siam by the new revolutionary government of Cambodia. The crew was interned.

The last time the United States flag had suffered that kind of indignity was in 1968, when the U.S.S. *Pueblo* was captured by North Korea. It had taken ten months of negotiation to free Captain Lloyd Bucher and his crew. The American public found that demeaning and infuriating.

The *Pueblo* was an electronic spy ship, while the *Mayaguez* was merely a merchant vessel, carrying a cargo of commercial and military goods from Hong Kong to Thailand. And in the wake of recent American setbacks, the Ford administration decided that this time Uncle Sam would draw first and negotiate later.

Within a matter of days, a 1,100-man marine force was airlifted to a base in the neighboring country of Thailand; from there, it was immediately launched into battle. In a brief, furious engagement, the *Mayaguez* and its thirty-nine-man crew were freed at a cost of thirty-eight American lives—fifteen killed in battle, twenty-three in a helicopter crash.

Later there was some evidence the Cambodians had been on the verge of releasing the captives without a fight. If true, it gave the White House no second thoughts about the speedy, drastic course of action it had taken.

"That incident," Gerald Ford maintains, "was a shot in the arm to American morale at home and at the same time was certainly a warning to our enemies and a reassurance to our allies." The international niceties were taken care of by a routine apology to the Thai government for the unauthorized military use of its territory.

The *Mayaguez* incident was only a mild foretaste of life in a world that showed little respect for either military might or moral authority and less for the rules of civilized behavior. In the next ten years, the challenges continued and the decisions only got tougher. It was not just because the image of American power had shrunk but because the realities of power were also changing.

The nuclear edge which the United States had held for three decades was definitely gone. And now Americans could also feel the economic underpinnings of power shifting and buckling beneath them.

Room at the Top

The United States had had plenty of time to get used to the idea that nuclear supremacy, unlike diamonds, was not forever. There had been stirrings of alarm ever since the Sputnik phenomenon of the late fifties and its offshoot, the alleged missile gap. As the Kennedy administration quickly discovered, that was a false alarm. Even in 1972, Nixon may have been overanticipating when he assumed in heading for the Moscow summit that the Soviet Union by then had achieved nuclear parity. Some Russian sources insist it didn't actually happen until the late 1970s or even the early 1980s.

Whenever it happened, it was no surprise. The Soviet Union was known to be building up its nuclear stockpile. Sooner or later it would match America in overall destructive power.

On the other hand, the idea of a challenge to the American economy, that colossus of the postwar world, was so startling that it was harder to grasp. So were its cold-war implications. For the economic pressure wasn't coming from the Eastern bloc. If anything, the Communist system was being left further behind in that branch of the global competition.

Number Two

When it comes to sizing up the Soviet Union, the veteran British diplomat Sir Frank Roberts is reminded of a nineteenth-century maxim that "Russia is never either as strong or as weak as she looks. In the West, we are always going from one extreme to the other," he observes. "We begin to knock at the knees and think [the Russians] are seven foot six. And then we find they're not. And then we go to the other extreme and say their economy is about to break down tomorrow morning, which it's not."

Clearly, the Soviet economy was not in a state of imminent collapse. Nor was it standing still. The gross national product would approach $2 trillion by the mid-eighties—not much more than half the U.S. figure but still second in the world.

From the brighter, dressier look of the crowds on the streets of Moscow and Leningrad, from the new button-down style of Soviet diplomats and their increasingly well-coiffed wives, from the pictures on Soviet television, it was becoming evident that Russia was no longer just a society of drones in babushkas and rumpled suits, harnessed to a turbine-and-tractor economy. The Soviet Union was finally entering the age of the consumer.

But—the weakness behind Russia's apparent new strength—it was entering at least two decades behind the West and almost that long behind the promise first issued by Nikita Khrushchev. And into this new era the Soviets were bringing all the problems that had traditionally plagued their economy: low productivity, poor quality, perpetual shortages.

A few years into the eighties the Soviet Union would be producing over one million private automobiles a year—more than five times the figure Khrushchev achieved. But it took 25,000 people, including 10,-000 production workers, to turn out 183,000 Moskvitch cars—a number that General Motors could match with only 6,000 employees, of whom 5,500 were production workers.

A change in the overall Soviet diet—more meat, less starchy food—reflected an advance in the standard of living, just at the time affluent Westerners, in the pursuit of fitness, were cutting down on meat and discovering the virtues of carbohydrates.

An American correspondent visiting Moscow in the mid-eighties for the first time in twenty years noted as the biggest difference that "the queues are shorter." The Soviet press continued to be full of reports complaining about the quality of clothes, appliances, housing. A Moscow woman summarized the consumer economy in a single terse sentence: "Nothing fits, nothing works, everything leaks."

In one significant area, the Soviet economy not only failed to advance but moved backward. Historically an exporter of grain, Russia became dependent on the world market as the huge collective farms repeatedly fell short of national targets, sometimes by as much as 25 percent.

RICHARD M. NIXON

There are no examples of success on the part of the Soviet Union any place in the world. Soviet economies simply don't work. Not in America. Not in Cuba. Not in Asia. Our system, with all its faults—I mean that in the broadest sense: free *systems*—do work.

Measured by their own standards, Communist economies were not quite the sweeping failure that this suggests. East Germany—once Khrushchev's Berlin Wall went up and the drain of manpower and currency was stanched—experienced a lesser version of its West German neighbors' "economic miracle." As for Cuba, a U.S. State Department publication notes that "the real standard of living of the Cuban population, particularly the rural folk, has improved markedly since the Revolution and especially since 1970."

But it was certainly true that most governments adopting the Soviet economic model shared in its failures. North Korea lagged far behind the southern half of the country, which developed into a "little Japan." Communist Vietnam distinguished itself by becoming the poorest nation of Southeast Asia.

"Communism as the way to quick and miraculous solutions to society's evils," observed the leader of one of Vietnam's prosperous non-Communist neighbors, Lee Kwan Yew of Singapore, "got a rude debunking from what's happened in Vietnam, Cambodia, and Laos and from its disappointing performance in China. . . . If what it leads to is boat people and refugees, hunger and privation, and war and more war, then it isn't the golden age."

The economic part of that lesson was not lost on some East-Bloc governments. One of the most striking developments of the post-Saigon decade was the loosening up of Communist economies and the introduction of practices that, a decade earlier, would have been considered capitalist heresies.

In China, farmers and factory managers were permitted to sell at market prices whatever goods they produced in excess of their quotas. Family farms were being restored. No fewer than one million state stores and factories were designated to be turned loose to make their own way in the marketplace. China was enthusiastically importing capitalist know-how to set up and manage various new industries. Among the new enterprises was a Maxim's restaurant and a Great Wall Sheraton hotel. The country was showing all the signs of a new consumer spirit. In a society with a penchant for numbering things—"The Eight Principles," "The Four Beards" (Marx, Engels, Lenin, and Stalin)—there was a new arithmetic centering on "The Three Bigs"—refrigerator, TV set, car.

Even in the Soviet Union—too deeply committed by ideology to adopt capitalist measures officially—an increasing share of the economy operated "underground," promoting the development of a small but visible new middle class. Whole state factories were illegally leased and run after hours by private entrepreneurs, some of whom did well enough, making clothes and furniture, for example, to open substantial bank accounts in the West. Whole apartment buildings were put up by private contractors, buying their materials on the black market and hiring workers outside the framework of the (theoretically all-inclusive) central plan.

Perhaps the most successful of all the Communist societies was Hungary, which was thriving on an economy that was 10 to 20 percent private. The government actively promoted the capitalist idea by encouraging individuals to start small firms—businesses with fewer than twenty employees.

ARMAND HAMMER
Chairman of Occidental Petroleum Corporation, New York

The only way socialism works is when it's mixed with a certain amount of capitalism, and I think Hungary is an example. I go there very often, and I meet with Mr. Kadar [Prime Minister Janos Kadar].

Hungary not only feeds itself but exports food, and they have more freedom in Hungary than in any of the other socialist countries. For example, there's no border between Hungary and Austria. Austria is a capitalist country, and Hungarians can go back and forth without visas, without passports. In fact, many of them leave Budapest in the morning, drive to Vienna and have a good meal, see the opera or the ballet, and all come back. Nobody runs away from Hungary.

When I said to Kadar, "You've made a success because you've mixed socialism with private property and incentives—with capitalism," he said, "No, not capitalism. Human nature."

The New Rich

In the new economic reality of the post-1975 period, Communist countries played the role of customers, not challengers. The competitive pressure which the United States was beginning to feel came from within the Western bloc. It was the payoff, beyond all expectations, of America's postwar policy of rebuilding the Western allies and its wartime enemies as a bulwark against the advance of communism.

An observant traveler could have picked up the signals of the new competition from his or her hotel bill or restaurant check. For American tourists, accustomed to cheap luxuries in the world marketplace, experienced a shock of disbelief when they checked into hundred-dollar-a-day hotel rooms in London, Paris, or Frankfurt and paid the tab for two-dollar cups of coffee in Europe's charming little cafés. And when the tourists flew home, they went through U.S. customs empty-handed, untempted by the hundred-dollar sweaters or the five-hundred-dollar briefcases they had been offered in the shop windows of the Continent.

At that time, the alert traveler would have noticed, the European scene was taking on the prosperous, dynamic look that Americans had long associated with their own country. Along quaint village streets, the traditional little greengrocers, *épiceries,* and *lebensmittel* were being crowded out by lavish new American-style supermarkets. The kitchens of working-class homes were being equipped with dishwashers, just like American tract houses. Europe's cities had acquired traffic jams and parking problems, phenomena once limited to America, the birthplace of the automobile culture. And the cars crowding these European streets were no longer predominantly Fords or apologetic little Volkswagen Beetles or rickety French *deux chevaux;* increasingly, they were sleek, substantial, though still relatively small vehicles being turned out by the millions on the automated assembly lines of companies like Fiat and Peugeot. There was even a sprinkling of the new, fuel-efficient little competitors made—astonishingly—in Japan.

On weekends, the highways were crowded with leisure-bent vacationers and with thriving bourgeois—real-estate developers, mail-order merchandisers, electronics manufacturers—heading for their second homes in the Loire Valley, the Auvergne, or the Bavarian lakes. The newspapers carried columns of ads for condos on the burgeoning resort coasts of Spain. The parking area for private planes at the Stuttgart airport was beginning to look like Tulsa or Fort Worth.

And if Americans could no longer afford to buy in Europe, then Europeans seemed to be busily buying up great chunks of America. Hotels, department-store chains, factories, and farmland passed into foreign ownership at a greater rate than American business was investing abroad.

This unfamiliar panorama reflected facts and figures that were too much for mere economic charts; they announced a new era in world history. Some of its most significant features were these:

• *The United States, for decades the world's biggest and busiest supplier of products to other countries, was gradually being forced over to the other side of the counter, becoming more of a buyer than a seller.*

In 1970 U.S. trade showed a negative balance—imports exceeding exports—for the first time in the twentieth century. For the rest of the decade and into the next, the red ink continued to flow off and on, mostly on. Among the imports were 38 percent of the nation's requirements of oil (in 1960 only half as much came from outside) and amounts ranging from 60 to 90 percent of strategic materials like cobalt, chrome, manganese.

• *American productivity, the very hallmark of the nation's economic superiority, was gradually being matched by competitors.* The value of goods turned out by the average U.S. worker in a single year continued to increase, but at a slower rate than before, a slower rate than in competing countries.

In 1950, it took three German workers to turn out as much as a single American; by 1980, it took only two. In Japan, in that same period, the ratio was cut from seven to one down to two to one.

• *The American economic powerhouse, which produced a staggering 60 percent of the whole world's total of goods and services in the late 1940s, was now turning out just over 20 percent.* That was still a huge proportion of a total that had grown tremendously over the decades. But the reduced figure represented the bottom line in a new world economic order. For America's share was now roughly matched by Western Europe—that is, by the group of ten countries (later twelve) whose economies had been linked, with America's blessings, by coordinated trade and tariff policies as the European Economic Community or Common Market.

By the middle of the 1970s, Europe had replaced America as the world's greatest trading power, the leading exporter of goods.

Europe, not America, stood as the most dynamic economy in the world, its gross product increasing more than twice as fast as America's. Its star performer was West Germany, which had regained its prewar economic status although reduced to two-thirds of its prewar size. But even historically poor countries like Italy, Greece, Portugal, and Spain were sharing in the new wealth.

Overall, the economic power of the free world had burgeoned immensely by the middle of the 1970s, and America's remarkable economic growth was very much a part of it. The great change was this: that America, once pretty much the only player in the poker game, now had to share the table with its allies.

Rise of the Rising Sun

As remarkable as Europe's postwar development was, it was in some ways exceeded by the performance of the former Pacific enemy, Japan. Yes, Japan—that overcrowded little island society, practically devoid of all natural resources, with a historic reputation for producing little but dime-store products—economic trivia.

AKIO MORITA
President and co-founder, Sony Corporation

I was walking down a street in a very hot summer [in Europe, in the early fifties], so I stopped at a small café. I had an ice cream, and a small bamboo umbrella was put on the ice cream, and the waiter said, "This is from your country."

I was very much disappointed that an umbrella represented what we make in Japan. So on seeing this and hearing this, I made up my mind we should change [the image of] "Made in Japan." That's why we decided to make a very high quality product, even a little bit high in price. We thought: *Unless we make a good product which the general public likes, we cannot get a good reputation for made-in-Japan products.*

In '53, we got the first license for transistors, which an American invented. I clearly remember when I signed the patent licensing contract with Western Electric, and the licensing engineer advised me the only thing we could make with a transistor then for consumer use was a hearing aid. "So," he said, "why don't you make hearing aids?" But when I got back to Tokyo we discussed [the advice], and everybody believed that hearing aids could not be big business. So we put all our money in and worked very hard with the scientists and engineers. Finally, we came out with a new transistor which could be used for a radio.

I brought that radio to this country. I visited many dealers, distributors. That time, all these people laughed at me because they said nobody would buy such a small radio. But I believed that you have so many radio stations and all the different programs are always on the air, so why shouldn't everybody have his or her own radio to listen to his favorite program? I think we succeeded to sell a new idea or new concept of the radio.

But we had a big problem [with] our company name: Tokyo Tsushin Kyogo Kabushiki Kaisha. I found no American can pronounce that name correctly.

So that's why we wanted to find [a better] name. Firstly, a name that we thought up and, secondly, the name should be an international [word] and, thirdly, the name should be pronounced the same all over the world.

So we studied many different languages and dictionaries, and we found in Latin *sonus*—"sound"—and the English word "sonny boy."

We thought: *We are a group of sonny boys in the sound business.* We decided to make it short. We created S-O-N-Y.

In those postwar years when Morita and his colleagues were trying to get a foothold in the world market, the Japanese got little encouragement at the governmental level. Takeshi Watanabe, Japan's first diplomatic representative in Washington, remembers being advised by Secretary of State Dulles that Japan ought to concentrate on developing markets in southern Asia because it would never be able to produce anything it could sell to the United States or against American competition in other parts of the world.

But Japan soon began to benefit from a combination of U.S. policies, historical accidents, and native qualities. The democratization process initiated by the occupation proved to have economic blessings. By proscribing military development, the new "peace constitution" freed the country's finances for economic purposes. Land reform lifted Japanese farmers out of serfdom and gave political leaders a constituency for conservative economic policies. It also helped expand the domestic market, giving native industry a broader base than it otherwise would have had. At the same time, by making Japanese agriculture less efficient as a competitor against foreign produce, it forced the country to concentrate on industrial exports.

American military procurement in Japan during the Korean War made up the bulk of the country's exports in the early fifties; it gave the economy a quick boost. The industrious Japanese people—conscious of the need to make up for their lack of raw materials by intensive labor—took it from there, with help from the Tokyo government.

Many important industries like steel, shipbuilding, and banking were initiated by the government and then turned over to private enterprise. The auto industry, emblematic of Japan's success, was another, having been developed by the government before the Second

World War to produce military vehicles. It went private afterwards with continuing government subsidies in the form of benevolent tax programs. The subsidies enabled Japanese companies to underprice their products against world competition.

Japanese businessmen matched government in their creativity. They took lessons from American experts in quality control and, like Sony's Akio Morita, they studied foreign markets assiduously. Meanwhile, their businesses benefited from the labor-management harmony that is part of the tradition of paternalism. That tradition is composed of job security plus benefits like company housing, lunches, and recreation programs, on one side, and employee loyalty and moderate union demands on the other.

Under these conditions, the Japanese economy developed at a rate that American policy makers never foresaw. In the mid-seventies, two decades after Secretary of State Dulles consigned Japan to a purely regional role as a kind of supply shop for southern Asia, the flag of the rising sun was muscling out the stars and stripes in fields that American industry once dominated as if by U.S. patent.

The Japanese were practically monopolizing the American market for TV sets and other kinds of electronic equipment. They were cutting deeply into the domestic sales of American auto manufacturers while replacing Detroit as the world's leading exporter of motor vehicles. Japan was the world's foremost builder of oil tankers and other ships. And Japanese steel was outselling the American product not only in the world market but even in the U.S.A.

Overall, in terms of GNP, Japan by the late seventies had become the world's number-three economic power, well ahead of West Germany and not far behind the Soviet Union.

Strains on the Alliance

The dazzling new economic prowess of Europe and Japan strengthened the Western alliance overall, but inevitably it created tensions among the members. American business reeled with the surprise blow of unaccustomed competition; American workers felt it in the form of disappearing paychecks. Perhaps two million jobs were lost over a ten-year period as whole industries began to slip down the tubes—textiles in the South, electronics in Texas and California, even that historic foundation industry of the U.S. economy, steel.

All these were victims of pressure from high-quality products turned out by lower-paid workers under national policies designed to give their country's exports an edge in the world market.

Those policies became issues between the competing nations. NATO meetings that a decade or two earlier would have revolved around arms, strategy, and defense budgets now took the form of debates over interest rates, beneficial tax structures, and protective tariff levels—all factors affecting the price tags carried by competing exports. While facing the Communists as a bloc in the cold war, the Western Allies fought "auto wars," "pasta wars," even "chicken wars" among themselves.

A Japanese financial expert explained the frustrations of American leaders in the eighties with a reminder of the problem his own country faced in the fifties and sixties: "At that time, the U.S. was a very good poker player in the world trade game. Every time we played, the Americans got all the chips. It would have been very hard to continue that game unless they redistributed [the pot]. But now the situation is reversed—the Japanese are getting all the chips."

He chuckled—an expression of empathy mixed with satisfaction.

The dynamics of competition—the thrust toward new markets and new sources of raw materials—drove the Western nations into economic ties with the East. Nixon's détente policy had spurred new trade agreements between the United States and Russia; American grain and farm machinery were being exported to the East in substantial amounts.

But Western Europe was geographically closer to the Communist countries and had a prewar history of trade with them. In the seventies it began to flow again at a modest but increasing rate—a significant economic penetration of the Iron Curtain.

Fiat of Italy built an auto plant for the Soviets and sold them earthmoving equipment. The French built chemical plants and sold computer hardware. German engineers got a $13.3-billion contract for a 1,500-mile pipeline to carry natural gas from the Soviet fields in the Caucasus through the Iron Curtain and into Western Europe.

Clearly, the cold-war relationships were becoming more intimate, more complicated. In the 1960s a summit meeting meant a consultation of Soviet and American leaders. In the seventies, Chancellor Helmut Schmidt of West Germany and French President Valéry Giscard d'Estaing began having independent summit meetings of their own with Soviet leaders.

The Oil Weapon

Increased economic power had the curious effect of making the Western alliance more vulnerable. For the engines of its high-tech economies were devourers of energy. They ran on oil. In the strategic world scheme of the 1975–85 period, oil was a weapon—ultimately perhaps less powerful than nuclear bombs but certainly more manipulable.

The weapon lay in the hands of the Arab countries of the Middle East, which together accounted for about one-fourth of the world's production. The weapon was pointed straight at the West. The United States had its own reserves to fall back on in a crunch, but the other Western Allies were practically defenseless. The one exception, Britain, was just starting to tap the difficult, limited North Sea fields in the early seventies.

The Communist bloc, on the other hand, was relatively immune to pressure. The Soviet Union's production, slightly larger than the Arabs', was more than adequate for the less advanced economies of Russia and its satellites. The Arabs were in a position to blackmail the West; with the right connections in the Middle East, Moscow would be able to use Arab oil for the same purpose.

The possibilities of the situation had emerged with startling clarity one day in October 1973. It was the day the Nixon administration began to airlift emergency aid to Israel, beleaguered by advancing Arab armies in the Yom Kippur War.

Calling on the NATO allies to join in the emergency effort, Washington was rebuffed by every country except the Netherlands. The allies even refused permission to fly war matériel over their territory, delaying emergency aid to Israel by four precious days. The European nations felt they simply couldn't afford to alienate their oil suppliers.

Almost instantly, the United States felt the first blow of the oil weapon. The Arab nations imposed an embargo against oil exports to the U.S. (the Dutch, for their pains, suffered the same penalty) and vowed to reduce their output 5 percent a month until Israel surrendered its 1967 conquests. OPEC, the Organization of Petroleum Exporting Countries—a cartel of governments put together by America's own protégé, the Shah of Iran—seized upon the shortage artificially created by its own members to start raising the price of crude oil. It began with a steep increase of 70 percent.

These measures threw America's auto-oriented society into a panicky skid. Overnight, the tradition of cheap gasoline ended in America as prices at the pump took off from the standard 30 cents a gallon and kept climbing. Soon they were double that figure—higher when and where gas station operators thought they could get it. The lines of cars waiting to get at their pumps—sometimes a mile or two long in metropolitan areas—told them they could. The oil companies raised the pressure still further by manipulating supplies to the retailers, claiming shortages where, from later evidence, none yet existed.

A New Jersey gas station owner recalls the frenzied mood of the public in tones of disbelief: "Gasoline became the most important thing in their lives. They were sitting here from three, four o'clock in the morning, waiting for us to open the station at five. They were anxious, they were irritable. [There were] fist fights, arguments often. There were offers made of booze, favors by women—which I didn't take advantage of."

The panic abated only after a year, when it became evident that the supply of petroleum products was not about to dry up. But there were penetrating, lasting effects on the economy. For one thing, the American public began looking with increasing favor on the small, fuel-saving Japanese cars. That kicked Detroit's problem of foreign competition into a higher gear.

Even more significantly, the jolt of high oil prices—affecting practically everything from crop fertilizers and plastics (and, therefore, food and its wrappings) to household heating bills and industrial kilowatt-age—speeded the upward spiral of inflation that had been launched by spending for the Vietnam War. High-priced American exports took a further beating in the world market. The dollar declined. Interest rates soared, and the lagging growth rate of the economy slumped still further.

The world economy suffered even heavier blows. Countries that had little or no oil of their own had to pay a heavy price to keep their economies humming. Some third-world countries had to borrow heavily to keep up the flow of the imports they lived on—borrowing at inflated interest rates in order to meet the inflated prices. Argentina, Brazil, Mexico, and the developing countries of Africa practically mortgaged their economies. Panama wound up so heavily saddled with foreign debt that it took 74 cents out of every dollar the country produced just to pay it off.

These dramatic effects had not yet begun to unfold when, at the beginning of the 1975 oil crisis, the British Labour party's leading expert on defense and finance, Denis Healey, pronounced it a watershed event. "For the rest of the century," he told an American visitor over a glass in his tiny office in the House of Commons, "world events will be shaped not by military factors but by economic pressures, especially by the Common Market's need for energy."

Like most such forecasts, that one proved too sweeping to be entirely true. But there was no question that through the rest of the 1970s and into the 1980s, when the United States strained to exercise its considerable military power, it found itself looking into the muzzle of the oil weapon.

It was a period that began with an effort toward moral leadership but gradually yielded to disillusionment.

·23·

CARTER'S WAY

One of the purely domestic results of Watergate was a law that re-formed the traditional system of financing presidential election campaigns. Essentially, it replaced large individual and corporate contributions, the candidates' traditional source of funds, legitimate and shady, with rather generous federal grants. The basic idea was to break the grip that party leaders and their "fat cats" exercised on the voters' choices of candidates—another example of the antiestablishment spirit of the times. The new system of campaign financing would open up the party primaries to utter outsiders.

To dramatize the situation with an extreme example, a 1975 network TV documentary showed the declaration of candidacy by a mild, youngish (fifty-one) southern Democrat with no experience in national politics, no recognition outside his own state of Georgia, where he had served as governor—and so, presumably, no possible chance of winning his party's nomination. His name was James Earl Carter, Jr.

The next year Jimmy Carter was elected President of the United States.

His victory represented a rejection of the imperial presidency exemplified by Johnson and Nixon. It was the perfect expression of the accumulated distrust of the political establishment—of strong centralized authority administered by professional politicians with their suspect methods and their dubious values.

Jimmy Carter personified visible, understandable government—even a kind of *anti*government—operated on the basis of homey vir-

274

tues. It was a spirit expressed in his folksy personal style—the insistence on the nickname by which he always introduced himself to American voters and foreign heads of state alike; the cardigan sweaters he wore for television interviews and FDR-style fireside chats; his liberal, socially oriented form of born-again Christian faith, which coincided with the widespread revival of religious belief in various forms—not only charismatic Christianity but also Jewish Orthodoxy, offbeat sects like Sun Myung Moon's Unification Church, and quasi-religious cults like Scientology.

The new spirit was embodied in policies that renounced the cold-war values under which the nation had conducted its international affairs for three decades. From now on, the Carter administration assured the American public and the world, the military and strategic complexities cherished by professional diplomats and policy makers would be subordinated to simple human concerns.

In May 1977, President Jimmy Carter declared, "We are now free of that inordinate fear of communism which once led us to embrace any dictator who joined us in that fear."

JIMMY CARTER

In that speech, which was my first major speech as President, I was trying to show that our foreign policy ought to have a positive, confident, and—if you'll excuse the expression—a moral basis.

And so the thrust of the speech was human rights, and I wanted the American people to understand that I, as their President, would no longer predicate what we decided on hundreds of issues on an inordinate fear or concern about the Soviet Union. That we would approach the Soviet Union with a hand of friendship but also a hand of supreme confidence. That our own system of government in a peaceful competition would prevail because we had all the advantages on our side, in my judgment.

The corollary of that policy was a deemphasis on America's relationship to the Soviet Union and a greater stress on other areas of the world, where the United States proposed to reestablish its leadership by moral example instead of sheer power.

The Moral Weapon

Setting a good example was no easy burden in an imperfect, power-driven world. The nation's own instincts of pride and self-preservation were often at war with the desire to do right, and these instincts were subject to manipulation for political purposes.

When the administration proposed to end a historic complaint against Yankee imperialism in the hemisphere by giving up control of the Panama Canal, the resistance in Congress summoned up images of the Alamo and Bunker Hill. The waterway was a heart-warming memento of American power in a time and place when it was expanding without challenge. To surrender it now would be a painful retreat, as some expressed it, in the face of a Communist threat to American military and economic interests. The canal, after all, was within bomber range from Cuba.

That argument begged the question.

The Panama Canal was obsolescent, a strategic dinosaur. It was too narrow for the big nuclear-powered aircraft carriers that were the nucleus of the modern fleet or for the mammoth supertankers of the oil era. And it wouldn't take a Cuban bomber to put the locks out of commission—one grenade in the hands of a saboteur could do the job.

The canal had been cut through the narrow isthmus by American engineers in the Teddy Roosevelt era, early in the century, under a treaty imposed on the infant republic of Panama by force. The document, giving the United States virtual sovereignty over the canal and the surrounding canal zone "in perpetuity," was an affront to Panamanian independence, a focus of deep emotion shared throughout Latin America, and the subject of serious negotiations since the 1960s.

As the issue moved toward a climax, President Carter observed, the Panamanian people "were as obsessed with those negotiations as we were with the hearings on Watergate."

Against the warning din of opposition on Capitol Hill, President Carter brought the negotiations to a climax by signing a new treaty with Panama's president, General Omar Torrijos Herrera, in September 1977. It remanded the canal to Panama as of the last day of the century—though an amendment insisted on by Senate critics as the price of ratification gave the U.S. the right to use military force, if necessary, to reopen the canal if it should become obstructed.

The world being as complex as it is, even Carter's benevolent act of signing the treaty involved a degree of moral compromise.

JIMMY CARTER

Torrijos was a tough leader of Panama. Many people called him, in the unfortunate debates of the Panama Canal treaty, a tinhorn dictator. But I had a great admiration for him. He was like a sergeant who had been promoted to president. He loved his country; he was very courageous personally.

When we assembled with the representatives from twenty-one nations in Washington to sign the Panama Canal treaty, President Torrijos and his wife and Rosalynn and I were in a little private anteroom getting ready to march on the stage to sign the treaty. And as he began to move toward the stage, he stopped, turned around, burst into tears, put his head on his wife's shoulder, and sobbed for a minute or two. He finally got himself composed, and he turned around to me, quite embarrassed, and said, "Mr. President, this means so much to me I couldn't control myself." He said this in Spanish. Rosalynn and I speak enough Spanish to communicate.

Later, when we had finally gotten the treaty ratified after the most difficult political battle of my life, I went down to Panama to exchange the documents, and we had a private breakfast, just Omar Torrijos and I and the interpreter there. And he said, "What can I do for you?" And I said, "I would like to see Panama be a democracy."

And he said, "In my lifetime you will see a democracy in Panama." And I said, "With free elections?" He said, "With free elections."

And he kept his promise.

In the Carter administration's effort to redefine the global competition, human rights were the expressed value, and U.S. aid became the moral equivalent of Arab oil. But human-rights criteria were hard to apply to foreign policy. As Leslie Gelb of the Carter State Department recalls the persistent dilemma: "If a country such as the Philippines was mistreating its citizens, did that mean we should reduce its aid from $50 million in military credits to 43? Or 20? How does one balance that off against our need to maintain naval bases in the Philippines?"

Officials appointed by the President to enforce the human rights policy found themselves in conflict with State Department officials.

PATRICIA M. DERIAN
Human-rights advocate
1977: Assistant secretary of state
for human rights and humanitarian affairs

There were a few people who just thought it was a damn-fool idea and really goofed up foreign policy, that diplomacy really had two main interests, military and commercial, and that was hard enough. And you certainly shouldn't be worried about what a government [did] to its own citizens. That was their business.

When you want to pay somebody off in a hurry because you want a base or you want your communications to run through their place or whatever, you really want it, you want it now, and, by George, you don't want to be bothered with trifles! So pulling the human-rights seat up to the table was sometimes a struggle.

In the beginning, there was a lot of denial about human-rights problems in Argentina and everywhere. The Latin American Bureau [of the State Department] position was essentially: they had a terrible problem with terrorists and guerrillas and they are only doing, as a government, what they are obliged to do—there's a reason for torture, summary execution, all those naked bodies stuffed in garbage cans, disappearances, the whole ghastly thing.

So the bureau came to me after I'd been at the department a very short time and suggested that I go to Argentina. Without telling me that they thought that if I went there and talked to these reasonable killers and torturers, that then I'd lay off.

Well, I met with Videla [Lieut. Gen. Jorge Rafael Videla], who was the head of the army and the so-called president of the country, and with Manserra [Adm. Emilio Manserra], who was head of the navy. We met at a place called the Navy Mechanical School, which was a site of ghastly tortures in Buenos Aires. He [Manserra] said, "No, no, no—that's what the Communists will tell you!" And I said, "You know, I've seen a floor plan of the floor below us, where people are tortured. I could probably describe the equipment and what goes on. In fact, as we're sitting here, there are probably people being tortured now." And this enormous grin swept over his face.

I had with me a [State Department] officer who was an opponent of the human-rights policy. And it was a chilling moment, and it was obviously a horribly affecting one for him, because he really did look as though he's been electrified. It was a case where they denied it in the beginning and finally admitted everything. And said, "So what?"

When I went to El Salvador, when General Romero was the head of their government, we had a very exclusive talk about human-rights violations—people getting their heads cut off with knives and their thumbs tied together and state terror being practiced. And it was a very long talk. Several hours. At the end of it, he leaned back in his chair and shook his head and said,

"It's a good thing they send a woman to talk about things like this. Men's voices are much too harsh!"

It was not any kind of a compliment. Nobody was prepared to have someone look them in the eye across the table in an official way and say, "Because of these practices of your government, our government is not going to do the following things."

ANDREW YOUNG
Mayor of Atlanta, civil-rights advocate
1977–79: U.S. ambassador to the UN

I remember the ambassador from a Latin American dictatorship coming to me privately, saying, "President Carter has to keep the pressure on. It makes our governments uncomfortable, but it makes all the people of the world love America. And the people will prevail."

And that's one of those [countries] that now does have a civilian government.

The Carter agenda, it soon became apparent, was based on an unrealistic view of the world. The third world, in the comment of a veteran foreign diplomat, "was being exaggerated as a power factor and rather idealized in sentimental terms." The human-rights policy may have had its triumphs in Latin America, but it didn't produce the same results everywhere. In active cold-war arenas it was harder to apply. The threat of a cutoff in aid to the repressive revolutionary government of Ethiopia, for example, produced no result but to drive that African country definitively into the Communist orbit. And no amount of reassuring presidential rhetoric could dispel the looming presence of the Soviet Union.

"In practice," recalls the former State Department insider, Leslie Gelb, "we began to concentrate very quickly on U.S.–Soviet relations just as everybody else had done. Before the first year was up, the pressures of world events, the inevitable competition between us and the Soviets, just washed other issues to the sidelines."

Rediscovering Russia

The Russians appeared receptive to Washington's attention, but they weren't happy about the form it took at first.

GEORGI A. ARBATOV

I think it was made absolutely clear that our government would be ready to deal with the new administration in the most constructive way. Brezhnev even, I would say, went out of his way and made a special speech just to point out the major issues between us and to show the Americans that there was a green light, that we could go on.

But the first thing he [Carter] did to the Soviet Union was to send through the embassy [the U.S. embassy in Moscow], using official channels, a personal letter to one of the Soviet dissidents.

You know, human rights is an issue like motherhood. Everybody is for human rights. We made our revolution for human rights.

We consider it to be tremendously important for human rights [to think about] your homeless, about your unemployed, about your blacks. But we cannot base our governmental policy and our negotiations with your country on the condition that you change your system.

Jimmy Carter's personal letter to the dissident scientist Andrei Sakharov was the first shot in a continuing volley of human-rights fire aimed directly at the Kremlin. Where President Ford, out of concern for détente, had declined to receive the anti-Communist Russian exile writer Aleksandr Solzhenitsyn, one of the early guests of the Carter administration was another dissident, Vladimir Bukovsky. The U.S. embassy in Moscow invited Soviet citizens to a screening of *Doctor Zhivago*, a movie banned in their country. Official protests called attention to arrests and trials of dissidents and to the cases of "refuseniks," Soviet citizens who were denied permission to emigrate. The convictions of two Soviet Jews whose cases had been widely reported in the American press, Aleksandr Ginzburg and Anatoly Shcharansky, were met by the cancellation of high-level official visits. In an attempt to enforce human rights objectives, trade embargoes were imposed on U.S.-built computer hardware and on oil- and gas-exploration equipment bound for the Soviet Union.

The basis of the human-rights pressure on Moscow was the Helsinki Agreement of thirty-five nations, including the Soviet Union and the United States—a treaty that had been years in negotiation and finally signed in 1975, during the Ford administration. While ratifying the postwar boundaries of Europe—in effect, formally renouncing the phantom policy of rollback—that treaty also pledged respect for "fundamental freedoms including freedom of thought, conscience, religion, or belief."

Traditionally, in East-West relations, human rights had been considered a taboo subject, to be handled with the greatest delicacy and often indirectly, like sex among the Victorians. The West German government, for example, in effect was buying the freedom of individuals from across the Iron Curtain by giving East Germany trade and financial concessions in return for easier emigration policies.

HELMUT SCHMIDT
Economist, editor
1974–82: Chancellor of West Germany

Europeans, whether they are French or Italian or British or German or whoever, value the rights of the individual as do you Americans. But we knew we couldn't change the situation, for instance inside the Soviet Union, just by a snap of our fingers.

We didn't wish to get into a propaganda war on top of the hostile situation that we already had had for thirty years.

RICHARD M. NIXON

Lecturing [other nations] on ideology, lecturing them publicly on their internal policies, is a mistake. Privately, you can indicate to them that if they were to adopt a more liberal policy with regard to emigration and so forth that it would be very helpful in other fields. Publicly, lecturing them may make us feel better, but it doesn't do anything for the dissidents.

That is not the way Jimmy Carter saw it. For, in 1978, the Soviets began to ease their restrictive immigration policies. That year 30,000 refuseniks got their exit permits—Jews, Baptists, other religious and political minorities—as against the usual number of 10,000 or 15,000. In 1979, emigration rose to 51,000 before the gates were slammed shut again.

The easing of emigration could have been because the Kremlin simply decided to change its method of dealing with the internal problem of dissidence—by exile instead of imprisonment. But Carter remains convinced that the improvement in the lot of Soviet citizens was at least partly the result of the pressure from Washington.

The Revival and Relapse of SALT II

It may well be that the Kremlin accepted the loss of 81,000 souls as the price of getting something they wanted from the United States— even if it took a little gritting of Soviet teeth to put up with Jimmy Carter's virtuous style. However reluctantly, Moscow recognized that human rights were Jimmy Carter's theme.

"Everybody wants to find a main tune," observes *Izvestia*'s former Washington correspondent, Melor Sturua. "We knew that President Carter had to find the main tune of his administration, and he found human rights like President Reagan found Star Wars."

What the Soviet Union wanted from the United States, perhaps as much as the grain and other trade goods it was now importing regularly, was a military form of détente. There were negotiations in the works on a variety of arms-control measures including a ban on weapons of chemical warfare; an extension of the nuclear test ban to cover underground testing; restrictions on outer-space weapons; and a reduction of conventional forces in Europe. But the main area of negotiations was strategic weapons—essentially the long-range nuclear missiles that Americans and Russians would presumably fire at each other if World War III should break out.

The second Strategic Arms Limitation Treaty (SALT II), about 90 percent negotiated during the Ford administration, stood incomplete, a victim of presidential-year politics. Jerry Ford had felt obliged to back away from it himself in 1976 when, in the words of one observer, "he heard thunder on the right in the form of the campaign of Governor Reagan," his challenger for the Republican nomination. But when Ford—who gained the nomination but was defeated in the election— handed over to Jimmy Carter, he urged the new President to continue negotiating, with the object of getting revised terms that could satisfy the recalcitrant Senate.

Arms control—which would become the headline issue of the cold war in the 1980s, the main test of East-West relations—is a field as full of jargon and special references as professional football. But it doesn't take a knowledge of high-tech weaponry to understand what made it so hard to sell to some elements in American political life.

SALT II as originally negotiated by the Ford administration imposed equal ceilings of 2,400 on the total number of strategic-missile launchers that would be permitted to each side. Not on the missiles themselves, not on the warheads in which they packed their explosive punch, but on the various delivery systems: ICBM silos on land and submarines cruising the seas; long-range aircraft capable of reaching the other side's homeland with a load of nuclear bombs; cruise missiles (which were really a form of "pilotless plane" or "robot bomb," powered by their own engines rather than launched by rocket).

But the ceiling was really a lot higher—the restrictions a lot looser —than it appeared. For the two sides were given leeway to develop some new weapons systems, and over half of each country's stock of missiles could be MIRVs—that is, could be loaded with as many as ten separately aimed warheads, each zeroed in on a different target.

The Soviet preponderance of big MIRV-type land-based ICBMs was a source of worry to many on the American side—never mind that the United States had an edge of its own in other categories. Another worry was that traditional problem of verifying any agreement made with the Russians.

It was in response to these concerns that President Carter launched a personal effort not merely to complete SALT II but to renegotiate its basic terms.

PAUL WARNKE
Washington lawyer, arms-control advocate
1977–78: Chief U.S. SALT negotiator

We were asking them [the Russians] to cut very, very drastically into their land-based large intercontinental missiles without compensating reductions in the areas in which we had the edge. We had more concerns about their ICBMs because they are very large, they can carry more warheads, they are getting increasingly accurate.

What the problem is is that because of the geographic situation of the Soviet Union, the preponderance of their strategic forces is in the large, land-based ICBMs. They've got about 80 percent of their strategic warheads in that force. We have, by contrast, something like 30 percent of ours in the land-based ICBMs and more than half in submarine-launched ballistic missiles.

Now, the Soviet Union does not have the option of going to sea to the extent that we do, because of their geographic situation. They don't have ready access to the ocean. We of course have got these two immense coasts. Not only that, but their submarines are noisier, and they're not able to be at sea anywhere near as much of the time. So that they will continue, in my opinion, to base most of their strategic warheads on land. And we have to recognize that.

Now, they have made major concessions in that regard. They accepted, in [the revisions of] SALT II, lower ceilings on the land-based MIRVed ICBMs. But they won't cut the guts out of their force, and we can't expect that they will.

One of the real problems that we've had in negotiating with the Soviet Union is their preoccupation with secrecy. And it's a preoccupation that predates the Bolshevik Revolution. If you read accounts of people trying to deal with the czars back in the seventeenth, eighteenth, nineteenth centuries, you find that this preoccupation with secrecy is basically a Russian trait.

Now, as a consequence, we had great difficulty getting the Soviet Union to accept something that we thought was quite routine, and that was the exchange of a data base. We wanted a listing by both sides of all relevant categories of strategic weapons. The Soviet Union fought that for years.

And I can remember, finally, when the Soviet side accepted that. It took a trip back to the Soviet Union by Minister [Vladimir] Semenov. And he finally came in to Ralph Earl, who was the deputy head of the delegation, and me and said, "I am now authorized to exchange the data base." And then he said, "You realize that you've just repealed about four hundred years of Russian history." And then he further said, "And maybe that's not a bad idea."

It took two full years of arm wrestling across the negotiating table, but Soviet and American experts finally agreed on revisions of SALT II. It remained only for the national leaders to complete the document and sign it as the central event of a summit meeting in Vienna.

Carter and Brezhnev, like Kennedy and Khrushchev, had been conducting a personal correspondence almost since the beginning of Carter's presidential term. The American leader sometimes wrote his letters in longhand "because," he explains, "I wanted him to know they came directly from me. When I got a reply back from him, it was obviously written by a large committee because the letters quite often expressed just the Soviet line."

In person, at Vienna, Carter found the Soviet leader considerably more sympathetic. It should have been America's turn to play host at a summit on United States territory, but the closer European site was chosen as a concession to Brezhnev's frail health. Carter was moved when, as the two leaders started down a steep flight of stairs after their first meeting, Brezhnev, with no apparent embarrassment, put his hand on Carter's shoulder to steady himself. With the Soviet chief in a position of frank dependency on his younger American counterpart, they went to face the waiting international press.

JIMMY CARTER

I was thoroughly conversant with the details of SALT II, which is one of my characteristics as an engineer often criticized.

As was my custom, I got up quite early every morning; and when I was preparing to meet with a foreign leader of significance to us—Begin or Sadat or Deng Xiaoping or in this case Brezhnev—I had a large globe by the side of the President's desk; and I would try to put myself in the position of that foreign leader and look at the world as Brezhnev must look at the world from the Kremlin.

We look at the world with great confidence. We have a mighty nation, adequate food supplies, a stable government. Our system of government is admired by many other countries. We've got warm oceans on both sides. We've got friendly Canada and friendly Mexico to the north and south.

But if you look at the world from the perspective of the Soviet Union, it looks quite different. Then you can understand why the Soviets are almost paranoid as they look out at frozen oceans and a very limited food supply, at uncertain allies to the west and at a feared enemy, so-called—China— on the southern and eastern border.

So I tried to understand how Brezhnev would look at the SALT II issue and modify my own proposals to accommodate his needs as much as possible.

One thing is that we look on the nuclear arsenal of our potential adversaries, seeing only the Soviets' weapons. From the Soviet side, they look upon the weapons of the United States, the weapons of China, the weapons of Great Britain, and the weapons of France. They see four nuclear nations who are all potential adversaries. So you have to understand that the Soviets' perspective is different than ours.

But even accommodating that difference, I felt that the SALT II terms were highly favorable to our country and not unfavorable to the Soviets.

SALT II was signed by Carter and Brezhnev at the Vienna summit in June 1979. Before the ink was dry, the smearing process began on Capitol Hill. Senate critics in both parties attacked it as an act of "appeasement," the attacks sharpened by the imminence of another presidential election campaign. Political hopefuls were looking for issues to start riding, and the Communist threat was always an effective one.

The President was in no position to mount an effective counterattack. His standing in the public opinion polls was almost as low as Nixon's Watergate level. The public was smarting from the sting of inflation—5 percent in 1976, almost double that rate in '78, rising to 13 percent the next year. To a large degree, it reflected continuing OPEC boosts in oil prices.

The administration seemed powerless to prevent the Arabs' economic insults; in fact, its Middle East policy, benevolent toward Israel, further provoked them. And Carter's energy policy—aimed not at increasing supply but at cutting down consumption by tax and conservation measures—irked the public and hardly did much to enhance his popularity.

Carter's executive style discouraged public confidence. He had a habit of shifting and reversing policy positions; it became as much of a Jimmy Carter trademark as his human-rights evangelism. It reflected an open conflict within the administration, personified by the perpetual tension between a hard-liner, national security adviser Zbigniew Brzezinski, and the secretary of state, Cyrus Vance, who embraced détente and deplored the tendency to emphasize military approaches to cold-war issues.

The President never seemed to seize control of the elements in this conflict but always to be at their mercy. "The core problem inside the Carter administration," as it was defined by one State Department insider, "was that most of the senior officials did not have a clear idea where the President really stood. Our sense was always that Mr. Carter himself had no real ballast inside him."

Carter had arrived in office with an avowed horror of the growing worldwide sales of arms, but foreign military sales reached a new level during his administration. His firm support of Israel was crossed by an anti-Israel vote of the U.S. delegation in the United Nations—from which the administration hastily and confusedly backtracked. UN Ambassador Andrew Young was forced to resign after a conciliatory move toward Israel's sworn enemy, the Palestine Liberation Organization. Carter publicly favored a comprehensive ban on nuclear testing, then switched sides. The administration conducted a long and difficult campaign to persuade the European allies to endorse the development of a controversial new battlefield weapon, the neutron bomb, only to have Carter abandon it himself on the very eve of a NATO meeting at which it was to have been adopted.

Even the absolute value, human rights, proved to be flexible. The repressive governments of Argentina and Ethiopia were penalized; the repressive government of South Korea continued to get U.S. support.

It was as part of this zigzag pattern that President Carter undermined SALT II even in the process of negotiating it.

As opinion polls showed during Carter's first year in office, his efforts to deemphasize the East-West conflict were widely interpreted as evidence of that hereditary sin imputed to Democratic leaders: "softness" toward communism. In attempting to prove his toughness, Carter began to assume a stance that was almost the opposite of his original position. By hyperbolic rhetoric and provocative timing, he not only emphasized the cold-war relationship but dramatized the element of threat even where it did not exist.

"We will match . . . any threatening power. . . . We will not allow any other nation to gain military superiority over us," Carter declared in 1978 at a time when he was trying to get arms-control negotiations on track. And soon after: "The Soviet Union can choose either confrontation or cooperation. The United States is adequately prepared to meet either choice."

In speaking of SALT, he adopted the code words which the opposition used to signify the very impossibility of a trustworthy agreement with Moscow: *"dependable, verifiable"* arms control.

He began to treat "détente" as a dirty word; like Jerry Ford before him, he pointedly stopped using it in public.

The final stage of SALT negotiations with Moscow was postponed at the end of 1978 in favor of a meeting in Washington between Carter and China's Vice-Premier Deng Xiaoping, to normalize relations with Beijing. That action, in January 1979, completed the process begun by Nixon in 1971. Its timing suggested the building of a common defense against the country—the USSR—that Carter was about to make his partner in the arms-control deal.

And before leaving for the Vienna summit, Carter announced that the Pentagon would proceed with the development of a vast, expensive new concept in strategic weapons: the MX mobile missile. Instead of just keeping a missile poised in an underground silo, the MX system would rotate an ICBM among a whole network of launchers, keeping on the move in order to present an elusive target to the enemy's counterforce.

The MX was denounced by the Russians as a violation of the intent, if not the substance, of SALT because it would make verification more difficult. It seemed to put the Carter administration in the same camp with those opponents of SALT who felt that no agreement with the Russians would be trustworthy—you always needed a hedge.

The Russians soon began developing a controversial "hedge" weapon of their own—a new version of the ICBM. Meanwhile, the Kremlin was also doing its usual damage to the prospects of détente by pursuing its policy of supporting "wars of national liberation"—that is, revolutions from the left—in Africa. That was only consistent with the Kremlin's infuriating practice of compartmentalizing its relationships with the West—taking provocative actions in one area while seeking accommodation in another. In all fairness, it was also a practice they seemed willing to tolerate on the part of the United States —as when they met with Nixon at the summit and initiated the process of détente just after the American bombing and mining of the Soviet's ally, North Vietnam.

The *coup de grace* for SALT II's prospects during the Carter administration was a domestic blow, a standard piece of anti-Communist politics. It was delivered on Capitol Hill by a member of the President's own party. That was the disclosure, in the summer of 1979, of the presence of a Soviet brigade in Cuba—a discovery made and trumpeted by Senator Frank Church, a Democrat seeking reelection in Idaho, who was on the defensive because of his liberal record in foreign affairs.

The Soviet unit of about 2,600 men had apparently been on the island for years—presumably a holdover from the Kennedy–Khrushchev era. There was nothing noteworthy about the situation. But once the issue was raised, Carter fell in step with it. As usual, he was so busy covering his rear that he never managed to advance. The administration suspended its pursuit of SALT II ratification in the Senate.

By the time that noise died down, other, more troublesome sounds were heard. They came from events in the Middle East—first in Iran, then Afghanistan. American power and prestige were challenged, and the East-West relationship was violently disrupted. SALT II—a treaty representing the world's most advanced hopes for curbing the threat of mankind's destruction—was soon to be put on the shelf.

·24·

TRIALS IN
THE MIDDLE EAST

When the United States celebrated its two-hundredth anniversary, on the Fourth of July 1976, the year of Jimmy Carter's election, the main event of the bicentennial ceremonies in New York was a procession of majestic, tall-masted sailing ships up the Hudson River. It was more than a birthday salute. Perhaps subconsciously, it was also a nostalgic gesture toward a time before fuel played such a large and consuming role in the life of the nation and its citizens.

By 1976, as part of the American auto-driving public, you would have become accustomed to paying all of 60 cents a gallon for gas. If you were also part of the house-buying public, you would have found that mortgage rates had inched up to 9 percent. Prices everywhere were inexorably on the rise even while the economy itself—as measured by GNP and unemployment—was slowing down. The interlinked economies of the entire Western world were in the same boat —a gas-guzzling powerboat.

The energy problem—essentially, the oil policies of the Arab countries—was at the root of the world's economic concerns. It demanded that governments deal with the continuing instability of the Middle East.

The Camp David Adventure

Since the end of the Yom Kippur War, the United States had managed to exclude the Soviet Union from a significant role in the Middle East. This was done by a combination of strenuous diplomacy

289

and favorable local circumstances. As Nixon's, and then Ford's, secretary of state, Henry Kissinger had plied a busy shuttle between Washington and the Middle Eastern capitals and had succeeded in brokering a disengagement of the two main antagonists, Israel and Egypt. The Egyptian president, Anwar el-Sadat, helped things along —from an American viewpoint—by disengaging himself from his former patron, the Soviet Union. Egypt's resident unit of 20,000 Russian military and technical advisers had been firmly evicted from the country.

The Carter administration took the baton and began pushing for a comprehensive settlement in the Middle East, to include all the conflicting parties—countries whose territory Israel was hanging on to or who were still at war with the Zionist state. Washington even proposed to involve the Soviet Union in a settlement. As sponsor of two Arab governments, Syria and Libya, Moscow remained a potential source of troublemaking as long as it was excluded. The American initiative bogged down almost at once when Israel refused to recognize the Palestine Liberation Organization as the representative of the Palestinian people. The Israelis were determined not to open diplomatic doors to a force openly pledged to Israel's destruction—a policy which the PLO was carrying out by acts of terrorism.

President Carter, in abandoning the effort for a comprehensive settlement, appealed to Sadat to keep the peace momentum going, and the Egyptian leader responded with one of the most dramatic gestures in recent statesmanship. The head of the largest and most dynamic of Arab nations—leader of the forces that had opposed Israel's very existence for three decades and planner of their most recent war of extinction—Sadat flew to Jerusalem one weekend in November 1977 to meet with the head of the Israeli government, the one-time anti-British guerrilla recently elected prime minister: Menachem Begin.

Sadat's overture was so little expected that the Israeli government, hastily making preparations to receive him, had trouble rustling up an Egyptian flag and the music to the Egyptian national anthem.

When, some time the next year, negotiations between the two sides reached a sticking point, Carter stepped in to play the role of moral broker.

As a studious Christian, Carter had a profound interest in the Holy Land. He invited the two leaders, with accompanying advisers, to join him in wrestling with the problem in the quiet of Camp David, the rustic presidential hideaway in the Catoctin Mountains outside Washington. "Some sort of a kibbutz with a lot of trees" was the way it looked to Begin's foreign minister, Ezer Weizman.

Camp David proved to be an extraordinary adventure in personal diplomacy.

For thirteen days, the basic business of the United States was run in Washington by Vice-President Walter F. Mondale, while Jimmy Carter immersed himself in the affairs of two Middle Eastern countries, conducting international relations in an atmosphere that combined the intensity of a religious retreat with the informality of a summer camp.

"We never had had negotiations walking in a forest," observes Sadat's foreign minister, Boutros Ghali. "This was new for people who have spent their lives negotiating around a table and with paper." The sight of the President of the United States riding a bicycle and the experience of having breakfast and lunch every day with people he was accustomed to regarding as antagonists, Ghali recalls, were enough to shake up the professional diplomatic mind-set.

But it was not easy to find common ground between the two Middle Eastern leaders: Sadat, the British-trained career soldier, rawhide-lean and dapper with his impeccable London tailoring . . . and Begin, the underground fighter with his open-collared workingman's style of dress. Sadat was a strategist with a global view, impatient about details; Begin's horizon was Israel, he was a stickler for protocol, and he was, in Carter's description, "obsessed with minutiae, with semantics, with individual words."

On the day the meetings were scheduled to end, with a helicopter ready to lift the participants out of Camp David, Carter still didn't have an agreement.

JIMMY CARTER

We had a deadlock. Begin had rejected one of the major proposals that was crucial to any sort of agreement.

As we prepared to depart from Camp David without any success, he asked me to autograph some photographs of me and him and Sadat for his —Begin's—grandchildren. There were eight of them, I believe. So he sent them over, and I guess he expected me just to write my name on them. But my secretary had gotten the names of all Begin's grandchildren individually, so I took quite a bit of time and personally [inscribed] each name and signed my name to the photographs.

I decided to walk over and give them to him and tell him that I appreciated what we had tried to do and I was sorry we had failed.

I walked up on the porch—he was in his room by himself, also feeling very sad—and he came out and said, "Why did you come to my cabin? I would have come to your cabin." I said, "No, I wanted you to have these photographs."

He took them and started turning around. He glanced down and saw the name of his grandchild, and he turned back to me and said, "Would you come into my cabin, off the porch?"

He looked at each grandchild's name and called the child's name out, and then the next one and the next one. Eight times he did this. And by the time he was finished reading just the names of his grandchildren, his lip was trembling, and he had tears in his eyes. And we began to talk about the future of the world for our grandchildren if we didn't have peace. And we parted. I went back to my cabin.

In about fifteen minutes he sent word over that he had accepted the issue that he had previously rejected, and it was from there that we went on very quickly and concluded the agreement.

In some respects the Camp David accords proved to be less of an agreement than a misunderstanding. The Israelis did not leave the West Bank, the Gaza Strip, or the Golan Heights. Nor was the cause of self-determination advanced for the people of those areas. Begin, in fact, reinforced his government's hold on the disputed territories by building new Israeli settlements.

But the Sadat–Begin agreement, formalized in a 1979 treaty, was the first gesture of real peace in an area at war since 1948. It returned the Sinai to Egypt and opened up civil relations between the two countries that were central to the Middle East problem. Embassies were established; trade began to flow; tourists began to travel by bus across borders that, for several decades, had been closed off like a little Iron Curtain.

ABBA EBAN

The fact is that Camp David was signed with a very lucid knowledge of its limitations. It's a very characteristic theme in diplomacy that each of [the three parties] signed that document with a different thought in mind.

Mr. Begin signed that document saying, "I'm now giving up Sinai in order that I will not give up one single square inch of territory anywhere else."

Sadat signed it saying, "When I've got the Israelis to loosen up on Sinai, I'm going to get them to loosen up on the West Bank and Gaza as well." The United States was rather closer to the Egyptian view—that the Camp David agreement was worth having in itself but would be even more worth having if it became an exemplary beginning for a further process.

Sadat remained hopeful that he could tempt "my friend Begin" into further concessions by the offer of "sweet Nile water" in a joint irrigation project. But a widening opposition within his own government got in the way of those plans.

Camp David remained a kind of unfleshed skeleton of Carter's hopes for the Middle East. Nevertheless, Abba Eban, for one, regards it as "certainly one of the major breakthroughs for international conciliation . . . a sudden eruption of successful and resourceful democracy. The United States got everything right. It was the right thing to do, to see that Egypt was the center of the Arab world, not Syria, not Lebanon, not the Palestinians."

Within a matter of months, the focus of American attention in the Middle East was forcibly shifted to two other countries, where American policy was faced with frustration and American prestige with failure.

Hostages and Partisans

Iran and Afghanistan. Two countries occupying a kind of transitional space on the geopolitical map—the area extending from the borders of the Soviet Union in Central Asia to the oil lands of the Persian Gulf.

Afghanistan, inland, is mostly untamed mountain tribes and untapped mineral resources. Iran, on the Gulf, is petroleum—the world's fifth-biggest producer in 1979 (after the USSR, Saudi Arabia, the U.S., and Iraq).

The two countries share little except a religion, Islam; a border; and exposure to the Soviet Union, the northern neighbor of both. When they burst into the 1979 headlines with unpredictable force—first Iran, then Afghanistan—the events had only a slight connection. But they set up a kind of echo effect in the American psyche, conditioned as it was by decades of cold-war experience and sensitized as it was by the frustration of Vietnam.

Iran, of course, was America's anchor in the Islamic world. The ruling Shah was the creature of the CIA-sponsored coup of 1953. To Americans he remained *"our* Shah," a comfortable anachronism—a figure out of the *Arabian Nights* in a version translated by computer, a Middle Eastern despot with high-tech interests, bent on westernizing his country.

Shah Muhammad Reza Pahlevi was familiar to the American public from his periodic appearances on network television—a man of intense, vulpine good looks; an interest in industrial development, technical education, and modern armaments; and a compelling way of talking about the dreams and visions by which he ruled. With his building program for factories and schools and with $15 billion in purchases of American jet fighters and other up-to-date arms in the mid-seventies, he was prodding his country into a headlong leap from Arab feudalism into the postmodern world. Jimmy Carter toasted him as an "island of stability in the Middle East." His country was used as an electronic observation post for monitoring Soviet missile tests.

It was a shock to United States policy makers when in 1978 the Shah became the object of massive protests in the streets of Teheran and other Iranian cities. In hindsight, Washington's unswerving commitment to the Shah is explained by one foreign service veteran as an example of "lock-in"—the inability of a government to escape its preconceptions even in the face of evidence that things are changing. For —again in hindsight—it seems clear that the very program of westernization which Americans found so reassuring about the Shah was undermining his control of the country, undermining American interests with it.

Iran's vast oil revenues were the basis of a Texas-style development boom which benefited a thin upper crust but did relatively little for the rest of the country. It created a new urban middle class without giving them a political voice in the Majlis, the parliament, which operated under the Shah's repressive control. And it devastated the large rural lower class, whose lives were wrenched out of shape by the elimination of small farms and the dislocation of villages in the forced development of agribusiness.

All except the top echelon suffered from the effects of inflation which came with the boom, and all were affronted by daily examples of corruption and high living. Big new resort-style hotels, big houses with swimming pools, big cars pulling up at expensive restaurants with groups of Iranian wheeler-dealers being entertained by foreign contractors with unlimited plastic to spend—all these standard images of the go-go business style were superimposed on the traditional Islamic scene.

They ran counter to a conservative current that was moving through the Arab world with increasing force. As in the West, a fundamentalist religious movement was stirring. Its main source of strength was in the Muslim sect called Shi'a, which preaches a puritan ethic emphasizing self-denial and martyrdom as the means of entry to a blessed life in the hereafter.

The Shi'ite movement had originated in the seventh century A.D., soon after the death of Islam's founder, the prophet Muhammad. Ever since, there had been periodic local eruptions against the Sunni mainstream. This latest manifestation was spreading like fire through the modern Arab world—a world in which countries import labor to work their oil fields and refineries; in which the faithful make pilgrimages to the holy city of Mecca in passenger-jet planeloads, and oil sheikhs sometimes distribute wealth among their subjects in the form of free TV sets.

Well established in Lebanon, Syria, and Iraq, the Shi'ite faith was also preached to increasing numbers of believers by the *mullahs* (teachers) and *ayatollahs* (priests) of Iran.

"Some people like myself simply did not know that much about the fundamentalist aspects of Islam," confesses Carter's secretary of state, Cyrus Vance. "I think all of us sort of underestimated the ultimate strength that it would have."

The unsuspected power of Islamic fundamentalism was displayed on the streets of Teheran in 1978 in demonstrations demanding the return of an exiled ayatollah, an anti-Shah leader named Ruhollah Khomeini. The Carter administration considered making overtures to Khomeini at his base in Paris but still had hopes for the Shah and was reluctant to do anything that might pull the Persian rug out from under him. By September the Shah held control only by martial law.

As pressure mounted and the repressive tone of Khomeini's program also emerged, national security adviser Zbigniew Brzezinski urged Carter to promote a preemptive takeover by Iran's military. But the President—in Brzezinski's description—"felt that the United States should not interfere to such an extent in the affairs of a sovereign nation."

By January 1979 it was too late to do anything. The Shah, in failing health, was forced into exile. The monarchy was overthrown in favor of a republic avowedly dedicated to Islamic principles and headed by the bearded patriarchal ayatollah.

The new government announced itself with a reign of terror in which more than 8,000 people were executed. The officer corps of the armed forces was purged; political opposition was violently repressed; religious minorities—Muslim sects as well as Christians and Jews—suffered campaigns of vandalism against their cemeteries and places of worship. The puritanical strain of the new regime was expressed in bans against mixed bathing and broadcast music and laws restoring the traditional subservience of Muslim women.

In foreign policy the regime took an explicitly anti-American position, identifying the United States with the Shah and also with Israel as the occupier of territory that was home to the Palestinian Shi'ite brothers.

To many members of one dynamic element in Iranian society—the students—America was also the source of authority that was sometimes humiliating.

MOORHEAD KENNEDY
Educator
1978–79: Economic officer, U.S. embassy in Teheran

Everything they were studying in school—so much of it, anyway—was of American origin. One engineering school in Iran taught in English. Here were the heirs to the world's oldest culture forced to become little Americans in order to succeed in their professions. Part of the revolution against the Shah and the expulsion of America was simply this: "We are not about to become second-class Americans. We are Iranians." And to Americans this is a shock. Because we are the nation that everybody wanted to emigrate to.

In February, a group of anti-American student demonstrators stormed and occupied the United States embassy in Teheran for some hours until an official of the revolutionary government persuaded them to clear out. For months afterwards, the anti-American atmosphere continued to build in Teheran while the Shah moved from country to country seeking sanctuary and medical treatment. The Iranian crowd demanded his return to face revolutionary justice. They also demanded the surrender of his wealth, much of which was presumably invested in the United States.

When, finally, with some reluctance, the United States agreed to admit the Shah as a medical patient, the demonstrations in the streets rose to a fever pitch.

In Washington, at three o'clock on a Sunday morning, November 4, 1979, an officer of the State Department's Middle Eastern bureau got a phone call from the embassy in Teheran (where the time was 10 A.M.) reporting that "Iranian mobs are pouring over the walls, and the embassy is under siege."

The Teheran embassy was not just a building but a kind of American village of twenty-seven acres within a walled compound containing a football field, swimming pool, and tennis courts. The trespassers had no plans beyond another brief, symbolic occupation of the premises. But this time they were encouraged to stay put by the acquiescence of the Khomeini government and by elaborate daily demonstrations that made public heroes of the occupiers—demonstrations that were staged in the streets outside the embassy walls, where they played to the worldwide news media. When the camera crews packed up for the day and the crowd dwindled, the cause was taken up by passing drivers, honking their horns as a signal of support.

Inside the compound, sixty-two Americans were being held hostage to a cause they scarcely understood through circumstances even harder to explain.

MOORHEAD KENNEDY

I sometimes wonder about the institutional framework of our government and what happens to common sense. A marine [who had just arrived] in Teheran was still suffering from jet lag when he went into captivity. Why were people still being sent out there? Why didn't we destroy the files?

A marine was saying—I guess it was the Wednesday before, or Thursday before, the takeover—"Hey, man, we're going to have an Alamo!" A Teheran banker said to me, "For goodness sake, don't quote me by name in your reports because one of these days those students are going to break in and take over your files and I'll be in deep trouble."

On Wednesday before the takeover, I remember saying to an old Teheran hand, "Look, the students are taking over hotels for student dorms, and the government can do nothing about it. If they're taking over hotels and the government's doing nothing, what will they take over next?" And it never occurred to me: I was sort of denying reality to make the next leap.

Even after we had surrendered, after they'd blindfolded us, after they tied my hands and were leading us downstairs, I kept denying it to myself. I had seen that flood approaching the embassy—students with looks of rapture on their faces, which, as I thought about it afterwards—was told by some of them—meant they were hoping the marines would shoot, because they were all psyched up to attain martyrdom and get on the express elevator to paradise. I should have known, but there's some very strong feeling in the human psyche that denies reality. It's what every psychiatrist tells you happens to victims of mugging or rape.

And so, even the first day when the students cracked down on us to assert their authority, we were very unruly. I led people whistling "Rally Round the Flag." I sat blindfolded. I refused to take my shirt, my tie, or jacket off because, after all, you don't take a diplomat hostage—so it must be of very short duration. And thinking: *My gosh, I've got a dinner party tonight. Very chic Iranian hostess. How do I get word to her?*

As hours passed, and then days and weeks, with Kennedy and his fellow diplomats still held captive, State Department officials talked among themselves about some sort of American military action against Iran. An American naval force was sent as far as the Persian Gulf. But as one ranking officer on the State Department's Middle Eastern staff notes: "Applying military force to press a government to make a decision assumes that there's a government there to make a decision. And at Teheran at that time, the Revolutionary Council was not a coherent decision-making body, and we couldn't see that it would respond to the application of punitive force in the way that any constituted government might."

JIMMY CARTER

I could envision the Iranians taking our hostages out one by one and executing one of them every morning at sunrise. So I sent word to Khomeini, "If you put a single American hostage on trial, we will stop all trade and commerce between Iran and the outside world. If you injure or kill a hostage, we will respond with military attacks on your country." We sent this message through the Swiss embassy, which was acting for us, also through the leaders of Great Britain, France, Germany, Italy, and Japan to make sure Khomeini got the word.

The takeover of the embassy had produced two dramatic images, recorded by the omnipresent TV cameras, which became painful logotypes of the event. One was the burning of an American flag by a jubilant group of Iranian students. The other was the procession of

Americans in blindfolds being led in helpless captivity from one of the buildings in the compound. Those scenes seared themselves into the American consciousness.

The next month, December 1979, Washington's sense of threat was heightened when the Soviet air force began landing planeloads of paratroopers in the mountainous country bordering on Iran—the republic of Afghanistan.

Afghanistan is one of those places that used to exist in the Western mind mainly as a setting for Kiplingesque adventure stories about the days of the British raj. Its role in nineteenth-century history was as a buffer, a wild frontier, separating the ambitious empire of the Russian czars from the British sphere of influence in the Middle East and India. The object for both European powers was to keep each other from gaining the upper hand in the Muslim tribal kingdom occupying the high ground of Central Asia.

During that continual thrust and parry, the Afghan capital, Kabul, was occupied a couple of times by British troops. But after World War I the independence of Afghanistan was established, and the country managed to maintain that status by playing one power off against the other. First, it was Britain against the Soviet Union. After World War II, when the United States assumed the British mantle, it was America against the Soviets.

In the 1950s, as Washington extended its alliances around the world, the U.S. government made a substantial military commitment to one of Afghanistan's neighbors, Pakistan, and that prompted Kabul to turn rather decisively in the direction of Moscow.

With the increase of Soviet influence, a Communist party was established in Afghanistan. Early in the 1970s, the monarchy was overthrown in favor of a leftist republic. But within a few years the new government began to loosen its ties with Moscow while exploring new relations with Pakistan, China, and Iran. A Muslim fundamentalist movement surfaced, preaching its message of opposition to foreign influences. And in 1978, a struggle for power broke out among various leftist factions. There was a series of political murders. The government was unseated by a military coup, which led to the establishment of a pro-Soviet "people's republic." But the new regime's control was tenuous. The politics of the country were in turmoil. There were repeated acts of guerrilla violence against the government.

When, in December 1979, Moscow sent the first Soviet paratroop units to occupy the airfields around Kabul, it could have been viewed as an act of desperation by Brezhnev to prevent the loss of a near-satellite. Soviet sources claim that the Kremlin had resisted several earlier appeals for help from the pro-Soviet leadership in Kabul and that the occupation was finally carried out only after the United States moved naval forces into the waters off nearby Iran during the hostage crisis—a possible overture to American intervention in that region. Officially, the landing of Soviet troops in Afghanistan was a defensive move.

NIKOLAI MOVCHAN
Soviet Army defector; publishing-house employee in New York
1982: Sergeant, Red Army antitank unit in Afghanistan

Essentially, what we were told is that we'd be sent there to defend the new Republic of Afghanistan against external aggressors. We were also told that we were being sent there in order to defend the southern borders of our own country. What it came down to was that we were going to be fighting American, Chinese, and Pakistani mercenaries.

Once we got to Afghanistan, the fairy tale about these so-called mercenaries wasn't told as often. We were simply told, "Hey, guys, this is war; and if you're not going to shoot, they're going to shoot at you!"

I did not participate in combat, but I was stationed on guard duty. Our duty was to defend our platoon from the "Duschman," which is a term meaning "enemy."

Our entire regiment was surrounded by a minefield. One time I remember two Afghan civilians wound up in the minefield, and one of them was blown up. A discussion began around the subject, well, was this Afghan just a peaceful civilian or was he a Duschman; was he an enemy; was he a member of the *Mujaheddin* ["holy warriors," the anti-Soviet partisan movement]? And I remember being told that there were no peaceful Afghans in this country, that they were all enemies; they were all Duschmen.

When Sergeant Movchan of the Red Army walked away from his unit and crossed over to the Afghani side, he took asylum in a village where, he found, everyone was armed—"old men, wives, children"—some with antique rifles or pistols, some with grenades or automatic weapons.

What the Russians had done in their occupation of Afghanistan was to create their own Vietnam. Acting in the name of ideology, they had intruded upon independence—and in the particularly fierce form it often takes in isolated mountain regions.

During the next five years, at least 100,000 Soviet troops were kept pinned down in Afghanistan by the resistance of the people—along with another 40,000 or so held in reserve just across the Soviet border. The Soviet air force destroyed whole villages by saturation bombing, killing an estimated 1 million people. Perhaps as many as one-third of Afghanistan's 15 million population fled the country, taking refuge in Pakistan and Iran. If the United States had not been arming the anti-Soviet partisans beforehand, as the Kremlin charged, then the American arms supply began openly now, mainly by way of Pakistan.

Until the invasion of Afghanistan, there had been no such overt move by Soviet armies since the occupation of Prague in 1968. All through the seventies, the Kremlin had been content to pursue its interests by political means or through proxy forces. So the international shock was a severe one.

The violation of Afghanistan's independence, coming just at a time when the United States was tormented by feelings of impotence over events in nearby Iran, was regarded by some American leaders as opportunistic and provocative.

The impact on President Carter was visible in the stern expression on his face and the belligerent tone of his words. Treating the Soviet move almost as an act of war, he responded with a dire warning: "An attempt by any force to gain control of the Persian Gulf region will be regarded as an assault on the vital interests of the United States and . . . will be repelled by any means necessary, including military force."

It was a warning that would be hard to back up since the nearest American military base was 1,600 miles away, in Turkey.

According to the Kremlin, the supposed Russian threat to the Persian Gulf was a phantom. When the American industrialist Armand Hammer later challenged Brezhnev on that issue, the Soviet leader responded, "That's nonsense." If the Russians were aiming at the Persian Gulf, he went on, "we could go through Iran—it's much easier for us."

Washington obviously saw the Middle East map in a different perspective. Describing the Soviet move as "the most serious threat since World War II," Carter called upon Congress for a 15-percent boost in his own record-high military budget—an explicit response to Afghanistan.

There was talk of restoring the draft—a move that only a few years ago, in the wake of Vietnam, would have seemed like an act of political suicide for any proponent. This time there was considerable support among the young—along with the expectable stirrings of a new draft-resistance movement.

In the public debate over the Afghanistan crisis, such incendiary watchwords as Munich and the Holocaust were invoked.

Military experts linked the brazen Soviet move in Central Asia with what was described as a "tremendous" overall buildup of Soviet arms.

The chairman of the Joint Chiefs of Staff, General David Jones, emerged from a morning briefing and pronounced the state of the world as "not too good." He called attention to the Russian superiority in megatonnage of missiles and, in spite of the U.S. lead in numbers of weapons, foresaw "a difficult period in the early eighties." He added reassuringly: "I do not predict nuclear war."

SALT II, the strategic arms control agreement that Carter had signed months before but that had run into trouble in Congress, was given up for dead.

The American specialist on Soviet affairs, George Kennan, the original author of the containment doctrine, considered the official response to events in the Middle East with dismay, commenting: "Never since World War II has there been such a far-reaching militarization of thought and discourse in Washington."

A Soviet journalist, Aleksandr Bovin, who served as Brezhnev's speech writer at the time, sums up the Russian reaction to those Washington developments: "Carter went into hysterics and didn't think about Soviet-American relations. For us, détente was more important than Vietnam. For Carter, Afghanistan was more important than détente."

In measures considerably short of military force, as no threat to the Persian Gulf developed, the United States embargoed grain shipments to the Soviet Union and boycotted the 1980 summer Olympics in Moscow. Carter failed to carry the Western allies along in this tide of sanctions. Most of them sent their athletes to Moscow and declined to join in trade sanctions against the USSR.

The hostage crisis in Iran, meanwhile, was developing into a nerve-racking war of words, silences, and economics.

"The United States," President Carter declared, "will never yield to international terrorism or to blackmail." But the hated Shah was forced to leave the United States after cancer surgery; briefly accepted into Panama, he moved on to Egypt, where he soon died.

That didn't end the Iranian demands for vengeance and for seizure of the royal properties overseas—demands mostly voiced by the Teheran crowds while political leaders were infuriatingly mute on the hostage issue or gave out contradictory signals.

Using what little leverage it had, the Carter administration froze the estimated $8 billion of Iranian assets in the United States and boycotted Iran's only significant source of revenue, its oil.

Like the whole Western world, the United States was already taking painful blows from the oil weapon. OPEC had taken advantage of the political upheaval in Iran to raise the price of crude by 15 percent; as the crisis deepened, the price was raised again, this time by 50 percent. Before long, the price of gas for American motorists would reach the unimagined level of $1.50 a gallon. Japan, which depended on Iran for a full 12 percent of its oil supply, was concerned about a calamitous slowdown of its high-speed economy. Oil-spurred inflation was sending shudders through the societies of the United States and Western Europe; it was tearing at the vitals of third-world economies.

And the hostages remained at the mercy of their student captors while, with maddening deliberation, the Ayatollah Khomeini proceeded to organize the government of his Islamic republic. From time to time, the American public was given tantalizing glimpses of the captives in televised scenes, which were scrutinized for clues as to their welfare and the prospects for their release.

Almost six months into the crisis, in April 1980, the Carter administration finally—desperately—attempted what the American public demanded: to do *something—anything*—rather than just wait as if America were as helpless as the hostages.

From an aircraft carrier in the Persian Gulf 600 miles from Teheran —the nearest American position that could be safely established—a long-shot rescue effort was launched. Four months in rehearsal, it was complex and audacious: eight big Sea Stallion helicopters plus support aircraft heading for a staging area in the Dasht-e-Kavir, Iran's Great Salt Desert, there to rendezvous for a two-stage raid on the embassy another 250 miles away.

The plan would have to be carried out in perfect secrecy and with perfect timing. Any alarm might result in the execution of the hostages instead of their rescue.

The plan never came to the test. Three of the eight helicopters developed mechanical trouble en route to the staging area.

COLONEL CHARLES BECKWITH
Security consultant
1980: Commander, hostage rescue mission

Very quickly we had busted into the Iranian air space. We had gone into their country, and we had landed at a predesignated area out in the desert. And darkness was upon us. And then a bus arrived which was filled with elderly people and very young people. It wasn't a threat to us. We were just going to load the people onto the C-130s and fly them out of Iran, then reintroduce them the next night.

[But] then, unfortunately, there were only five flyable helicopters. I guess a lot of people asked the question: why didn't you go on with five? Well, that would have been ludicrous. Which twenty-two, twenty-three people do you pull off and say, "You don't go"? Every man with me had a job to do. Some had two or three. It was that well rehearsed and that surgical of an operation. And we stated early on in the planning of this operation: without six flyable helicopters you can't go forward.

A lot of people say they made that decision, and everybody that said they made it can have credit for it. But I was standing there on the desert floor when I was asked, "Would you go forward with five flyable helicopters?" I said, "Hell, no!" And if I was asked again, I'd say the same thing.

On the desert floor, in the darkness of an April night, the rescue mission was scrubbed. But the bad luck wasn't over. On the takeoff for the retreat to the carrier, another helicopter collided with a C-130 cargo plane loaded with fuel. Eight crewman were killed, their bodies abandoned with the wreckage.

The American public was demoralized by a failure that had put an end to all hopes for a rescue; the hostages were now scattered in new hiding places. *Time* magazine commented on the deflation of the American ego: "A once dominant military machine, first humbled in Vietnam, now looked incapable of keeping its aircraft aloft even when no enemy knew they were there."

The British historian Paul Johnson calls this moment "perhaps the lowest point of American fortunes in this century."

It was more than six agonizing months later, in November 1980, that the hostage crisis began to unwind as the Khomeini government, finally in place, began to enter into serious negotiations.

With the government of Muslim Algeria serving as intermediary, the painful and humiliating process of bargaining for American lives got under way. Essentially, the terms were: an American guarantee of nonintervention in Iran, return of frozen Iranian assets, and release of Iran from damage claims by American companies and individuals against the Iranian government.

What had finally broken the crisis and spurred the negotiating process was neither the power of the United States nor the moral force of world disapproval but an extraneous event in the Middle East: the outbreak of war between Iran and its neighbor, Iraq—a war that in the next six years would show no sign of abatement. Its impact was so disruptive that Iranian oil production, already in serious decline, was thrown into a tailspin. In one year it fell almost by half, and soon Iranian motorists were driving across one of the world's most extensive pools of petroleum on rationed gas.

On January 20, 1981, the 444-day hostage crisis came to an end when fifty-two Americans were flown out of captivity from Teheran on an Algerian passenger jet. (The rest of the original number—some blacks, some women, one man suffering a neurological disorder—had been freed in previous months.)

The release came on the Inauguration Day of a new President. Jimmy Carter had carried the rebellion against the imperial style of presidency too far; he had proven a little too humble. And having identified the American mood as a kind of "malaise," a crisis of spirit, he was held responsible for that crisis by the electorate.

The day after Carter left office, he flew to Germany to greet the returning hostages on behalf of his successor. He had been routed at the polls by the Republican candidate, Ronald W. Reagan, who exuded confidence in the American future, expressed defiance of America's enemies, and promised to restore the country's damaged prestige.

For all their political differences—Reagan was a conservative ideologue, in contrast to Carter's moderate Democratic lineage—the two men had brought to the recent campaign similar views of the East-West competition. Much different from the picture Carter had presented only four years earlier, it was the perspective in which the nation as a whole was coming to view the world of the 1980s.

"This action of the Soviets," said Carter, speaking of Afghanistan in one of his final foreign-policy statements, "has made a more dramatic change in my own opinion of what the Soviets' ultimate goals are than anything they've done in the previous time I've been in office."

In one of his first foreign-policy pronouncements as fortieth President of the United States, Ronald Reagan declared: "I know of no leader of the Soviet Union since the Revolution and including the present leadership that has not more than once repeated, in the various Communist congresses they hold, their determination that their goal must be the promotion of world revolution."

America's relationship with the Soviet Union was being defined once again primarily in terms of danger.

A decade of détente was over. America would seek its security in the world by way of containment and confrontation as it had early in the cold war.

·25·

CONSERVATIVES
IN COMMAND

Like Jimmy Carter before him, Ronald Reagan arrived on the Washington scene as an outsider in fact and in spirit. Both men made the leap to the Oval Office from a governorship without the benefit—or handicap—of experience in Congress or the cabinet. Both brought a kind of outsider's approach to the conduct of foreign affairs. Good-by to the shenanigans of traditional diplomacy—*they* would be guided by principle. With Jimmy Carter it was human rights. With Ronald Reagan it was conservative ideology, in which the free-enterprise system was proclaimed as the only atmosphere in which human rights could truly live and breathe. Conservatives made no apology about advancing the American viewpoint.

JEANE KIRKPATRICK
Political scientist
1981–85: Ambassador to the UN

[In] the very first discussion in the Security Council after I arrived, there was a resolution that condemned Israel for firing back across the Lebanese border after the Israelis had been fired on by the PLO from Lebanon.

Now we said, "No, we will not accept such a resolution. Not only will we not vote for it, but we will not abstain on it"—which the previous administration had been doing. We said, "If it's going to deplore Israeli shelling, if it's going to regret Lebanese-Palestinian dead, it must regret Israeli dead and the prior shelling of Israel." We made clear that we would, if necessary, veto that.

307

People understood that there was a new team in town after we had done that.

The assertive, sometimes strident new American was the Reagan administration's way of translating its 1980 mandate, expressing a conviction about America's role in the world. For the Reagan election was partly a rebuff to Carter and his conduct of foreign policy, which was seen as vacillating and ineffectual. But it was also an expression of the same impulses that had elected Carter four years earlier. It was a reaffirmation of the post-Watergate spirit and the growing aversion to big government—the milieu and the product of professional politicians.

Curiously, in numbers of employees, the growth of the federal payroll in the three decades from 1950 to 1980 was a relatively modest 40 percent; the big increase, by far, was in state and local government, which had tripled. But Americans were certainly justified in their impression that Washington had much more influence over their lives than ever before.

The minimum wage may have made sense at one time; now, as some Americans saw it, the law simply guaranteed the wages that *other* people got paid no matter how inexperienced or unskilled. There were federal regulations that forced plants in your town to shut down or move because they couldn't maintain the quality of air the employees breathed or control the toxicity of industrial waste products. There were laws on how fast you could drive your car and judicial guidelines that determined whose children your kids went to school with. Birth control and abortion had federal sanctions, and there were politicians in Congress who wanted to license your shotgun. You paid for all these restrictions, willy-nilly, with your increasingly heavy and complicated taxes.

You were required to help support somebody else's illegitimate children; at sixty-five, you would join them as a ward of the government and a patient of its infuriating health-care bureaucracy. Human nature being what it is, the beneficiaries of the system resented it perhaps even more than the better-off citizens who mainly supported it.

Some of the benefits were at once too obvious and too subtle to measure: the gradual opening up of a once rigidly color-bound society; the increasing absorption of disadvantaged and handicapped individuals into the mainstream; the continued remarkable broadening of the American middle class.

What counted in most people's lives—what caused many to reject the whole experience of government activity instead of trying to refine it—was the damned persistence of problems which big government had not only failed to solve but was widely blamed for. The persistence of chronic poverty—15 percent of the American population still living below the economic subsistence line, one out of twenty on welfare. The persistence of social blight like teen-age pregnancies and the pernicious drug traffic. Above all, the persistence of crime, which made personal security an issue taking precedence over national security in the agenda of the 1980s.

Cold-War Fundamentalism

It was the special genius of conservative ideology that it could relate all the unpleasant and threatening aspects of American life—even transfer them—to a foreign antagonist. From the earliest days of the cold war, the conservatives had presented an image of the Communist state not merely as an oppressive system but as the ultimate form of the dangers surrounding Americans at home. It was as if poverty, drugs, illegitimacy, and crime were not the result of malfunctions in American society but the products of an alien system that had somehow taken root here. In the conservative view of the world, the view represented by Ronald Reagan, the most immoral and most hostile of all the forces loose in our time was big government at its biggest: the Soviet Union.

Yet the high point of Soviet-American relations since World War II had occurred in the presidency of another professed anti-Communist, Richard Nixon, who had turned out to be pragmatic about dealing with the rival superpower.

STANISLAV MENSHIKOV
Adviser to Central Committee, Communist Party of the Soviet Union

A number of people came over between Mr. Reagan's victory in November 1980, and January 1981, to try to convince the members of the Soviet government that he was, in fact, pragmatic. And that for that reason we should not hurry with anything we may have had in mind in the way of foreign policy actions.

These were quite authoritative people—Senator Percy [Illinois Republican, Foreign Relations committee leader] and General Scowcroft [national security expert in several administrations] and other people.

These are serious men, so we did wait for a while. And without great hope, but we did.

What we got was a new rhetoric.

As a presidential candidate, Ronald Reagan had taken the traditional cold-war view of communism as a monolithic enemy. "Let us not delude ourselves," he said. "The Soviet Union underlies all the unrest that is going on."

As President, far from following Nixon's lead in pursuit of détente, he seemed bent on fending off any such possibility by his rhetoric. At times he appeared to be going out of his way to attack the Soviet antagonist, as if the risk of an accommodation was ever-present and the American public needed constant reminding of the danger from the international left. The rhetoric was pure cold-war fundamentalism.

The Soviet leaders, he declared, "reserve unto themselves the right to commit any crime, to lie, to cheat" in order to attain their objective, which he defined as a "one-world Communist state."

He described the Soviet Union as "a society in which everything that isn't compulsory is prohibited," as a system having "no respect for human life, for the dignity of an individual," as "the focus of evil in the modern world."

The hard line extended straight through his circle of foreign-policy advisers, including people like General Alexander Haig, secretary of state in the original Reagan cabinet, and Richard Allen, the President's first national security adviser. It hardened still further when it reached the Pentagon, where Caspar Weinberger held sway as secretary of defense. Weinberger soon developed a record of taking positions to the right of the President at crucial junctures, as if his appointed mission was to keep his chief from backsliding. "If the movement from cold war to détente is progress," the secretary once observed, "then let me say we cannot afford more progress."

The Pentagon needn't have worried. Not until well into his second term did President Reagan show any inclination to deal with the Kremlin on the great East-West issues. In fact, it was only months before the end of his first term that he even met any high-ranking

Soviet official face-to-face. In foreign affairs, the new administration was preoccupied with situations in which American self-esteem had suffered recent insults—and where the chances for retribution looked good.

Confrontation in the Hemisphere

When the policy makers of the newly installed Reagan administration unrolled their maps of the Western Hemisphere in 1981, what they saw was a pair of countries freshly colored a disturbing shade of red. One was the tiny Caribbean island republic of Grenada, the other the Central American country of Nicaragua—both the seats of recently established leftist governments. In addition, there was a left-wing guerrilla insurgency in progress against the government of El Salvador, with help from sympathetic neighbors in Nicaragua.

What the Reagan administration proceeded to bring about in the hemisphere was described as a confrontation between the United States and the forces of international communism. Even more, it was a confrontation between conflicting elements in American political life and their conflicting views of the danger. On one side, the conservatives, newly entrenched in the White House. On the other, the foreign-policy liberals in Congress and their hemisphere allies.

RICHARD STONE
Retired senator and diplomat
1983–84: President Reagan's special envoy to Central America

To blink away the Russian ships and the Bulgarian ships and the East Germans and the PLO and the other forces that are in there, in Nicaragua and elsewhere—as well as Castro's people—is to blink away reality.

CARLOS ANDRÉS PÉREZ-RODRÍGUEZ
Latin American political leader
of the moderate left
1974–79: President of Venezuela

There is no doubt that there is Communist infiltration in Central America. There is no doubt that advisers from the Soviet Union, Cuba, and other countries in the Communist nucleus are present in Cuba. There is no doubt that Nicaragua has been slipping away toward the Cuban-Soviet bloc. But it is also true that the problem in Nicaragua and the problem in Central America is not communism, and it is also true that there is no strategic danger—that there is no danger to the security of the United States. And it is also true that Nicaragua is not a strategic objective of the Soviet Union.

The greatest mistake [of recent American administrations] was pretending that the Latin American problem was communism, not the problem of the exploitative oligarchies in our countries and the negative interference by U.S. capital in the political life of Latin America.

America has played such a dominating role in the political and economic life of Central America that almost everything important that happens there has some connection to the United States and its imperial past. That was true of the Sandinista revolution, which gained control of Nicaragua during the Carter administration and became a major target of Reagan's foreign policy.

The movement took its name from a political hero of the left, Augusto César Sandíno, who was instrumental in ending the occupation of the country by American troops in the early 1930s. His achievement was ephemeral. Within a few years, American influence was firmly reestablished by the accession to power of the Somoza family, which was closely connected to U.S. economic interests and to the government in Washington. General Anastasio Somoza Debayle, the third successive member of the dynasty to occupy the presidency, was unusual among third-world leaders in disdaining any pretense of non-alignment. He declared himself four-square for the United States and the Western alliance.

Somoza was just the kind of Latin American ally that has traditionally supported American interests while giving the United States a bad name. The family and its friends profited enormously from American agribusiness concessions—coffee, cotton, sugar, beef—as well as from domestic sidelines in gambling, prostitution, the construction business, and various devices for tapping government revenues. In the description of a Nicaraguan banker, for the Somozas "the country was only a mechanism for investing abroad." Increasingly, the regime alienated the middle classes by making it difficult to do business or pursue a professional career without paying off the authorities.

A disastrous earthquake, which all but leveled the capital city of Managua in 1972, yielded a bonanza for Somocista land speculators and developers in the form of $32 million in U.S. emergency aid from

Washington. For most Nicaraguans, the disaster was one more terrible event in a chronology of hard times.

Political opposition, which previously had been fragmented, was gradually pulled together under the leadership of the Sandinistas. Using the economic weapon of general strikes, they raised a serious challenge to the Somoza government, which responded by trying to suppress the opposition through intimidation and force wielded by Somoza's national guard.

The Carter administration was now faced with the standard cold-war dilemma: whether to try to save an undemocratic government it could count on or join forces with an unpredictable revolution with inclinations toward the left.

As usual, Washington chose the first course, trying to extract human-rights reforms from the regime as the price of continuing aid. But in that situation, political liberties probably wouldn't have counted for much without serious economic reforms. And since any strong pressure from the United States might destabilize the government it was trying to save, the administration's efforts were relatively slight. So was Somoza's response.

In 1978, after the murder of an opposition spokesman, the publisher of the Managua newspaper *La Prensa,* the country erupted in civil war.

The beleaguered Somoza regime unleashed the national guard in a campaign of atrocities—kidnappings and massacres were confirmed by a team of outside investigators from the Organization of American States and the private human-rights organization Amnesty International.

The brutality failed to save the regime any more than American aid had. By mid-1979, the Sandinista-led revolution overpowered the national guard and drove Somoza out of the country. His departure was speeded by Washington, which by now recognized his defeat as inevitable (though some American conservatives charged Carter with having "lost" Nicaragua as Truman had been charged with losing China).

With Nicaragua devastated by the war and its treasury looted by the departing Somozas, the United States extended aid to the junta that now ruled the country in the name of the Sandinista revolution. And the junta, under Daniel Ortega Saavedra, at first pursued a policy that was relatively benign to American interests. Nationalization was mild, and strikes against American companies were discouraged.

But before long relations began to decline. The new government in

Managua was having no luck with the economy. It began to tighten controls on business. It also began trying to cut down a rising opposition. Censorship was toughened; a delay of five years was announced before free elections would be held. Eventually, in 1984, the elections were held, and Ortega was confirmed as president with 67 percent of the vote. But meanwhile, reports began to emerge from Nicaragua of disillusionment with the revolution, arrests of its critics, repressive actions by Sandinista troops.

Congress tried to tie strings to the aid program, requiring the Sandinistas to give up their support of rebels in neighboring El Salvador. The Sandinistas responded to that by turning to the Communist bloc for help. It was not a change of direction but, as the incoming Reagan administration saw it, an expression of the true spirit of the Sandinista revolution.

JEANE KIRKPATRICK

The same week that the Sandinistas came to power in July 1979, Cuban military advisers began arriving in Nicaragua. Within the first six months, it undertook to destabilize the government of El Salvador. Within the first nine months of its existence, five of the members of the junta in Nicaragua traveled to Moscow, where they met with Chernenko and Gromyko and signed a party-to-party agreement between the Sandinista party in Nicaragua and the Communist party in the Soviet Union, in which the Nicaraguans committed themselves to support all aspects of Soviet foreign policy in the world including the invasion and occupation of Afghanistan and the development of revolutionary governments in Latin America.

During this period, the United States was providing a very large amount of economic aid to the government of Nicaragua—something like $115 million in economic aid during that eighteen months.

In case there was any doubt among Americans as to what the Sandinistas were up to, Nicaragua was flatly identified by the administration as a Soviet satellite and military base. It was being developed in a buildup that the President described as "greater than could ever be justified from the standpoint of defense." Some of the arms, he said, had been identified by serial number as "weapons left behind by us when we left Vietnam."

Managua, with an influx of East-bloc advisers, was described as a city with a "Soviet suburb" and as "a kind of terrorist capital for not only the Western Hemisphere but for the world."

"The Americans must have different maps," a British observer remarked wryly, "on which places like Cuba and Nicaragua are about twenty times bigger than they are on our maps."

Drawn to realistic scale, Nicaragua comes out about the size of Iowa both in area and in population (3 million). Its army numbered 25,000. Administration opponents, resisting what they felt to be an anti-Soviet stampede by the White House, argued that the Sandinistas actually received most of their arms from friendly pro-Western nations in this hemisphere and that the Soviet Union had shown some restraint about supplying weapons to Nicaragua—no less restraint, anyway, than the United States in Afghanistan.

If the Sandinistas were seriously interested in keeping the channels open to Washington, then they were indiscreet in their foreign relations, to say the least. As the traffic increased—Managua–Havana, Managua–Moscow—in trade and diplomatic exchanges, the image of a second Cuba took shape, and the Reagan viewpoint gradually gained headway on Capitol Hill.

Within the first year of the Reagan administration, aid to the government of Nicaragua came to an end. Congress balked at supporting provocative CIA measures like the mining of Nicaraguan ports, but the President kept pushing another program: aid for counterrevolutionary forces in Nicaragua—the so-called contras.

There were serious doubts about the merits and the prospects of the contras, reflecting the presence among them of elements from the old, repressive Somocista national guard. For a period of two years—1984-86—Congress explicitly banned military aid to the contras (though it did approve a "humanitarian" allocation of food, clothing, and medical supplies). The administration, not to be denied, secretly solicited arms for its protégés from private sources on the political right and from foreign governments—such unlikely sources as Saudi Arabia and the Sultanate of Brunei.

Meanwhile, the administration kept up the alarums about the Central American danger, kept up the pressure. Eventually, grudgingly, in the summer of 1986, Congress approved $100 million in military aid for the contras.

That kind of pressure from Washington might not topple the leftist regime in Managua, might not even force it to accept anti-Communist leaders into the ruling coalition, as President Reagan disingenuously suggested. But it might at least divert the Sandinistas from their activities in support of the insurgents in El Salvador, just across a narrow bay on Central America's Pacific coastline.

El Salvador, unlike "lost" Nicaragua, was still savable. The running warfare between the army and the guerrillas in that country during the late 1970s and the beginning of the 1980s had been characterized by savage acts and equally savage reprisals. One headline event was the killing of four Americans—three of them nuns—in an act attributed to government troops.

The Salvadoran government was a military-civilian coalition dominated by the right. The Carter administration had not had any great success in extracting liberalizing concessions from the regime (Assistant Secretary of State Patricia Derian and her human-rights efforts notwithstanding). Over a thousand political murders in one year were ascribed to right-wing "death squads" operating with official sanction. When the Reagan administration came in, it concluded that El Salvador was worth investing in nevertheless as a bulwark against the left in Central America.

The rationale for supporting repressive government in one country, El Salvador, while trying to undermine it in another, Nicaragua, was supplied by the articulate UN ambassador, Jeane Kirkpatrick, when she drew a distinction between "totalitarian" governments—those friendly to the East bloc—and those that were merely "authoritarian" and favored the West.

When the acceptably authoritarian government of El Salvador announced free elections to be held in the spring of 1984, American liberals predicted a ballot-box scam that would simply legitimize a right-wing regime. Some further suggested that, given a free choice, voters would elect a government of the left. They were confounded when voters turned out in large numbers and—apparently not intimidated either by right *or* left—decisively chose a moderate government in elections monitored by observers from various countries, including the United States.

The President elected by El Salvador was José Napoleon Duarte, an engineer with a degree from Notre Dame, an appreciation of both Carter *and* Reagan for advancing the welfare of Central America, and benign feelings toward the United States in spite of one humiliating memory from his five years of living in this country. Once, on a trip to New Orleans, because of his dark complexion, he was required to sit in the segregated balcony of a movie theater.

Although in no sense eliminated, the guerrilla threat in El Salvador began to subside. And the new government passed an important test in 1985 when the political right disputed a victory of Duarte's moderates in elections for the National Assembly, and the powerful military establishment refused to back the challenge.

El Salvador had been saved from both threats, left and right—though for how long, no one could safely predict.

The tiny island of Grenada off the northern coast of South America provided an opportunity to do more than avert another foreign-policy loss. Here, in the autumn of 1983, the Reagan administration found a chance to achieve what the American public desperately hungered for in their years of frustration and impotence, the years of Vietnam, Iran, and Afghanistan—a chance for a victory.

The government of Grenada—a former British colony smaller than most American national parks, with the population of Cedar Rapids, Iowa (110,000)—had been taken over by a leftist coup in 1979 without causing much notice. Maurice Bishop, the leader of the coup, became premier.

In October 1983, the Bishop government in turn was dislodged by a militant Marxist faction, and the premier was killed. Within a week of that development, U.S. navy ships landed an invasion force of 2,200 men—1,900 Americans and 300 from Caribbean neighbors of the Grenadians. The ostensible reason was to protect the safety of 1,000 Americans on the island, most of them medical students.

The main opposition to the invasion came from 600 lightly armed Cubans engaged in building an airfield. American officials claimed it was designed to receive an airborne occupation by Castro as the next step in a Communist thrust toward South America.

The American operation was completed in a week or so, and a centrist government came to power in Grenada. In that brief occurrence, in that tiny space—the smallest country in the Western Hemisphere —American conservatives found a meaning far beyond the scope of the event itself. For Grenada was the first territory ever retrieved from Communist control by force in the decades of the cold war.

Setback in Lebanon

The Middle East was a tougher proposition.

Even in the days of unchallenged empire before World War II, the Middle East was a puzzle to Western governments.

A British diplomat, a veteran of those bygone days, once compared the performance of the European powers in that area of the world to "vicarage tennis"—the game as ineptly played on English church lawns, where having the serve, normally an advantage, was regarded as a *dis*advantage because the server was sure to lose by double-faulting. Being in charge of the Middle Eastern countries, as Britain used to be, was just such a disadvantage.

When Dale Dye, a public information officer in the U.S. marines, was sent to Lebanon on duty in 1983 and was met by an English-speaking liaison officer in the Lebanese army, he asked for a briefing so he could get right to work.

"My friend," he was told, "you have been in the Middle East for five minutes. You probably now understand as much as you are going to understand. From here, it's all downhill."

Dye's unit was part of an American peace-keeping force of 1,400 that was dispatched to Lebanon along with British, French, and Italian contingents to replace an Israeli occupation force.

For the Americans, it was not really a cold-war situation. It did not present a potential gain or loss of territory or influence to the Communists, although some of the principals were clients of Moscow. But it had cold-war overtones because the American involvement was part of the Reagan administration's assertiveness in its relations with the rest of the world. It was intended to serve notice on any antagonist that the United States once again stood ready to make its weight felt in any situation that threatened America interests, including the fundamental interest in a stable world order. And including the Middle East, where the United States had been treated so unceremoniously by a regional power—Iran.

If that was the message, it was garbled in Lebanon.

That Connecticut-sized country was a maelstrom of internal conflicts that would swallow up any outside party venturing into it. Once known as "the Switzerland of the Middle East"—a haven of prosperous neutrality and an outpost of Western culture, mainly French—Lebanon had been wrecked in recent years by a baffling and interminable civil war. It was a conflict that had not so much sides as interlocking components—religious, political, socioeconomic, even tribal.

The country had once been held together by a constitutional balance of power between the Christian and Muslim (mainly Sunni) political establishments. But as the Muslim population majority continued to grow, it splintered. It now comprised three main groups—Sunni,

Druse, and, at the bottom of the economic and social ladder, the fastest growing of all: Shi'ites. In the armed struggle for power that ravaged Lebanon in the 1970s and 1980s, each of these religious groups was represented by its own militia.

Stirred into this explosive mixture was another incendiary element: the Palestinian exiles—300,000 of them, making up more than 10 percent of the population. Most of them lived in a cluster of housing developments (referred to as "camps") around the capital, Beirut. Their military-political arm, the Palestine Liberation Organization, had East-bloc support. Their *raison d'être* was war against Israel. Unwelcome to the government, they could not be dislodged—for fear of offending their sympathizers in other parts of the Arab world.

Some of the conflicting factions, furthermore, were divided within themselves. The Shi'ites, for example, had tribal branches that were not always in harmony. And a substantial group of Palestinians was at odds with the leadership of Yasir Arafat.

The militant activities of the Palestinian guerrillas, the PLO, had brought two outside forces into the picture. One was the Israeli army, which staged its invasion of Lebanon in June 1982, to put a stop to guerrilla attacks across their border. That, in turn, brought in Syria— another Soviet client. Its troops now remained in position, even after the Israeli withdrawal, in support of the anti-Arafat branch of the Palestinians. An endlessly interlocking problem.

No wonder an arriving U.S. marine would have trouble understanding the Middle East. The experience of the American melting pot, with its colorful mix of ethnic neighbors, was no preparation for this welter of uncompromising politics, religion, and ancient feuds.

At first, the marines treated Lebanon in the open-handed style the Yanks traditionally use with foreign peoples. They made friends with Shi'ite families in the suburbs around the Beirut airport, distributed candy and little American flags to the Arab kids, built them a playground. But within months the Americans found themselves just one more part of the problem.

In late August 1983, the fraternizing stopped and the marines were driven under cover when Druse artillery began lobbing shells into the American positions. On a morning in October, a member of a pro-Iran Shi'ite group called Islamic Jihad (*jihad* being Arabic for a holy war) drove a truck loaded with explosives on an anti-American suicide mission. He drove it through a barrier and into the wall of a massive concrete bunker that served as a marine barracks.

JOHN SHARNIK

ROBERT JORDAN
Editor of navy publication
1983: Major, U.S. marines, on duty in Beirut

It was a little after six o'clock, and I'd decided I'd sleep another half an hour before I got up. I must have dozed off when all of a sudden there was this loud flak explosion, and I woke up and I saw everything flying around the room. You know, you tune your ear to the various types of ordnance, and I had never heard anything like that in Vietnam or Beirut.

I ran across to my office, and I checked the phones, and they were all dead. Well, they went down to the Battalion Landing Team headquarters. And [a staff sergeant] came running up, and his eyes were real big, and he said, "Major, the B.L.T. is gone!"

I couldn't conceive of the B.L.T. being gone—this four-story concrete building. Each floor was a foot of reinforced concrete. The roof was three feet thick. The PLO, the Syrians, the Israelis had all used it as a strong point at one time or another.

So I started walking faster, and I looked over, and there was a hedgerow to my left, and every leaf had been blown off. And I looked up, and there were pieces of stuff just blown through trees—girders and ammo-can covers and everything. And as I came around the corner of this hedgerow, I looked out, and I could see the Beirut International Airport tower, and you couldn't see that before. The B.L.T. building had been reduced to one story. Everything was covered with a fine gray ash, almost like the pictures you saw of the Mount St. Helens' eruption.

And [a sergeant] came up, and he said, "Major," he said, "be careful. You can't tell where the bodies are." And as I walked down, I noticed the debris was about three to four feet deep, and mixed in with this were parts of human beings, and the only way you could tell was they were bleeding.

I think that the criticism, the soul searching, the self-flagellation that we went through to try to pin the blame on somebody for this—it was kind of like a rape victim, you know. Instead of saying, "Why did they perpetrate this against the marines who were there in a peace-keeping role?" it was, "Well, what did we do as a nation to deserve this attack?"

Well, what we did as a nation to deserve this attack was to stand up for the freedom of the individual, stand up for peace.

There were 241 American bodies in the debris of the marine barracks and another eighty wounded.

The sounds of soul searching in America, however, were soon drowned out by the noise of further developments. Fighting broke out between the contending factions of the PLO; Arafat and 4,000 loyalists were given safe passage out of the country to sanctuary in Tunisia.

That provided the merest pause in Lebanon's many-sided civil war. Two months later, in early February 1984, Shi'ite and Druse militia opened a joint assault on Christian neighborhoods of West Beirut, and the Americans were drawn into the violence. As the marines came under the heaviest fire they had yet experienced, President Reagan ordered them withdrawn, and U.S. navy ships began shelling the Muslim artillery positions.

The other international contingents also pulled out, and Lebanon was back in the throes of the bloody turmoil that seemed to be its inescapable fate, with or without American intercession.

The United States was hardly to blame for the setback, but the sound of American naval guns firing against Arab villages would probably not be forgotten.

Confronting Terrorism

Intervention in the Middle East was an attempt to reanimate the American image—to project that air of towering authority once again. In the end, it only reminded Americans of the limits of power in the modern world. It also brought the United States directly into contact with one of the most disruptive forces in that world—one that crossed cold-war boundaries with unnerving elusiveness. That force was terrorism.

MUAMMAR QADDAFI
President of Libya

When Palestinians face their enemy, Israel, in fact, they face the United States of America. That means this occupied Palestine that you call Israel is like a state of the United States of America. We are obliged to look for an ally to face this superpower. And, of course, the Soviet Union is our friend.

When the Lebanese fought to liberate their country from Israel's occupation, America accused them of being terrorists. Any just struggle for freedom and independence, America considers it a terrorist action. So they accuse me of being a terrorist. Okay—terrorist. I support any just cause in the world. I support the struggle for freedom of all peoples in the world.

American policy is responsible for these terrorist actions. They have no way of dealing with America face to face—only by hand grenades and by things like this. But these people—Palestinians or Lebanese—are obliged to do this because they have no means of discussing the problem of freedom with America.

Kidnappings, bombings, murders, hijackings, the taking of hostages —these acts of civil violence were practiced all through the 1970s by various dissident groups—leftist, nationalist, religious—throughout the supposedly civilized world. Arab terrorism became the most active force. It spread beyond the boundaries of the Middle East in two shocking incidents. At the 1972 Olympics in Munich, eleven Israeli athletes were kidnapped and murdered. Four years later, 103 passengers on a hijacked El Al jet were held hostage—and then rescued in a spectacular Israeli paratroop operation at an airport in remote Entebbe, in the central African nation of Uganda.

In the 1980s, Arab terrorism broadened its anti-Zionist focus and became a form of warfare against the West, with the United States the major target. In June 1985, Lebanese Shi'ite thugs hijacked a TWA jet with 145 passengers and a crew of eight, killing an American on board. They shuttled the plane back and forth between Beirut and Algiers while negotiating for the release of 766 Shi'a prisoners held by Israel in a nerve-racking transaction that went on for more than two weeks before the passengers were ransomed.

In one of the most outrageous of all terrorist acts, the Italian passenger ship *Achille Lauro* was hijacked on a Mediterranean cruise with about 450 aboard. Again, an American was murdered before the pirates surrendered in an Egyptian port two days later.

Moorhead Kennedy, one of the victims of the most protracted terrorist incident, the 444-day captivity of Teheran embassy employees, had an opportunity several years later to ask one of his captors for an explanation. "What did you hope to accomplish?" Kennedy asked.

The terrorist, who had by now become deputy foreign minister of Iran, answered: "At least, now people know where Iran is"—a statement that Kennedy translates as, "You'd better take us seriously."

Terrorism, in the phrase of George McGovern, the former senator and presidential candidate, is "the third-world's answer to the superpowers. They don't have submarines; they don't have nuclear weapons; but what they do have is the capacity to harass and strike fear into the hearts of citizens from the superpowers."

Terrorism struck on behalf of many different causes, but the Reagan administration identified it as fundamentally an instrument of international communism. When Nicaragua linked its fortunes with the Eastern bloc, Managua became, according to Jeane Kirkpatrick, a sanctuary for "representatives of the PLO and the Libyans and the Red Brigades in Italy and the Baader-Meinhof Gang [Germany] and the Spanish Basque ETA and the Argentine Montoneros and the Colombian M-19 and so forth—naturally also the FMLN in El Salvador."

The only significant terrorist groups left out of that accounting—perhaps inadvertently—were the Irish Republican Army, the Puerto Rican separatists, and an East Indian protest group.

As terrorist incidents became an almost daily occurrence—in 1979–80, there were 150 plane hijackings, aside from bombings, kidnappings, and so on—American diplomats and soldiers on foreign duty, American businessmen, and tourists all began to feel constrained by the omnipresent threat of violence. Even at home, the President's security became a matter of concern. (He had been wounded in a nonpolitical assassination attempt by a psychotic American in 1981.) The question of how to combat a secretive, often faceless, enemy occupied and frustrated American political leaders in the mid-eighties.

Libya became the major focus when United States intelligence sources identified Qaddafi as the Kremlin's main proxy in sponsoring, training, and directing world terrorism. As part of the administration's assertive stance in foreign affairs, Washington began to flex its muscles on Libya's doorstep by conducting naval exercises in Mediterranean waters claimed (insubstantially) by the Qaddafi government. Challenged by Libyan planes, the Americans shot them down.

The American policy reached a violent climax in April 1986 when U.S. aircraft bombed two cities, Tripoli and Benghazi, causing civilian casualties. The raid was in retaliation for a series of brutal incidents in Europe, the latest a bomb blast at a discotheque in West Berlin frequented by American servicemen. Several GIs were among the casualties.

With the air raid—and with well-planted rumors of further raids—Washington aimed to do more than just punish Libya and discourage further violence. The aim was nothing less than to provoke an uprising against Qaddafi and bring down his government.

With the exception of Britain, Washington got no help in this campaign from the European allies, still concerned about relations with one of their major oil suppliers. In fact, they went to some lengths to avoid being associated with the U.S. efforts against Libya.

Qaddafi was no hero to the American public, but even at home the administration's strong-arm policy was controversial. First there was the humane issue—the civilian air raid victims. Then there was the difficulty of pinning down the responsibility for any particular terrorist act. Terrorism by its nature was a chaotic and unruly force. Moscow was sometimes a victim. Four Soviet embassy officials in Beirut were kidnapped in 1985 and one of them was killed. Even Qaddafi's role was unclear. Only about 5 percent of terrorist incidents could actually be traced to Libya. Indeed, Iran and Syria were found to be pulling the strings in many acts of violence.

Finally, there were running arguments about what methods actually worked in dealing with this shadowy threat to individual security. Proponents of outright force as the best answer often cited the example of Israel with its record of success in liberating hostages by military means and its policy of swift retaliation. But the record was widely misread. In the 1985 TWA hijacking, for instance, Israel ended up meeting the terrorists' demands by releasing the Shi'ite prisoners.

ABBA EBAN

There was a belief that until recently we had a 100 percent record of not giving any transaction to the terrorists. That isn't the case at all.

Where we could have a military option, we fought them—successfully at Entebbe, successfully with [another hijacking, involving a Belgian airliner]. We tried to fight them in Munich, with tragic results.

But where we could not reach them with our force, we definitely did a deal. And one oughtn't to be sanctimonious about it. The United States, I think, has got to learn that there isn't an overall formula. Sometimes you can get at them and punish, and sometimes you can't.

Prevention is about 90 percent of the cure. The idea that you can put people on the moon and you can't insure that 326 people getting on an airplane don't have guns—that is so ludicrous. [Or] that you can't create a technique whereby people can't smuggle machine guns into a transit air terminal. [Or] that you can't penetrate the terrorist movements with your intelligence activities.

I hope the United States will understand that so long as political problems are involved you cannot get 100 percent results against terrorism.

Tighter airport security, better intelligence, quick and punishing retaliation—nothing proved to have more than limited effect on the surge of terrorism, and almost any conceivable policy was a minefield.

There were tripwires buried everywhere in a deal by which the United States, in partnership with Israel, tried to spring some American hostages in 1986 by selling arms to the renegade government of Iran. It flouted the Reagan administration's avowed principle never to do business with terrorists or their sponsors. And it had a spinoff— profits from the arms sale were diverted into aid for the contras of Nicaragua—that violated the expressed will of Congress on Central America at that time. Possibly, it violated the law as well.

Never mind the historical precedents by which American leaders at least since Woodrow Wilson had circumvented the policies and laws of their government in pursuit of what they considered to be the national interest. Never mind that the Iran-contra affair was hardly more clandestine or illegal than the Kennedy administration's covert war against Castro. At least the Cuba campaign failed in secret; the arms deal was an *obvious* disaster. Worse, it revealed the White House in disarray, with officials of the CIA and the National Security Council operating out of sync with the State Department. The revelations proved so explosive that the Reagan administration was practically brought to a standstill late in 1986.

Meanwhile the Cold War and its major imperative—relations with the Russians—had caught up with Ronald Reagan.

Dealing with the "Evil Empire"

In spite of Reagan's anti-Communist rhetoric and his confrontational attitude, the first half of the eighties proved to be a relatively stable period—if a standoffish one—in Soviet-American relations.

Some observers ascribed this to the "Reagan luck," which seemed to be a significant component of his presidency, along with personal charm and a persuasive platform style. And it seemed true enough that the Soviets were kept off balance during this entire period by an extraordinary sequence of accidents. Leonid Brezhnev's frail health overtook him in 1982, when he died at the age of seventy-six. His successor, Yuri Andropov, died at seventy after just fifteen months in office. Then Konstantin Chernenko, ill from the time he took over at seventy-two, lasted barely a year. Mikhail Gorbachev, who became general secretary of the Soviet Communist party in March 1985, provided an unusual new element of youth at the top of the Kremlin hierarchy. He was just fifty-four—exactly twenty years younger than Ronald Reagan.

Conservatives had another explanation for the Kremlin's relatively quiet behavior. The Soviets, according to General Haig, "don't care what we say. They're only impressed when we express a willingness to sacrifice for an objective, whether it's rebuilding our arms or defending our allies when they're threatened. They don't care what we 'imperialists' say. They only care about objective reality—what we do and what we demonstrate the willingness to do."

What the Reagan administration did in confrontations with the Soviet Union was sometimes provocative but rarely reckless.

At the time Ronald Reagan took command in the White House, there was one active cold war front—one situation in which the Soviet Union was directly engaged in extending control beyond its own borders. That was Afghanistan. There the White House continued the Carter administration's policy of restraint, limiting its support of the freedom fighters to symbolic shipments of light, relatively innocuous weapons.

By the end of Reagan's first year in office, there was another potential front: Poland. A terribly mismanaged economy had produced the worst of all combinations in that country: stagnant industry, a huge government debt, persistent consumer shortages, and soaring prices.

Hard times prompted the rise of a dissident labor movement, Solidarity, under the leadership of a tenacious organizer named Lech Walesa. With 9.5 million members by 1981, Solidarity was the largest social force in the country, after the Catholic church. Animated by the recent elevation of a Polish cardinal, Karol Wojtyla, to the papacy as John Paul II, the church also contributed to the rising national spirit in Poland.

Solidarity's widely supported strikes all but paralyzed the faltering economy in 1981. The power of the independent labor movement was challenging the power of the Communist regime itself, and Soviet intervention on the model of Hungary in 1956 and Czechoslovakia in 1968 seemed imminent. That probability was headed off only by drastic action on the part of the Polish leadership in the form of a military takeover under General Wojciech Jaruzelski.

By imposing martial law on the country in December 1981, the new regime cleared the streets and sent the workers back to the shipyards and factories. Some of the liberalizing concessions made to Solidarity, giving it a voice in economic decisions, were revoked. The union leadership was gagged and harassed by police actions; ultimately Solidarity itself was outlawed.

Washington responded to these repressive measures by leveling economic sanctions against the Warsaw government and some months later extended them to Moscow by blocking a deal for sending American gas and oil technology to the Soviet Union. The European allies refused to pull back from their increasing trade relations with the Soviet. Within a matter of months, the United States withdrew its sanctions against the technology deal and—under pressure from midwestern farmers—also gave its blessings to renewed grain sales to the Russians.

As it would later confirm in dealing with terrorism, the Reagan administration had at least a touch of pragmatism in its principled makeup after all.

Still, for much of its first term, the administration continued to resist the idea of doing business with what the President called the "evil empire." That jaundiced view of the Soviet Union was reinforced by a horrifying occurrence in the summer of 1983 when a Boeing 747 passenger jet bearing the logo of the South Korean airline strayed over Soviet airspace near Siberia and was shot down by a Soviet SU-15 fighter. The airliner was en route to Seoul with 269 passengers, 61 of them Americans. All were killed.

Moscow's original defense was an attack—the charge that KAL flight 007 was engaged in espionage for the United States. The Russians backed off that preposterous accusation only to the extent of claiming that their air defenses had confused the flight with American intelligence traffic in the area.

The second claim was apparently true, but Washington, in effect, charged the Russians with deliberate barbarity. "There is no way a pilot could mistake this for anything other than a civilian airliner," the President insisted.

Apparently, a Soviet pilot could and did. Lengthy investigations by American journalists showed there was ample reason for confusing KAL 007 with U.S. military intelligence flights in the area at the time and that the Soviet pilot, contrary to orders, fired a fatal shot at his target without identifying it visually.

The damning fact remained that the Soviets never saw fit to apologize for taking such harsh measures against an accidental violation of their air space.

"There have been numerous times," Ronald Reagan pointed out, "when other planes, including theirs, have intruded in ours, and we've never shot them down."

Still Alive: Arms Control

Among liberals as well as conservatives, there were few illusions left by the 1980s about the character of the Soviet system. But there was a continuing pressure on the administration to deal with the Soviet leadership as the only way to come to grips with the ultimate threat to world security: nuclear weapons.

The irrepressible concern about the arms race was expressed in a movement for a nuclear freeze—a flat halt to the production and deployment of atomic weapons by both sides—which was spreading in Europe. Derided by American hardliners as "marchers with their faces painted white," the movement won the endorsement of 140 congressmen and some prestigious senators like Democrat Edward Kennedy and Republican Mark Hatfield. Almost three-quarters of a million Americans came together in New York's Central Park in a demonstration against the continuing arms race.

At the time the Reagan administration took office, in 1981, SALT II —the strategic arms control agreement as revised and completed by Jimmy Carter and Leonid Brezhnev—was still on the table, signed by both leaders but unratified by the United States Senate. The new administration, calling the treaty "fatally flawed," made no effort either to get it approved up on the Hill or to renegotiate it again with Moscow.

The politics of arms control has been one of the great disillusionments of life in the cold war. For while almost every American leader has paid lip service to a reduction in armaments and many have recognized it as a national goal in itself, in the political arena it has often been treated as at best a kind of bargaining exercise and at worst a Communist plot.

PAUL WARNKE
1977–78: Chief SALT II negotiator for Carter administration

Either an arms control agreement improves our national security or it doesn't. If it improves our security, then we ought to ratify it, entirely apart from the fact that the Soviet Union does other things that we don't like.

The question I'm asked most frequently when I try and support the arms control process is basically, "How can you trust the Russians?"

My answer is: you can trust any country and any individual to act in its own self-interest. And they [the Russians] have a self-interest in not being destroyed in a nuclear war.

The debate over SALT II was and remained an impenetrable circle —hard for the civilian mind to break into—of doomsday scenarios and technical arguments over the different capabilities of different weapons and the countercapabilities of counterweapons.

In the 1950s, when the United States held a vast lead in nuclear power, the Bomb had been thought of as an instrument of "massive retaliation," a weapon the United States could bring to bear against Soviet cities if the Kremlin should ever be so rash as to provoke a third world war.

Gradually, as the Russians began to build up a substantial nuclear arsenal of their own, that vision gave way to the notion of "mutual assured destruction"—of a nuclear exchange in which the two sides would devastate each other's societies. In this scenario the United States still held an advantage because its decisive edge in missiles would enable it to "out-destroy" the Russians.

More recently—with nuclear parity and with the greatly improved accuracy of missile guidance systems—a "counterforce strategy" had emerged in which the prime targets in a nuclear war would not be the economic and population centers—not the cities and industrial plants —but the missile bases. The first objective in a nuclear war would be to spike the enemy's guns, leaving him incapable of wrecking your cities and leaving his own cities defenseless against the threat of your destructive power.

The basic facts of life in the age of nuclear parity were these:

1. The Soviet Union had bigger missiles, capable of carrying heavy payloads of multiple warheads (MIRVs).

2. The United States had *more* warheads, wedded to smaller, more accurate missiles.

3. Both sides had enough of everything to blow each other to smithereens.

But for the opponents of SALT II the bottom line was this: that the treaty would leave the Soviet Union with enough warheads and enough missile launchers to—theoretically—carry off a first strike against the United States, enough to take out practically the entire force of American missile silos and still have plenty left over. If the United States responded by launching cruise missiles and firing nuclear salvos from submarines, the Soviet Union—theoretically—would still be in a position to threaten American cities with destruction.

Not only was the Soviet Union capable of inflicting this sort of terminal damage on the United States, but, in the Reagan administration's view, it was quite willing to take the risks that went along with it.

"Unlike us," the President said, "the Soviet Union believes that a nuclear war is possible, and they believe it is winnable."

The charge was a loose bit of anti-Communist rhetoric, made in the face of repeated policy statements to the contrary by Soviet leaders. "To count on victory in a nuclear war is madness," Brezhnev told his fellow party officials at the twenty-sixth Communist party congress in 1981. Each of his successors echoed that idea. Possibly they were trying to lull the United States into a "false sense of security" with those words, as an administration spokesman said they had done with the arms treaty. But, if so, the Soviet leaders were also deceiving their own constituents, to whom most of the statements were addressed.

On the contrary, it was one of the disturbing aspects of American conservatism that many of its adherents took a rather sanguine view of nuclear war. Some religious fundamentalists among them were insulated from nuclear fears by their view of Judgment Day as the ultimate showdown between Good and Evil—a cataclysm that the faithful would survive in the hereafter. Members of a conservative cult of "survivalists," some religious, some not, were engaged in arming and supplying themselves to outlast Doomsday in wilderness hideaways.

That scenario clearly belonged to the lunatic fringe of American political life, but it was dignified by a deputy undersecretary of defense, T. K. Jones, who projected an image of hardy Americans evacuating cities under nuclear attack and safely digging themselves in beneath a wooden door and two or three feet of dirt.

The administration only reinforced this fantasy by disclosing plans for delivering the mail after a nuclear attack.

In the official view, a nuclear war would never be started by the United States but might well be launched—or more likely, just threatened—by the Kremlin while it held that much-debated lead in land-based strategic missiles. As Alexander Haig put it in his fluent Pentagonese, previous administrations "had permitted anomalies to develop in the critical area of strategic power—and I'm talking about the instantaneous, hard-target-capable ballistic-missile area, which gives you a twelve-minute-or-so response time and which holds hostage all of our counterforces, both submarines in port, aircraft on airfields, and our silos, and which today the Soviet Union could destroy with only 30 percent of the ballistic power they've accumulated over the past twenty years.

"Now, that is an incitement towards a flirtation with first strike against the United States!"

Instead of trying to negotiate the threat away—if indeed it was a real one—the administration chose to match it. The first order of business was a buildup of the American military force, with emphasis on two strategic weapons: the cruise missile and that hide-and-seek version of the ICBM, the MX system. Nor would the navy be neglected; the fleet would be expanded by one-third. The projected bill for this muscle-building program: a mind-boggling $1.8 trillion over five years.

From that point on, the story of the Reagan administration became a three-way tug of war between the defense budget, domestic programs, and tax-cutting policies. The outcome was an increase in federal spending in five years from $591 billion to $960 billion and a tripling of the deficit—this by an administration presumably elected to fight a war against big government and its spendthrift ways. But liberal critics were confounded when, instead of the jolting inflation they foresaw, the cost-of-living curve actually began to flatten out.

The military buildup extended to Europe, where the NATO alliance was explicitly committed to a "two-track" policy—arm while discussing arms control. Talks aimed at reducing nuclear weapons on both sides of the Iron Curtain were going on in Geneva—the INF (for Intermediate-range Nuclear Forces) negotiations. They were characterized by propaganda ploys rather than genuine negotiating offers.

The Kremlin was playing to the European gallery—the Russian bear costumed as a dove. Washington's main interest was to hold the Russians at bay while persuading the European allies to accept deployment of the Pershing II, a new and improved intermediate-range missile. It was an answer to the Warsaw Pact's new and improved SS-20, which, in General Haig's phrase, "threatened every capital in Europe."

Late in 1983, the INF issue moved toward a crisis. West Germany accepted the Pershing II, deployment began, and the Soviet delegation walked out of the Geneva INF talks.

Meanwhile, President Reagan had tossed a kind of sugar-coated bombshell into the arms-control process with an announcement earlier that year: "I call upon the scientific community in our country, those who gave us nuclear weapons, to turn their great talents now to the cause of mankind and world peace, to give us the means of rendering these nuclear weapons impotent and obsolete."

What the President was suggesting was the possibility of a national "shield" against enemy missiles. It might be achieved, he had been told by scientific advisers including the redoubtable Edward Teller, with high-technology weapons based in space.

Congress was asked to approve a five-year $26-billion research and development program called SDI—the Strategic Defense Initiative. The President sometimes referred to it—emphasizing its announced purpose of lifting the nuclear threat from human existence—as "my dream." Some critics amended that to "the President's dream machine." Mostly it was known as "Star Wars."

The nickname suggested a kind of science-fiction fantasy. Like some other Reagan "follies" that turned out to be facts—noninflationary tax cuts, a freely elected government in El Salvador—this one insisted on being taken seriously. Science fiction or space-age ordnance, Star Wars became one of the most seriously discussed issues of American security —eventually so treated by administration critics as well as supporters. The Russians treated it with consternation.

Nuclear parity between the superpowers was the basic assumption of arms control. It was, as the disarmament specialist Paul Warnke points out, what brought the Soviets to the negotiating table in the first place—"Nobody wants to negotiate from a position of inferiority."

But parity was a condition that would take some getting used to. American conservatives were clearly uncomfortable with it, and so were many of their more liberal countrymen. A British historian, Peter Calvocoressi, refers to "this feeling [on the part of many Americans] that you could be safe only if the Russians were a good way down." Aleksandr Bovin, the influential Soviet journalist who served as a Kremlin adviser and policy maker under Brezhnev, makes almost the same point: "I don't think the Americans were psychologically prepared to accept our equality."

Official statements from the Soviet leadership accused President Reagan of pursuing a "militarist course" aimed at regaining the nuclear lead. Whatever the objective, SDI was clearly the lodestar of his course.

Like President Jimmy Carter with human rights, President Ronald Reagan had found his "main tune" in Star Wars.

In crude terms, Star Wars was a concept involving space vehicles that would use laser beams and other "ray weapons" to cripple and disarm incoming nuclear missiles in flight. The problem was, according to one arms control expert, Paul Warnke, that "there is no available technology—in fact, there's none in sight and there's no real prospect we can ever achieve it."

Then why the alarm?

Why were the Russians exercised about Star Wars, much as they had been, for example, about the flight of East Germans to the West before the building of the Wall?

Why were they perturbed about a project that was benign in its announced purposes and most likely would prove ineffectual?

From the Soviet viewpoint, Star Wars was by no means "benign" and "ineffectual." It stirred the same shudders of apprehension in the Kremlin that Washington once felt about the Soviet's embryonic ABM —the antiballistic missile defense of Moscow. If by any chance the space shield did work, it would give the country that owned it the ultimate nuclear advantage: the chance to deliver a crippling first strike without worrying about a retaliatory attack.

Even if Star Wars didn't pan out as a workable defense system, the R and D process was sure to throw off some new technology that could be applied to the development of new *offensive* weapons. That was the idea the Russians conveyed in pointedly and consistently referring to SDI as "cosmic strike weapons." Star Wars belonged to the field of high technology, in which the Americans were past masters and the Russians lagged. And high tech also meant high-priced. The whole strategic arms race would be "ratcheted up," and at the astronomic new level of spending, the Russians could not hope to keep pace.

Star Wars and the Kremlin's panicky reaction to it emphasized once again the difficulty of reaching serious East-West agreements in a world ruled by distrust—a world created by the Bomb and by four decades of Soviet outlawry in postwar Eastern Europe . . . in Berlin and Cuba, Africa and Afghanistan.

HENRY KISSINGER
1974: Negotiator of basic SALT II agreement as President Ford's secretary of state

Arms control is a means, not an end, and it involves technologies which are so esoteric that the average person—and, I suspect, the average national leader—can't really understand it. When the technicians argue in Geneva, it's very hard for the policy makers to break the deadlock. And therefore I have always believed that a political understanding has to precede an arms control understanding.

I happen to believe that the basic instinct of President Reagan was correct: You cannot base the security policy of a country on the premise that security is achieved by keeping your population totally vulnerable, [when] any accident will lead to the destruction of untold millions of people.

It seems to me totally absurd that the Soviets maintain that offensive weapons should be limited but one should have no right to have defensive weapons at all. If we have no defense at all, no amount of [arms] reduction is going to improve the situation. In 1962 President Kennedy thought we were facing Armageddon when we had 3,000 warheads. Now each side has anything between 10 and 15 thousand warheads, depending on how you count.

By all expectations, Star Wars should have stopped arms control dead—stopped all progress on an issue that many average persons do consider an end in itself since it is life or death to humankind.

The President's dream was a worthy one, but if Star Wars became a reality, it would almost certainly violate the ABM treaty, signed by the Nixon administration, which became the basis of SALT. The new technology would require tests of nuclear-powered devices, so Star Wars would also preclude a comprehensive test ban ending *all* nuclear explosions, underground as well as above ground. This was something East-West negotiators had been pursuing for more than two decades.

But arms control remained a live issue—even if at first a dormant one—because the Soviets were obviously serious in wanting a military détente and because American Presidents are moved by instincts that take precedence over ideology.

From the beginning, while rejecting SALT II as a snare and a delusion, President Reagan had declared he would abide by its limitations so long as the Russians did the same—a tacit concession that the treaty was of some benefit to the United States after all. When hard-liners in the Defense Department later urged him to abandon the treaty altogether, he resisted them (though eventually, late in 1986, he authorized a breach of SALT II—one more cruise-missile-equipped bomber than the treaty allowed). Meanwhile, he indicated, he was prepared to talk with the Russians about a *serious* approach to the arms-control problem—not SALT but START, signifying a Strategic and Tactical Arms Reduction Treaty. The key word was "reduction" in place of mere "limitation."

It was not until 1985—with the beginning of Reagan's second term in office and the accession to power of the young new Soviet leader,

Mikhail Gorbachev—that the process began in earnest. The Russians returned to the Geneva negotiations on the missiles in Europe (INF) after a lapse of fifteen months. Secretary of State Shultz and Foreign Minister Gromyko conferred about arms control in Vienna. And Reagan agreed to meet with Gorbachev at the summit.

PRESIDENT REAGAN

We now have redressed our military capability to the point that the Soviet Union does not have an undisputed superiority of such nature that they could deliver an ultimatum, "Surrender or die!"

I think our own buildup has been very beneficial in this regard. I could use a cartoon that appeared in some the papers to illustrate that—a cartoon of two Soviet generals, and one of them was saying to the other, "I liked the arms race better when we were the only ones in it."

Well, they're not the only ones in it. They have seen the alliance hold firm —the NATO alliance. They know that there is not going to be any easy picking off, one at a time, of nations in Europe—or very many places in the world, for that matter. They have not actually advanced any place in the last five years.

I believe them when they say they don't want a war. But if we and they can sit down and then both of us by deed confirm our words that we are living together in the world—we don't have to love each other—there may be times in which the two of us as the two biggest powers can have an influence to keep peace in the world.

Beyond Cold War

The first Reagan-Gorbachev meeting was held in Geneva in November 1985—a couple of smalltown boys, the Soviet leader observed companionably, in a position to do "great good and great harm."

At that time and during the following months, the whole range of East-West issues was aired—in small face-to-face meetings, in rooms populated with experts, and in the world media. The superpowers were engaged in a new phase of their relationship, a step beyond confrontation but far short of détente. It was an era of dialogue. Almost in spite of themselves—in spite of expressed doubts and low expectations—they found some important differences narrowing.

On the knotty question of strategic missiles, the Soviets seemed to agree with the basic American proposition that world security required reductions in the big land-based ICBMs—even though the cuts would weigh against the Russians.

What once looked like an American propaganda trick became the basis of a serious discussion on European missiles. It was a so-called "zero-zero option"—eliminate both the Soviet SS-20s *and* the West's Pershing IIs.

And President Reagan acknowledged the Russians' problem with Star Wars by proposing to limit the project to research, postponing actual deployment for a period of years.

Some of these emerging agreements might mature sooner or later and pay off in arms-control treaties. It was still too early in the dialogue to be sure. If it did happen it might allow East and West to advance to the kind of uneasy coexistence they seemed to be working toward in the early 1970s.

But could they ever move beyond that to a condition of genuine peace? Or had the very idea become obsolete in our time—like cheap gas and safe neighborhoods?

Could East and West ever achieve Henry Kissinger's prescribed state of "political understanding" so long as they held such conflicting views on how to improve the world—the Communists by revolution, the West through stability and personal freedom?

An average person searching the headlines of the mid-eighties for portents would have to conclude that the signs were far from promising.

On the eve of Ronald Reagan's 1985 trip to the Geneva summit, his defense secretary, Caspar Weinberger, wrote him a letter—which was carefully leaked to the press—urging him to beware of taking any steps toward an agreement with the Russians.

And on the eve of his trip to a kind of mini-summit with Gorbachev in Iceland in the fall of 1986, Ronald Reagan—that paradigm of anti-Soviet conservatism—found it necessary to assure his countrymen that he had not gone "soft on communism."

Ideology and political rhetoric were still part of the American leadership's cold-war baggage—a dead weight on a trip to the summit.

On the Soviet side, the discouragements came less from their rhetoric, which often radiated good will, than from their deeds, which were sometimes diabolical. The Iceland meeting followed a dismal episode in which the Soviet government seized an American journalist in Moscow, charging him with espionage, and in effect used him as a hostage to secure the release of a Russian arrested as a spy in New York.

In the headlines of the mid-eighties, the searcher for portents would find some hopeful words about Afghanistan. The Russians indicated they were willing to discuss the issue—willing to consider a withdrawal from that battered country in return for international guarantees about its future.

But even before that trouble spot could be settled, another potential one was emerging: South Africa, where Communist influences were at work in the black nationalist movement, ready and willing to exploit the black majority's yearning for liberation from *apartheid* and poverty.

Moscow's Aleksandr Bovin raises the specter in unambiguous terms: "Suppose there was an uprising in South Africa, and those blacks that are being subordinated and suppressed—what if they asked for help? What would we say—'No, we will not help you.'? Of course not!"

How to respond to challenges like that is a question that troubles the West.

What guidance is there in four decades of cold-war experience? What have we learned from our own history?

American life-style penetrated Iron Curtain in the 1980s, along with Western economic influences. Pepsi-Cola became a favorite in Moscow, while McDonald's franchises are being planned for other Iron Curtain capitals. *(UPI/Bettmann Newsphotos)*

Camp David colleagues—Sadat of Egypt, Carter of U.S., Begin of Israel—celebrate the payoff of their efforts. Signing of a formal Egypt-Israel peace treaty at the White House in 1979 ended a state of war that had lasted for more than 30 years. *(UPI/Bettmann Newsphotos)*

In failing health, Soviet leader Brezhnev steadies himself on President Carter's arm at 1979 Vienna summit. *(UPI/Bettmann Newsphotos)*

Scarcely a year before his shocking downfall, the Shah of Iran was toasted by President Carter as "an island of stability" in the Middle East. *(UPI/Bettmann Newsphotos)*

Leader of the Islamic fundamentalist revolution that displaced the Shah of Iran in 1979: Ayatollah Ruhollah Khomeini. *(UPI/Bettmann Newsphotos)*

Exultant students in Iran burn an American flag in 1979 seizure of U.S. embassy in Teheran. This scene was an overture to the 444-day hostage drama. *(UPI/Bettmann Newsphotos)*

American hostages being paraded through the grounds of the U.S. embassy in Teheran after it was seized by Iranian students. *(UPI/Bettmann Newsphotos)*

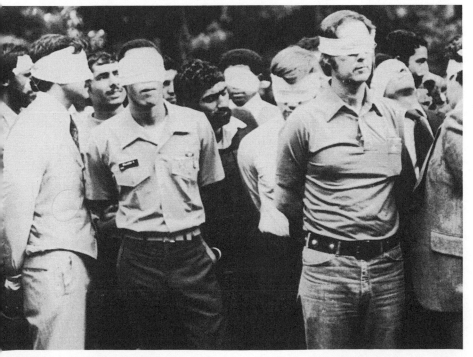

Khomeini justice: A firing squad acting in the name of the new revolutionary government of Iran carries out death sentences against separatist rebels and former police officers of the deposed Shah's regime. This scene characterized repressive acts of the revolution. *(UPI/Bettmann Newsphotos)*

Lightly armed Afghan guerrillas, sometimes switching from motorcycles and other vehicles to horseback for operations in mountainous countryside, kept an estimated 150,000 Soviet troops tied down in their country and along its borders. *(UPI/Bettmann Newsphotos)*

Dismantling a legend: Sign quoting Chairman Mao is taken down from a Beijing building in 1980. As the late Chinese Communist leader was being downgraded, the economy was also retreating from the rigid collectivism of his revolution. *(UPI/Bettmann Newsphotos)*

Liberated Iran hostages, flown out of Teheran to U.S. air base in West Germany, were greeted there by ex-President Carter. *(UPI/Bettmann Newsphotos)*

Labor movement called Solidarity challenged Soviet-dominated Polish government in early 1980s. *(UPI/Bettmann Newsphotos)*

Sandinista militia, mobilized for a 1983 demonstration in the streets of Managua, the Nicaraguan capital, to protest anti-Sandinista statements by President Reagan. *(UPI/Bettmann Newsphotos)*

Wreckage of marine barracks in Beirut buried American hopes of imposing peace on fragmented country of Lebanon. Suicide bombing by guerrilla faction linked to Iran claimed lives of 241 Americans in 1983. *(UPI/Bettmann Newsphotos)*

Shadow of Arab terrorism fell over 1972 Olympics in Munich, West Germany, when hooded gunmen captured members of the Israeli team and held them hostage. Eleven athletes were killed in rescue assault. *(AP/Wide World Photos)*

An MX missile—one of the controversial issues of strategic arms discussions in early 1980s—emerges from its hiding place under 5 feet of earth and 10 inches of concrete in test of the experimental system. *(UPI/Bettmann Newsphotos)*

At their first summit, President Reagan and Soviet leader Gorbachev sit together during the closing ceremony, but talk with their interpreters during the 1985 Geneva conference. *(UPI/Bettmann Newsphotos)*

·26·

FROM THE FORTIES
TO THE EIGHTIES

Four decades hardly make a ripple in the sixty centuries of human history, but they feel like a long time in the life of a generation.

In 1945, when World War II ended and the cold war began to emerge, no human being had ever ventured more than eleven miles from the surface of the earth—the altitude record achieved in a balloon. Nobody had ever received a heart or kidney transplant; no one had ever heard of AIDS. Cigarette smoking was sometimes condemned—as a messy habit that could shorten an athlete's wind. The health threat that all parents feared for their children was neither tobacco nor drugs but polio, for which there was no vaccine.

A salary of $10,000 a year put a man in the executive class; his wife didn't work. The average job paid less than $50 a week.

There were just 5,000 homes with television in the United States, and in all of civilization there was exactly one McDonald's. Frozen foods were not yet on the market. Air conditioning in homes or cars was a rarity. Nobody had yet written with a ballpoint pen or slept under an electric blanket. The first "electronic brain" or "computing machine" had recently been built; it filled a gymnasium.

Among the influential movements of our time that did not exist in 1945 were environmentalism and consumerism. There was not a single female member of the New York Stock Exchange, no female ambassador of the United States in any foreign capital, no female judge in a state or federal court. Only ten cities had major league baseball teams, the westernmost being St. Louis, and not one of them had ever knowingly fielded a black ballplayer. "Whites Only" signs were prevalent throughout the South, and all-black schools were commonplace in urban neighborhoods throughout the country.

In that blessed year of Victory over the Axis, which turned out to be Year 1 of a much longer conflict, there was no Wall in Berlin, no Federal Republic of (West) Germany or (East) German Democratic Republic. Among the other countries that did not yet exist were Pakistan, Israel, Vietnam, Cambodia, and Grenada. The United States was the only nation in the world with nuclear weapons. A man who was soon to become secretary of the air force, Stuart Symington, recalls that at the time "the United States had at least eighteen months to get ready for a war. We had the two greatest allies a country's ever had in the history of the world—the Atlantic and Pacific oceans. Now we'd be lucky to have eighteen minutes."

A Pentagon official of more recent vintage, General Alexander Haig, gives the current figure as twelve minutes.

Professor Dean Rusk, sitting in his study at the University of Georgia on a summer day in the mid-1980s, looks back on the early years of the cold war—the years of the Marshall Plan, the Berlin airlift, and great decisions in the United Nations—as a halcyon period in the life of an American generation.

It was a time of inspired altruism, when, he recalls, "we came up with over 3 percent of our gross national product" for various foreign-aid programs. "Today," he goes on in the matter-of-fact tone diplomats learn to use even when they are feeling sadness or regret, "today you can't get one-half of 1 percent of our GNP for such purposes. Well, you see, in those years just after World War II, our minds and spirits had been purged in the fires of a great war, and we were thinking at our best. We were prepared to make an effort in those days which apparently we haven't been willing to make since."

If the ghosts of Harry Truman and Winston Churchill, who were leaders of the free world in those early years of willing sacrifice and cooperative effort, returned in the 1980s to confer over their strategic maps, they would have found the boundaries changed in one dramatic respect—and changed for the better—though some would argue that it had less to do with the West's effort than with the inexorable forces of history. That development, of course, was the detachment of China from the Soviet bloc.

Otherwise, Truman and Churchill, those two old speakers' platform companions and poker opponents, would have suffered some disappointments, though probably no serious shocks.

The original cold-war boundary, the Iron Curtain Churchill warned of in his Fulton speech, remained stubbornly unchanged by four decades of conflict—unchanged for better or for worse. Poland, Hungary, Czechoslovakia, Rumania, Bulgaria, East Germany all were once "part of the European family and now no longer are," as the secretary general of NATO, Lord Carrington, laments. But neither was the Iron Curtain quite the impenetrable barrier it once had been in terms of trade, travel, and communications. And the satellite nations were experiencing degrees of independence that would have been hard to imagine in the dark years of the 1950s.

Meanwhile, on the Western side of the boundary, no other European countries had gone under. And, as Dean Rusk observes, "no member of NATO has been subject to attack since NATO was born."

In the Middle East, if American power had recently been under challenge, then Russia's had measurably declined. While losing out in populous Egypt, the Soviet had gained only tiny Yemen, unstable Libya, and what one Middle East diplomat calls "half a foothold in Syria," which persisted in policies of its own making.

A number of other third-world countries had joined the Communist camp during the lapse of American power—or was it only American inattentiveness?—in the 1970s. The list included Vietnam, Laos, and Kampuchea (formerly Cambodia); Ethiopia, Angola, and Mozambique; Nicaragua and Afghanistan.

Each of those casualties was mourned in the West as a death in the family, though not all the Communist gains were losses to the side of free nations. Some were an exchange of one form of repression for another. The sad truth of history is that freedom may not be the inevitable fate of the entire human race; some peoples have a tradition of tyranny, the Russians among them. But it is also true that nations die hard and the triumph of an alien power or its system is often illusory.

There would be no blinking at the Soviet footholds in Africa and the Western Hemisphere. The persistence of Soviet influence in Cuba would certainly be discouraging to the two old leaders of the transatlantic alliance. But they would be aware that long-distance relationships are hard to exploit for a power with a limited navy and a faulty economy.

Churchill would take note of what one of his former foreign service officials, Sir Frank Roberts, later ambassador to Moscow, had to say about the third-world's role in the cold war:

"As long as these countries were wanting to free themselves from colonial rule, obviously they looked to anybody for support. Today they're looking basically for economic assistance, for economic development, which the Russians can't give them. None of these countries want to buy Russian goods. The only things the Russians have to sell them are arms, by and large. So that there is a community of interests between the third world and the West, in spite of all the quarrels, that doesn't exist between them and the Soviet Union."

There is a way of measuring progress in the cold war besides territorial gains and losses. That is by the advance of wisdom in dealing with a global conflict in which the margin of catastrophic error has been reduced to twelve minutes.

Listen to the voices of some individuals looking back at the cold war from the vantage point of 1985. They speak from their own experience in the great, continuous war of ideas—and sometimes of arms—that gripped the second half of the twentieth century.

ROBERT S. MCNAMARA
1961–68: Secretary of defense

To this day, both the Soviet Union and we are misjudging the capabilities and intentions of each other. I believed then and I believe today that the Soviets will take advantage of weakness, and it's absolutely essential that we maintain in the West strength such that they do not believe they can achieve political or military advantage by threatening the U.S.

What I don't believe today and I didn't fully believe then is that they threaten to dominate the world.

SIR FRANK ROBERTS
1960–62: British ambassador to the USSR

The whole of Russian history consists of Russia always pushing in where it was safe to do so and where a door had been left ajar but very rarely of Russia breaking down doors or taking risks. So it's very important we don't give them the impression that they are strong enough to get away with things.

ABBA EBAN
1966–74: Israeli foreign minister

The Soviets will test America very acutely and very sensitively. But they are fully capable of retreat without a sense of humiliation or despair. They retreated in Cuba. There was a similar retreat in '74, when the United States shook a fist. The Soviets didn't react hysterically. They said, okay, just send some UN observers [to the Middle East] and that will be a substitute for Soviet forces.

Well, that's nonsense—UN observers are the opposite of Soviet forces. But they'd found a face-saving way of retreat.

COLONEL HARRY SUMMERS
Military historian

Someone said, only half in jest, that the first thing that would happen to the Soviet Union if they started a nuclear war with the United States is that they'd ruin their own grain reserves, and they'd also cut themselves off from Western technology. There's a lot of truth in that.

One of the problems we have today when we talk about the use of military force is that most Americans have in their mind as the model of war World War II. Total and unconditional surrender. The one thing that the American people want is a quick victory and a very clear-cut resolution.

In any conflict with a nuclear-armed adversary, we're not going to have that. We'll stalemate the battlefield, and then diplomatic action is going to be necessary in order to bring it to a conclusion. That's very frustrating for the American people.

RICHARD M. NIXON

The United States no longer seeks nuclear superiority. But we must insist that the Soviet Union, which is an offensive power, not have nuclear superiority.

Why? Not because the Soviet Union's going to lob one into the United States or lob its SS-20s into Europe and destroy it. The reason we must avoid nuclear superiority on the part of the Soviet Union is to avoid nuclear coercion, where the Soviets would be able to do to us what Kennedy did to them in '62, what Eisenhower did to them in 1956.

One final point. The Soviet Union isn't responsible for all the problems in the world. The Soviet Union isn't responsible for hunger and famine as a result of poor crops and drought. The Soviet Union isn't responsible for the disparity in income between the producer nations of the world and the consumer nations. The Soviet Union isn't responsible for the new kind of violent terrorism that is sweeping through the Mid-East and the Persian Gulf.

And, therefore, we must find a way to deal with these problems and not think that if only we could be strong enough to face down the Soviet Union everything is going to be fine.

GEORGE MCGOVERN
1972: Presidential candidate

One of the basic problems with our policy in these years since the end of World War II is that it has been guided largely by what we're against rather than what we're for. It's fear of communism rather than faith in democracy and faith in freedom that guides American foreign policy.

THEODORE SORENSON
1961–64: White House special counsel

The underlying error of American foreign policy during the last forty years was to underestimate the forces of nationalism in the Third World. The United States ought to be, as it once was, a shining star to those forces of nationalism. Instead, too often the United States is looked upon as the Yankee colossus, the one who's always interfering to prop up the status quo because we are fearful the Communists will come in and exploit the other side.

RONALD REAGAN

It is true there has been a kind of confrontational thing with one erstwhile ally, the Soviet Union. But that doesn't mean that we succumb to the idea of the inevitability of conflict. We keep on trying in the hope that they too will realize that their system will be better off if we decide to live in the world together without conflict.

GERALD R. FORD

Détente, whether you use the word or not, is the best policy for the United States vis-à-vis the Soviet Union.

DEAN RUSK
1961–69: Secretary of state

In 1985 we put behind us forty years since a nuclear weapon had been fired in anger, despite several serious and even dangerous crises. We've learned during those forty years that the fingers on the nuclear triggers are not itchy, just waiting for a pretext to fire. We're learned that Soviet leaders have no more interest in destroying Mother Russia than our leaders have in destroying our beloved America.

Now, that's not a guarantee for the future. We and the Soviets should not play games of chicken with each other to see how far one can go without crossing that lethal line. And we have to watch the level of rhetoric between our two countries, because if that rhetoric becomes too virulent over too long a period of time, there's always the chance that one side or the other will begin to believe its own rhetoric, and then we could have problems.

Throughout human history, it's been possible for the human race to pick itself up out of the death and destruction of war and start over again. We shan't have that chance after World War III—there won't be enough left. So, at long last, the human race has reached the point where it must prevent that war before it occurs.

The basic lesson of the cold war seemed to be that with the tremendous growth of military power since World War II, its very usefulness had declined. It could be neutralized by nationalism, as in Vietnam; or by terrorism, as in the Middle East; or by the threat of nuclear retaliation. It was something rarely to be used but mostly just *kept,* like financial credit, as a means of negotiation.

So the cold war entered its fifth decade with the two major antagonists still confronting each other without shooting. They seemed to be *trying* to trust each other, to believe something they would not let themselves accept before: Both were now willing to believe there was no intention of pushing the button by the other side. The dialogue, focusing on arms control, was being conducted mostly in reasonable, businesslike terms. The rhetoric was notably restrained.

Although the 1985 summit in Geneva was pretty much another "psychiatric" session, like Geneva in 1954, the Soviet and American leaders found themselves in accord that nuclear arms offered nothing but disaster for both sides. The 1986 Iceland meeting reached the very threshold of incredibly far-reaching agreements on arms reductions. The two sides were discussing serious proposals for the total elimination of strategic weapons (or at least of ICBMs—there was some disagreement about that afterwards) when the talks broke down over the Star Wars issue.

The two sides blamed each other for the breakdown with some vehemence, but without the traditional tone of malice and distrust that characterized past failures. What seemed important to both sides was not to score propaganda points but to keep the dialogue going.

After four decades, there was still no truce to the cold war, but there were moments when the antagonists sounded almost like allies again, facing a common danger.

INDEX